D0339367

The Road from Damascus provides a street-level view of a so-called "terrorist" nation—a view that gives the lie to accepted wisdom in the United States. Syrians, the author discovers, are intelligent, gracious, fair-minded, and utterly in love with American culture—even as they decry what they see as the excesses of US foreign policy.

It was a rough few years in the Middle East: suicide attacks, hostage-taking, hijackings. In 1985 the terror spread to Europe, and Americans were among the victims. The following year the United States responded by attacking Libya. Commentators said that Syria was next.

In Seattle, Scott C. Davis was curious. Did Middle Eastern people hate us? How true were media stereotypes which condemned Muslims, Arabs, and Syrians?

Davis flew to Damascus. Two hours after arriving, he took a hotel room with a Muslim "fundamentalist" and found himself using his mountaineer's compass to answer technical questions: Exactly how many degrees to Mecca?

Two weeks later in the shadow of a great Crusader castle, Davis and a local teenager ran from the *mukhabarat* and took shelter in a stone house on the cliff side. After dark the teenager played disco on a Korean boom box, and Davis gave bump dance lessons to six Muslims including two women. While the dancers shook, the cows in the room below shuffled and moaned.

A few weeks later in a dry town at the edge of the Euphrates, Davis was invited to play chess by a Kurdish soldier on leave. The night was cold, and the soldier pulled a sheepskin cape over his shoulders for warmth. As the game progressed, the soldier taunted the 241 US Marines killed in Beirut four years earlier. At checkmate Davis learned that the taunts concealed respect, sorrow, and an inescapable comradeship.

On his first night in Syria, traveling on a rickety transit bus into Damascus, Davis had been overcome with apprehension. Weeks later, returning to Damascus from hard travel on the eastern steppe, Davis welcomed this city as a safe moorage, a quiet resting place, an enduring home.

"The Road from Damascus *is more than travelogue, it is odyssey . . . Insight, humor, and offhand eloquence are on every page of this book.*"
—Al-Jadid Magazine

"In 1987, five years after the Hama massacre, and with Syria seemingly on the brink of war with Israel, a naïve Davis made his first visit. Fourteen years later he returned to find the country radically different: less militarized, less uneasy, less frightening.

"Refreshingly candid about his pre-1987 ignorance about the Arab world and about his sometimes overblown but very real fears, Davis chronicles his meetings with Christian, Muslim and Jewish members of all stations of Syrian society, painting a cultural portrait that is vivid, moving and wise in its humble, wide-eyed approach."
—*Publishers Weekly*

"*The Road From Damascus* deserves to be read by Arabs all over the world. These are terrible times. Politicians posture for the public, while armies lacerate silent victims—those speechless men and women whom Franz Fanon called the 'damned of the earth.' With great humility the author restores the voices of these forgotten sufferers. He does so simply because their voices speak the truth. The truth can also be found in the words of Scott C. Davis."
Le Renouveau, Tunis

"There's a widespread belief among non-Americans that most US citizens are an insular-looking lot . . . But there are exceptions to the rule and Seattle construction worker, writer and mountaineer Scott C. Davis is among them."
—*Irish Examiner*

"Every word that Davis writes is a bold contradiction to the ignorant and superficial thinking that rules American foreign policy."
—*Ad-Domari*, Damascus

"Meticulously observed. Davis went far off the beaten path—into side streets and mountain villages—and saw a Syria that escapes nearly all Western travelers."
—*Talcott Seelye, Former US Ambassador to Syria*

"An excellent read, with an important message. Much more than an amusing travelogue, it is really a crash course in world cultures and a reflection of the author's unique personality, humor, and warmth."
—Benjamin Beit-Hallahmi, author of *Original Sins*

"In this remarkable journal, Davis describes with unerring detail and honesty his headlong plunge into the rich, complex, and ancient land of Syria. Deftly written and fast-paced, the book brings out vividly the human face of the Syrian people."
—Paul J. Hare, Middle East Institute

"It is my dearest wish that *The Road from Damascus* should clear some of the smoke and debris left by 9/11 and make way for a clearer perception of at least one Islamic country."
—*Palestine Chronicle*

"Scott C. Davis saw many things in Syria, recorded them in his mental archive, then went back to the United States and wrote a book that reveals tremendous affection for Syria . . . *The Road from Damascus* bucks the tide of anti-Syrian sentiment in the United States."
—*Al-Thawra*, Damascus

"At the end of his first visit to Syria, Davis met with the Patriarch of Antioch, who reminded him that according to the Bible, St. Paul experienced his conversion via a vision of God on the road to Damascus. But, as Davis learned during his second visit to Syria, it is not the vision of God that a seeker receives on the road *to* Damascus that is important but rather how the seeker puts it into practice in life (i.e., how he or she walks the road *from* Damascus).
—*Library Journal*

"In a period inundated with books about our region by specialists—and putative specialists—it is refreshing to read a travelogue by an avowed non-scholar."
—Jerusalem Post

"Here is an American, who is not only so bold as to travel alone in a country in the Middle East at a dangerous time, but also has the *moral* courage to keep an open mind about a nation and its people who are declared *pariahs* by his government. This book is an extraordinary perspective of one American who is deeply religious in his own way, yet one who has the humility and magnanimity to recognize humanity and decency wherever he sees it."
—*Indian Link*, Sydney

"The terrible events of 9-11, the surging violence in the Middle East, and Syria's centrality to the Arab-Israeli conflict, all add to the importance of this book."
—*Somali Times*

"At the end of his 1987 journey the writer has what can be called a mystic experience. As a former mountaineer he had conceived of the arrival at the Roman Bridge as reaching a summit. Now Davis realizes that it truly is a bridge: a means to cross over to the other side and view the world through the eyes of "the other."
—*Rambles*, a Cultural Arts Magazine

"*The Road from Damascus* is a nuanced book . . . an honest, eloquent, and perceptive narrative of personal experience, set into a readable and convincing historical and political context."
—Dr. Laurence Michalak,
University of California at Berkeley

"... wryly humorous, idiosyncratic and detailed ... endearing in its self-disparaging honesty ... Davis unfolds a present that is almost lost to Americans ..."
—Montreal Muslim News

"Ultimately what emerges from *Road From Damascus* is a profound sense of community . . . this book overcomes fear—fear of the unknown, fear of loneliness, fear of being foolish, fear of emptiness—to reinforce the need for openness, acceptance of difference, and the need for humility in order to understand others.
—*Montreal Muslim News*

". . . quite amusing, nicely drawn, and exhibiting the author's eye for detail and comic pacing."
—*Daily Star,* Beirut

"Davis gives us compelling portraits of the people he meets. Indeed, he is excellent in personalising his Syrian contacts, in reaching out to ordinary people who struggle to make a living and to lead fulfilling lives under an authoritarian regime."
—*Banipal,* London

"*The Road from Damascus* is not just remarkable, it's the sort of book that should be on every college reading list in America."
—*The Star,* Amman

THE AUTHOR

Scott C. Davis was born in 1948 in Seattle, graduated from Stanford in 1970, and now lives with his wife, Mary, in Seattle. He serves as the US correspondent for Damascus-based *Ad-Domari* magazine—the first independent publication in Syria since 1963. His writing has appeared in the *New York Times*, the *Christian Science Monitor*, the *Exquisite Corpse*, and other publications.

Davis's first book, *The World of Patience Gromes: Making and Unmaking a Black Community*, won the Washington State Book Award. His second book, *Lost Arrow and Other True Stories*, won the KCAC Literary Award.

Davis has edited and produced a distinctive collection of essays by 75 new writers. *An Ear to the Ground: Presenting Writers from 2 Coasts* was endorsed by Horton Foote, Vaclav Havel, and Arun Gandhi who also contributed essays to the volume.

For more information visit scottcdavis.com.

THE ROAD FROM DAMASCUS
A Journey Through Syria

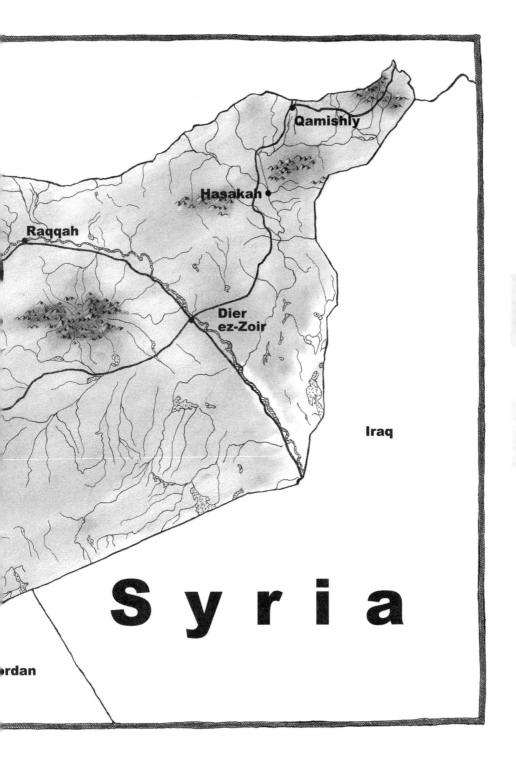

Qamishly

Hasakah •

Raqqah

Dier
ez-Zoir

Iraq

Syria

rdan

THE ROAD FROM DAMASCUS
A Journey Through Syria

Scott C. Davis

 Cune

This book is dedicated to the memory of Fateh Moudarres.

The Road from Damascus:
A Journey Through Syria
Cune Press, Seattle, 2003

© 2003 by Scott C. Davis
All Rights Reserved
ISBN 1-885942-84-2 (Cloth)
First US Edition
3 5 7 9 10 8 6 4 2

Future Editions
ISBN 1-885942-86-9 (Leather)
ISBN 1-885942-53-2 (Paper)
ISBN 1-885942-65-6 (Electronic File)

Portions of this book originally appeared in slightly different form in the *Exquisite Corpse, Ad-Domari (The Lamplighter)* (in Arabic translation), and on NPR affiliate KPLU (based in Tacoma, Washington). This edition is a revision of the First Foreign Edition which was released in 2001.
For artists, see Credits.
Photos by author except as noted.

CIP
1. Syria--Description and travel. 2. Syria--Social life and customs. 3. Davis, Scott C., 1948 Journeys--Syria. I. Title. DS94 .D28 2003 915.69104'42--dc21   2002005170

Copies of *The Road from Damascus* are available for purchase at your local independent bookstore. Also available online or toll free: www.cunepress.com; (800) 445-8032. Bookstores: Find the Cune Press Catalogue at www.cunepress.com.

This is a work of nonfiction, based on detailed notes and photographs that I took during my travel in Syria primarily in October-December 1987 and January-February 2001. I have also included political updates based on my travel to Syria in January, July, and October 2002.
In this volume I have used actual names for Youssef Abdelke, Zouhair Dabbagh, Ali Farzat, Walid Ikhlassy, Fateh Moudarres, Archbishop Matta Roham, Mamoun Sakkal (as Hasan the architect), Abu Taleb, and for public figures. The names of others have been changed to protect their privacy. No composites have been used.

The Road from Damascus is part of the Bridge between the Cultures Series from Cune Press. (Jesir al-Thaqafat.) For more: www.cunepress.com

Cune Press
PO Box 31024
Seattle, WA 98103

We wish to thank the Salaam Cultural Museum for its support.

Table of Contents

Maps & Illustrations

Photographs

Papers & Objects

On Arabic

The representation of Arabic words in English is an inexact science—the source of unnecessary confusion for readers of English. Before traveling to Syria, for example, I never grasped that the English words "Moslem" and "Muslim" refer, in fact, to a single Arabic word. The same is true with "Mohammed" and "Muhammad," "Koran" and "Quran."

Another thing that confused me were the varying transcriptions for the definite article. With most Arabic words the proper "al-" or "el-" is used (as in al-Jazira, the island). However, in actual speech the article is slurred when the word that follows begins with certain consonants (called "solar letters"), and so the article can be transcribed into English differently. For example, in the towns "Ar-Rasafa," "Dier ez-Zoir," and "Jisr esh-Shughur," the prefixes "ar-," "ez-," and "esh-," refer to the same Arabic word as "al-."

The approach I have taken is to follow the most common modern practice for popular writing. Thus I have used the contemporary "u" in words such as "Muslim," "Muhammad," and "Quran." I also have followed the practice of transcribing the proper "al-" as it is spoken in names such as "Dier ez-Zoir." When necessary, I have sacrificed logic to accommodate current usage. The political group Party of God or Hezbollah (as transliterated by the *New York Times)* to my mind should be transliterated Hezballah so that readers can see the *"Allah"* in the name or Hezbullah for phonetic accuracy (there is no "o" sound in Arabic). However, I have followed the lead of the *New York Times* because it will be familiar to many readers.

Since September 11th many readers have heard of Osama bin Laden, traditionally transcribed as "ibn Laden" or "son of" Laden. When transcribing other Arabic names that follow the "son of" form, I have preserved the traditional "ibn" because my examples are medieval and this spelling will be more familiar to readers of medieval history.

On Politics

The story I have to tell is about people, ideas, history, and culture. All of these have political implications. So I offer the following notes for those non-specialists who wish to know more about the political associations of the people I met in Syria, and who want to sharpen their sense of the modern political terrain in the Middle East.

Lay readers often think of Syria in a general way as an "Islamic" state. Not true. Although eighty-five percent of the Syrian people are Muslims, Syria is a secular state fiercely opposed to Islamic extremism. Syria's ruling clan prefers to keep mosque and state separate because they are Alawites, an Islamic minority widely persecuted in years past. The regime's archenemies are conservative Sunni Muslims, sometimes identified as the Muslim Brotherhood. In the late 1970s radical Muslims engaged in political assassinations in Syria, throwing into doubt the regime's ability to secure public order. Ultimately, the regime reasserted control following the 1982 revolt in Hama which the army suppressed with great loss of life. In the last year Muslim leaders have been freed from prison in an effort to mend these wounds.

Given the regime's antagonism toward politicized Muslims within the country, it is ironic that in recent times Syria's primary ally has been Iran, which *is* an Islamic state. For years Syria stationed 50,000 troops in Lebanon and thus helped Iran maintain the Hezbollah as a political and military force. In return, Iran has lent financial aid to Syria. One more reason to make common cause: for years Syria and Iran have shared Iraq as a common enemy.

Since 1963 Syria has been ruled by the Baath party. Over the years Party members who lost out in Syrian power struggles fled Damascus for Baghdad. This explains some of the friction between the two Baath regimes. In 2001, however, the Syria made overtures to Iraq in hopes of easing tensions and increasing oil revenues.

You would think that Syria's Baath regime would have been receptive to Communism during the heyday of the Soviet Union. Baath doctrine has a socialist cast. And the regime's proudest accomplishments include land redistribution and the bringing of electric power, roads, and schools to the villages. What's more, for years Syria received armaments and aid from the Soviet Union.

Yet the Syrian regime during Soviet times viewed Communism as a mortal threat, second only to politicized Islam. In 1987 I met a Kurdish youth who said he would be arrested if the police discovered his copy of Lenin's writings. Some Syrians joked that Soviet advisers in Syria had always been confined to their bases to prevent them from spreading their ideology whereas American tourists (read "CIA") were given free run of the country—never mind that the United States backed Israel.

Syria would seem to be a logical American ally. It has a large Christian population, a long history of religious tolerance, an enlightened attitude toward women, and for more than a century has been sending emigrants to the United States. Middle class Syrians with American educations are exerting steady pressure for economic opening and civic reform. A decade ago Syrian troops joined Allied forces in Operation Desert Storm. In recent years Syria has forced radical Palestinian groups with offices in Damascus to disavow violence or to leave the country. The regime has prepared Syrians to accept a "peace of the brave" with Israel, and most Syrians view peace with Israel as necessary and inevitable. More recently, Syria sent condolences to the United States in the wake of the September 11th events and provided intelligence to the CIA that saved American lives.

The sticking point in US relations with Syria is the Hezbollah. Syria is still using this Shiite military force to fight a proxy war against Israel along one small portion of the Lebanese-Israeli border.

The Hezbollah was formed following the Israeli invasion of Lebanon in 1982. Its organizers included some of the same "students" who held Americans hostage in the US embassy in Teheran three years earlier. Its members are Shiite Muslims largely based in Lebanon's southern countryside. For years the Hezbollah was the bright hope of the Iranian clergy who wanted to export an Islamic revolution to Lebanon and then to the world. By now the fires have cooled, yet Iran still funds the Hezbollah and still uses them to exercise political influence.

Lay readers may need to be reminded that Iranians (or Persians) are not Arabs. Although the members of the Hezbollah in Lebanon share a Shiite Islamic faith with their Iranian sponsors, the two groups are different races and have different native languages.

Another wrinkle: Many Arabs are not Muslims. Also, Islam is distinct from Arab culture. In evaluating any faith, Islam included, it is important to separate the influence of a specific culture from the essentials of the religion. Some commentators, for example, observe that American Muslims seem to be evolving a practice of Islam that is quite different from that based in traditional Arab culture.

Syria, like nearly all Arab governments, operates as a security state—critics would say a "dictatorship." Syrians, however, hope for change.

Before his death in June 2000, Syrian president Hafez al-Asad "froze" the state of emergency under which the country had been ruled since 1963. Asad's British-educated son Bashar has succeeded his father and urged reform. He released political prisoners, opened the banking system, cracked down on corruption, allowed independent newspapers, authorized private universities, and more.

I attended a freedom forum in Damascus in February 2001 that was organized by Riad Seif, a Member of Parliament who belongs to a prominent merchant family. Ordinary citizens gave rousing speeches in favor of an independent judiciary and other elements of "civil society." Since then Riad Seif, Riyad al-Turk, and others have been arrested (Seif was sentenced to five years' imprisonment in April 2002), and new publications appear to be subject to "guidance" or restrictions by the required government distributor if not censorship. On the other hand, events in 2002 give hope: a cabinet reshuffle in January that brought in ministers educated in the West; a purge of conservative bureaucrats in March; public airing of the ministers' plans in July; a water conference with world experts in October.

I am surprised in the wake of the 9-11 attacks to hear Syria mentioned as a target for US bombs. Congress has passed a measure that would restrict visas to Syrians, and a far more punitive measure is currently before Congress. Rather than chastising Syria, it would make more sense for the United States to complete the last work needed to cement a peace deal between Syria and Israel. Peace would create stability in the region, and it would give a lift to Syrian reformers, including Bashar al-Asad, in their efforts to defeat a corrupt bureaucracy, establish the institutions of civil society, and open the economy.

To the Reader

The point of this book is the humanity of men and women in a country that the US State Department has branded a "terrorist nation."

I am writing about the ordinary people of Syria, and they are a way for me to pose questions about my own country. If Americans live in a democracy, then why don't the principles of fairness and decency that apply to our domestic life apply as well to our foreign policy? Who decides how the US acts abroad, members of the political and moneyed elite or ordinary citizens? How can Americans condemn our enemies overseas when we have little idea of the US actions that have triggered their enmity? When will the doors open so that Americans can face the full truth of our actions in the world since 1945?

Fairness and decency—do these principles still apply to our domestic life? In the wake of September 11th, the US administration has made dozens of large and small decisions to limit the Freedom of Information Act and Fourth Amendment rights. The Attorney General, for example, has announced that he has the right to label any individual a "combatant" in the war on terror, to deprive the accused of all civil rights, and to act without court review. Are the secrecy, arrogance, and contempt for civil liberties that have long characterized our foreign policy now poisoning domestic policy as well?

In my experience, Americans know little about the lives of Middle Eastern Arabs and Muslims. Following the September 11th attacks and the current violence in Palestine, fear and ignorance are the dynamic behind American public opinion. As I write, more than a year after September 11th, the impulse of the citizenry is to give government leaders carte blanche in foreign affairs.

The issue of the moment is the proposed US invasion of Iraq. Members of the administration are touring the talk shows, whipping up the fear of the populace. *60 Minutes* reports that many of the facts they use in their arguments are false. Still, they have been effective. The evening news reports that in a recent survey, a majority of Americans wrongly identified Iraq as the cause of the September 11th attacks.

A few years ago tens of thousands of people were slaughtered in

Rwanda and the Balkans while the US stood by. Why did the US not act decisively then? Why is military action imperative now?

Did the public ever really learn what happened the last time the US attacked Iraq? Since the Gulf War, hundreds of thousands of children and elderly people have died from diarrhea, the calculated result of US bombing of water treatment plants—which we did in order to "put pressure" on the regime and to "give bite" to the sanctions.

I imagine that very few Americans would have approved this strategy. No need. The decision was made on our behalf, without our knowledge, and the US media has never covered this story in depth. As a result, most Americans are unacquainted with the grim results that occur when misguided think-tank strategies are tested on real men and women. Can we count on the promises of today for a clean, quick "regime change" any more than we should have trusted the Gulf War rhetoric which promised laser-guided accuracy?

Sad to say, policies created by a few insiders against a backdrop of public indifference or ignorance are often the wrong policies. They have unintended effects. They backfire and harm the United States. And they ruin the lives of innocents in foreign lands.

Why did I come to the Middle East? In 1986 Libya and Syria stood accused of sponsoring terrorism. In May the United States responded by bombing Libya, killing fifteen people including Qaddafi's infant daughter. Commentators suggested that Syria was next. By December Syria was routinely denounced for harboring the world's worst renegades. Still, I had trouble jiving the TV image of Syria with the one Syrian whom I knew. In Seattle, I had built a restaurant designed by Hasan the architect. He was mild, fastidious, courteous to a fault—a Poirot, a real fuss-budget—and a family man who indulged his daughters. Was he typical of Arabs in the Middle East? Or were they, on the balance, violent people bent on martyrdom?

"I've got to go and see for myself," I announced. I had spent a decade building my construction business and needed to take a break. As a destination, the Middle East seemed more adventurous than, say, Hawaii. I wanted to meet the people I had seen in the news.

One more thing: I was angry because, coming out of college, I had worked hard to put my life in order. The hatred and killing in the Middle East, geographically distant as it was, nevertheless distorted my mental world. The Middle East defined the possibilities for human behavior. Cruelty, fear, and revenge were kept alive in my life in Seattle because they dominated the story that came out of Ramallah, Jerusalem, and Tel Aviv.

"The world's leaders have failed to solve the Middle East conflict," I thought, "despite those hefty salaries they have been collecting. I guess I will have to do it myself." This was a vain thought, typical of a carpenter convinced of his can-do prowess.

"I am joking," I told myself.

Yet as my journey progressed I found that Syrians constantly restored the mantel of responsibility that I had so quickly shed. "We must think, and pray, and yearn for the ideas that humanity needs to survive," Syrians seemed to say to me. "Ultimately individual men and women, not experts, not power brokers, achieve peace."

Why Syria? This country is a microcosm of the Arab Middle East. What I learned in Syria, I felt, would apply in some measure to all Arab countries. Also, I had an advantage with Syria. The contacts that Hasan the architect provided could help. This country had amazing ruins and very few tourists. Even more compelling: Syria had dozens of cultures and subcultures developed over five thousand years' time, probably unmatched in the world for a country of its size. Syria was a cultural storehouse—the Amazon rain forest of raw cultural material.

I wanted to isolate the special capacity that enabled men and women of different races and faiths to live together. In Syria I sensed that I had the best chance of finding the answer for which I was searching.

I also wanted to write about my journey, and I hoped that Syrians would honor this endeavor. As it turned out, I met many Syrians who encouraged me to put my travel to literary use. In the old Crusader seaport of Tartus, for example, I took tea with a local English teacher, a short, plump man who listened to my itinerary, then interrupted.

"You must have a purpose for your travel," he said. "Something for humanity. I think that you should write a book—not a funny book, but wise, very wise. In the Middle Ages, before a man wrote a book he traveled the entire world, talked to the people, saw the customs. Only then did he sit down to write. Syria—it is the world. All the philosophies, all the history, all the peoples of the world are here, right here, in our small country. You see, you speak, you make a note. Then go home and write a book of wisdom."

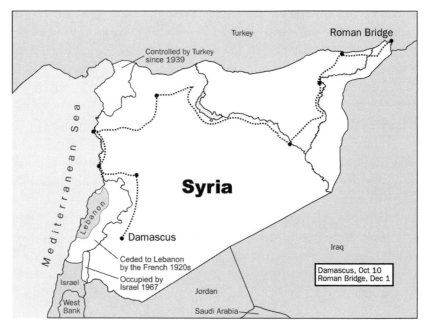

From Damascus to the Roman Bridge.

PART ONE

Temple of Zeinab
A Week in Damascus

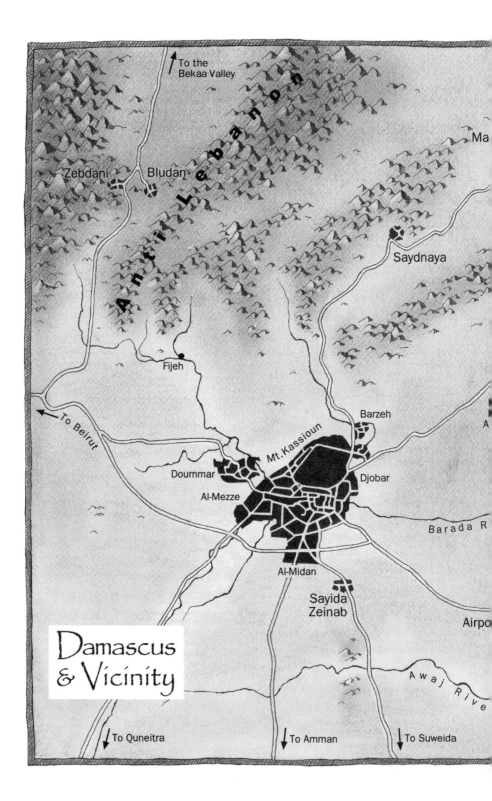

Damascus
& Vicinity

1 — Trapped in a Can

SEATTLE. FRIDAY, OCTOBER 9, 1987.

One Friday morning while I was brushing my teeth I considered my situation. The remodeling job I had promised to complete was done, and I had no immediate commitments. I was booked on a three o'clock flight that would take me to Europe and then to Damascus. "I can still cash in my plane ticket," I thought. Did I really want to go to Syria?

I had made many noble declarations over the years. Nothing ever had come of them, and at a certain level I did not really expect to carry through on my Syria proposal. Yet something was different this time because, over the previous nine months, I found myself taking steps—learning a little Arabic, acquiring a passport, applying for a visa. I talked to my Syrian friend Hasan, who gave me the names of associates in Syria—as did Rita, my travel agent, and Alex Bertulis, another Seattle friend who had traveled in Syria. Also I asked travel advice of Robin Wright, a journalist who had lived in the region.

I found myself thinking, "Syria? I *do* need a break." I had kind of promised Hasan to take some art books to his friends in the country. Besides, I'd gotten a cheap fare, so I probably could *not* cash in my plane ticket. On the face of it Syria was not entirely logical, yet on this morning it was the easiest thing to do.

The decision was made, and I had only an hour or two. I shoved underwear into the bottom of my expedition pack, dropped in Hasan's art books, plus some note pads that I'd assembled, a camera, a tape recorder, more underwear, a pair of slacks, a map, my woodsman's compass. I folded my blue blazer on top and lashed down the flap. My wife was calling for me by now, and I grabbed my passport and traveler's checks on the way out the door. At the airport I was late. I kissed my wife, waved to my parents, and ran to the airplane. As we taxied onto the runway I had the strange feeling that the doors of an immense, heavy vault had just swung shut. My plane lifted off, and I found myself thinking: "This evening I won't be home for dinner."

I was not a seasoned traveler. In fact I scarcely had left town for the previous fifteen years. I never quite grasped the point that a trip to Syria meant leaving home. I felt guilty for not being on the job. When I remembered how long this trip was supposed to last—not a week or two, but three months—I became nauseated, overcome with the notion that I might never return to the life I was leaving. I strained against the seat belt, a victim of my own unfortunate plotting. There was no easy way to reverse plans that had been put in motion. A few hours from now, when we touched down in Denmark to make connections, I couldn't just catch the first flight home. There were vague complicating factors, sunken thoughts buried in the black, watery depths of my mind. I sensed that Syria was not an accident. Syria was something I needed to do.

We were flying now over bare northern reaches, land and water and pink haze on the horizon. I looked out the window, tears rolling down my face. I loved my home, my work, my routine. These were the things that nurtured me. I loved my wife and relied upon her. Normally she steadied me—only now she was back home in Seattle. I missed her already, the more so since we were not on especially good terms. She had opposed this trip, silently, for a year, and I had no idea why. I hoped she would be waiting for me when I returned.

The evening meal came and went, and our captain asked us to pull the shades on our windows. The lights in the cabin went down, and passengers grew quiet and began to sleep. The night, however, was artificial. I cracked my shade, looked across the top of the world, and saw red at the edge of the sky. When I had boarded the airplane, the careful divisions of work and leisure that composed my life came apart. Now the normal patterns of day and night had become confused as well. There was nothing I could do. In my youth I had climbed mountains. Hiking to the base of a great cliff, I had felt strong and in charge of my fate. Now, nothing of the sort. I was being sucked along by forces that I could not control. I was an animal trapped in a can, carried for transplant to the other side of the world.

2 — Soldiers

The airport was modern, yet the walls were drab, and the floors were stained and gritty. I was tired, disoriented, and anxious. I knew about recent bombings where the terrorist Abu Nidal—allegedly following Syrian direction—had blown to bits travelers in the Rome and Vienna airports, travelers whose only crime was to come too close to the El Al counter. I had also heard of government actions within Syria. In Hama in 1982, following a wave of killings by right-wing Islamic extremists, Syrian troops commanded by the President's brother Rifaat al-Asad had quelled a revolt, turned the artillery on the city, then sent in the death squads—something like ten thousand died. In Jisr esh-Shughur men in uniform had set up field tribunals where people had to stand in line twice: once for the military judge, a second time for the firing squad. In Palmyra people had been jailed, waiting to be judged. Then Rifat's Red Berets landed in helicopters and made short work with grenades and automatic weapons. I had been informed that the secret police—who came in nineteen different flavors—were far worse than uniformed troops.

Now that I was in Syria, I had reason to be anxious. And I had trouble separating my fears from reality. I had not slept for two days. My mind raced. I found myself projecting my own mental whimsy, daydream, and nightmare onto the people around me. I needed to get through customs and find my way to town. I needed to sleep.

Ahead of me in line was a Texan who wore blue jeans and cowboy boots and was returning to work on an oil installation in the desert. He had been here a year earlier when Reagan decided the Syrians were terrorists and ordered US companies to leave. This allowed European companies to make money on Syria's limited oil deposits. We wanted the business, but did not want to take Syria off the terrorist list. So, apparently, we had decided that it was OK to do business with terrorists as long as they had at least some oil. I talked to the Texan for a minute while I grew more and more uneasy about the soldiers, four dozen of them—fierce-looking men in khaki.

They had us surrounded.

I averted my eyes, because I was the one they were looking for. My passport stated my occupation as carpenter, but actually I was a creative writer—carpentry was just something I did during the week to throw people off the track and, also, to earn a living. So here I was, traveling on a tourist visa, with false information on my passport, and what did I have in my blue nylon expedition pack hidden under a thin layer of T-shirts? Note pads, that's what. If the soldiers found my note pads, it would be the end. People in Seattle had cautioned me, but I had not listened. Up ahead, travelers were opening their bags for inspection, and I saw no obvious way to avoid disaster. I looked at the floor and kept my mouth shut. When I had completed this line, I forced myself to walk, slowly, to the next.

The military men were closer now, and I wondered at their formation. They were not surrounding us precisely, but seemed to be standing, almost at random, in the spaces where we were not. Suddenly I understood: their lines were staggered in a combat formation, so that a single enemy bullet could not kill two men—they were on guard against armed invaders, not creative writers.

Syria was still at war with Israel, a foe of exceeding cleverness. The Israeli lines were a few miles up the road at the Golan Heights, yet, as any armchair tactician could tell you, the Israelis fought according to principles of maneuver and surprise. They would not do the obvious. For example, they'd never drive their tanks down the highway for twenty minutes until they reached Damascus. Instead they'd do something a little offbeat, like fly into the airport on a commercial airliner and take taxis into town. It was clear to me now. Syrian troops had massed at the arrival gate to check a possible Israeli advance.

After fifteen minutes my line began to move. I couldn't see the Texan. He had short-circuited the whole procedure by waving a few papers in the face of an official.

After nearly an hour in what the US media and State Department termed a "terrorist" nation, I was still breathing. But the soldiers puzzled me. I peeked for a moment at the one nearest me and saw that he wore a glazed expression. So did the others. A few minutes earlier, I had recognized the brutal soldiers of years past. But now I understood that these soldiers were different. They were killing time.

Later I realized that this was my one sane observation all evening. Like most successful military rulers, Syrian President Hafez al-Asad kept track of those in the country who were for him and those who were against him, the Ins and the Outs. The Ins worked for the government and spent their time sitting in overstuffed chairs in offices or standing in uniform at the airport. The Outs did not have jobs and spent their time playing backgammon in coffee houses.

Looking more closely, I saw that the customs officials were only giving the luggage a quick glance, nothing thorough. My chances of getting through were good, and now I felt embarrassed at my alarm. I had never seen so many people in uniform up close. They were intimidating. But I needn't have worried. They were merely customs officials, not real soldiers at all, and only a few carried weapons. Their closest links were not to the army, but to the secret police. The secret police?

That's the way things worked in Syria. As soon as you got calmed down about one danger, you discovered another that was deeper, more subtle, more insidious.

3 — Saleh

I felt alone and lost. I did not have a single acquaintance in this country. I had no reservations, and no idea where I would spend the night. The simplest procedures were beyond me. How, for example, did you get to town from the airport?

I made it past the second customs booth, but the last table was crowded so I sat on a bench to wait. Next to me was an Indian wearing a dark blue suit. His beard was trimmed short, his hair carefully parted, and I took him for a businessman.

"The customs," Saleh said in a low voice, "is a waste of our time. Must they scowl at us? And why does it take four dozen men to do nothing?"

I, too, saw the dirt, the broken walls, the uniformed officials standing around while passengers waited in line. But I preferred to remain silent. Syria, like other countries, had dungeons.

"A sad operation," Saleh continued, "but this is only the

bureaucracy. The Syrian people are friendly. Of course, there is the problem of taxis and hotels." Fortunately, Saleh had a plan: we could split the cost of a taxi and a hotel room. "I can prevent certain murder," he said.

In the next room we claimed our bags and then opened them on a low platform for inspection. The officials waved me on but were puzzled by Saleh's Ugandan passport with its numerous Iranian visa stamps. Saleh argued back and forth: he was a British resident, from London. As Saleh spoke with our customs man, I glanced into the foyer. Swarthy men in jeans and dirty army jackets pressed their faces against the glass that separated us. They had a hungry look and were sizing us up, giving our baggage the eye, blocking our exit. Were these a loosely organized group of terrorists or simply freelance thugs?

"Taxi drivers," said Saleh.

Eventually Saleh smoothed things over with customs, cleared the doorway, then adopted a blank, menacing stare and led me through the taxi-driver-gauntlet.

In a few minutes we made the front entrance, decided to forego a taxi, and boarded a city transit bus—dingy, dirty, and empty except for an African woman in an orange gown. Saleh and I took a seat and, to keep an eye on our bags, placed them on the seat beside us. Soon the driver appeared, however, and scolded us. We moved our gear to the baggage space at the rear. Half a dozen men came aboard, Arabs who used the rear door and crowded in the back near our luggage. Others used the front door. It was late, I was tired, and these men had a sinister air about them. Every so often Saleh looked back. Had our baggage been cannibalized?

"Tell me about your business," I said to Saleh.

"I am a travel agent, based in London, but my family lived in Uganda. I was in London as a student when Idi Amin expelled the Asians and confiscated our property. It is fortunate that my father was visiting me at the time—he could have had trouble leaving."

I remembered Idi Amin, the flamboyant, moody dictator who reportedly tortured and murdered more than 100,000 of his country-men. "You have a suitcase," I said, "but also boxes."

"These contain special books from a printer in London. I have brought them for my friends in Damascus."

Several more men had entered from the rear, pushing against those who had come before and calling to their friends in front. The aisle behind us was packed tight. The men were young and hostile. The bus driver should have scolded them instead of Saleh and me. But now this keeper of rules had retreated to his seat and was staring out the window. I felt in danger, and, as our ride progressed, the situation grew worse. My only hope was Saleh. Yet he seemed oblivious to the danger—preoccupied with obscure history and politics.

"Part of my job is to meet many people," Saleh said. "I book special flights, especially to Damascus and Teheran. This is how I picked up my few words of Farsi." Across the isle were two young men, more clean cut than the others. One began talking with Saleh in Farsi, and a few minutes later Saleh explained.

"He is an Iraqi who fled for his life to Syria eight years ago and now finds work in an airline office in Damascus. Many have fled Iraq, for Saddam's men like to murder Shiite Muslims, except of course they first rape the women. Especially they abuse those whose families have come from Iran such as this fellow. He has come to the airport to meet another Shiite, the man sitting next to him, who is here on pilgrimage."

Saleh's friend leaned over. "Karbala, Karbala," he said.

"He is describing the pilgrimage," said Saleh. "Fifty years after the death of the Prophet Muhammad a great battle was fought in the desert near Karbala, a city in Iraq. Hussein, the grandson of the Prophet, was slain and his sister taken captive and brought here to Damascus where she lived out her life. Once a year we mourn in our homes or at temples. So this is the reason that his companion has traveled such a long way from home."

As Saleh spoke, another four or five men climbed aboard. They were rough and careless and shouted and laughed and pushed one another into empty seats while the rest of us pulled back from the aisles to keep from being bruised. The most malicious of the lot was an enormous young man who sneered and cackled as he walked down the aisle, then abruptly swung into the seat behind me. This guy was huge, and I could feel his hot, stale breath on the back of my neck. He worried me. I turned and looked back to check on our luggage and found myself staring at his midsection. I lifted

25

my eyes—he was glaring at me. I gave him my "international understanding" expression—a friendly look that I had been practicing at home in front of a mirror. He grunted and I turned back to Saleh. "Who are these guys?" I asked. Saleh spoke with his friend for a moment. "These are from Libya."

The previous April the United States had bombed Tripoli at night, capping an exchange of insults and provocations between Reagan and Qaddafi. US officials said afterward that the purpose of the raid was not to assassinate Qaddafi. On the other hand they would have been pleased if he had been killed accidentally by the bombs targeted on his sleeping quarters. Now, past midnight on a bus in Damascus, I couldn't count on these Libyans to appreciate such a fine distinction.

The bus driver closed the front and rear doors, and we slowly pulled away from the curb. The street was curved, we came to a military checkpoint, then moved along a straight road in the dark—no highway lights—and I could see stunted trees in the weak wash from the headlights. We were thirty Libyans, one black African woman, two Iraqis, Saleh the Indian businessman from London with a Ugandan passport, and me. What of Saleh?

"Why have you come to Damascus?" I asked.

"The exact reason began fourteen hundred years ago," he said.

"At Karbala?"

"Yes. The ashes of the daughter of Ali were buried in a tomb, which now rests in a small village called Sayida Zeinab or the tomb of Zeinab, which is outside Damascus."

"Is this from the Quran?" I asked.

"No, no my friend," said Saleh. "The Quran was dictated by Allah to the Prophet Muhammad before this. If you would like to read this book I can make a special gift to you."

"You have a Quran with you?"

"I have three dozen Qurans, in my boxes. But these are in Arabic. I will have to send you one in English."

Behind me the big Libyan spoke in Arabic. I turned around. His travel bag was on his lap, open. He pulled out a can of beer, nodded at me, and popped the top. I didn't drink and, until this moment, had taken comfort in the idea that Muslims did not drink either.

"As I was saying," Saleh continued, "every year Muslims come from all over—three or four thousand of them—to attend the

Arbyeen, or fortieth day after the death of Hussein, a festival of four days, a remembrance of this dear man and the sadness of his death. Shiites, especially, remember him."

"What are these Libyans doing here?" I asked. "Are they coming to the festival?"

"No, no," said Saleh. "They are simply on holiday. Things are strict in Libya, but in Damascus the rules are much relaxed. At home in Libya these ones must be silent and respectful and kind to the poor and strangers. But here no one knows them, no one cares. They can make a nice riot for a few days."

The Libyan leaned forward and spoke to me. "Deutsch?" he said. "German?"

I was wearing Levis and a plaid button down shirt. I had promised myself I would neither flaunt my nationality nor conceal it. "American," I said. "I am from America."

"*Amerikee,*" said the Libyan. He crushed his beer can, threw it on the floor and reached in his bag for another. He popped the top and took a swig. "*Amerikee, Amerikee,*" he said to himself. Then he called to the rest of the mob in the front of the bus, "*Amerikee,*" and pointed at my head. I inched down in my seat and tried to look friendly.

"*Ayyy. Amerikee,*" the Libyans in front answered.

"*Amerikee, Amerikee,*" the big one announced to his friends in the rear.

"*Ayyy,*" they responded, adding some phrases in Arabic that described, I sensed, some crude procedures that they would like to perform on my body. The Libyans in front laughed and added details of their own. The big one grunted.

I nodded my head and smiled. "Nice to meet you," I said. The Libyans sneered. The big one shoved his beer can under my nose. I turned back to Saleh.

"Of course, we also remember the death of Hussein's older brother," Saleh said, "and in the background of it all is the treachery done to Ali, Hussein's father. Do you know him?"

Saleh jabbered on, the Islamic scholar and missionary to the end, explaining how the Sunnis had done the Shiites dirt over a thousand years before—not that he was keeping score. "This man is my protector," I thought. "But who will protect him?"

Saleh's Iraqi friends from across the aisle had been following his spiel. Now one of them leaned toward me. "And where have we Shia—what you call Shiites—been?" he asked. "Out. Out."

"Yes," said Saleh. "The Shiites—ever since the murder of Ali—have been out at the edges, never corrupted by the wealth of empire. We have been few, the Sunnis many. Of course all Islam is one. These Libyans are one with us as well, brothers in the faith. Though, at this moment we are subdued, thinking about the sad events of fourteen hundred years ago, and they are thinking of the women of Damascus."

The bus accelerated gradually until it was hurtling along in the night, and still it accelerated. I did not like my Libyan companions, but we were in motion now, they grew quiet, and my fears shifted from the comparative order of this bus to the angry disorder of the city that lay before us, the city I had learned about on television news, the world capital of terrorism, the home of Abu Nidal, the cruelest man alive—a city where any evil was possible at any moment. Soon I would be walking the streets, aimless, disoriented, at the mercy of those who lurked in the shadows. I turned to the window and saw a road sign whip past and nothing more, no lights, no moon, flat blackness that was murky from the dim light of the bus. I was nauseated and cold, shaking a little, fear and weariness and not-knowing. I wanted to sleep but I needed to stay awake, to stay alert. Our bus was ragged and out of control. Where was the driver? I glanced forward but it was too much effort to pick him out. I looked out the window again, looked at the edge of the road, blurred as it shot past. Behind me I could hear the Libyans grunting and cackling, and my protector, Saleh the Shiite, mumbling in a foreign tongue. The African woman was silent, the bus rattled, and the engine was loose, loud, and fast, running wild and blind, pulling into the night and carrying us along with it.

I thought about the home I had left behind, the places I had known, the people who had wasted love on me. My life had been going smoothly, working on the job, working at home, moments of leisure, and all the time people knew who I was, my family, my friends, small associations built over the years. In this vast world I had scratched out a little place for myself. Then, suddenly, I had made travel plans, and now I was captive to those plans. I was on the other side of the world, in the night, alone. Could I ever find my way home? I closed my eyes, opened my mind, and searched the universe for comfort. But none was to be found. "I will never return," I thought. "I am lost, we are all lost, on a rickety bus rushing into darkness."

4 — Prayers

At home in Seattle, I had formulated a principle for safe travel in Syria: avoid Shiite Muslims. The fanatics who had held Americans hostage in our embassy in Teheran in 1979 were Shiites. At the moment, Shiites in Beirut were holding half a dozen Western hostages—minus whoever had been tortured and killed. My architect friend Hasan was a Syrian and a reasonable man. Of course, he was a Sunni Muslim.

My first discovery in this so-called "terrorist" nation, however, was that Shiites, for all their bad habits in the matter of hostage taking, were a far sight better than drunken Libyans. Saleh the Shiite, for example, was not my idea of a threat. Still, he was a fundamentalist who liked to visit Teheran. Did this man, who appeared so mild, secretly lust for martyrdom?

Our airport bus parked in the center of town, and Saleh's Iraqi friends guided us to the al-Boustan Hotel, a thirty-year-old building in downtown Damascus where a porter showed us a tiny room on the seventh floor. The porter was an old man dressed in a synthetic uniform that was losing its shape, and the room did not look much better. Still, the night manager was asking thirty-two dollars per night (the tourist hotels required payment in hard currency: dollars, British pounds, or marks). Saleh scowled when he saw the room. Our inspection complete, the porter led us back to the lobby. I was exhausted, ready to sleep. But Saleh was energized.

"I have thoughts about the price," said Saleh. He spoke to the night manager, a slender, dark-haired man of twenty-five who stood behind the counter. "Such a small room, barely with space to breathe. Under the circumstances I think we should pay no more than fifteen dollars." Saleh stood facing the night manager, looked him straight in the eye, and spoke firm, urgent words. Saleh's stance and his words, however, were undercut by his fingers—the fingers of his right hand could not keep from drumming on the counter, apropos of nothing, whenever Saleh stopped talking—a zany accompaniment to the night manager's replies.

"You do us great honor to seek accommodations with us," said the night manager in crisp, British English. "You must know, however, that we have our established rates and that it would be irregular and unprincipled of me to deviate from them."

"You have your rates, but surely they apply to full size rooms with enough oxygen to sustain a guest for an entire evening."

"The room is small but entirely sufficient. We keep it available for emergencies such as yours, when travelers come to us late at night with no place else to stay and beg us for a small space in which to rest themselves for the evening. And of course we offer the same banquet at breakfast as for our guests in other rooms."

"We are foreigners," said Saleh. "We are guests in your country, your city. We are, in a way, guests in your home. Has not the entire world heard of Arab hospitality? Is it not proper to give us the very best you have, to take the slippers from your own feet to give us comfort?" Saleh's fingers began to drum once more. The night manager glanced down for a moment, then looked back at Saleh.

"You speak well and you must know how my heart has sorrow for your late arrival this evening and your carelessness in the matter of reservations."

"How long does this go on?" I said to the porter. He didn't speak English, but caught my meaning and shrugged. In a few hours Saleh was supposed to be at the shrine outside town—the burning, spiritual purpose of his visit and a must for this Muslim fundamentalist—yet he seemed to have forgotten.

"Yes," said Saleh. "But let us consider that half the night is gone, which should bring a commensurate deduction in the price of the room."

"As you undoubtedly understand," said the night manager, "I am a person of great authority in this hotel during the evening, but I do not set the rates and I do not have the power to alter them."

"Look," I said. "I'll pay the difference. I haven't slept for two days." Saleh stopped drumming for a moment and held up his hand for silence.

"You must admit," said Saleh to the night manager, "that it is late and unlikely that anyone else will rent this room for the night. If we do not take it for fifteen dollars, then no one will take it. Under the circumstances, do you feel that your superior would rather you collected fifteen dollars, or nothing?"

I began to carry our bags to the open elevator. The porter held the elevator door. I shoved my passport across the counter to the night manager and tugged on Saleh's sleeve.

"Tonight, since my friend is tired, we will agree to stay in shameful conditions at this inflated price of thirty-two dollars which amounts to robbery, assault, and three sex crimes added in," Saleh smiled. "But in the morning we will speak with your superior to ask for a deduction. And in consideration of your desire to keep your position at this establishment, we will not tell him of the grievous difficulties and aggravations that you have caused to come down upon our heads. And for this favor of silence on our part, we must insist that your porter immediately transform our room into spotless condition, with a suitable bed for my friend, and all the amenities that travelers in our position have a right to expect when they put down one half their year's income for a simple night's lodging."

Saleh placed his passport on the counter, smiled, drummed his fingers one last time, and followed me to the elevator. On the seventh floor we carried our bags around the corner to the door with our number on it. Inside was a suite: a small foyer with four doors, one to our room, one to the bath. We assumed that the other two doors led to linen closets. The porter removed one of the stuffed chairs and brought in a folding bed and mattress. He returned with sheets and blankets, and I began to help him make the bed. "What are you doing?" Saleh said to me. "You must never help people such as this. When you assist them, they only work more slowly."

"You must move quickly," said Saleh to the porter. "At present you are a sloppy worker with no pride in your job. You bring this hotel, which is low enough already, to even greater depths." Saleh's tone was sweet, and he had an impish smile on his face. Something was going on that I did not understand. The porter paused, looked up, and seemed to listen. "Oui, Monsieur," he said in a whisper, and went back to making the bed. I felt for the porter, but there was nothing that I could do. When he left, I chided Saleh.

"No, no," said Saleh. "I am far too gentle. You should listen to the people with whom I normally travel. They make me sound like an angel. You see, the hotel workers play a small game for their amusement and sometimes make bets. They wait to see if a guest will accept their sloppy work—they are testing the guest, forcing him to show his prejudice toward third-world people, that he sees their worst and thinks that they are helpless to do better. We have paid for excellent service, the hotel workers have excellence to give, and we honor them by calling their bluff and insisting on our money's worth."

For Saleh, argument was play. He had argued with the night manager and now with the porter. The next day he would argue with the manager, various bus drivers, the proprietors of local restaurants. Sometimes he scored: the manager would grant us a five-dollar deduction on our night's lodging. But money was not the issue, and often there was something ridiculous in his demands. Who but Saleh, faced with a bus fare of eight cents, would bargain for a lower rate? However, no matter how contrary his words, Saleh always displayed a playful, light tone.

I couldn't find towels, so Saleh offered to search the closets in the foyer. He opened one door, but couldn't see anything until he hit a light switch and found himself staring at a man and a woman naked in bed—an unthinkable breach of privacy in this Muslim land. It turned out that the room was not a closet but a bedroom. Saleh muttered apologies, retreated, and suggested that I go down to ask for towels rather than test the fourth door.

By the time I returned it was nearly 3:00 AM. I was tired. Saleh had shoved back the coffee table and unrolled a prayer mat on the few square feet of open floor. At the head of the mat was a small, rectangular piece of stone. "I have missed many prayers today," said Saleh. "I don't feel right."

"It's late," I said. "Maybe you should give it a rest and try again tomorrow."

"No, no. We are supposed to pray five times each day," Saleh said. "Only those Sunnis usually combine afternoon and evening prayers, cutting corners, not right at all. As Shiites we must keep each prayer." Saleh was matter-of-fact, a professor explaining his faith to a student. He was, as usual, oblivious to the circumstances.

He retrieved a small, green box from his suitcase, opened it, and removed a silver compass with buttons to hold and release the needle. In the box were extra needles and a folded instruction sheet. The compass was manufactured specially for Muslims traveling in heathen lands. "One must face Mecca," Saleh explained. The instructions listed the magnetic deviation from true north and the compass bearing toward Mecca for many of the world's great cities. Damascus, however, was not included.

"What would the deviation be for Damascus?" Saleh asked.

"Magnetic north is above Newfoundland," I said, "so from Seattle it is twenty-one degrees east, and from here it would be something to the west. Unless, of course, we have come far enough around the world that we would be pointing back east again." Saleh seemed to think that I knew what I was talking about.

I unfolded a map of the Middle East on my bed and on top of it placed my own compass, a large, liquid-filled model with a clear plastic base. The sighting mirror had broken off. "This is a Swedish compass," I said. "I used it in Alaska. The first thing to do is orient the map." I was avoiding the question of deviation.

"But your map," Saleh noted, "does not extend as far as Mecca."

"This complicates things, but I remember Mecca being about down here," I poked my finger into the blanket, "somewhere below this cigarette hole."

"I should be accurate," said Saleh, "however in emergencies I think a forty-five degree margin of error would be acceptable."

"So we have oriented the map," I continued, "and Damascus is here and Mecca approximately here. In my opinion you should be praying at just about this angle," I gestured toward the corner of the room.

"Here?" Saleh pointed his left hand, fingers extended, thumb up.

"A little to the left," I said, "and that should bring you a lot closer than forty-five degrees." I was a child of the American West, a man-of-action, you could say—at least I'd watched plenty of man-of-action movies. I was pleased to find that even this Muslim fundamentalist needed what I had to offer.

"Thank you," said Saleh as he turned his mat, moved his stone and knelt. He took a couple of test bows to get the stone the correct distance from his knees so that his forehead would touch it perfectly when he leaned forward. Saleh needed lights on, so I lay down on my bed to scribble a few notes while he proceeded, first kneeling upright and repeating words to himself, then bowing and touching his forehead. After a few minutes the porter came in. Saleh was bowing away from us and seemed scarcely aware of the man's presence.

The porter handed me the towels and began to leave, then stopped. Something about Saleh's prayer bothered him. He stood and waited. At last Saleh looked his direction. The porter motioned for him to shift his rug. Saleh stood, moved the mat, and looked back for approval. The porter motioned him a little farther to the right, and Saleh complied. The porter smiled and bowed slightly. The rancor of their earlier exchange had utterly vanished—and now I realized that it had never existed outside of my mind. They exchanged *Salaam Alekhems*, the porter left, and Saleh resumed his prayers.

Saleh's mat was now oriented parallel to the side street. Damascus, in one of its incarnations, had been laid out by the Romans. Thus Saleh was facing directly south, about twelve degrees off course by my calculations. I was about to say something, but hesitated. I was enjoying myself but it was late. This comedy would have to end.

I stepped over Saleh's feet on my way to the bathroom where I took a cold shower. When I returned it was nearly 4:00 AM. Saleh had finished his prayers. "I feel very much better," he said. "I have missed three prayers today, which is inexcusable, and now I am late with my night prayer but I have done my best.

"I was in flight from Frankfurt at the proper time for the night prayer. I was going to roll out my mat and kneel down in an aisle but I thought that the stewardess might become excited. In Europe they always object about Muslims hijacking airplanes."

Saleh glanced at his watch and decided to wait up an hour so that he could perform his morning prayers at the proper time. I thought this plan unwise. How could he endure a four-day pilgrimage if he did not get his rest? I offered to set the alarm on my wristwatch. Saleh agreed and got under the covers. I fiddled with the alarm, and he was asleep before I turned out the lights.

The alarm woke me at 5:00 AM. I yelled at Saleh, turned on the light, and yelled again but he did not respond.

"*Allaaaaahu akbar!*" The call to prayer blared from the public loudspeaker outside, the eastern tonalities distorted by an amplification system that was too squawky for my taste.

I grabbed Saleh's foot and yanked.

"It's time for your prayers," I said. "Are you awake?"

"Yes, yes, very much so," Saleh replied. He blinked his eyes against the light. I returned to my bed, turned out the light, and got under the covers. At 10:00 AM I woke to the sound of cars, buses, and trucks on the street below. Saleh was still asleep. Beneath the comic facade he was serious about his faith. He had come a long way for a religious purpose, was trying his best to get everything right, and now he had botched his first religious duty of the day. "Poor man," I thought. I expected him to be agonized with guilt. I shook him. "You've missed your morning prayers," I said softly. "I'm so sorry. It's entirely my fault. I should have properly wakened you." Saleh sprang from bed.

"You and I have paid dearly for breakfast," he announced. "The manager would love to have us miss our meal. We must go quickly."

5—To Me, Syria Was a Mountain

I was twenty-two and a Stanford senior when a friend from college and I climbed a new route on El Capitan in Yosemite Valley. The "Heart Route" we called it, for the prominent heart-shaped feature on El Cap's west face. For ten days we lived on the sheer granite face. We slept in hammocks, suffered close calls with falling rock and threatening storm. Since then seventeen years had passed, I was nearly forty, and I hadn't climbed a mountain in years. What I missed most from mountain climbing was the way it forced me to pull together every scrap of "who I was"—every physical, emotional, intellectual, and spiritual resource—in order to accomplish a single, crisply defined goal. I was older now and did not want to compete against my former self. I needed a challenge which would equal in its own way the summits of my youth.

The mountain climbers I remembered from Yosemite now rafted rivers in Asia and sailed boats around Patagonia—interesting expeditions. Most over-the-hill mountain climbers, however, took fewer risks. They preferred to trek through remote areas with paradisal beauty. My notion of the ideal expedition for this retired climber was to revive the old spirituality, to live hard, bivouac on ledges, suffer a little, learn from the peak. I was looking for adventure, something closer to Asian rapids and Antarctic currents than blissful reveries in Shangri-La.

Still, fast rivers and choppy seas were not quite what I was after. An expedition such as mine needed to enter an extreme realm, but not necessarily a physical extreme. After all, there were no more blank areas on the chart in this age of satellite mapping. Nowadays, uncharted realms were cultural. Risks were psychological. An expedition into the unknown might as well take place in crowded cities as in isolated places of wind and waves.

Two or three centuries ago, European explorers traveled to distant lands, mapped what they thought of as empty spaces and made notes on the curious behavior of the so-called "savages" who lived there. The soldiers and colonial administrators who followed, rationalized the whimsy, intuition, and daring of the explorer and turned his feats into solid coin for the mother country.

Up close, the civilizing process was coarse and bloody—we now call it imperialism, racism, and genocide. The civilizing work of colonial powers made you think that, for all their advanced weapons and complex schemes, they were the real barbarians. In modern times the indigenous peoples who somehow managed to survive colonial rule were emerging, demanding their due, and a world wrapped in hypocrisy was groaning and cracking under the strain.

I suppose that the courage of yesterday's explorers could be separated from the colonial implications of their expeditions. Still, modern day adventurers who sojourned in the Karakorum, Antarctica, or other distant corners of the earth—woman or man against nature—seemed like doddering generals fighting the last war, a pretend war. Real battles were raging, and my idea was to move into the heat and smoke. The battleground I chose was the third world—a web of human striving and despair that said more about our future than our past. But where in the third world? Something specific was eating at me. I could only scratch this itch by visiting a particular third-world location. And so I had come to Syria.

6 — Fear

I had been in Syria for only a few hours and had been sheltered from this culture by a more experienced traveler in Saleh. Yet already I was jittery. In Syria in 1987 fear was a plain, day-to-day emotion, unexceptional and scarcely worthy of comment. It filtered experience. It was a feeling that I carried with me every moment.

In the United States I had never lived in fear of the government. But in Syria things were different. The security forces were strict and seemed to think that citizens and visitors alike were guilty of some crime. At any moment, on the slightest pretext, they could descend and call the guilty one to account. In Seattle I talked to a Palestinian who told me he had been sitting in a Damascus coffee shop with his sister one day when two young men wearing red berets took the next table. (They were members of Rifaat al-Assad's feared Defense Companies.)

"*Shouf al-bizaz,*" said one, Look at those breasts. He nodded in the direction of the Palestinian's sister.

"*Bidi aneekha,*" said the other, I want to have her. These remarks continued until the Palestinian no longer could ignore them.

"*Shu hada al-kalam?*" he said, What kind of talk is this? In an instant the two Red Berets dragged the Palestinian onto the street, punched and kicked him, and threw him into their jeep.

"*Ila al-Jebel,*" one said, To the mountain. The "mountain" was Red Beret headquarters and, for the Palestinian, it promised to be a one-way trip. At this moment the owner of the coffee house ran out and pleaded for the life of the poor foreigner who, the proprietor explained, simply did not know the respect due to Red Berets.

The Red Berets threw the Palestinian on the sidewalk and drove off. His sister called a cab, and they drove from one hospital to the next seeking help. When hospital attendants learned the cause of his wounds, they refused to treat him. At last his sister found a dispensary in a Palestinian refugee camp at the edge of town. She had her brother stitched and splinted. "Then, quickly," the Palestinian told me, "she put me on a plane out of the country."

I heard another story from Farouk, the academic and Paris coffeehouse philosopher who read and critiqued the manuscript of my Syrian adventures. Before his years in Paris, Farouk had left his home in Tunisia to study in Damascus.

"I was walking through the Souk al-Hamideyeh," he said, "and my hair was a little long in back. Three guys grabbed me, put a gun to my temple, and dragged me to a house where they kill people. I looked like another man, a Syrian Communist who they were after. They were about to shoot me right there, and I was crying and holding out my ID from my country. But they wouldn't listen, and wouldn't listen. Then one glanced at my ID. So they threw me in the street. I left the country that afternoon and never have returned."

In Syria in 1987, from hour to hour, a person never knew if he or she would be challenged, detained, or interrogated. During the weeks of my journey, most days would pass without incident. Yet every hour was filled with tension.

The Syrians I met seemed to think that their government, for all its shortcomings, was better than one formed by members of the Muslim Brotherhood. I couldn't substantiate this impression, however, for the first rule of travel in Syria in 1987, a year after the bombs in Rome, Vienna, and Berlin, was never to talk politics. Foreigners who complained about the government—even in private gatherings—could expect to be confronted by the secret police the next day and told to leave the country. Citizens who criticized the regime risked far worse.

Syrians, hoping to cement a friendship with an American, gave me their names and addresses and asked me to send them postcards from America. They put themselves in jeopardy, and so did those who assisted me by paying my bus fare, inviting me for tea, or asking me to eat a meal with them or to stay the night. Syrians became my accomplices in the crime of literary note-taking. In Syria in 1987 a foreigner who traveled from place to place and jotted down observations was considered a spy. These spies were divided into two categories: journalists who spied out in the open, and agents who spied undercover. I thought about applying for a visa as a journalist.

The trouble was, as a journalist I would have been given no more than ten days in the country and would have been followed. That left me no choice but to travel as a tourist and trust that my bags would never be searched. I would have to write my notes in secret, make carbons, and send them home in small batches. The police had agents in the mail rooms who inspected packages heading to the United States. I could expect that my mail would be read, and that at least some dispatches would be destroyed. So I would have to keep my originals. If they were discovered, I would get a quick trip out of the country at a minimum.

The Syrians whose names and addresses I carried would be interrogated in their homes by the police—a shattering and degrading experience. Reports would be filed, and evidence of guilt placed in the official record, ready for retrieval. Of course it was possible that I would meet Syrians whose situations were tenuous or whose enemies were looking for the right moment to press their advantage. Then, what I feared most: a person's name in my notebook could be the pretext for his or her imprisonment, torture, or death.

"Never, under any circumstances, travel in a third-world country with misleading information on your documents," said Robin Wright. Robin was a journalist and author with the *Los Angeles Times*. She had spent years in Beirut during the troubles. The day before I left Seattle, I needed encouragement, so I called her. "You are bound to do something which seems suspicious. You are bound to be picked up by the police. And then, when the police find that you have lied on your visa application, it will be taken as proof of guilt."

Even if I escaped the secret police, Robin pointed out, culture shock and the difficulties of finding my way in a third-world country would make short work of me. "Do you speak Arabic?" she asked. "Or French? Do you have friends in Syria?"

"Not really," I said.

"And you never have been to the third world before?"

"That's right."

"You are making a mistake," she continued, "and it's not too late to change your mind. In Syria you will be lonely and lost and unable to function. The filth and squalor will make you sick. The simplest things will be impossible. Everything takes time, and a Westerner can't get anywhere. Officials will suspect you. You will be followed. Hotels run a hundred fifty dollars per night. Your trip will be total disaster, a brief but very expensive disaster."

The day before, I had also received a briefing from my travel agent, an Arab who had lived in Syria for several years and returned every so often to visit relatives. She told me of the scrapes that other tourists had gotten into with the Syrian secret police—like the Englishman whom she just barely saved from prison: he had taken a photo of a bird—unfortunately the bird was sitting on a sign that read in Arabic, "Military Zone, Photos Forbidden." As I said good-bye, I noticed that she was trembling. Was she afraid? "You were impulsive," she explained later, "and you had such a big mouth. It's hard for me, calling long distance, to get someone out of a Syrian jail—and that supposes I can even find him."

7 — Looking for Free Digs

Ten and a half hours after arriving in a supposed "terrorist" nation I was still breathing. I had escaped the drunken Libyan and his raucous companions on the bus, and I had survived a night alone in a cubicle with a fundamentalist Shiite Muslim. OK, I admit that Saleh was no threat. He was a Shiite, but reminded me more of Laurel and Hardy than Khomeini and Rafsanjani. Saleh was endearing. I wanted to adopt him. But now I had another worry. I was afraid that Saleh would botch his pilgrimage and otherwise fail to make the grade as a good Shiite.

Other than my worries about Saleh, things were going fine—as long as I stayed in our hotel. The streets outside were pure carnage, horns honking, brakes squealing—and was I hallucinating or did I hear pedestrians shouting at the trucks, then screaming as they ricocheted off of fenders? Did I see policemen dragging the injured from the roadway in an attempt to keep traffic flowing? On the sidewalks below our window I saw many men. I wondered if they were desert nomads with knives who in the past had ambushed camel trains but now had found easier pickings in town around the hotels? My hotel was safe, if over-priced. The porter and even the night manager had been gentle and friendly. I was half-convinced, however, that any attempt to leave the al-Boustan would bring nothing but trouble.

When Saleh and I returned to our room from a breakfast of apricot jam and crusty flatbread, I grabbed the phone, half-expecting smoke as I lifted the receiver—but no, it seemed to work. At thirty-two dollars per night, my trip would last only three weeks, so I needed to find free digs. I could teach English to pay for lodging. But where to begin the search? Instead of plunging blindly, I decided to work through channels. My travel agent had given me the phone number of Saad Shalabi, a Syrian with an office in Damascus. She didn't know him well, and I didn't know him at all. But I had nothing to lose, unless you count my freedom and my physical well-being. I was afraid that this Muslim would hate me and turn me over to the secret police for a visa violation. I took a deep breath and dialed. I heard a voice in Arabic, then English: a recording. It was Saad, speaking on a telephone answering machine. I left a message after the beep.

While I waited for a return call, I would assist Saleh. He needed to get to the temple, but lacked a sense of direction. His little round compass was worse than useless, and no one was available to assist him. As much as I feared the chaos beyond the firm walls of our hotel, I feared more for my amiable boy zealot. Saleh would protect me from the swirling currents of Arab culture. I would protect him from himself.

My friends in Seattle had predicted that I would be taken hostage in Syria, probably within three days of my arrival. They had heard on the news about Terry Anderson and the other Western hostages who languished in Beirut, and they knew that their captors were Muslim fundamentalists—Shiites, but more particularly members of the Hezbollah, a radical Shiite fringe.

If Shiites as a group were not dangerous, this special segment, the

Saleh snapped my picture in front of the al-Boustan Hotel.

Hezbollah, was a genuine threat. For one thing, they had executed several hostages a year earlier, after our air strike on Libya. Still, I wasn't worried. An international border separated Syria from Lebanon, a border which I did not intend to cross. For that matter, the State Department had forbidden Americans to enter Lebanon. What I did not know, however, was that once a year—on the very weekend I arrived in Damascus—members of the Hezbollah came en masse to the temple of Zeinab on the outskirts of town. All the better to celebrate the martyrdom of Hussein. Saleh was innocent and unwitting. I never could have guessed that he would lead me into the arms of the Hezbollah.

8 — Enemies of the West

Saleh and I rode buses in circles for two hours until we happened on one which took us to a small town on the outskirts of Damascus whose sole industry was the temple of Zeinab. With casualties rising in the Iran-Iraq war, the shrine had grown ever more popular. The Iranian government gave women all-expense-paid trips to Sayida Zeinab as compensation for the loss of their sons in battle.

The temple had minarets, a tiled courtyard, and a shrine with two enormous gold doors enclosing the tomb of Zeinab. The place had cost a mint to restore, but Iran had picked up the tab. In all, it was perfectly sized for an intimate mass meeting.

By the time we arrived, Saleh had missed two prayers. He hurried into the inner sanctum while I sat on low marble steps on the south side of the shrine and rested my head on my knees. The sun was pleasant, and I was beginning to sleep when I sensed movement. I looked up and saw five young men, their faces two feet from mine.

"Who are you?" their leader said in English.

"I am an American. Who are you?"

"We are the Hezbollah." I had no obvious means of escape, so I smiled. "Nice to meet you," I said.

The young men stared at me for a few moments, then one looked at the others and smiled slightly. I had expected snarling terrorists, but I sensed that these young men had been raised well by good mothers. They introduced themselves, we shook hands, and they began to teach me the error of my ways.

"Imam Khomeini says, 'Our war is with the American government, not the American people.'" Muhammad was a student and spoke good English. "We love the American people," he continued, "but the government—we will strike the white palace." He adopted a defiant pose.

"Ahh, the white palace," said Jamal. "Crush the white palace."

The white palace? The young men thought it inappropriate that the president of a country as magnificent and mysterious as mine should live in a mere house. They admired the power of Americans but marked us down on matters of style.

"The white palace has ships and bombs, but they can't defeat us," said Muhammad. "We have our God. If we die in battle we go to Allah." They were posturing and later admitted that, as students, they never actually had gone into battle.

"Everyone is against us. The Russians, the French, the English, the

The Hezbollah handed me a poster with the logo of the Iranian Revolutionary Guard: an assault rifle held aloft above a globe and a Quran.

Almany or, as you say, Germans. And Reagan. He sends the battleship, shoots big bombs into villages, explodes buildings, and kills children. The children that got killed, what did they do to him?

"The Israeli devils pull down our villages in south Lebanon and make captives and do terrible things to the women, things so sad I cannot tell you. And the Israelis let Christian militia kill hundreds in Beirut, in the camps, women and old men and little boys, people in the camp where they came when they did not have a home. The Israeli tanks look for the Palestinians and instead blow us up.

"You in America don't know us. You don't know me until you know my brother who is dying in south Lebanon."

"What do you think of Iran?" I asked.

"Iran," Muhammad said. "Irangate." In the United States the Iran-Contra scandal had dominated network news for the month before my departure. It was a fair bet that some of the TOW missiles that the United States had sold Iran had been shipped to Beirut, to enable the Hezbollah to destroy Israeli tanks. A newspaper in Beirut had originally broken the story, so it made sense that they would have known. But I never imagined that Muslims in Beirut saw the American TV coverage which local stations, to satisfy their large, Christian audience, pulled down from the satellites. "On television we saw Irangate," Muhammad continued. "Did Reagan win in Irangate?"

"Of course he won," I said. "Nixon was run out of office for doing a lot less. Reagan, on the other hand, rode off into the sunset like an American hero."

"Do you know Ollie North?" I asked. Muhammad and Jamal threw out their chests and flexed their muscles. "Ollie North, Ollie North," they chanted. They had watched his congressional testimony. "Ollie is Rambo," said Jamal. I would have expected them to despise Colonel North, a professed enemy of terrorists, a man who claimed to be on Abu Nidal's hit list, yet they seemed to admire him. Whom else did they admire?

"Sylvester Stallone," said Jamal. "Sylvester Stallone for president." Jamal owned all of Stallone's movies on video, the Rockies and Rambos. The mullahs told young men like Jamal about sacrifice and heaven and the will of Allah before sending them into battle in south Lebanon. But their model of manhood, it seemed, was molded at a more visceral level by the well-muscled American actor.

Four passageways led from the courtyard at the temple of Zeinab.

Only later, when I had come to know Jamal and Muhammad better, did they inquire about another American adventure hero: Chuck Norris.

"Is *Delta Force* true?" asked Muhammad. "The American Army, does it have commandos trained just to kill Muslims?"

I tried to explain that the bodies which fell left and right in this Chuck Norris movie (based on an actual airline hijacking which ended in Beirut) were not Muslims—they were bad guys, and no one need be offended. But Muhammad and Jamal were not offended, really. It was more as though their feelings were hurt. They believed my country to be the wealthiest and most powerful and most free of any nation. They admired it and were happy to be featured—even as enemies—in movies alongside the great Chuck Norris. They simply wanted respect.

After a few minutes' talk, Jamal and Muhammad invited me to walk with them around the shrine. Women—many of them clad head to toe in black gauze *abiahs*—had spread blankets on the covered promenade at the edge of the courtyard and sat amidst their bundles while they watched the younger generation walking past.

A man with a battery-powered megaphone began to chant. Several other solemn-faced men stood in a circle. They took a hopping step and reached their right hands toward the center of the circle, then thrust their chests forward and slapped right hand over left breast.

"Hussein, Hussein," explained Muhammad. "They are having sorrow over Hussein."

I was wearing Levis and was easy to identify as a foreigner. When other pilgrims approached and challenged me, Jamal and

Muhammad interceded. "He's OK," they said in rapid Arabic. "He's with us."

Saleh and I stayed at the temple until ten o'clock, then caught a bus back to Damascus and the al-Boustan Hotel. It was nearly midnight and I was ready to sleep, but Saleh was restless and hungry and felt the need to explore. We marched into the gloom and wandered until Saleh found a sidewalk sandwich shop which was closed, although the weary shopkeeper was still there, cleaning up after a long day. Saleh convinced the man to fire up his equipment in order to feed us. By now I was hungry, but I'd have to wait because Saleh insisted that the man fix us horizontal kebab with chips even though this shop offered only vertical kebab and rice. At last Saleh had to concede the point, and I thought we were going to eat, but there was one more thing. This meal was priced at thirty lira or about one dollar and twenty cents, excessive to Saleh's mind, so he argued furiously for a reduction of eight cents. Eventually the shopkeeper was swayed. He cooked the meal, we ate, said good-bye, and returned to our hotel.

It was three o'clock and Saleh wanted to stay awake for the sake of his morning prayers. I convinced him to sleep and set the alarm on my wristwatch for 5:00 AM before shutting off the lights. I was pleasantly exhausted and fell into a sound sleep.

9 — My Summit

I had come to Syria to meet many different kinds of Syrians. Otherwise, I had no plan.

During my first days in Damascus my lack of planning had paid dividends. Saleh the Shiite, the temple of Zeinab, and my unlikely Hezbollah friends Muhammad and Jamal never could have been anticipated. On the other hand, I sensed that I couldn't wing it for long. I needed a geographic objective.

What in Syria was my summit?

Syria is burdened by an illogical geography which Syrians blame on the French and British who rigged the boundaries in the Levant after World War I. Syria's rivers disappear into Iraq and Turkey, the summits of its mountains are in Lebanon, its railroad line crosses two intervening countries before it gets to Mecca. Rivers, mountains, and railroad lines had worked for other travelers in other countries. But they wouldn't work for me.

Looking at my tourist map, however, I did see one possibility. In the far eastern tip of Syria, closer to the former Soviet Union than to the Mediterranean, a stone bridge arched over the Tigris: Jisr Roman. It had been built by Romans at the site of an ancient ford used by Alexander. It linked West and East. It was a way station on the Silk Road to China, a portal to the elevated, arid steppe of Central Asia. Syria had always been an intersection of trade routes. It prospered when borders were open, withered when they were closed. A feature of the ancient transportation system was an apt symbol for this country. The Roman Bridge would be my summit.

There was a quick route to the Roman Bridge from Damascus, made possible by modern highways. But this would have meant avoiding most of the inhabited portions of the country. I chose instead the traditional route that followed the watered grassland of the Fertile Crescent that vagabonds from Abraham to the military man Tamerlane the Great relied upon to support their herds as they traveled. The route traced an arc from Damascus, up the coast to the city of Aleppo, and down the Euphrates to its confluence with the al-Khabur River. Only then did it turn to follow the Khabur upstream north and east through desert and steppe to the Roman Bridge.

Success in reaching Jisr Roman was not a given, far from it. I would have to master all the intricacies of travel in this third-world nation. In addition, I faced a whole range of complexities that a wealthier traveler could have avoided.

Of course the Roman Bridge had its own special difficulties. It was located in al-Jazira, a remote area between the Tigris and Euphrates rivers—positioned at the intersection of three countries. For hundreds of years al-Jazira had been a haven for fierce brigands and smugglers who preyed on travelers and merchants. The place always had been difficult for the authorities to police. These lands were heavily populated by Kurds, and the Kurds were looking for a pretext to revolt—as they had been for centuries. Things were simmering, and a bloody guerrilla war had broken out just across the border in Iraq and Turkey. The Syrian districts heavily populated by Kurds had not yet gone up

47

in flames, presumably because the Kurds were using Syria as a base and supply depot with the tacit approval of the Syrian government (which had its own reasons to oppose the Turks). Still, there was no love lost between the Syrian government and Kurds.

In Damascus, a couple of years before I arrived, a dozen Kurds had marched on the sidewalk carrying placards, lodging a protest. A couple of policemen walked over and—Tear gas? Batons?—pulled out their AK-47s and machine-gunned the entire group. At least that's how an American friend, who had been studying at the university nearby, told the story. And Damascus was tame compared to the district surrounding the Roman Bridge. Police in al-Jazira were in combat mode, prepared for insurrection, fearing for their own safety, and were in no mood to welcome tourists.

10 — Only One Thing

DAMASCUS. MONDAY, OCTOBER 12.

At 10:00 AM the phone rang. As I tried to make sense of the commotion on the other end of the line I realized that Saleh was out cold. I had shaken him at five o'clock, but instead of rising he had pulled the blanket over his ears against the blaring call to prayer. "Wrong number," I shouted into the phone, then hung up. The phone rang again, and by now my mind was more clear.

"For you." I recognized the voice of the desk clerk. "It is Monsieur Shalabi."

An hour later Saleh and I were sitting in the office of Saad Shalabi, a blue-eyed Arab whose once-blond hair was now silver gray. Saad had been born in Damascus, had taken degrees in civil engineering at colleges in California, and spoke perfect English. He motioned Saleh and me to sit on the leather couch in his office while he settled into the swivel chair behind his walnut desk, lit a cigar, and quizzed us on our visit. He was Sunni, Saleh was Shiite, yet both were Muslims who had lived in the West. They talked as though they had known each other for years. They traded tales of travel in the Gulf and exchanged business cards. When it was my turn to talk, I elbowed Saleh.

"My friend is looking for a situation," Saleh explained. "A way to provide services for his lodgings, so that he may extend his visit. When he travels to the coast and to Aleppo he will need to stay in hotels, which will be expensive, but unavoidable. And of course he will visit the market like all tourists and pay a little too much for imitation goods to take as gifts to his wife and family. In order to afford these future necessary expenses he was hoping to obtain a base in Damascus where he could stay for a very modest price. Actually, free would be good."

A day earlier, before I'd met Jamal and Muhammad, I'd had jitters at the thought of Saad Shalabi, whom I thought would be my first Arab acquaintance. I feared that he would be hostile, a cynical basher of America. I was surprised to find that Saad loved my country despite what he perceived to be its flaws. What's more, he seemed determined to offer every possible courtesy. "I have a place for you to stay," said Saad in delicate, refined English. "It is primitive, scarcely suitable, but it is yours if you choose. And please let me give you a tour of Damascus, later, at the end of the week."

I was puzzled. Why was Saad so eager to assist me?

As my journey progressed I would witness this phenomenon time and again. Arabs, even those who were poor, assisted me in large and small ways. Was it considered good luck to help an American? Perhaps they thought I would return the favor at a later date. In the end, however, I was forced to accept a less complicated conclusion. Arabs are generous people who feel good about themselves if they are kind to strangers. With Saad there was an added twist. To host me affirmed his status as an international man, an Arab with local roots who nevertheless had mastered the language and culture of a distant country called America.

That afternoon Saad met Saleh and me in front of our hotel and drove us to a farm he owned on the outskirts of Damascus, three miles from the temple of Zeinab. His father had purchased fifty acres with fruit trees as an investment in 1957. Saad gave me a key to the stone farmhouse, introduced me to the Eritrean student who occupied the caretaker's quarters, and advised me to keep my distance from the mongrel which was chained inside the compound's steel gate. I could stay as long as I liked, leave baggage here while I toured, and in return I was required to do nothing at all. I was the guest of Saad Shalabi, who apologized once again that he had nothing better to offer.

I left my bags in the farmhouse. Then Saleh and I rode into Zeinab with Saad who let us out near the temple. I went to the driver's window and thanked him. "This is nothing," Saad said. "And only one thing I ask."

"What's that?"

"Do not give my name. Not to the police, not to anyone."

11 — Literary Ambition

On the road from Damascus to the Roman Bridge I wanted to meet Syrians, to learn how they saw America, to find out if they were terrorists filled with hate or were real human beings with hearts, souls, and minds of their own.

My journey was straightforward, yet it was overlaid by a thicket of ambitions. And these ambitions—not the secret police, the bad hotels, or the complex tongue—were my largest obstacles.

You've heard about the stereotypical American tourist: He has an intense job at home, never takes a break, and is completely overworked. The instant he *does* leave on vacation, however, he immediately develops a hobby which he pursues with as much intensity and single-mindedness as his job at home. It's impossible to relax in the company of this American. On my Syrian excursion it was my misfortune to be saddled with just such a companion. I was forced to travel, in other words, with myself.

My prime ambition was to write a book about this trip. Once I had arrived in Syria, my greatest chore was to turn my days and nights into character, dialogue, and plot. I had read my Paul Theroux. I knew that the traveler's itinerary provided his plot. "What a cheap way to write a book," I thought. "Take a trip, create a story, write it down." The idea appealed to one who labored over his words. What I had not fathomed was the small problem that any misstep in my itinerary would bend my plot out of shape. Literary form, to my mind, also demanded Big Moments at the beginning and the end of the narrative. Also the book needed a dénouement.

If I was worried day by day about Syria's secret police, my literary fears were equally pervasive. How to create a plot of verve and insight? How to develop tension, conflict, and resolution? And, at the dénouement, how to provide an insight suitable to the occasion? I worried that I would do or say something that would fail to capture an inviting plot twist or would destroy a plot that, until that point, had been flowing quite nicely.

What was required, I reasoned, was educated spontaneity. In advance I had studied Syrian history and culture just enough, I supposed, to hone my instincts for the profound—not so much as to rob my travel of whimsy and surprise. On the road, I knew, I would need to quickly decide among opportunities of the moment. When faced with two mysterious paths, I wanted to follow the one that led to an ancient palace, not the one that led to a McDonald's. (I prayed that Syria did not have a McDonald's.)

12 — The Patriarch of Antioch

In Seattle, paging through a picture book on Syria, I had seen a photo of a magnificent-looking man with a frizzy beard cut square in the ancient style, a cap of black silk, and flowing robes. This was the Patriarch of Antioch, leader of the ancient Eastern Orthodox Church, who embodied a tradition going back to early saints and martyrs, to the Apostles, and to Christ himself.

I imagined that the Patriarch was a man of humanity, a voice of reason in the midst of madness. His title recalled Abraham, the patriarch of the Bible who was the father of Jews and Christians through his son Isaac, and the father of Arabs through his son Ishmael.

I decided to take a few hours and find the Patriarch of Antioch. Wouldn't it be great if he gave an invocation for my journey? Something serious, profound, quotable. A piece of literature needed a formal opening. The Patriarch of Antioch was undoubtedly a busy man. Yet in ancient times Eastern leaders had held public audience where the humblest subject could come forward to beg judgment or favor. According to the caption under his photo, the Patriarch continued this tradition every Sunday after Mass.

"The Patriarch of Antioch?" asked Saad Shalabi. "You can find him in the old city, I am sure. But where, where in the old city?"

"I must ask my friend the lawyer. He is a Christian." Saleh and I followed Saad to the neighboring office.

"*Marhaba,*" I said, Greetings.

"*Ahlen wasahlen,*" the lawyer replied, I bid you welcome.

Since I had virtually exhausted my Arabic, and the lawyer did not speak English, Saad began to translate.

"He says *which* Patriarch of Antioch? There are two, the Greek Orthodox and the Syriac."

The photo in the library book had shown one Patriarch, not two. "For my purposes," I said, "either Patriarch would be fine."

The lawyer got the translation and mumbled some more. "What are your purposes?" Saad relayed.

"I just wanted to say hello," I said. Saad frowned. "I mean, I've heard that he is a great religious leader, and I thought he might have some words of guidance and insight that I could carry back to my country. In the United States, well, we are steeped in materialism, you know."

Saad translated. The lawyer seemed to like the idea of saving America from its sins. "*Mumkin, mumkin,*" he said.

"It is possible," translated Saad. "He will make inquiries and we should contact him again in two days."

After my interview with Saad Shalabi and his lawyer friend I was upbeat because this country seemed to be developing in a literary direction. In two days I would meet the Patriarch and receive my invocation, quite a coup. With such a high-toned yet offbeat opening, how could my book fail to capture the interest of the reader?

And, next on my list, an unpleasant task, a showdown with the immigration police. My visa was good for six months, but my travel permit—that other, crucial piece of paper—allowed me only two weeks. If I passed muster, the immigration police would extend my travel permit, and I would be free to begin my journey to the Roman Bridge. In the meantime I would hang with Saleh at the temple of Zeinab.

13 — Army of the Faithful

The terrace around the courtyard was covered edge to edge with blankets and, as evening came on, pilgrims packed in until the courtyard was a moving, circling mass of humanity. I found Jamal, the Hezbollah member from the day before who now seemed like an old friend. We didn't mind being seen together—you could say we served as one another's trophies. He was my terrorist, I was his imperialist. Beyond that, he was a nice guy. He hooked his arm in mine, and the two of us walked and talked and fended off the curious as before.

By now several thousand pilgrims filled the temple. Each corner had its own circle of young men who did a three-step hopping dance, thwacked their chests, and shouted in unison. The sound of two dozen hands landing against two dozen chests was solid. The chanting was a high, lonely solo, the life of Hussein, his joy his passion, his sacrifice against the thud, thud, thud: the solid earth, the sun, the moon, the stars.

The young men seemed childlike, superior not in their religion but in their culture. I envied their capacity to dance, sing, and chant without self-consciousness and wondered how many centuries had passed since men and women in the West could believe in God without excusing themselves or offering footnotes in a vain attempt to satisfy skeptics.

I saw a woman in a wheelchair with her right leg in a cast. In making her way through the crowd she approached an august sheik in long silk robes from behind, rammed him in the rear with her extended plaster leg, quite on purpose, then demanded his apology. Was this feminism at work? Did this sheik have a reputation for arrogance? Was this woman simply tired of being ignored while forced to live in her wheel chair, below eye level? I wanted to know more and started to follow her, when my quest was interrupted.

"*Allaaaaaahu, akbar!*" The muezzin, or prayer leader, was dressed in a white robe and turban. In a few minutes the entire courtyard was covered with prayer mats and kneeling figures. Jamal excused himself,

The walls of the temple were decorated with posters. This one depicts Musa al-Sadr, an Iranian Shiite leader who disappeared under mysterious circumstances on a trip to Libya.

and I moved toward the exit.

Those few pilgrims who wished to continue circling were forced to the perimeter where a small pathway remained between the mats placed in the courtyard proper and the blankets in the covered terrace. Halfway to the exit the last passageway closed before me, like winter ice over the Arctic Ocean. I stood still, surrounded by people bowing to touch their foreheads. Then a boy passed me and walked nonchalantly across mats, blankets, and clothing toward the exit. Another pilgrim followed. As an American, however, I needed to be more discreet. I spotted a stray patch of uncovered courtyard, then jumped for it. Women in scarves looked up as I attempted to balance on one foot while searching for the next landing zone, and in a few minutes I managed to reach the edge of the courtyard without stepping on anyone.

I left the temple for the shopping district, and when I returned Jamal grabbed me by the arm. "A big man," he said, "the *imam*. I have the *imam* for you." I had told Jamal and his friends that I was looking for a cleric who could elucidate the fine points of Shiite doctrine. Jamal led me to the southwest corner of the courtyard and, a few feet away, I saw a noble-looking older man. He wore a fine, white gown and a brown cape and walked quickly past. Close behind were half a dozen young men, who dressed like other pilgrims but had the darting eyes of bodyguards. "Fadlallah," said Jamal. "This is Muhammad Hussein Fadlallah."

A week earlier, at home in Seattle, I had learned about Fadlallah and the quiet feud he had going with the CIA. I read a review of the new Woodward book that depicted the CIA as inept and heavy-handed in its Middle East operations. He charged that the agency had spent one million dollars setting off a bomb in Beirut in March 1985 to kill the Hezbollah leader, this same Fadlallah. The bomb, hidden in a pickup truck parked on the street, destroyed a block of high-rise buildings and killed dozens of people, many of whom had just left a nearby mosque. The slaughter of innocents was not the idea behind the bomb, but in the espionage business, apparently, it is hard to get every detail just right. For example, the detail that Fadlallah was not at home when the bomb went off.

In the wake of the September 11th tragedy, Americans are asking why Arabs and Muslims in the Middle East sometimes seem to hate the United States. One irritant is the US definition of terrorism which, to many Middle Easterners, seems arbitrary and self-serving. When Israel strikes the West Bank with F-16 fighters it's called "self-defense." When Palestinians respond with the more primitive military means at their disposal, it's called "terrorism." The car bomb which the United States exploded in Beirut received scant notice in the US media. But to the people of Beirut it's a case of US sponsored "terrorism," plain and simple.

Fadlallah and his entourage turned abruptly and entered the shrine. The young men who composed the rear guard turned and walked slowly backward into the temple. They glared at us and clutched their garments where, I thought, their automatic weapons were concealed. Jamal's heart was in the right place, but he had overreached. Fadlallah was important and busy and nervous. A conversation with Fadlallah had never been a possibility.

At ten o'clock I said good-bye to Jamal, found Saleh, and walked to the shopping district across the street from the temple. I was talking with Saleh when the party began to break up. The crowd moved out of the shrine and into the streets, surging across curbs and

An artistic rendering of the word Allah, printed on a card I received at the temple of Zeinab, was also a national symbol found on the Iranian flag.

sidewalks, scraping the shuttered walls where shops had closed for the night, encompassing the last carts of sidewalk vendors. The crowd moved with cohesion and strength as though it had a heart that throbbed and shuddered with life. The singer chanted into a megaphone, the crowd in unison shouted its response while young men beat their chests in time. This was an army on the march, a ragged army of the faithful spilling into the streets of the village. Overhead I heard the chop chop chop of a military helicopter.

Saleh returned to the shrine to spend the night, and I found a taxi back to Saad's farm.

14 — Martyrs

Earlier in the evening, when Jamal was searching for some of his friends, I had struck up a conversation with Qasem Shehab, a short, dark-complexioned man of twenty-two who wore a faint mustache.

Other members of the Hezbollah had wanted to strike the white palace. But Qasem was a veteran who had fought the Israelis in south Lebanon. He was jaded, faintly skeptical, and although he enjoyed performing chants with his friends, for him the slogans were empty of meaning. Qasem Shehab was worried about his future and was desperate to find a way out of the Middle East. Perhaps I could help.

"Why not go to the US embassy," I said, "and ask for a visa?"

"The embassy is in Christian Beirut," he replied. "If I go there I get shot."

Yes, of course. But I doubted that I could do much to help. On the other hand, I was curious. Had Qasem ever killed another person? "No," he said. "I never do that."

"Didn't you kill any soldiers from that other country? Did you kill civilians on purpose or by accident? Isn't killing what soldiers are paid to do?"

"I killed no one. Only the enemies of the Islamic Revolution."

Qasem was young and although he was a college student he was not intellectually facile. He had served as a soldier, not a suicide bomber. He had fought Israeli troops. It was other members of the Hezbollah who fired rockets into Israel that killed indiscriminately. So why was I suggesting that he was a terrorist? Qasem was not interested in all this political talk. Yet his few words made clear that he considered the Shiites of South Lebanon to be victims of Israeli aggression since the Israeli invasion in 1982. He thought of the Hezbollah as the defenders of South Lebanon. What could he say that would make me understand?

Qasem led me to the passageway at the west exit tunnel and pointed to a poster bearing the photograph of a young man. "This is Ali Daril, from Beirut. He was married, then after fifteen days Israelis killed him in south Lebanon." Qasem pointed to a second poster. "Muhammad Naja, a student in Beirut. On summer vacation, three days out of school, he was captured in south Lebanon. Later, in Israel, we found his body."

Qasem Shehab wore an amulet with a photo of Khomeini.

We walked back into the courtyard. "In the village of Ansar in south Lebanon are many friends of mine. The Israelis keep them in jail like dogs."

I had read of Israeli excesses in south Lebanon. But what of the pretext, the incident that brought the Israelis into Lebanon, that bit of handiwork by Abu Nidal? One night in London, after a party at the Dorchester Hotel, someone had put a bullet into the head of the Israeli Ambassador. There was blood on both sides.

We slowly circled the shrine, stopping for a moment to chat with Saleh, then continuing our tour. "We were asleep," Qasem continued. "All the Muslims in Lebanon were asleep. We made prayers and houses and gardens and did not care about Palestine. But the Israelis invaded and woke us. Imam Khomeini woke us. The Islamic Revolution must fight until victory." Qasem seemed tired and spoke without emotion. After a while he interrupted his litany. "Mr. Scott," he asked, "can you go to the embassy here and put a visa application for me?"

15 — Sitting on the Floor

Qasem Shehab and the other pilgrims thought of the festival as an act of worship. At the least, I had to concede, it was magnificent theater. Looking back now, however, the most touching moment happened a few blocks away from the shrine itself.

On Tuesday morning I met Saleh in the village of Zeinab. He hadn't slept, and his blue shirt was wrinkled, although his suit seemed in good shape. He was accompanied by Qasem Shehab who led us to a small rental house nearby. We walked through a courtyard into a room with a single piece of furniture, a sofa positioned near the window. Qasem asked me to sit on the sofa, while he and the other young men arranged themselves on the mats at my feet. Later I thought about the symbolism.

Traditional Arab furnishings consisted of carpets and pillows. Whether in a tent in the desert or a mud house in a village, Arabs sat on the floor. But in modern Syria, Western style furniture had long been a mark of status, and by now the only people who sat on the floor were working-class folk who could afford little, if any, furniture. Qasem Shehab and his friends were poor. If they entertained a Syrian of elite status—the son of a landowning family, for example—they would not have expected him to sit on the floor. And now they had an American guest, in their pantheon several classes higher.

Saleh tried to sleep on a foam mattress in the corner while the young men translated one of the chants that they had performed at the shrine.

> My God, my God, until we see al-Mahdi,
> Save for us Khomeini

"Who is al-Mahdi?" I asked.

"He is the last *imam*," said Qasem. "A very important one, like a prophet."

"Not precisely." Saleh roused himself in the cause of correct theology. "Muhammad is the Prophet. There are no prophets after him." Having clarified this point, Saleh returned to his mattress.

"So where is al-Mahdi?" I asked.

"He is here," said Qasem.

"In Damascus?"

"Yes, and Beirut."

"No, no." Saleh could not sleep. "Al-Mahdi is present among us, but we cannot see him. He is the twelfth and final *imam* who disappeared under mysterious circumstances many years ago. When he appears again, he will fight the sinners. Muhammad is the Prophet, then the *imams* start. Imam Ali, the son-in-law of the Prophet, was the first. Then came his son Hasan, then his second son Hussein, on down to Muhammad al-Mahdi al-Mountazar, to use his proper name."

"So we say, save for us Khomeini," Qasem continued, "because we need him like a father until the final *imam* comes to us." (At the time of my travel, Imam Khomeini was still alive and in power in Iran.) Qasem and his friends demonstrated this chant, beating their breasts with perfect timing, shouting in unison. They were the first generation of their families to live in the city and attend college. They were close to the land and to each other. Their religion was still the dance, the passion, and had not yet grown cold, refined, intellectualized. Saleh, the London sophisticate, tried to chant along with them but he beat his breast tentatively and out of time whereas they were solid and unquestioning and precisely on the beat.

"Those Lebanese," Saleh said later, "amazing."

At noon we broke for prayers and, an hour later, met again in the rented house. The young fundamentalists had purchased roasted chicken, flatbread, and two sodas in cans. "We ask you to take this lunch with us," said one of them to me, "because Islam is a very good religion."

As an American I was a celebrity to these young men. Their only first-hand experience of my country was a military one in which the United States and its people appeared to them to have enormous arrogance. Other countries, they pointed out, sent spies or diplomats or assassins to Lebanon, but only the United States sent a battleship. I had read press reports. The USS Missouri had stood far out to sea and lobbed huge shells, 2,400-pound "flying Volkswagens" that landed in country villages. These young men argued that such shells killed and

Were Qasem Shehab and his crew a bunch of carefree guys on holiday, or were they the awesome cadre I had seen at the temple chanting their sorrow over the death of Hussein?

maimed people at random—did not distinguish between those who loved the United States and those who hated it. To the members of the Hezbollah, the battleship showed that America did not have high regard for its enemies, did not, in fact, care who they were. Qasem and his friends had demonstrated one of their favorite chants—then apologized for its refrain: Death to America.

Qasem and other young fundamentalists appeared to be terrorists of awful conviction preparing their own martyrdom. But a little below the surface Qasem and his friends seemed to have a different mind altogether. In the morning I had sat on the couch, but now that it was lunch I followed the young men across the room and took a place with them on the floor. I sat on a foam mattress, leaned against the wall, and the young men sat beside me and spoke back and forth to Qasem in fluid Arabic as they laid out the meal. When his friends stopped talking for a minute to cut the chicken with a spoon, Qasem told me what they had been saying. "They cannot believe that you, an American, sit with us on the floor."

16 — I Fight an Iranian

After lunch Qasem Shehab and I returned to the temple where I walked and talked into the night. At eight o'clock, Qasem and I were at the south entrance when a young friend of his, a mischief-maker who had earlier mimicked Saleh's clipped accent, ran up with the latest news. "Saleh," he said, "has lost his shoes." The mischief-maker pantomimed the holy man from London scolding the keeper of shoes. Qasem laughed. Saleh had entered the shrine for prayers and, as required, forfeited his shoes at the entrance booth. The shoe keeper tossed Saleh's polished black oxfords in a pile with three hundred sorry looking pieces of shoe leather, the footwear of other pilgrims. Some of these shoes had spilled from the pile, others had been pushed into corners, and it was possible that Saleh's were among the strays. On the other hand, the possibilities for mistaken identity were great. The mischief-maker suggested that Saleh would have to inspect the shoes of several thousand circling pilgrims if he was to locate his own. Soon Qasem and his pals were making wagers.

Qasem and I continued to walk, with Jamal and Muhammad running interference. Every so often, however, I ventured forth on my own and was forced to defend myself in halting Arabic to one hostile, suspicious young man after another. I was making friends, yet the effort tired me and made me irritable. Normally I am a peace-loving guy, especially when outnumbered three thousand to one. Now, however, I was beginning to lose my cool. At ten o'clock I met a young man, an English major at the university in Beirut, a member of the Hezbollah. He offered to shoot me with his AK-47 if only I would come to Beirut to make this pleasure possible. At midnight I met a rude young man who mocked the US Marines killed in Beirut by the Hezbollah suicide bomber, and succeeded in exhausting my last traces of good humor. I was annoyed at these Muslims, tired of playing the compliant American. My survival instincts were still alive, however, so I kept my mouth shut and hurried toward the exit. But where was Saleh? I needed to say good-bye. I turned back and found him standing below the clock, a look of triumph on his face: he had found his

A frieze of dark blue tile surrounded the temple courtyard.

shoes, wedged in a corner beneath a heap of sandals. I congratulated him and excused myself for the evening.

At that moment a dozen grim-faced young men blocked my exit. The men stepped aside to reveal a dark, sinewy man with close-cropped hair, some kind of tough guy, an Iranian—bitter and angry, a man with no light in his eyes, a hollow man. In a few seconds twenty people encircled us, then fifty. The Iranian and I faced each other in a small opening in the center of the crowd. Saleh had been trailing me, and I glanced to my right but I couldn't spot him, then I saw him ten paces behind me, caught in conversation with a religious man wearing spectacles, oblivious to my predicament, unreachable. I looked back at the Iranian.

"Iranee Amerikee," shouted the young men. *"Iranee Amerikee. Yala, yala,"* Fight, fight. The shouting became a chant and the chant repeated again and again, growing louder, swelling until it filled the courtyard. It was hot and I was tired, so tired, my head aching, I was losing my grip. Still the chant continued, on and on, insinuating, hypnotic and I began to lose it—noise, color, the pressure of bodies crowding around and, in the center of my vision: the Iranian. He seemed no longer to possess his own mind. He seemed emptied of will, a vessel for the malice of the crowd. I had come to this festival as an observer—it had seemed a good idea at the time. Now, I felt like a child beaten by waves. I was nauseated, shivering, dripping sweat. I was going to pieces—but not the Iranian. The crowd affected him in a different way. It focused him, gave him a center, gave him control. His head was down, his eyes narrowed, and he seemed to grow in stature as I watched. I thought that he was preparing himself for some ultimate test, some act of glory.

A few weeks earlier the United States had entered the Gulf in an effort to protect Kuwaiti tankers from the Iran-Iraq war. The Iranians had objected and had run their torpedo-laden patrol boats into our path. On the preceding Thursday our helicopters had sunk one of

Verses from the Quran were inscribed on the frieze.

these boats. On Saturday the Iranians responded with sneak attacks. Now it was Tuesday. People on the streets in Damascus watched TV in sidewalk sandwich shops and knew what was happening. They were up-to-the-minute. And now they were waiting for the American response. Especially for Hezbollah and Iranians on vacation, these incidents were fresh evidence of American treachery. Was I an opportunity for revenge?

Many in the audience had been like Jamal and Muhammad, friendly after the first few moments. But this crowd had sucked up the friendly faces. Now, as I watched, the Iranian slowly raised his head, opened his eyes, and stared straight at me. He lifted his head as though to speak and then paused—it was like a knife going through the crowd: silence, utter silence. And then he spoke quick, fierce words. By now Saleh had caught up with me. He translated. "Imam Khomeini says, 'Our war is with the American government, not with the American people.'"

At this moment, preparing to be slaughtered, I did not need a cliché. If I am going to be mauled in Damascus, I thought, at least let's be honest, there is a lot of hate between Iran and America, a lot of unfinished business.

"The hostages in Teheran in 1979 were American people," I replied in English. "So were the Marines in Beirut in 1983. So is Terry Anderson who, right now, today, you've got chained to a radiator somewhere in Lebanon. You have tortured Americans, killed Americans. Isn't this war against my people? If not, then tell me, what is?" Saleh grabbed my arm and cut in. "I must translate," he said and began babbling in Farsi. After a few minutes I tugged on his sleeve and eventually he wound down and turned to me with an explanation.

"I told him that you said you have great love for Imam Khomeini and the utmost respect for Islam, that you have observed the sincerity of the believers at this temple and . . ."

As Saleh continued to tell me the words that he had put into my mouth, I turned to the Iranian. Suddenly he lunged, his two thick hands gripped my neck, and he was pulling me down. In a flash I realized that I was being sucker-punched—an Islamic sneak attack. I was contemplating a countermove when, instead of a knee to my groin, the Iranian delivered three wet kisses, left cheek, right cheek, left cheek. Then he backed away and, facing me, gave a thin smile and then bowed slightly. The young men, now a hundred strong, cheered. I wiped the slobber from my cheeks. Getting kissed in public was painful enough, but to be kissed by a man, and an ugly one at that, was more than I could bear.

The Iranian grabbed my arm and led me through the crowd with Saleh trailing. We pushed and dodged until we reached a passageway and ran through it to make our escape. On the sidewalk outside the temple the Iranian again smiled and bowed slightly, then disappeared into the gloom.

17 – Saying Good-bye

DAMASCUS. WEDNESDAY, OCTOBER 14.

On this day, I was supposed to visit Saad's lawyer friend, yet it had not been a formal appointment. I had gone to bed at two o'clock the night before, slept in late, eaten breakfast on the roof. Now that I was ready to roll, it was eleven o'clock. From Saad's farm the trip to town would take two hours because I would have to walk a mile to the bus stop, then wait up to forty-five minutes or more for the next bus to come along. The ride itself would take at least an hour. Offices in Damascus closed at 1:00 PM for the midday meal, so I would not arrive in time. I would try the lawyer in a day or two.

That evening was my last at the temple. Things were subdued, the festival was winding down. Qasem Shehab and his friends already had left, but I found Jamal and Muhammad and said good-bye. At the end of the evening Saleh explained that he was leaving to visit a friend in the Gulf.

On Thursday, I met Saleh at the shrine at noon. The place was empty, and torn posters fluttered from the walls. Saleh ducked into the inner sanctum for a quick prayer, while I swatted flies and watched an old woman tossing abandoned shoes into a wheelbarrow—other pilgrims had been less fortunate than Saleh in the matter of missing footwear.

At the airport Saleh and I sat and waited for baggage check to open. This part of the airport was bright and clean, unlike the gloom and dirt on the other side the night we arrived. The sun was out, and I could see an interior courtyard with light streaming down and high ceilings, intricately painted, like a tapestry. Across from us Bedouin women sat with their children. They wore colored scarves and *thoubs*, traditional gowns of heavy black cloth, carefully embroidered in bright colors: blue, purple, and red. One woman must have been nursing. Her full left breast hung down the front of her dress, and she seemed in no hurry to conceal it. When I saw her I knew that I had been duped. Like everyone else in my country I had accepted the stereotype of the cloistered Arab woman. None of the reports I had seen on the Middle East explained that, in airports, some Arab women bared their breasts.

Now the time had come to say good-bye.

"Fly to London on your way home," said Saleh. "Study further into Islam. Finance is no problem. In Muslim lands the religion is eighty percent. You need the religion to understand the people."

"Sure," I said.

"Really," he said. "You have no idea why you came to Syria. But I know why. You did not come to Syria by accident. Not at all."

"Oh," I said.

"You came here to serve humanity. There are real people here, real lives. People here are asking you to see them, know them, believe them. You are in Syria because there are men, women, and children in this land who need what you have to give.

"You have a future in the third world. You can rent your house in the States and come here and teach English and support yourself and your wife very well. You can have a child. You can help the Shiites. You can help the third world from within. There does not have to be aid from Britain and the United States, not only.

"What else could you want in life? Do you want a lot of cars and houses and flashy things, a lot of money? I don't think so.

"You are open. Openness is a powerful thing. The people you see are your people, your kin, your brothers and sisters, your sons and daughters. The third world is your calling. Why did you come to Syria? Allah brought you here to heal your ignorance, to bless you and to bless the people of this land."

"Yeah," I said.

"Like every Western traveler you think you are looking for a shining vision. You are such a romantic. You want to hear the words of God. This is fine, seek your mystical vision, enjoy yourself. But please wake up the next day and look at the people of this land. They will tell you something more important than mystical insight. They will tell you how to live.

"You still don't see this? That's OK. Don't decide anything yet. Walk the road from Damascus. Go to cities and villages, hilltops and river valleys, meet educated people and people who are simple and plain and live close to the earth. Meet men and women of every faith, every race, every occupation. They will tell you why you are here and what you should do to serve them. Allah will speak to you in their words, their hands, their faces, their eyes. Listen to them and think as you travel. By the time you return to Damascus, you will know the truth of what I say."

Tears ran down my cheeks. I hadn't slept much for four days, and Saleh's words surprised me, moved me, laid me bare. The man touched my heart. Even so, I have to admit, I was also thinking of something less profound: a small problem of a literary nature. Saleh had stolen the lines that I had reserved for the Patriarch of Antioch. This was supposed to be the first Big Moment in my book, now it was wrecked, and, since my genre was nonfiction, I could not undo it. Saleh had grabbed my typewriter, so to speak, and written himself into the starring role. My journey across the country would begin in a few days and the words of the invocation were being uttered—not by a hoary Christian dignitary—but by a Shiite Muslim in a business suit.

Saleh was a bumbling, boyish man, always in trouble. Still, it struck me that I had needed him far more than he had needed me. Now I would be alone in Syria. Could I cope?

In Seattle I knew a former Navy pilot who had flown two hundred missions over North Vietnam. He told me how he had hated the way the military, in his initial training, had broken his spirit, made him crawl—only to put him in a frame of mind where he could learn a few lessons very, very well. "Looking back," he said, "those lessons saved my life. I would not have survived without that rough, crude, abusive beginning."

This country, so different from my own, was a painful place to be. I was the odd one in the crowd, the person who drew stares, the outsider. I was uprooted, languishing in a boot camp of the soul. Would I learn lessons? Would my life be saved?

I walked with Saleh toward the gate. We passed a booth with a sign announcing in Arabic and English "Mandatory Airport Tax." I told Saleh about the tax, and he walked a few steps toward the booth, then stopped. The attendant had stepped away for a moment, which, to Saleh, indicated that the tax was voluntary. "Such a tax is foolish," Saleh said. "I must not pay it." He turned again, and went through the gate.

I walked toward the door. Saleh should have been off to his plane by now but something told me that he was still in sight, caught in debate with customs officials who had seen him skirt the Airport Tax, in peril of missing his flight, obsessed with the point he was making and oblivious to all else. Saleh needed me. I turned—but he was nowhere to be seen. Saleh was on his own now, and so was I.

PART TWO

الشام

Cham Palace
A Second Week in Damascus

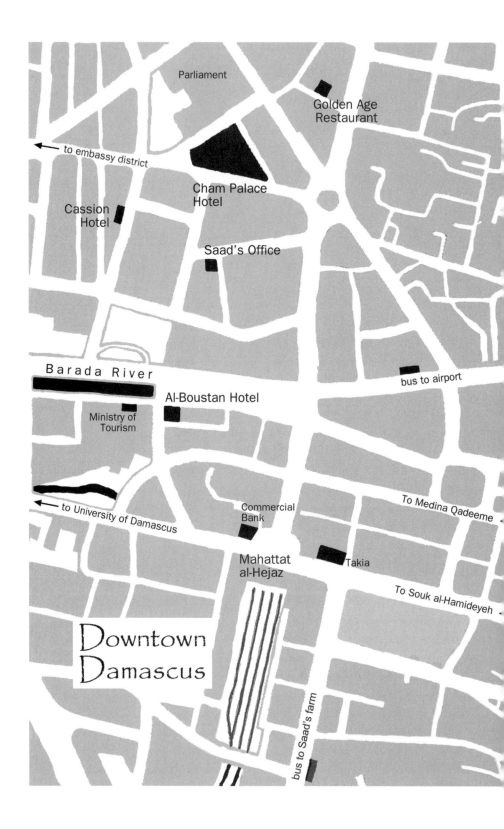

Parliament

Golden Age
Restaurant

to embassy district

Cham Palace
Hotel

Cassion
Hotel

Saad's Office

Barada River

bus to airport

Al-Boustan Hotel

Ministry of
Tourism

to University of Damascus

Commercial
Bank

To Medina Qadeeme

Mahattat
al-Hejaz

Takia

To Souk al-Hamideyeh

Downtown
Damascus

bus to Saad's farm

1— Innocent Souls

While planning my trip to Syria, I searched the stacks at the University of Washington library. Their collection on contemporary Syria was weak. Yet I found a number of books that awakened images of the ancient land. The Syria of my imagination was a place where mystics wandered the streets begging for coins and Sufi dancers chanted and went into trances and spun faster and faster until they brought the spirit of God crashing down upon themselves and everyone who watched.

The Lebanese whom I met at the temple of Zeinab were not mystics, yet they danced and chanted and seemed to lift themselves, if not into a trance, then into a state of exaltation. Qasem Shehab and his friends were spontaneous, emotional, and sincere. As a businessman accustomed to the grind, I was amazed by men who still knew how to play. That's what appealed to me about the Middle East. I'd heard that in this region intellectuals challenged you to leave the comfort of your profession or academic specialty and wade right in: Chautauqua on the Mediterranean. In this war-weary land, people had recognized that human beings who spoke from the heart—not technicians or specialists—were the crucial ingredient of civilized life.

Unlike Syria's ancient mystics, America's businessmen (at least the ones that I knew) did not stand up at their banquets and dance. And sometimes I thought that my country's intellectuals—especially those protecting carefully carved professional niches—also hesitated to let loose and speak from the heart. That's modern life for you. At the turn of the century organized professions began to appear and soon they ruled. The ingenious Yankee farmer who repaired his own threshing machine, built his own house, and served as lawmaker when the need arose was gradually replaced by the scientific farmer with chemical fertilizers and hybrid seed, the mechanic, the craftsman, and the career politician. In the world of ideas, thinkers were forced to develop credentials, to establish specialties, and to delimit their musings on reality. Historians who had once told grand stories now felt compelled to count and calculate. Thinkers in literature and the humanities tried to act like scientists. What ever happened to the Victorian ideal of the "educated amateur" who could probe reality with his or her own intelligence and humanity? What happened to poets such as Walt Whitman who could stuff the entire American experience into a single poem? And what of Herman Melville? He gazed into the heavens, and wondered, and knocked on the door of God's tomb. Which makes me think. If the author of *Moby Dick* could stand up and dance, then why have modern thinkers lost courage?

Herman Melville and Leo Tolstoy (another favorite of mine from the 1800s) felt that ordinary people could understand the most real and powerful forces at play in the universe. Melville and Tolstoy were not technicians themselves, but seemed to think that their words were more than polemic or amusement, that they were a serious instrument with which to probe reality. When you get to the bottom of it, Melville and Tolstoy believed that reality was spiritual and therefore could be understood by laymen and women who brought their own spiritual capacities to bear. Art and religion—music, dance, storytelling, painting, prayer, penitence, fasting—were not palliatives, decoration, or entertainment but the leading edge of human inquiry into the problem of being.

If I had become an automaton for the sake of my work, that was one thing. What bothered me was the possibility that I had sold out to a vague, modern cultural presumption that art and religion—untidy, difficult, inefficient—were simply an immature phase of human development that we had shed as our culture rose into a gleaming, precise, quantifiable adulthood.

In my youth I had admired Henry David Thoreau. For that matter, I thought of El Capitan as my equivalent to Thoreau's Walden Pond, a place of isolation and self-denial which enabled a person to see more clearly. I was especially attracted to Thoreau's idea of the "busk," a means of personal cleansing taken from a primitive tribe: each year tribe members burned all their possessions. Today the idea was impractical (the possessions which most dominated my life, for example, were owned by the bank). But couldn't I accomplish a busk of my own simply by leaving Seattle for a few months, leaving everything, everyone?

I am a progressive Christian. Remember the Vietnam War and the protests of the Reverend William Sloan Coffin and Robert MacAfee Brown? In college I heard these two men speak. MacAfee Brown was one of my advisors. They defined a Christianity that was engaged and, to me, had three parts: high-minded spiritual thinking; an awareness of injustice, poverty, and suffering; action in the world. During my travel in Syria, in the top of my blue nylon expedition pack, I carried a copy of the Bible in the rich and allusive King James translation. Every day I read for a few minutes from Psalms, from the Gospels, from the Epistles of Paul. Still, I am a construction worker, not a saint. In moments of frustration I might utter a few choice words. On the other hand, in truly difficult situations I would pray.

Thoreau, Gandhi, Tolstoy, the Apostle Paul: these writers believed in the virtue of the essential man, unsullied by the materialism of human life. I agreed, and yet I went a bit farther—had I picked this up from Rousseau?—because I believed that men and women who lived beyond the reach of Western culture were innocent souls untainted by the greed and sensuality of consumer society and the driving, linear imperatives of the hard-charging business world. After a dozen intensive years building my construction business, I was exhausted. I was convinced that a journey among such people was what I needed. I would escape the tyranny of my possessions and lose my ambitious calculating businessman's persona, I reasoned, in the clear-eyed innocence of a foreign land.

2— Saad Shalabi

If the Lebanese at the temple of Zeinab were spontaneous, emotional, and almost medieval in their clannish attachment to one another, Saad Shalabi was reserved. If they were primitive and passionate, he was reason itself. If they gave flight to my dreams, he was the rock upon which my dreams foundered.

Saad Shalabi was fifty years old, of medium build, and fine-boned, almost delicate. Judging from his looks, he had a capacity for precision. Saad was a charming man with a dry wit and a live-and-let-live attitude—courteous, pleasant, and warm. Yet he played his cards close to the vest. He was an engineer who preferred fact to speculation, a masculine being who didn't talk about his emotions. You'd never catch Saad walking down the street arm-in-arm with another man.

Sometimes Saad was busy or distracted or not feeling well and was sealed up even tighter than usual. At times like these I found myself wondering what I had done wrong: had I failed to observe some courtesy or botched my Arabic beyond hope of redemption? Later I realized that I had done nothing wrong—this was just Saad's style. I liked Saad. He was a pleasant man, but I couldn't begin to understand him until weeks later when a chance occurrence enabled me to see behind the facade.

Part way through my journey I returned to Damascus for a couple of days to do laundry, banking, and pick up supplies. Saad was on a business trip and, in his absence, his brother visited the farm. Rafiq was a slender man, taller than Saad, with dark hair, brown eyes, and a gift for conversation. Like Saad, his English was perfect, for he too had been educated in the United States. I caught a ride with him into town, we began to chat, and eventually the conversation turned to his older brother.

"What do you think of Saad?" he asked.

"He's OK," I said. "Your typical engineer, very cut-and-dried."

Rafiq laughed. "In Syria," he said, "things are not always what they appear. Saad is an engineer, but also he is a Sufi, a visionary, the heir to the leadership of the Damascus *mawlawi*—you know the *mawlawi?*" I confessed my ignorance, and he continued. "In America they are called whirling dervishes, religious men seeking God who spin and spin in circles in the pavilion."

By now Rafiq was maneuvering his car through the crowded streets of downtown Damascus. "Here it is," said Rafiq, "the *takia*, the apartment building where the *mawlawia* once lived. You see down below a courtyard where the dancers performed."

Rafiq pulled over and I stepped across the sidewalk. Stairs led down into a walled courtyard, covered with tile, which was shaded and cool. I returned to the car, and Rafiq pulled out into traffic. "Our father was the leader," Rafiq continued. "Each dancer wore a tall, brown fez and a white cape. When the dancers spun, their capes flared."

Later, after returning from his business trip, Saad opened up a little. He gave me an article with the history of the Sufi sect that was founded in Konya in what is now Turkey by Jellal ed-Din Rumi who died in 1273. That same year, Marco Polo was returning from China, and Damascus was still picking up the pieces after its run-in with the Mongol horde. "I would have been a dancer myself," Saad explained, "like my father and also my grandfather. But in 1949, three years after Syria was free, the government banned all religious orders and confiscated their property. My father was forty-six. It's hard to begin a new career at that age."

The choice bits of downtown real estate owned by Saad's family would have been a nice prize for the bureaucrats. Had the government used religion as a cover for more earthly motives?

Saad's farmhouse was built of limestone blocks and featured a decorative iron front door.

"My father knew the twirling dance technique," continued Saad. "It is very difficult to spin so fast, and it requires years of practice. But who was hiring dancers? My father also knew real estate from his work managing the holdings of the *mawlawi*. So he became a developer, purchasing lots and constructing a hotel, a hospital, and other buildings. That's why I do not dance for a living. Instead, I calculate soil loads."

Even though I now knew about the *mawlawi*, Saad still was difficult to figure. It wasn't until two years later, when Saad visited Seattle, that I finally understood: the key to Saad Shalabi was his family.

Saad had come to California for college and afterward married a Damascus woman. He took her to live in Palo Alto where he had a job with an engineering firm. It was the middle 1960s, and real estate prices were rising quickly. Saad spent his spare time hunting down real estate and eventually put some deals together that seemed, in his judgment, to be good opportunities. They certainly would beat anything in Damascus. Back home the Baath party had recently come to power and begun land reform and other measures designed to break the power of the urban merchant and land owning class. His father had done well in the boom of the 1950s, but if the family's money was to grow it was now time to invest in another country. His parents considered Saad's proposal and went back and forth on the idea. Ultimately they agreed that the family could face ruin if they did not develop business interests outside Syria. Still, they turned down his request. "My mother," Saad explained, "told me this: 'If you buy real estate in California, our finances will be secure—but you will stay in America, you will make your life there, we will lose you.'"

"Was she right?" I asked.

"My mother was perceptive," said Saad. "Of course she was right."

Saad came home, settled in Damascus, and hoped that the government-controlled economy would allow enough construction to keep an engineer busy. He purchased a coring machine from America, mounted it on the back of a Ford pickup, and for a time found work testing the soil for large buildings. After the 1967 and 1973 wars with Israel, the Saudis pumped money into Syria, and the Soviets added a little more. In ancient times Syria had thrived as a trading center, and trade had picked up under the French and in the first years following independence in 1946. But under the Baath party (which took power in 1963) the border with Iraq had been closed, and with it access to Iran and the Persian Gulf. The Baath also restricted currency dealings, so it was difficult to finance trade. The Syrian economy perked along while outside money was coming in, but lacked an engine of its own. Eventually the Soviets cut their aid, and later the Saudis followed suit. Inevitably the economy slowed, and Saad had plenty of time to contemplate the choice he had made.

Every so often Saad visited California and found that his business judgment had been sound. The properties he had liked had dramatically increased in value. Ownership would have led to other business deals, and there was far more work for a soils engineer in the San Francisco Bay Area than in Damascus. As it was, Saad and his family had made a nice life for themselves in Damascus. His wife far preferred Damascus as a place to raise children, and so did Saad. It was safe in Damascus, street crime was almost unheard of. Teen drug use, gangs, unwed mothers, guns in the schools, teen suicide were nearly unknown. In Damascus a woman alone could walk the streets after midnight without fear. Children grew up slowly and had time to be children. Damascus was a stable, family town, but it was no place to advance one's career. Saad's farm lost money every year, and his engineering business provided a service which was no longer in demand. What happened to the money his father had made and saved and invested? "The businessmen of Damascus," said Saad, "most of us are drawing down our principal. Every year we find ourselves a little more poor."

A day after dropping Saleh at the airport, I met Saad in his office. "Most Americans," I said, "think that people over here are deranged fundamentalists with curved knives clenched between their teeth."

"I've given up trying to educate Americans," Saad replied. "When I was a student in California one guy asked if my father owned an oil well. Everybody in California thinks Arabs own oil wells. 'No,' I told him. 'Those of us who do not have oil wells have camels. My father is a used camel salesman.' He believed me, of course.

"And Americans think it's so dangerous over here," Saad continued. "How many murders do you have in Washington, the US capital, in a year?"

"Four or five hundred," I said.

"Well, Damascus is about the same size and here we have three or four murders a year."

"Three or four? You're kidding."

"Really. We don't have violence because we have strong families. And families solve other problems, too. Like old people. I got some other professional men together and we donated money to create an old age home in Damascus like I had seen in the United States. Our problem? We couldn't find old people to move in. Only after months of searching did we find one old woman."

Saad laughed and leaned back a little in the swivel chair behind his desk. He smiled a casual, off-center smile, as though he was pleased at his success in educating one more American.

"And you mention the Shiites," Saad continued. "When I grew up there was no distinction among Muslims. We didn't say, 'He's Shiite, he's Sunni.' Only now, with Khomeini, has this started again as it was in ancient times. The Iranians try to divide the people of our region in a political move with religion as the cover. Almost all wars use religion as a pretext. That's how you motivate people to kill themselves."

Saad's office and his person were perfectly in order, but the man himself was relaxed. He leaned back again, gave me his casual smile, and gestured vaguely with his hand. We are pals, he seemed to be saying, despite all that divides us. At other times Saad smoked a cigar, usually a Davidoff. Cigars were one more thing that Saad had brought back from California—his way of nodding to the West and, perhaps more important, to the East, to the overzealous and xenophobic members of his faith.

"The Umayyad Mosque here in Damascus—that's our main mosque, the big one," Saad continued, "was built on the site of a large Christian church."

"A church?"

"Yes. The builders of the mosque kept the baptismal font from the church as a sign of respect.

"People don't realize that to be a Muslim you first must be a Jew and a Christian. Christianity continues where Judaism left off, and Islam continues where Christianity left off. We believe that Jesus was a holy man. Jesus was taken to God and will come again through one of the spires of the Umayyad Mosque," Saad gave a slight grimace, "so the story goes.

"When I was a child I used to go to church with my Christian friends, and we would watch girls together. Christian girls, you see, don't cover up so much as the Muslims. In California, before San Jose State, I went to the University of the Pacific in Stockton, a small Christian college. I pledged AKA. I had fun. One day a guy was shooting me with a squirt gun, so I sneaked behind him and poured a pitcher of milk over his head. That's fraternity life for you. In the classroom, as a Muslim, I had insights into the Bible that the teachers found helpful. They gave me a scholarship."

"You're kidding."

"Really. I also noticed that in the United States there are many conflicts between different Christian denominations, but Muslims here are not so splintered, not against each other."

Saad wore a three-piece suit that had been made, I guessed, in London. His tie was perfectly knotted and pushed tight to his collar.

On days when he intended to visit his farm or a construction site, he wore slacks and sport shirts. To me his clothing was unexceptional. But to ordinary folk, to the young men I had seen at the temple of Zeinab in ill-cut jeans and shirts, Saad was instantly recognizable as a member of the elite.

Later Saad commented on the construction boom going on a few hours drive to the south in Amman, Jordan. "In the 1950s," said Saad, "the boom was here in Damascus, the energy, the commerce, the tourists, and Amman was completely dead—just a village with goats in the streets. Now our economy is closed, and the situation is reversed.

"These days," Saad continued, "you have to know how to talk to the bureaucrats. What little construction we have is tied up in government."

"In Seattle," I said, "there are codes and inspectors crawling all over the place."

"I don't mean codes to strengthen the building," said Saad, "or safety laws to protect workers. I mean the government gives the work to the architects and the construction companies. Even so it's slow. The Jordanians are friends with the United States, but we picked the Russians. Such a mistake. No one ever got rich being friends with the Russians. We are not a wealthy country, and our cousins to the south—well, we spend most of our money getting ready for the next battle." Syria is about the size of my home state of Washington, yet it had half a million men in arms—two-thirds as many active soldiers as the US Army. Syria spent sixty percent or more of its annual budget on the military and intelligence services, whereas the United States spent half that.

"Would you say that this government is efficient and honest, or what?"

"Let me put it this way," said Saad. "Last week I went to East Germany—"

"Wheeling and dealing?"

"Well, we were wheeling but they weren't dealing—such a contrast to West Germany. East and West Germans are the same family but their brains are washed differently. In the West, people are quick and adapt easily, but in the East the people are lethargic and sometimes, I think, corrupt—like they make money by taking advantage of their government position—"

"In East Germany they take bribes?"

"Or fees, or whatever. This is not a political matter. It's simply human nature."

"Is it the same in Syria?" Bribery and corruption among government officials was a common complaint leveled by Syria's out-of-work merchant class. One friend of Hasan's had imported goods from Europe and failed to pay off a city official. The irate bureaucrat set him up, framed him, and he ended up in prison.

"Everything is fine here in Syria," he said, avoiding my question. "But my point is that the man who can take a risk and make a profit is the man who can get something done. We used to have many such people here in Damascus—the traders in silks and spices, the middlemen between Europe and the East. But now it is difficult to trade because you can't take Syrian currency out of the country to exchange for dollars or marks. So what can you use to pay for goods and raw materials? How do you get loans in hard currency to feed the business? Only the government trades now, not private companies. Government, that's where the money is."

The politics of Syria had many nuances and complexities, yet it was not entirely wrong to say that the country was simply divided into Ins and Outs. I sensed that Saad had been lumped with the Outs.

Saad's bookcases had an oriental look to them. His desk, on the other hand, was expensive but undistinguished, the sort of thing one would find in an office in the United States. I imagined that many of Saad's college classmates were now sitting behind such desks, only in far more luxurious offices in California. I imagined that they were no more capable than Saad, but that they had earned small fortunes over the years while Saad spent days at a time waiting for his phone to ring.

3 — The Oasis

DAMASCUS. SATURDAY, OCTOBER 17.

In Seattle in 1986, inspired by news reports, I conceived of Damascus as a capital of terror. But I also had a subtler and less negative concept. I thought of Damascus as a medieval, walled city with narrow streets, hidden courtyards, and crowded bazaars piled with silks and spices. I imagined intricately decorated Damascus blades forged from secret blends of tempered steel that allowed a sword to be given a razor sharp edge, to have extreme hardness, and yet to bend and flex rather than chip and fracture. In my dreams I saw scarves created by Damascus weavers from strands of eastern silk, wispy and light as the air itself. I had read the story of the Crusader who confronted the Muslim leader Saladin, boasted of the fine steel of his sword, and hacked at a tree limb the thickness of a man's wrist, with one swing cutting the limb clean off.

"Our Damascus blades also keep a fine edge," Saladin responded. "Let me show you." He extended his sword with the edge turned up, then threw a silk scarf into the air. As the scarf fell across the blade it parted—cut by its own weight.

The medieval Damascus that lived in my mind was a place of noble words and gestures, a place of courtesy as well as danger. In my mind I saw merchants, traders, mystics, and shifty-eyed Bedouins. The city of my dreams was simple and severe: an oasis surrounded by orchards and desert. I hoped that upon reaching Syria I could somehow dispel the gripping truth of terrorism to find an ancient city of exotic yet gentle people.

My vision was Arabian Nights mixed with leftovers of colonial prejudice, an image passed down since Victorian times and given life in films I'd seen: *The Thief of Baghdad, Khartoum, Lawrence of Arabia*. A traveler with a feel for the mystery of a foreign locale prepares himself to make discoveries in that culture, and gives himself a position from which to look critically at his own land. Sentiment has its uses, and yet it tends to obscure. Saad Shalabi, the engineer, was anything but sentimental.

"In 1940," Saad said, "Damascus had one hundred seventy thousand people. Now, depending on the time of day, it has three million and many more in outlying cities."

"What does this mean?" I asked.

"We have had to adjust," Saad replied. "Many people have moved to Damascus from the villages, and so we have built new apartments in places like Zeinab which you have seen, and have made satellite cities where there was desert before."

We were standing on Mt. Cassion, the bare ridge of rock and dirt behind the city. As Saad pointed, I could make out the texture of human construction in the smog near the horizon.

On the ride up from town we had passed dozens of sentries with AK-47s—who knows what they were guarding—and wound our way through the exclusive Malke neighborhood. Atop a low shoulder of Mt. Cassion I looked away from Damascus at an enormous concrete building under construction on the next hillside—the new presidential palace, rumored to cost three billion dollars. Closer at hand was the Mezze prison where Salah Jadid, an old comrade of the president's and, along with Asad, a former member of the ruling triumvirate, had languished since 1970. When Hafez al-Asad took power, he pushed aside the older man. Rather than accepting a genteel exile as an ambassador, Jadid was defiant. Assad's biographer reports one story that illustrates Jadid's bitterness. "If I ever take power," Jadid is supposed to have said to Asad, "I will drag you through the streets until you die."

We turned and soon reached a viewpoint with an open air restaurant. "People can come here for a small holiday," Saad said, "to see the lights of the city at night and to entertain themselves."

Below us was Damascus, an awkward skyscraper called the Asad Tower, and a jumble of low-rise buildings stretching into the distance. Forty years ago my image of Syria had not been that far off the mark: Damascus had been an oasis surrounded by orchards. Yet now the land was covered with crudely formed concrete and stucco, and it was difficult to see where urban wreckage ended and desert began. Damascus had preserved *Medina Qadeeme*, the old town. Aside from that, however, it was just your average megalopolis. Like Los Angeles, Damascus could never get enough water.

"What about that canal in front of the al-Boustan Hotel?" I asked. "It stinks up the place. Right in the center of town."

"Sewage from the newest parts of Damascus, from Malke for example, feeds into the canal," said Saad. "But there is not enough flow. The Barada River and the Fijeh spring, which supply the city water network, have been low the last few years. It has been very dry."

I thought about the Barada River flowing onto the desert, sinking into the ground, polluting the water table. Saad later told me that the city fathers had hired a British firm to design sewage treatment plants and were asking the World Bank for financing. But these things took time. The city also needed roads and a reliable supply of electricity. This was infrastructure, a term I associated with municipal engineers in Seattle who were forever gobbling up the arts money for bridges. In the third world, I realized, there was no money for arts *or* infrastructure. Government could only afford essentials like presidential palaces, prison cells, and soldiers on every other street corner.

I wondered how the desert could support such growth. "Pumping," said Saad. "We have been pumping for twenty years and now the water table is falling. My farm in Zeinab needs water—in warm weather we must pump six hours each day and not far ahead there will be laws to restrict pumping."

Today Saad was driving his second car, an aging El Camino. On the way back to town, Saad switched on his radio which was tuned to a local station that played Western music. I listened to Janis Joplin singing "Me and Bobby McGee," and thought about water and desert.

Saad's fruit trees were irrigated with well water, distributed by a network of ditches. Where the ditches intersected, small steel gates regulated the flow.

Damascus had been a capital of terror on the night I rode into town with the drunken Libyan and his jeering pals, and the place was still big and strange. Although the city of fear was easing, much to my disappointment, it was not being replaced by the medieval town of my dreams. Now I was beginning to see Damascus as Saad the engineer saw it. And Saad did have a point. The orchards of the old town had been cut and the ground covered with pavement. Damascus was a modern city with trucks and cars and power lines strung every which way. It was a city in the desert, a metropolis running low on water.

4 — The Arab

In the morning I rose early, ate a small breakfast of hot lemonade and flatbread, and, after a couple hours' work on my Arabic, set out to purchase a watermelon.

I walked through Saad's orchard in the direction of a small village market. I was mumbling Arabic when I ran into Askia, the Eritrean student who served as caretaker. We sat on the wooden cover atop an "Arab" well, a hand-dug affair lined with cemented stones that was forty feet deep. "The *shebab*," Askia said, using the word for boys or children, "break the branches of the small trees to make sticks for play." As Askia talked I saw two men in red headdresses walking through the trees with their stringy-haired sheep. Saad had given them permission to graze. A little later two women from a nearby village walked past on their way to market. They were short, fleshy, and wrapped in cloth of many colors. One had tattoos beside her eyes and on the backs of her hands.

By now I could recognize a few Arabic words when Askia and his friends talked to each other. But these women were incomprehensible. *"Ana daraset al-Arabi,"* I told them, I am studying Arabic. Askia translated their reply: "If he wants to learn Arabic, then let him learn Arabic." They laughed and walked on. I wondered about their tattoos. "Those marks," Askia said, "are for beauty."

I continued to walk through farms and orchards and ground stripped bare for new, concrete apartments. Near Zeinab I came upon two policemen in white helmets and khaki uniforms.

"American?" said one. "And from here?" He motioned up the highway, the direction from which I had come. He would have understood a tourist walking from the town of Zeinab, for Zeinab was a tourist center. But why would I be walking the other direction? What had I been doing in the villages below the hills where, one supposes, radar and missiles were deployed against Israeli warplanes? The policeman had good questions, but the answer would have meant giving Saad's name. I acted as though I did not understand

Arabic, an easy role for me, and eventually the policeman motioned me on. After I had walked a couple of blocks my heart began to beat normally once again.

As I passed the temple of Zeinab, I saw a disheveled man in a red *kaffiah* or headdress walking slowly toward me, two burlap sacks over his shoulder. Suddenly I knew what had been missing in Damascus: street people.

The man in the *kaffiah* came closer, then stopped and swung his sacks to the pavement. He was about forty, had dark hair, and was imperfectly shaven. He began to speak, mixing a few words of English with his Arabic. *"Allmanie?"* he asked, German?

"Aesho bil Amerika," I explained.

"America good," he said in English. "Have you heard of our hero, a Syrian who lives in America, a *mulakim?"* He crouched slightly and moved his hands in front of him.

"A wrestler," I guessed. The man clenched his fists, then began jabbing at an imaginary opponent. "A boxer," I concluded, "he is a boxer." The Syrian boxer apparently had received a lot of press in Syria for his exploits in the ring. Later, I wondered what it did to a nation when its heroes chose to live in other countries.

After a few seconds the man relaxed and smiled and pointed a finger at his chest. "Once," he said, "*I* was a boxer."

"I bet you were good," I said.

"I was good."

He paused. "Now," he said, "I am not a boxer. I am only an Arab." He hoisted his sacks, turned slowly, his shoulders drooping a little, and shuffled past me down the street.

I wondered at the man's terminology. I had thought of all Syrians as "Arabs." Why did he use the phrase to designate down-and-outers, members of the underclass? The term came up again, near the end of my trip, in the desert town of Abu Zouhair on the Euphrates River. I took tea with a Bedouin who had left Abu Zouhair to work in the Gulf, saved his money, and,

In Zeinab I bought a bar of soap, made in Damascus, with a wrapper that surprised me.

Muslims did not like to be photographed—or so I had heard. These guys, however, saw me with my camera and motioned me over.

now that he had returned, hoped to start a taxi service. "The Gulf was far better than here," he said. "In the Gulf the European supervisors taught me to use a front end loader and other heavy equipment. I did well. Here, in Syria, no one will teach me. No one will give me a job. I am just an Arab."

Years later, in Seattle, Hasan the architect explained. "In Syria," he said, "you have three main groups of people. You have city dwellers who live in Damascus or Aleppo or another large city. These are *al-sunna* (people who follow the teachings of the Prophet) or as you call them Sunni Muslims and include merchants, landowners, or more recently people who earn their living in the professions such as Saad Shalabi. Also, of course, you have a working class of craftsmen and laborers. Then in the villages you have the next group, peasants or *fellahin*, who farm the land for a living. You saw *fellahin* in the small village near Saad's farm. And finally you have *bedu* or as you say Bedouins, who tradition-ally have been nomadic people.

"Back in the early 600s, in the beginning of Islam, Muhammad was a city dweller. He lived in Mecca and Medina where he worked as a businessman. He made trips, but they were business trips, not part of a nomadic life. We have in Islam records of the acts and sayings of Muhammad. *Sunna* we call them. And these *sunna*, among other things, tell how Bedouins came in from the desert to question Muhammad about his faith. The Bedouins are depicted as very different than city dwellers, unafraid to ask bold questions, more honest, and also more severe. These were people with a desert code of honor who, before Islam, were animists. In the *sunna* they are called *a'arab* which is the origin of the modern word Arab. Today in Syria *arab* can be used to refer to the descendents of the Bedouins.

"Of course now Bedouins for the most part do not live as nomads. They no longer make their money guiding caravans or even breeding camels (maybe in Tunisia, but not in Syria). Many have settled in desert villages along the Euphrates such as Abu Zouhair or in eastern lands on the other side of that river. A few, such as the boxer you met in Sayida Zeinab, have drifted to the big city where they have a hard time adapting. Those Bedouins who move directly from the desert are restless in the city, unaccustomed to a life with boundaries. Those who move from villages are completely alienated, for they miss the closeness and intimacy of village life. If this boxer came from the latter group, one would expect that he had no family in Damascus. And if he did, it would be a family that had moved to the city recently and was living in tenuous circumstances."

5 — Three Patriots

At the market I purchased a small, round watermelon, placed it in my day pack, and began walking back to the farm along the main road. A horse-drawn oil cart, driven by two teenage boys, came up behind. I climbed onto the small seat atop the oil tank and, as we rode down the shoulder, the two youths explained that they left home at 5:00 AM each morning to sell heating oil in the villages. Their only day off was Friday, the day of prayer. In Seattle, one friend of mine insisted that the third world was overcome by sloth and torpor (and why didn't those people get jobs instead of relying on our foreign aid?). Hasan the architect had insisted that the pace of life was far more relaxed in Syria than in the United States. That might be true of professionals and those who lived on inherited wealth, but Syrian working folk were like these boys—hard at it six days a week.

Walking the last mile to Saad's farm, I passed the open door of a wood shop where three men worked quickly at a large band saw—at a time of day that was supposed to be reserved for a long, indulgent, family meal.

A little farther on, an old man in a white gown and red headdress called to me from his gate: I was invited for tea. I followed him through the gate, across a courtyard, and into a room that was cool and clean. Four men wearing scarves and gowns sat on the floor and leaned against the walls. Two were old, two were young. They had completed their midday meal and retired to a living room for tea and conversation. They were relaxed and provided a traditional picture that contrasted with the frenetic activity next door at the furniture shop.

My host motioned for me to sit and poured dark coffee into a small cup. I drank, and they asked about my nationality, occupation, family, means of transport, and itinerary. I mumbled in Arabic while they helped me find words.

"*Allaaaaahu, akbar!*" The call to prayer began. A loudspeaker mounted on a water tower amplified a recording. Two of the men knelt in the center of the room and began speaking softly to themselves. I wondered at the simplicity with which they prayed.

"*Allaaaaahu, akbar!*" The voice of the muezzin was high and nasal, a haunting sound that evoked images of the past: low houses built of earth, rutted streets, a village well. The call to prayer continued, and my companions bowed forward on their mats.

> *Ashhadu an la illaha illa Allah.*
> I testify that there is no God but God.
> *Ashhadu an Muhammadan rasool Allah.*
> I testify that Muhammad is the messenger of God.

The soft chant of my kneeling companions seemed of a different order than the broadcast call to prayer. The recitation of the muezzin was perfect in every detail, the achievement of a practiced singer captured on modern recording equipment. In the past, each village would have had its own muezzin singing five times a day from the highest rooftop. The singing would have been imperfect, but live: an expression of faith from one member of the village to his neighbors. I supposed that electronics had fostered a star system. A few talented singers were recorded and became professionals, others were neglected. Now, I guessed, those who might have sung spent their days driving buses, shoving blocks of wood through band saws, or riding horse-drawn tanks of heating oil through the streets.

At length I made excuses and continued my walk. I passed a cement block wall with a ledge, in the shade this time of day, where three old men sat in gowns and *kaffiahs*, a teapot beside them. A few days earlier they had invited me to sit with them and, after exchanging formalities and pouring tea, had given me a message to take back to America. "The French," one said, "break a corner from Syria and make it for Turkey."

"Kalam saheeh," said another. "It is so."

"A good corner," said the third, "and the people all must come away." The French, it turned out, had given a choice portion of Syria's Mediterranean coast to Turkey in 1939 to keep Turkey from joining the Germans in World War II. The lost land included the port of Alexandretta and Antioch, from which many Christian residents fled to Damascus. (That's why the Patriarchs of Antioch lived in Damascus.) The land giveaway had occurred nearly fifty years earlier, but to these village folk the wound was fresh.

"Turkey is strong," continued the first man. "What can be done? Syria, she is weak."

At Saad's farm I carried my watermelon to the caretaker's quarters where Askia pulled a pan of vegetable stew from the table and began to warm it on a small propane burner. When the stew was hot he served it in a bowl and set a teapot to warm. As I ate, Askia took it upon himself to correct my views of Arabs.

"In America they say Syrians are cruel," Askia made a cutting motion across his wrist. "Not true. In Syria no one gets his hand chopped, his fingers chopped. In the Gulf maybe, never here. In Syria the Arabs are poor and kind. The government makes wars, but the people are friendly. I go into the village, and all the people come around me. I am a foreigner, but I am here, no trouble. Once in maybe five years you hear of a theft. A murder? Here you never have a murder." Iraqi saboteurs had a nasty habit of sneaking into Syria, then exploding bombs in public or throwing grenades at the Syrian president. Yet, as Saad had pointed out, the kind of vandalism and urban street crime that we had in the United States was unknown here. And Askia was right, Syrians did not mutilate criminals.

After dinner Askia and I walked around the compound and snapped photos of the farmhouse. "No photography in this direction," Askia said, waving across a field toward the road. "A little past our drive is something special. The men who wait there are not police with white hats, the ones who direct traffic. They are not the army. Something secret is there, men who are dangerous, very, very dangerous. You must be good to stay away."

Askia's parents in Eritrea were old and pinned down by the local guerrilla war. They survived on checks from their eldest son who worked in Saudi Arabia. Askia disapproved of war.

"One bullet of nuclear bombs," Askia said, "cost one billion dollars. I am not for war. I am a peace man, a hippie." Askia knew quite a bit about the United States, but also had questions.

"What were the hippies?" he asked.

"They were against the Vietnam War," I replied.

"That's very good."

"And they took LSD and other drugs all the time."

"This is not good, I think. What happened to the hippies?"

"After the Vietnam War was over," I said, "they started making good money and dressed in good clothes and lived the good life."

"Ah," said Askia, "the good life."

6 — Flames

DAMASCUS. TUESDAY, OCTOBER 20.

The next day I rode a bus into Damascus and found myself in an uncomfortable position. I was an American, walking the streets of this Arab capital, at the moment that the United States dropped bombs in the Persian Gulf. As I was passing a sandwich shop, I saw a television and heard the announcer speaking quickly in Arabic. Every third word was *Amerikee*. I knew something was up. That evening I checked into the Cassion Hotel. I wanted to attend a concert which would end late. And, in order to protect Saad Shalabi, I wanted to be checked into a hotel like a good tourist when I visited the immigration police one day later. In the lobby of the Cassion I noticed three men staring at the TV in the lobby. I sat down and joined them and soon was watching an Iranian oil rig in flames. The footage was in living color.

"The United States bombed the Iranians," said one man. "The damage is five hundred million dollars." At a time of conscious poverty among Syrians, my country stood condemned of wasting half a billion dollars in one day. I trusted that we would not do such a thing without a reason. Still, I had no explanation that sounded plausible here in Damascus. The men with whom I sat were mild and subdued, not the chanting "Arab street" depicted in our media. They were watching the news, talking back and forth, passing judgment on foreign governments—just as my friends and I did at home. And now they judged the US government to be wasteful, callous, and arbitrary. Still, they seemed to make allowances for me, an American citizen.

CASSION HOTEL
Damascus Tel. { 218117
{ 217797
Brazil St.

حمامات ساخنة
تدفئة مركزية
خدمة ممتازة
٢١٨١١٧
٢١٧٧٩٧
دمشق ـ هاتف
فندق قاسيون
شارع البرازيل ـ تجاه ثانوية
ابن خلدون وفندق أمية العبيد
وأهلاً وسهلاً

"You are one man, what can you do? It is not you, it is not your family. It is your government. Bad. Too very bad." My country, they told me, much as theirs, was governed by a few men who made decisions, dropped bombs on unknowing victims, then presented their actions as a *fait accompli* to the rest of the country.

These men were courteous. Still, I felt as though I had been slapped: weren't these the same phrases that my friends and I used to dismiss the actions of Arab nations? Then it struck me: we were not as fair as these Arabs. Our media rarely distinguished between the acts of Arab rulers and the sympathies of their citizens. When our leading newspapers or our State Department referred to Syria as a "terrorist nation," for example, we tarred not only the leadership but the entire populace. America had money and prestige. Yet in some ways we lacked the sophistication and goodwill of these working-class Arabs in a cheap hotel in Damascus.

A week later I found a copy of *Time* magazine which quoted the

State Department. This bombing was a "measured response" to Iranian gunboat attacks.

7 – The Good Life

DAMASCUS. WEDNESDAY, OCTOBER 21.

The people whom I met around Zeinab were friendly, generous, and curious about an American. They were quiet people, not brash or demanding. They were a bit distant—not chummy like Jamal, Muhammad, Qasem Shehab, and other Lebanese—yet they were not cruel or violent. None seemed bent on martyrdom.

In my wanderings around the town of Zeinab I met urbanized villagers who participated in the larger, city economy. The remnants of traditional village life, however, were plain to view, and—as my friend Hasan the architect later explained—this was my first glimpse of *fellahin*, Syria's ancient agrarian class.

I also had seen or detected city dwellers who depended upon the regime for their well-being—customs officials, airport security, soldiers on street corners. I had driven with Saad through the Malke District where a one bedroom apartment sold for a quarter of a million dollars. These apartments housed the nouveau riche, high level bureaucrats and officials, who grew wealthy from their association with the president. A dozen years later, when commentators spoke of the final difficulties in gaining a peace treaty between Syria and Israel, they noted that a peace treaty would mean opening the economy—a move which would undercut the administrative class that lived in the Malke District and would shift power back to the private sector. The opposition of this administrative class, or fear of the retribution that they would face once they began to lose power, was the real obstacle to peace.

In Damascus, the "private sector" referred to the traditional merchant and landowning class, urban folk, Sunnis—a group that had expanded to include professionals such as Saad Shalabi. These folks were currently somewhat in disfavor. The regime kept them on ice, ready and available in case a peace treaty were signed, borders were opened, and Syria returned to a market economy. In a brave, new Syria, the merchant and landowning class would be the key to economic survival. I wanted to know more and was quick to accept when Saad invited me to a gala at the posh Cham Palace hotel. Over the course of a long evening I learned that the good life which Askia dreamed about in America could also be found in Damascus.

I thought of the Cham Palace hotel as the unofficial capitol for the region and the city. (Cham or Sham is the Arabic name for the region and also one name for Damascus, the region's major city.) There were other fine hotels in Damascus—Syria's nouveau riche, for example, met at the Sheraton in the ritzy Malke neighborhood. But the sons and daughters of old merchant families came downtown to the Cham Palace.

The exterior of the Cham was polished red granite. Inside, the atrium was six stories high. Saad and I arrived in the banquet room and found crisp, white table cloths, polished silver, and plastic bottles of Boukein spring water. Soon the hall filled with guests, most middle-aged. The men wore three-piece suits, the women high-heeled shoes and evening dresses of conservative cut, Western styles, no veils or *abiahs*.

We sat down for dinner at nine-thirty to a first course of yogurt with mint, hummus, pepper sauce, tabooli, and cucumbers. I spoke to a single woman of fifty, dark-haired, a little heavy, and dressed in black. She was a language teacher who, like many in the crowd, belonged to the Damascus Friends Society, a civic group that was trying to preserve the old city. As we chatted, something caught my eye: a couple who looked as though they had stepped from a fairy tale. The man was an older gentleman, perfectly bald on top, with a full mustache, ruddy complexion, and noble bearing—Prussian looking. By his side was a young woman, slender and pale, a woman of striking beauty. They sat two tables away.

Next I spoke with the man to my right, a tall, gangly fellow with a crew cut, an engineer who had retired from the Syrian state oil company and who sat with his wife and daughter. A native of Homs, the industrial city in the center of Syria that served as the butt of the nation's jokes, he lacked Saad's panache. Still, he had done well, purchased a second house in Damascus, sent his son to the United States for college. He talked, in English, of Syria's oil industry. "The Iraqis," he complained, "have made too many bad things for Syria.

The Cham Palace Hotel.

We built a new pumping station, very modern, very expensive, on the line from Iraq's Kirkuk oil fields. We worked very hard, finished our pumping station, and then the Iraqis made a political move, an incident. Our president could do nothing but shut down the oil line. So our new pumping station sits, never used, and the Iraqis send oil north through Turkey."

I turned and glanced at the elegant old Damascus gentleman and his young wife. He sat with his shoulders thrown back, smiling at some remark. His face was big and lined, and his nose was strong and angular. He was sixty or so and seemed conscious of his own nobility. I imagined that for generations his family had been merchants of fantastic wealth which they kept hidden behind plain stone walls. The young woman was radiant: fair skin, dark brown hair, and fine, sculpted features. She wore jewelry and an evening dress, and she could not have been more than twenty-four years old.

I was talking to the language teacher now, but I wasn't listening to her, my mind was running in another direction. The young woman had bright eyes, a quick smile—a combination of innocence, vivacity, and reserve which made her sophisticated beyond her years. She startled me, made my heart skip a little, but it wasn't her, and it wasn't her man: it was the two of them together. They had not stepped out of a fairy tale, I realized. On the contrary, this grand old prince and his delicate wife were waving an invisible wand, creating a fairy tale—right here, right now. I looked about and saw a plain banquet hall, a collection of ordinary people. We were Cinderellas slowly warming to the possibilities of the evening.

Our musicians were known for their traditional songs including many from Andalusia, the Arab name for medieval Spain. "The Arabs ruled Andalusia for eight hundred years," explained the language teacher.

"Andalusia was the gem of the Arab empire," Saad added. "The Umayyads in Andalusia built mosques with domes and arches, very elaborate. We also built libraries, and that's how your Renaissance got going—Greek science and Arab math were translated from Arabic."

It turns out that medieval, Arab Spain had a special hold on the people of Damascus. For the finest Andalusian leaders had been Damascenes. They were Umayyads—as in the Umayyad Mosque, the big mosque in the old city that Saad had mentioned. Spain had been conquered by Moors (or Moroccans), an army of Arabs and Berbers. The most refined Andalusian nobility, however, were families who emigrated directly from Damascus. I always had thought of the Moors as barbarians who chiseled away at Christian Europe. But now I was sitting in Damascus, the seat of the Umayyad caliphate, and the Arabs in Spain seemed not so bad.

Aside from their Andalusian associations, I later realized, the songs were notable for their mystic elements. Some contained Sufi lyrics, and the musicians imitated the old practice of singing as a way of achieving lightness, vision, and an ultimate spiritual ecstasy or *sultani*. "They repeat certain words or sounds over and over again," Hasan's wife told me later. "They are like the Sufi dancers, the *mawlawi* who twirl and repeat a word while the music plays and almost go into a trance."

Our dinner had been cleared by now, and musicians stepped onto a

CHAM PALACE

Héritage et Tradition

Logo from the wine list at the Cham Palace. Only two of the sixteen beverages listed were "sans alcool."

low stage in front and unpacked their instruments. As I talked with Saad and the language teacher, the oil engineer pushed his chair back from the table, pulled his prayer beads from his pocket, and stared at the stage where one man was tuning an oud. He was silent, intent. Another musician began plucking at a canoon to put it in tune. After a few moments Saad fell silent, and the language teacher looked to the stage. I turned and glanced at my fairy tale couple. I had seen the young queen of the ball and her dark-suited man. Would the rest of us be transformed when the chorus began to sing?

I noticed one of the singers, a tall man wearing a *galabea* or full-length shift. His hair was dark and slightly receding, his mustache full and black and turned up sharply at the ends in a way that made him seem to be smiling. He moved about more actively than the others, his expression serious and alert. I picked him as the group's inspirational leader, the one whose esprit created an ensemble. The musicians were sitting in their places now and in front was Sabri Moudallal, the soloist and leader, a white-haired man wearing a tall fez and grasping prayer beads in one hand. Suddenly, the man with the smiling-mustache lifted his tambourine, and the audience grew quiet.

8 — Sultani

Sabri Moudallal nodded, the music began, and when the instruments and chorus dropped out, the old man sang alone. His voice was deep and hoarse, and he sang the same word over and over in a melodic line that rose and fell and rose again: *"Amani, amani, amaaani."*

At the end of a long run the old man paused, the sound system gave a squawk, the chorus took up a refrain that had an easy, swinging pace, and then the singer began to improvise on a single syllable: *"Ah, ahh, ahhhh."*

"The pain," said the teacher. "*Ah* means pain, and also, of course, it is just the sound." The old man milked the syllable, and the musicians followed him wherever he went. He paused and the chorus came in. "Patience in love," they sang. "Patience, patience. Patience in love."

The piece ended to applause, and then the man with the canoon played alone, dozens of quick notes like a herd of mice running across the strings. The tall, dark-haired singer came to the mike and gave praise. "The canoon is a difficult instrument," he said in Arabic. "It has seventy-one strings. And this is the best canoon player in all of Syria." The canoon played on, and the crowd interrupted after passages requiring special dexterity: *"Yanaweim! Yanaweim!"* Oh little ones, soft ones, they said, referring to the fingers of the canoon player. Then the melody changed pace, and notes came cascading down like water in a dry land. *"Ullluh,"* yelled one man in the audience, and I realized he was saying Allah, My God! The canoon was clear and precise, not painting a picture but taking one away, taking away the grim streets, the trash, the clouds of war that beset this country and leaving something pure and real.

The crowd was warm, but not enough for the old man. "These people from Damascus," he intoned, "they don't know that a lover needs encouragement." The crowd shouted back, *"Aewa, aeeewa!"* Yes, yes. He began another improvisation, *"Ya leili, ya leili,"* My night, oh my night. And then he began to sing: "Between the lover's acceptance . . ."

The old man told us again and again that something of great significance lay in the space between acceptance and rejection. What was it? When he finally gave the answer he sang quickly, and the language teacher could not make out the words. I thought of Saad, the hereditary Sufi mystic turned engineer, and the other people in this room. Education, good character, and hard work could not ensure their future. They were blocked, never in favor with the regime yet never, entirely, out of favor. Between acceptance and rejection was the life they lived.

I glanced back at the old Damascene and his bride. He was looking to the waiter while she watched the musicians, her elbows on the table, hands clasped beside her cheek. She moved slowly to the music, and by now I was moving with her. I was amazed by this music, these people, this city—an ancient city where ordinary citizens could be transformed into swaying souls with a single spirit.

By now it was midnight, the women were moving their hands in the air, men were dancing. The oil worker shook his head from side to side in rapture, the language teacher tapped the edge of the table in time to the music, and Saad smiled. I clapped and swayed and watched. On

The tall, dark-haired singer.

stage the tall, dark-haired singer stood forth from the chorus. He lifted his head. His mustache smiled. He raised his arms in the air and moved them slowly back and forth. Then he moved his shoulders and hips a little in time to the music. His movements were precise, without waste. I learned later that he was a man of limited means, a shopkeeper in the Aleppo market, an uneducated man. "This is my life," he seemed to say. He smiled, then dropped his arms and stepped back into the chorus.

The language teacher stood up and moved her chair behind mine. "That man across the room is staring at me," she said. "Now you will block his view and I can enjoy the music." I had heard about this: Syrian men liked to stare at women in public. The language teacher was a nice person, and it made me angry that some lecher should be so rude as to direct lascivious glances toward her without thinking that he could be ruining her evening.

The old man in the fez shook his prayer beads. "The eye can love many," he sang, "but the heart has only one." I looked behind me for the young woman but she had moved so that her husband blocked my view.

At another table a young man wearing tennis shoes and a T-shirt with ocean waves on the front stood and danced to the music, moving his hands, his hips. Then he unfolded a cloth napkin, stretched it tight, and moved it over his head from side to side. I had pulled my tie loose, and the place was going crazy, men jumping from their seats and moving in time to the music.

"We will be two spirits in one body," the old man sang. "God will save me from the pain of *ah, ahh, ahhh.*"

The singer improvised upon his pain, pursued the melody into the depths, the oud and canoon close behind, and the line of his voice was sinuous, the tone dark, and he probed deeper and deeper and then pulled back and circled and gathered strength and rose above the gloom. Now he approached a summit, and the oud and canoon followed, and then the instruments dropped away and the old man was alone on the shining heights, his eyes closed, and still his voice rose higher, then higher still, and his singing was *sultani*—a vision of things as they are, an ecstasy of body and soul and spirit. The audience was quiet now as he embellished this paradise, showing its color and shape and substance. And then he paused and dropped down and the crowd came alive, *"Allaah! Allaaaah!"* Soon the singer had returned to the everyday, the troubles of the lover caught between acceptance and rejection.

"My night," he cried. "My night, oh my night."

9 — Dancing

The song concluded and the musicians raced through four short numbers, local favorites judging by the expression of the oil worker who shook his prayer beads and slapped his knee in pleasure. Saad smiled his off-center smile and looked at me. The dazzling young woman behind us was still blocked from view by her husband, and the young man with the ocean waves on his T-shirt mopped his brow and sat down to rest while the musicians wrapped it up. The audience clapped and shouted.

"Shouf! Shouf! Shouf!" See, see, see what they've done.

Half the crowd left but Saad wanted to stay. About one o'clock the music began again with another soloist. By two the old man was back, slapping his hand up and down to get the music going and bringing the crowd alive. Men rose to dance beside their tables, and near us four young women waved their arms in the air in time to the music. The young man in the T-shirt was up and dancing again. Half the audience watched the singers, half watched the four young women, and we were bright and alive in the darkness of the city.

The drum and the canoon performed a tattoo, an Andalusian signature, and the crowd announced their support: *Aeeewa! Aewa!* I saw that the oil company worker and his wife and daughter had returned. He had taken off his coat in the heat, unbuttoned his vest, and was slapping his knee in time to the music.

The men who were dancing solo joined hands and started a line, dancing through the tables, pulling their companions into the dance, winding around the room. The music moved forward more quickly now, and the line of dancers wound its way to the front. A man at my table joined the line, but Saad stayed in his seat.

The music surged and throbbed, and the line worked its way around and had half gone by when I jumped from my seat, grabbed a hand in front and a hand behind, and became part of a long, human creature, a moving line of men. We made another circuit, then another. By now I was dancing, gettin' on down, dancing, dancing to the music.

The musicians leaned into their instruments, the sound intensified, and the tall, dark-haired singer stepped forth from the chorus with his smiling mustache. He danced and gave a high pitched, trilling cry, and then another and another. It was a Sufi exercise, and we were fragments of dust dancing in the glow of God's sun. It was the cry of a village woman welcoming a child into the world, the cry of wedding, the cry for husbands who have returned from the journey to Mecca. It was the yell of the *debka*, the line dance of the villages, and we were urban villagers celebrating our former lives, celebrating Andalusia, the flower of the Arab Empire, lost to the swarming, surging Christian barbarians of the north.

At last the old man stopped, bowed his head, and raised his hands in the air. The musicians stood, and the tall, dark-haired singer smiled. The audience clapped. I looked at the musicians and then at Saad: his suit coat was unbuttoned, but his tie was still perfectly knotted and tight to his collar. The crowd chanted in Arabic, "Look! At them! Look what they've done."

10 — The Bureaucrat

The next morning Saad Shalabi was bleary-eyed. I sat on the leather couch in his office and studied my small collection of Arabic words while he worked business deals on the phone. A couple of weeks into my journey, with the help of this sane man, I was beginning to put my life in order. I had learned to function within Damascus and could keep from getting lost as long as I stuck to the familiar corridors that lead from my bus stops to Saad's office.

I told Saad of my adventures with the Hezbollah at the temple of Zeinab, and at last he stopped me. "You think that these Lebanese are something great," he said, "but to me, they are *mejanin*, crazy."

One of Saad's friends was even more emphatic. Abed was a fifty-year-old former tank commander, a distinguished looking man with close-cut gray hair and a military bearing. He ran the Golden Age restaurant near Saad's office, and later I stopped to talk with him. "For centuries," Abed said in measured English, "we are traders, business-men, deal-makers. We will make a deal with anyone. You see that man sitting at the corner table, he is a Christian, a well-known actor. But he doesn't believe in Christianity any more than I believe in Islam. We appreciate religion and religious values, but we don't fast, don't pray very much. We are not fanatics. Faith is something that we sell to other people. In Syria, religion is for export."

"What about the Shiites?" I asked.

"The Shia or, as you say, Shiites of Damascus are different from those of Beirut or Teheran. Ours are not radical, but those of Teheran take it a bit far. In Islam there is no clergy class. It is prohibited. But the Shiites in Iran have a hierarchy with titles, of which 'Ayatollah' is the highest. It's ridiculous, just like the Christians with their cardinals and bishops.

"The Iranians are fanatics. They see things from one way. Wise people look at things from different sides. The Iranians are absurd. Fourteen hundred years ago Hussein was not a great man to face the Umayyad army at Karbala. He was unwise. So now young Iranians want to die for the memory of a reckless man? It is silly, the same kind of silliness that you find in Northern Ireland."

Next, I needed to visit the immigration police, across town near the University of Damascus, to get my travel permit. When I reached the immigration building, I stood on the sidewalk and watched a local entrepreneur, a man with a wooden camera stationed on a heavy wooden tripod who copied passport photos. The camera had a bellows in front and a box behind. The box had an eye piece on top and on the back was covered by a black cloth. The photographer opened his customer's passport to the photo page and used a rubber band to attach it to a small stand that extended a foot in front of the lens. Then he removed the lens cap with his right hand for a two count before replacing it again. The camera, of all things, had no shutter. But it did include—within the box—its own dark room.

After taking the picture, the photographer wriggled his hand around inside the camera box, then removed his hand and, on the right side, pulled out a wooden drawer attached to the bottom of the camera. He fished out a negative print, strapped it where the passport had been, then took another photo. This time he removed four positive images from the drawer beneath the camera. He washed them in a bucket of water nearby, dried them, cut them to size.

I turned and entered the immigration building, dark, bleak, and dirty. As I climbed the dank stairway, I marveled at the ingenuity of the photographer. In America I relied on cameras with moving parts—plus one-hour photo labs, photo booths, Polaroid cameras, all-night copy centers. Did I really have a clue how to function in this country? I skipped up the last stairs into an unlit hallway. The interior of this building was dreary, but my heart was light. In a few hours I hoped to be on the road, the first step of my circuitous trek to the Roman Bridge.

I found the correct office and sat to wait. I had worried for a week about the man I was to face, the immigration official who had the power to extend—or to end—my stay in this country. Would he be the stereotypical third-world bureaucrat, fat and distracted, casually swatting flies or picking at scabs while helpless tourists such as myself pleaded for favor? When my turn came to lean across the counter, I was surprised to face a man only a year or two older than I, a weary man who was, nevertheless, brisk, businesslike, and intelligent.

"I can't give you eleven weeks," said the officer in perfect English. "Fifteen days, only."

"But I need more time," I said. "How can I see the Syrian coast in fifteen days? And I want to go farther, all the way to the Roman Bridge."

"One month, then."

I went outside to get a photograph from the man with the wooden camera, and next purchased special stamps from another sidewalk vendor. Then I went back upstairs to get a signature from the headman. "Have a nice visit," the officer said.

In the afternoon I stopped again at Saad's office and asked if his lawyer friend had turned up anything on the Patriarch of Antioch. It was too late for an invocation, but I had been thinking ahead. What about a benediction, something formal to give my adventure a nice, crisp conclusion? I would locate the Patriarch now and set something up for the end of my trip.

Saad took me next door, and the lawyer informed us that the Patriarchs were having a conference this week to discuss the idea of combining their churches. Of course, that would mean only one Patriarch of Antioch. I wondered which one would lose his job. "Come back in a week or two," the lawyer said in Arabic. "I personally will arrange an audience."

Saad and I excused ourselves, and then I said good-bye to Saad and marched down the stairs of his office building. Outside Saad's office, as usual, cars were parked all over the sidewalk. I began walking to the bus corral, then thought better and caught a taxi.

11 — Minorities

I intended to travel in Syria's coastal region, following the northward swath of the Fertile Crescent. I planned to travel for a week, then to make a quick trip back to Damascus to pick up the clothes and gifts that I would need before continuing to Aleppo.

On the coast, I wanted to see Crusader castles, early churches, and ancient Phoenician sites. Yet I was less interested in things than in people. I wanted to meet Syria's most prominent minorities, and on the coast I was looking for Christians, Alawites, and Ismailis.

Years later Hasan the architect explained the shortcomings of my approach. "You are too concerned with Syria's minorities," he said. "And you will give readers a distorted picture of Syria. They will think that the minorities are the main thing, but they are not. For example, three out of every four Muslims in Syria is a Sunni. All together minorities are less than a third of the Syrian people. Yet you leave the impression that they are the majority."

I had to agree with Hasan. There *was* a large, open-minded, comparatively bland Sunni population in Syria—a silent majority whose faith lacked the secrecy, extreme doctrine, and exotic history which could give color and verve to a traveler's tale. The Sunnis were interesting, especially the urban Sunnis. But they were subtle. They were an advanced course. Once I had a feel for the components of Syrian society, I'd be able to explore the intricacies of Sunni culture. If I couldn't stuff that material into the current book, I'd write a second one consisting of conversations with leading Syrians—men and women who were distinguished by their ideas, their professional accomplishments, their humor. By the law of averages, the second book would be heavily weighted toward Sunnis.

The second book would also be more mental, more abstract. How many urban Sunnis drove smugglers' trucks across the desert and screamed at the border police who probed their cargo with long, slender, probing steel rods? How many Sunnis were waging grudge matches with the secret police and spent their afternoons running through the stone terraces of ancient hillside towns below Crusader castles as steel-gray men with AK-47s gave chase? Urban Sunnis were sedate. They did good or ill behind the scenes. They had been the system, the establishment, for centuries until Hafez al-Asad and the other members of his military triumvirate broke up their party in 1963. Today Sunnis still lived, worked, schemed, and created in ways that were sometimes virtuous, sometimes profound, but almost never cinematic.

Hasan had a point about Sunnis, yet I could have argued. Although he was correct about Sunni belief being dominant, religious doctrine and practice were only part of what defined a minority. Hasan did not mention that half of the Sunnis were minorities on other grounds than religious doctrine. I'm thinking of Kurds, Bedouins, villagers, Palestinian refugees, and various other groups, most of whom did not live in the cities and had an overriding ethnic, linguistic, or cultural loyalty. Kurds, for example, composed about ten percent of Syria's population. They yearned for Kurdish independence, loved Marxism, lived in remote northern villages, and were a far cry from the image of an educated Sunni city dweller. Bedouins and Palestinian refugees composed about six percent of the population and possessed very different loyalties than urbanized Sunnis. Thousands of Sunnis still lived in agricultural villages where their isolation, traditional way of life, and clan loyalties distinguished them from Sunnis in the cities. Saad Shalabi stands out to me as an example of an educated urbanized Sunni, but even he was only one generation separated from the *mawlawi*, the esoteric Sufi sect of which his father was the local chieftain.

Perhaps the strongest characteristic of Syrian society was its lack of a dominant national culture. Sunnis had the numbers, as Hasan pointed out, but too many Sunnis identified themselves in another way. People in Syria stayed home. At least, they did not move about the way that Americans did. Syrians tended to feel as though they belonged to the locality where they lived. Syria had television, but it had not yet molded the mind of the populace. The Baath party was in power, but its base did not extend far into the Sunni majority. Neither was there a dynamic cultural movement, an environmental movement for example, that cut across class, race, and sect to unite the people. And so it was that some commentators wrote about Syria's "empty center." Only in the mid-1980s had this center begun to fill as the sons and daughters of the traditional Sunni merchant and landowning class slowly intermarried with the sons and daughters of the Alawite elite that President Asad entrusted with power. The oft-repeated question among Syria watchers: after Assad's passing, would a strong national center emerge? Or would Syria fragment along ethnic and religious lines?

Syria's minorities made me curious. They were exotic or obscure and fitted into history in surprising ways. Each one, to me, was like an intricate Tolstoy novel—a complex cultural composition with its own texture, color, tone. Coming from the American melting pot, I was amazed at groups that maintained a distinct character over hundreds of years' time. I also sensed that Syria's subcultures had been preserved for a reason: they represented a vast gene pool of cultural possibility. Centuries from now, I imagined, the rest of the world would mine Syria's minorities for ideas, insight, style.

Alex Bertulis, an architect friend of mine from Seattle, had visited Syria and, like me, was interested in Syrians of all stripes. "Each wave of conquerors who came to Syria, each tribe of wanderers, each group of refugees left camps, villages, castles, bridges, cities, or people behind. You can still see the structures today, and the people are still there. The links have not been broken."

The minorities of Syria's coast who were positioned closest to

Damascus were the Christians who had lived in these hills since New Testament times. The two Christian establishments that I most wanted to visit, the convent of Saydnaya and Marjurjos (the Monastery of Saint George), had been built before the Muslim invasions of the seventh century, and more than four hundred years before the Crusaders won their first battle in Syria (when they breached the walls of Antioch in 1098). Syria's Christians included eleven sects, but I was interested in the four most prominent: Greek Orthodox, Syriac, Greek Catholic, and Armenian. The largest and by far the most powerful of these was the Greek Orthodox or Eastern Orthodox Church, traditionally based in Constantinople (current day Istanbul), whose adherents long had claimed it as the original "mother church" from which all other Christian denominations are derived. This assertion, as you can imagine, raised hackles—especially among the Syriac Church of years past.

Christian religious practice in the years after the passing of Jesus and the Apostles was individualistic and ecstatic. There was no canonized New Testament, no fixed liturgy, no priesthood or religious hierarchy. Individual churches were led by elders or "bishops" and were independent from one another. As the centuries passed, some church leaders such as Tertullian emphasized an individual's closeness to God. Others like Clement of Alexandria, however, emphasized authority and argued that Christianity needed greater organization if it were to survive and certainly if it were to become the official religion of the Roman Empire. By 200 a fixed liturgy and religious hierarchy had emerged, partly to counter extreme ecstatic movements. Church elders like Clement and his pupil Origen had been born to wealthy pagan families and had received an education in the Greek classics. Now they devised a closely reasoned theology which drew from Greek philosophy. As the centuries passed, Christians met in ecumenical councils to tighten their organization and theology. The tension between the desire for individualistic worship and the need for discipline continued, however, and periodically churches who chose not to abide by the pronouncements of an ecumenical council would split off from the main church. Those churches that were left, namely the churches who adhered to the edicts of the first seven ecumenical councils, composed the Greek Orthodox Church.

In 330 the emperor Constantine chose the Greek trading city of Byzantium as the capital of the Eastern Roman Empire and renamed it Constantinople. In 395 when the empire was divided into eastern and western halves, the Christian Church was divided as well. As the years passed the Roman Catholic (or Latin) Church expanded into Europe and adopted Latin as the language of its liturgy. The Greek Orthodox or Eastern Orthodox Church slowly expanded from the Middle East into the Balkans and Russia. Although we think of the Crusades as the effort of Western Christians to recapture the Holy Lands from the Infidels, the Fourth Crusade actually was launched *against* Constantinople (on behalf of Venetian trading interests). The Crusaders overcame the Byzantines, divided their empire and installed a line of Latin kings. The sacking of Constantinople and the theft of priceless icons and relics, plus Latin interference in the Greek Orthodox Church itself, aroused the hostility of the Eastern Church and ensured that there would be no reconciliation of the Greek and Latin churches.

The main competition to the Greek Orthodox Church in Syria had traditionally been the Syriac (in Arabic Souriyani) Church which emphasized individualistic worship and local autonomy over the strict hierarchy and authority of the Greek Orthodox. The Syriac Church was ancient. Its liturgy was expressed in the Syriac tongue which was derived from the Aramaic that Jesus spoke. In the earliest years this church was not differentiated from other Christian churches. In the fifth century, however, Syrian and Egyptian (Coptic) Churches took issue with the doctrines laid down in the council of Ephesus in 431 and the council of Chalcedon in 451 and split from the Eastern Christian Church. Two centuries later, when Syria and Egypt accepted Muslim governance, the possibility of reconciliation became faint. In modern times, as Saad's lawyer friend had explained, Syriac Christians were making amends and seeking reconciliation with the Greek Orthodox Church.

An alternative Christian faith was the far smaller and more recent Greek Catholic Church. It emerged in the mid-nineteenth century and consisted of Eastern Christians of Greek descent who established communion with the Roman Catholic Church.

Armenian Christians, whom I later would meet when I visited Syria's north, also had a church of their own, a national church established in about 300—which gave them the distinction of being the first Christian nation. Like the Syriac and Coptic Churches, the Armenian Church rejected the edicts of the council of Chalcedon. Through the years the Armenian Church remained in communion with the Syriac and Coptic Churches and maintained its independence from the Greek Orthodox Church. The Armenian liturgy was expressed in Syriac until 410 when an Armenian alphabet was devised.

As my taxi wove through midday traffic in Damascus, I pulled out my tourist map and located three Christian sites to the north of Damascus. As I've mentioned, I wanted to see two Greek Orthodox establishments, the convent of Saydnaya and Marjurjos. Also, I was interested in Maalula, one of three small villages where Aramaic, the language of Jesus, was still spoken. After visiting these Christian sites, I wanted to meet Alawites and Ismailis, two secretive Shiite sects that had formed at the turn of the millennium (just before the Crusades began). I looked again at my map and saw small Alawite towns on the hills overlooking the Mediterranean. For that matter, I noticed that the mountains themselves were named for the Alawites. After the Christians I'd try to meet Alawites. Then I'd do some sightseeing on the coast and, on my way back to Damascus, stop in the town of Masyaf, the fabled stronghold of the Ismailis.

An hour after leaving Saad's office I was on a bus riding north toward the ancient Christian convent of Saydnaya.

PART THREE

المنشقين

Heretics
A Week on the Coast

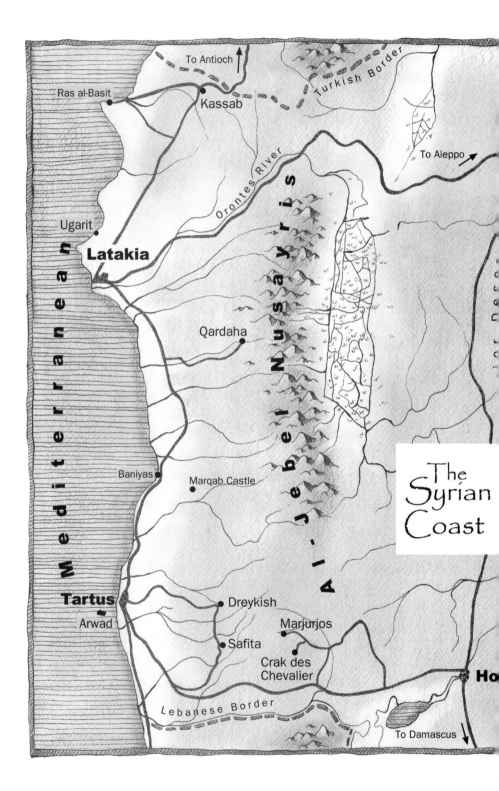

To Antioch

Ras al-Basit

Kassab

Turkish Border

To Aleppo

Orontes River

Ugarit

Latakia

Qardaha

Al-Jebel Nusayris

Baniyas

Marqab Castle

The
Syrian
Coast

Tartus

Arwad

Dreykish

Marjurjos

Safita

Crak des
Chevalier

Ho

Lebanese Border

To Damascus

1 — The Holy Icon

Desert rain fell from the sky and wetted brush and clay of the canyon lands through which we traveled. My bus turned from the valley and climbed an arid ridge to a steep rock summit capped with a palace of white stone: the Greek Orthodox convent of Saydnaya, operated under the Patriarch of Antioch. Saydnaya means "Our Lady" in the ancient Syriac tongue, and pilgrims afflicted with infertility have been especially attracted to the site and its holy icon.

The bus stopped, and I climbed a long flight of stairs to the convent's small, arched entry door. A few minutes later I was in the *sanctum sanctorum*, a small dark room with burning candles, black sooty paintings, and an altar. I saw a clay bowl, filled with clear olive oil. Floating in the center was a small raft with a wick that gave off a steady flame. It was very, very quiet behind these thick walls, and I felt as though I had walked back in time. A middle-aged woman wearing a white scarf entered the room. She lit two candles, placed them in holders on the altar, then knelt and grasped the altar and prayed. Behind the two small doors, according to tradition, was a silver casket containing the first of four icons painted by the Apostle Luke.

In the convent's early years the abbess had given money to a pilgrim on his way to Jerusalem. He returned with the holy oil painting or icon, having fended off attacking bandits with its power. Since then the paint had been rubbed and damaged by the kissing of nuns and pilgrims, and now the doors were kept shut. Jealous custodians of other shrines charged that the icon had been carried away to Italy by Crusaders and a copy left in its place, but the nuns insisted that they possessed the original. And pilgrims of all faiths, Muslims and Druze as well as Christians, confirmed the holiness of this object. They found Saydnaya to be a place of solace, prayer, and healing.

2 — Amazing Grace

"Will you stay with us?" Stephanie was a diminutive nun, wrapped in black so that only her face showed. On buses near the temple of Zeinab I had seen middle-aged Muslim women in full length, black *abiahs*, equally covered, but they seemed dull and weary. This nun was different. Stephanie pounced like a kitten grabbing a string. I replied to her in Arabic. She smiled and blushed, and hurried back the way she had come. In a few minutes she returned. "Follow," she said.

Saydnaya was established twenty years before the birth of Muhammad, nearly ninety years before the fall of Damascus to Muslim horsemen in 636. The convent was founded by Justinian I, the Byzantine (Eastern Roman) emperor, who was marching with his troops to attack the Persians. His soldiers were thirsty, and Justinian was looking for water when he saw a gazelle which led him to a rocky summit and then transformed itself into an icon of the Holy Virgin shining with light. "Justinian," the icon said. "Thou shalt build for me a church here on this hill." Then the vision faded and Justinian found a spring of sweet water. Before long the builders were cutting stone and dropping blocks into place. The year was 547. Soon pilgrims who made the long trek from Europe to Jerusalem were stopping along the way at Saydnaya.

The entry stairs at Saydnaya were chiseled from bedrock.

Mother Superior walked out of the kitchen. Behind her I could see large sinks and faucets, presumably fed by the spring that Justinian and his gazelle had discovered. "Stephanie," Mother Superior said, "was glad to greet you. She has practiced her English for many months in hope of speaking to an American or an English." Stephanie blushed.

Mother Superior was about sixty years old, craggy and warm. The possibility that I

The Saydnaya convent was filled with visitors, Muslim as well as Christian.

might not possess the proper religious pedigree did not seem to occur to her. "Our convent is busy," she said. "Here we have forty nuns living, and many pilgrims even now and more in the summer. If you wish to stay the night, we do not charge. We have a collection box in the sanctuary. The gratitude of our visitors provides for our needs." Of course, as I later learned, the convent owned properties in Syria and Lebanon that supplied the larger part of its income. Although they were glad to assist pilgrims, the nuns' chief work was caring for homeless children of all faiths in their orphanage.

Stephanie showed me to a cell with a bed, a small table, and a tiny window cut in the thick wall which gave a view of the valley below. Later in the evening, I met Stephanie in the courtyard. "Where can I find the Patriarch of Antioch?" I asked.

"In the old city in Damascus, there is a place where Saint Paul escaped over the wall in a basket. Nearby is where the Patriarch lives today."

A few minutes later several dozen fair-skinned teenagers clambered into the courtyard—a gust of conviviality and high spirits, boys and girls with a couple of chaperones on a mild carouse. The youngsters cooed and squealed at one another in Arabic, while I spoke with the chaperones and one or two of the older kids in English. Surrounded by stone walls, their laughter echoed like a hymn of innocence. Alone among his light-hearted friends, one young man had a dour look.

"I don't want to fight," he told me. "The Bible says, 'Thou shalt not kill.' But I must go to the army. What can I do?"

"You have to pray," I replied. "You are not opposing the government or the conscription law. It's really a mental battle against evil in your own heart. This morning I was reading from Ephesians, where Paul writes, 'Put on the whole armor of God.' If you attack and destroy fear, greed, lust, and other forms of evil in your heart, then God sets you free. Anything can happen."

"I don't understand," he said. "I am *against* war and fighting. Were you in the army?"

"Well, when I was about your age and facing the draft, the Vietnam War was going on, people were getting killed, it was serious. I applied to be a Conscientious Objector, but my draft board turned me down. So I appealed, and for eight weeks as I waited for my hearing, I prayed. I was really going through the wringer—I felt like Jesus in the garden of Gethsemane where he prayed and sweated blood while he was waiting to be taken and crucified. 'Father,' he said, 'not my will but Thine be done.' I was completely in anguish. Where did I belong? What should I be doing? Should I be killing women and children in Vietnam? I used a similar prayer to that of Jesus. 'Not my will, or my draft board's will, or anybody else's will, but Thy will be done,' I prayed. I read the Bible and a book by a religious thinker called *Science & Health* for three hours every morning and told God that I'd be happy to serve Him wherever He sent me. I laid myself out there—God's will be done.

"At last the day for my interview came. My mom drove me downtown in our white '63 Buick station wagon with tail fins, and I went in to see my draft board. The draft board consisted of 'citizens,' in this case old guys, World War II veterans, who had retired from their work as businessmen, very conservative, doctrinaire. I waited, and then they called me in, and I sat down in a heavy wooden chair across a table from them. The walls were a drab, institutional green, the lights were fluorescent and one of the bulbs sputtered a little, the floors were beige linoleum squares with lots of wax. The head guy glanced at my papers, like he was pretending to read them. (This draft board never read the papers that you gave them. If they had read mine they could have denied me on a technicality, since I stated that, if this were World War II, I would probably not have claimed CO status.) I was sort of looking around, trying to feel very gentle and pacifistic when actually I was pretty nervous. 'The next three minutes,' I kept thinking, 'are going to determine the rest of my life.' Then the head guy looked at me and frowned and mumbled a few words, scarcely comprehensible, and I asked him to repeat, and I still couldn't make any sense—this was business speak—but I got the idea that he was being rude.

"'Are you saying that I'm lying,' I said, 'that I just made all this stuff up?'

"'Yeah,' he said. 'That's it.' I had been praying my brains out for eight weeks. What did this guy know? I couldn't take it—I just snapped. I jumped out of my seat, clenched my fists and knuckled them into the table, and started screaming and shouting all kinds of incomprehensible stuff about my spiritual life.

"'I rely on God for everything,' I said. 'Absolutely everything. My car broke down in the mountains this summer. You would have called a tow truck. Not me. Of course, being the mountains, there was no phone. So I didn't call, I turned to God. I prayed for half an hour. Then the car started, no problem.

"'Who am I to say where I belong? I can imagine having a good experience in Vietnam and a rotten experience here in the States. It's not what I want, but what God wants.' I was sweaty and all red and totally raging, and as I screamed at the guy little bits of spit jumped out of my mouth and landed on the polished hardwood table. When I was done they showed me out, and I walked down the stairs to catch my ride back home. I felt as though a crushing burden had been lifted off my back. Of course I had said exactly the wrong thing. 'I'm nobody's idea of a pacifist,' I told myself, 'and I'm going to Vietnam. But that's OK.'

"Then a week later I got a letter with a form stamped Approved. I couldn't believe it. Later I talked to two different friends of mine from Seattle. They explained that they could never get approved as COs by our draft board, no matter how many times they appealed. They were meek, well-mannered, soft-spoken, and gentle. Nothing doing. Here I was just about to murder these old guys, I was so angry. Apparently my draft board figured that if I was ready to commit mayhem, I must be a sincere pacifist.

"So, you see, you can never predict. You have to just beat down evil thoughts in your own mind, place your life in God's hands, and prepare to be surprised."

As I spoke, I wondered at this young man and his schoolmates. They were of Greek descent, an enclave of Christians from Tartus on the coast. Their people antedated the Crusaders, antedated the Muslims. They were ancient Christians, the same Greeks to whom Paul had taken the Gospel. I was older than these young men, yet their tradition was original. I felt that they should be lecturing me, not the other way around.

The next morning I packed my bag. "I must go," I told Mother Superior.

"You should stay one more night," she replied.

"Today I need to see Maalula," I said. "They say that the people in Maalula still speak Aramaic, the language of Christ."

"It is true," she replied. "And there are caves in the cliffs where the Christians hid from the Ottoman Sultan's armies and a spring of healing waters and a very old church. There are many things to see, but you must not leave us without breakfast."

"I'm really not hungry," I said. I was famished, but I couldn't wait. I needed to catch an early bus. "

I need time to hike around Maalula," I said.

Stephanie gave me a tiny reproduction of Saint George slaying the dragon.

"At least, then, coffee."

While Mother Superior rushed to find coffee, Stephanie arrived and implored me to have some hot milk. My Arabic was not sophisticated enough to say "no" with courtesy, so I could only accept her invitation. She disappeared to fetch the milk. While she was gone, Mother Superior returned with a cup of brew. I drank coffee in alternate sips with the milk and, when I was finished, gave Stephanie a postcard of Mount Rainier and a cloth patch showing a ferry boat on Puget Sound.

"For me?" She smiled and blushed. "A moment," she said. In a few minutes she returned with two offerings of her own: a small plastic crucifix and a tiny reproduction of Saint George slaying the dragon in its own plastic frame.

The convent of Saydnaya was a place of hospitality, good will, and grace. Nuns like Stephanie saw the best in everyone. They encouraged me, uplifted me, and made me believe that Christ had indeed risen from the dead. Two days later I would visit Marjurjos (*mar* for Saint, *jurjos* for George) which represented the same Greek Orthodox denomination, the same religious doctrine. At the Monastery of Saint George, however, I would meet a priest who was angry, bitter, inhospitable, and who seemed to see the worst in everyone. He discouraged me, pulled me down, and made me believe that religious people were indeed capable of putting Christ to death.

I waved to Stephanie, then caught a bus to Maalula where I hiked to the holy spring, the church of Saint Sergius (one of the oldest churches in the world) on the top of the bluff, and spotted an old man in a *kaffiah* and Turkish pants ploughing a small plot. Then I hiked down past picturesque cliffside dwellings to the center of town. At noon I caught a bus heading north toward Homs where I transferred to another bus taking me into the coastal mountains and Marjurjos.

Mamoun Sakkal

Cliff Dwellings in Maalula.

3 — The Monastery
of Saint George

The coastal mountains. Saturday, October 24.
Our bus climbed lush green grassy hillsides above the Homs plain.
The scenery was great, but I couldn't appreciate it. I had been on
buses for five hours, explaining myself in Arabic to one passenger
after another, a major strain. I was tired, sinking fast, and still the
curious wanted to know: How much did my new Nike boots cost?
How much did I earn in America? When I could, I stared out the
window to discourage conversation. I was not used to Arabic or to
being on display. And I was concerned about a young man, serious
and silent, who had an automatic protruding from his rear pocket.
With the encouragement of Saleh the Shiite, I had come to think of
myself as a humanitarian, a lover of all kinds of people, not one to
get sucked into tribal rivalries and prejudice. But at this moment I
needed sanctuary and looked forward to resting among Christians.
(At this moment, I thought of Christians as my own people.) Our bus
rounded a corner on the hillside and, just in time, I saw a sprawling
stone building: Marjurjos.

Inside the gates I met a pleasant young man, an assistant named
Peter, who assigned me a cell and gave me a big, heavy key. I asked
about a parchment scroll, displayed in a glass case in the office. "A
letter," said Peter. "This is a letter written to the monastery by Umar,
a companion of Muhammad's who later became caliph. This letter was
sent to us and to others in 629, before the Muslims rode north from
Mecca. It promised that when they ruled our land we could continue
as before. We keep it, even today."

Later I learned that this scroll and others like it in Christian institutions across the Levant were one answer to an abiding mystery in
the region's history. How was it that Muslims from the desert were
able to overcome powerful, walled cities across the Levant? Scholars
surmise that the local Christians (called by scholars "Monophysites")
must have chosen Muslim administration of their lands as a way of
preventing their fellow Christians from the north—Greek Ortho-

Farming a small hillside terrace above Maalula.

dox Byzantines based in Constantinople—from taking over. There definitely were philosophical differences between the two Christian factions. The issue of contention: did Christ have one body (a single divine nature) as the Monophysites insisted or two bodies (a divine nature and a human nature) as the Orthodox claimed? The meaning of the debate was less arcane.

Local Christians preferred to find divinity through individual spiritual seeking or through their local churches. The Byzantines insisted that inspiration could occur only within the Eastern Church and its hierarchy. They were dictatorial, arrogant, and thought nothing of crushing small churches and scattering their members. This Christian conflict was big news in the Levant at the time and sometimes seemed to puzzle and bemuse the Muslims. One caliph invited representatives of the two Christian factions to his court, asked them to debate, and then offered solicitous advice on healing their rift—an odd example of interfaith dialogue. For my part, I wondered if the heavy-handed Byzantine mentality had survived to modern times. "Apparently not," I thought. "Stephanie and the others at Saydnaya were Greek Orthodox, the descendents of the Byzantines, and they were nothing but sweet."

Marjurjos had pigeons living inside the sanctuary and vines growing from window sills.

The scroll? The Muslims used it to smooth the way for their accession to power. "Under our administration," they were promising, "your lands and your religious practice will be safe." A scroll such as this would have an additional attraction to small local Monophysite churches, an implied promise, a deal-clincher. "We will keep the Byzantines off your backs," it said.

I toured the monastery, and then lightning, thunder. The clouds broke open, rain crashed down, and I took cover under the gateway arch. Peter joined me, along with a wiry albino—an animated, zany man, an employee who worked in the monastery's orchards and carried a wicked looking olive hook. The albino laughed and joked, but Peter was glum. When the rain stopped I resumed my tour and realized the cause of Peter's poor spirits: the place was falling apart—the courtyard flooding from the cloudburst, rain water streaking down the masonry beside broken downspouts, and inside the sanctuary, pigeons nesting on high, unreachable beams.

In the office again, I saw the head priest, wearing a blue silk robe, sitting at a desk below a color reproduction that showed Saint George driving his lance into the heart of a dragon. The priest was thirty-five, six feet tall, and solidly built. He had fair skin, dark hair, and a full beard trimmed short. His beard was terrific. I glanced at the picture of Saint George and tried to imagine the priest in shining armor astride a powerful white horse. He looked like a leader, yet something about him did not fit. It was his eyes. The head priest's eyes were vacant. I puzzled for a moment, then a thought occurred to me. "He is a dispirited man, not passive by nature, but a man of ambition and energy who has been thwarted, an unpredictable and dangerous sort."

Still, I did not believe my thoughts. For I saw a fine-looking young religious man who was the image of campus ministers I had known, long-suffering, mild, compassionate men who sat on the floor with students and talked for hours about all things. "He's OK," I thought. "And he might open up, sit with me in this ancient house of God, and speak of the great issues, of God and man, life and death. A talk with this man could serve as the philosophical heart of my journey. This is a priest, not a Patriarch, but he could carry the freight and then, at the end of my journey, the Patriarch could offer a few words to cap things off."

The head priest sat slumped forward a little, hands on the desk top, and looked at the wall across the room. An old priest, also wearing a blue robe, stood behind him and began to knead his shoulders, then to hit them with the sides of his hands. The head priest closed his eyes for a moment, tightened his face. An artery on his forehead stood out. Apparently things were not going well in the monastery business. Then the priest opened his eyes, looked at me, and nodded toward the old man. "Massage," he explained in English.

The bell rang for lunch. Peter joined us, and we walked through an empty courtyard below empty balconies that served empty cells. There was supposed to be a healing spring in the nearby hills, but its powers must have waned, for on this day I was the sole visitor. We descended to a small, dark dining room with a painting of the Last Supper and sat around the table. For the previous day I had been worried about finding the right bus and climbing aboard. I had not wanted to risk losing a day by stopping for food, since I never knew, exactly, how much time I had before my bus would pull out. I was starving. Aside from the milk and coffee offered by Stephanie and Mother Superior that morning, I had not eaten for twenty hours.

"*Tfadal*," the head priest said, Help yourself. I did not want to be rude, so I dished an especially small serving of rice and gravy. I was counting on seconds. I had eaten two bites when the head priest spoke again in Arabic. Peter translated. "We like Americans," the head priest said. "They give us many dollars. Heh, heh." The head priest's tone and his grating laugh said that he did not like Americans—that Americans, a people of immense wealth, had given him nothing. "And you. Do you have a good job in America? Do you have a lot of money? Have you ever thought about selling your car or your house and giving the dollars to do God's work in the Holy Land?"

I was still hungry, but now my stomach was in knots. I had met Muslims who were poor. Yet they invited me for tea, begged me to eat with them, and asked nothing, absolutely nothing, in return.

The head priest glanced at me as though evaluating my net worth. I did not reply to his inquiry and by now he seemed to realize that he was stuck with the worst of all visitors, an American who did not understand his own wealth, an American who would not donate the thousands of dollars needed to spruce up this stone pile. The head priest's mouth turned down at the corners, an expression of disgust. Then he looked back at his plate and used a piece of flatbread to push rice and gravy across its surface, his arm moving in short, angular strokes. He was wide awake, his sore back forgotten, and his face had taken on a slight reddish color. He looked decisive and strong, and I thought of a knight preparing for combat. He was a noble-looking man, cloaked in righteousness, and seemed to be playing to a vast audience. But there were only four of us in this room. The galleries of this monastery were dank, cold, empty. I forced myself to take two more bites, a small defense against his fury.

"What faith are you? Catholic, Orthodox, what?" The head priest's voice was flat and sharp. "I'm a Christian Scientist," I said.

Neither the head priest nor Peter could place it. The head priest turned his head and frowned. It seemed to be important for him to identify my heresy. "Something else about Americans," he said. "They are rich but they are wrong, all of them, very very wrong. There is the one true church, the Eastern Orthodox Church. So the Catholics of Rome broke away. And then Martin Luther, the Protestants, broke away from the Catholics. Tell me, why try to repair one mistake by making another mistake? Martin Luther should have come back into the fold. And now you see the sad pitiful outcome: all America is dozens of small, misguided churches—doing whatever they want, saying things, going out on their own, making many more mistakes." The head priest looked down at his plate, bowed his head slightly, and scooped the last of his rice with a wedge of flatbread. Then he looked up as though a sudden thought had occurred to him and spoke quickly with Peter in Arabic. At last he smiled and put his hands on the table, palms down.

"Your church has headquarters in Boston?"

"Yes, in Boston."

"We know this," he said.

The head priest dished a few *yalangi* onto his plate. I tried one, rice wrapped in grape leaves, found it a little bitter, but I was hungry and wondered at my chances of getting another. "You don't pray," he said and pointed to the bread on the table and then to the painting of the Last Supper on the wall. He exhaled slowly and with an air of utter satisfaction. "You are the ones who don't pray."

"We pray." I used a piece of flatbread to mop up the last streaks of gravy on my plate.

"Not in the church."

"Sure, in the church and out of the church."

"You don't pray in the church with bread and wine."

"No," I said.

"Our Lord and Savior Jesus Christ," he said, "commanded us to eat the bread as his body, and drink the wine as his blood. The hands of God break the bread, pour the wine." As he spoke he held up his hand for me to inspect.

I was surprised. At Saydnaya, Stephanie had made no issue of my faith. Her approach was Christian love overflowing, blessing everyone it touched. The head priest had a different approach, more like identify your enemies, then destroy them.

"I think of wine as inspiration," I said in a low voice. "And bread is an idea—"

"Wine, real wine, wine in a glass, not your idea of wine. Every day a thousand heretics are born." He gave me a look—rage, disgust, hatred, then extended his forefinger and jabbed it into the tabletop. "You must drink wine and eat bread and do this in the church."

"Well, ah," I said, "I see, I guess." I was churning inside, a long way from home, outnumbered, surrounded. History was alive here, and I was just one more Monophysite who valued a direct connection to God. He was the true Byzantine Church, a political and worldly power with priests, bishops, and archbishops who had been blessed by God and who, therefore, had a right to enforce the laws of God on others. I couldn't appreciate the history of this moment, however, because I was suffering. I felt like launching a withering riposte but I had been surprised, bushwhacked by "my own people" at a moment when I was desperate for sanctuary: exhausted, hungry, utterly vulnerable. No words came to mind.

Of course, there was another less noble reason for my silence: I was hungry, a single serving was not enough, and as the conversation developed and turned against me I kept watching—not the eyes of my attackers—but the food on the table. Instead of figuring out a clever comeback, I was angling for just a little more rice and gravy. "After a few volleys," I told myself, "the head priest will feel generous, will smile, and will dish me a big second helping." Then I watched in dismay as the assistant priest lifted the bowl of rice and shoved it back through the opening into the kitchen. The flatbread, gravy, and *yalangi* followed and there was nothing I could do to prevent it. "Stop," I thought. "Think about what you are doing. Be reasonable."

We walked outside. I was distraught. My body tingled with surprise, embarrassment, apprehension. In an Arab land that took pride in its hospitality, these guys had been the rudest imaginable hosts. They had been unkind to me and my country. They had dismissed my religion, my very highest beliefs, the things I held most dear. In my mind was an image of chewy, coarse rice and light brown gravy with a *yalangi* on the side.

The head priest marched up the stone stairs. He was in the lead, his eyes blazing, shoulders thrown back, head held high. He had killed the dragon.

4 — Escape

Saydnaya had been busy with visitors, but Marjurjos was too far from Damascus for day-trippers, and the sanctuary was empty. Traffic patterns had changed from the days when pilgrims walked on foot and needed lodging every twenty miles. Marjurjos was a monument to the faith of those who had lived here more than a thousand years before, as early as the sixth century. In a land of ruined cities, Marjurjos was just three warm bodies away from being archaeology itself.

I walked alone through the compound—at the gate I saw the albino, wearing a jagged smile, ripping off toward town on the monastery's tractor: standing behind, his robes whipping in the wind, was the old priest, the massage-giver. Otherwise, I saw nothing alive, nothing of interest. I sought refuge in my cell, a cave carved into limestone that was faced with thick limestone blocks and fitted with a heavy, wooden door. A single, small window looked onto the courtyard. I was hungry, tired, and nauseated, and I could not keep from thinking about the Inquisition. Religious hatred, out in the open, was new to me. I remembered Dostoevsky's Grand Inquisitor, the character in *The Brothers Karamazov* who incarcerated a stranger, and then ordered the man put to death. The stranger, it developed, was Christ, come again to save and heal the world. I had always thought of the church and Christ as allies. But now I could see that limestone blocks and tile roofs, not to mention sagging careers, were very different from the ethical teachings of Jesus. The ethical teacher said what was on his mind. He did not necessarily endorse institutions. He could cause problems. The execution of the ethical teacher was a sad concession to efficient administration.

Now I had met my own inquisitor and dreaded the thought of an evening with the man. Sadly enough, I had told Peter that I was staying. He had given me a key, I felt obligated.

Without warning, the cold silence was broken—from outside my door: a scream and another and another, screams of blood and rage. "They are coming for me," I thought. I checked for a means of escape, but my cell was solid stone. I peeked through my small window and saw across the courtyard a round-faced monk at the top of a flight of stairs, his face red with anger. I climbed on the bed to get a better angle, and the albino came into my line of vision. The monk was not after me but was waving his arms and howling at the albino (the only light-hearted man in this palace of gloom) who had pale red mud about an inch high on his tennis shoes. What had he done? Had he driven the tractor over a cliff and killed the old man? Or was it something minor, a petty irritation, paperwork improperly filled out?

The surly monk kept on, and his cursing reached a new level, like an aria nearing crescendo. The courtyard would have given magnificent resonance to forty pious men singing the mass. As it was, it magnified a song of venom and hate. The monk was really sticking it to the albino, demeaning him, rubbing his nose in it. The setting was right for murder, and I half expected the albino to slice at the monk's throat with his olive hook.

In a few minutes the monk stopped screaming as abruptly as he had begun. Did I really have to stay the night? I was a tourist, not a martyr. "I've seen about all I want to see of these Christians," I thought. "What's next on my list?" When the coast was clear, I grabbed my bag, handed my key to Peter, made a small donation, and escaped through the front gate.

5 — Kidnappers

CRAK DES CHEVALIERS. SATURDAY, OCTOBER 24.

After leaving Marjurjos I had a couple hours of daylight and no place to stay. In Syria the crime rate was extraordinarily low, yet an ancient tradition lingered: at night one did not wander beyond the walls of one's city or village. In medieval times, robbers and vagabonds roamed the darkened countryside. But I doubted that the modern state had this problem. It was age-old habit that kept Syrians close to their hearths at night. And ancient fear was reinforced in the present by the security needs of the regime: In the eyes of the secret police a foreign traveler wandering beyond the city limits, a traveler without lodgings, became a spy or terrorist the moment night fell. I was new in Syria, yet sensed that my situation was precarious. Still, after Marjurjos, I was tired of playing it safe. I hiked down the road—not to the hotel in the valley, but past the hotel to the mountain above and, on its summit, the great Crusader castle, Crak des Chevaliers.

Crusaders, as I have mentioned, came to the Levant beginning in 1098, captured coastal territories from Antioch to Jerusalem, then returned home. The few troops left behind could hold the conquered land only from fortified positions—and the Crusaders built hundreds

Half a mile from Marjurjos the sun burst through the clouds. I looked up and saw the great Crusader Castle, Crak des Chevaliers, silhouetted against the sky.

of them. Crak, the most famous of all, was built in the twelfth century in a position overlooking the Homs Gap—the only place from Antioch to Beirut where Muslim armies on the interior could attack the coast. Designed for two thousand knights, Crak repelled all assaults until the Mamluk army from Cairo laid siege, penetrated the outer wall, and, on April 8, 1271, tricked the defenders into surrender. Baybars, the Mamluk leader, forged a letter that requested the garrison to retreat to the coast, and the Hospitallers, credulous organization men, followed orders. At the time of its fall, Crak was defended by only three hundred knights.

Rain had wetted the land, the sun shone, steam rose from the fields: the air itself seemed to have been scrubbed clean. I caught a ride as far as the castle road, then hiked up the hill past dozens of children who stood before concrete or mud houses waiting for the return of fathers from fields in the valley below or from factories in Homs.

The road leveled out a bit, then grew steeper. Closely built houses extended to the base of the castle, then there were none—just the fortress with its broad walls and the green, grassy ridge top that showed in the photos in travel books. These pictures made it look as though the castle was all of a piece, created in a single stroke by a benevolent deity. In fact the castle was built block by block by people who had occupied houses below, just outside the frame of the photo.

Crak des Chevaliers.

The castle had been the local industry. The village had grown up to build and then to provision Crak des Chevaliers. Some workers were Arab Christians, others were Muslims. Most current residents of the village were Alawites, members of a Shiite sect who counted one of their own, Hafez al-Asad, as president.

How can I explain the position of Alawites vis-à-vis the rest of Islam?

Shiites were a minority within an Islamic world dominated by the Sunni faith. And Alawites, along with the Ismailis and Druze, were the most prominent offshoots from mainstream Shiism. (Alawite and Ismaili teaching developed from Shiite sources and Druze religious teaching emerged as a variation on Ismaili belief.) Each of these three minority sects had a secret religious doctrine and apparently mixed elements of Christian belief with Shiite teachings. Each of these sects emerged in the century or two before the Crusades began.

Saleh and his pals at the temple of Zeinab were my first Shiite Muslims. Shiites (from *shiate* Ali which means the party of Ali) were followers of Ali, the son-in-law of the Prophet Muhammad. The largest group of Shiites were called Twelvers, because—as Saleh had explained to me on the bus from the airport my first night in Damascus—they accepted the succession of twelve *imams* beginning with Ali. In old times the Shiites, as Saad Shalabi mentioned, had a running argument with the Sunnis. The Shiites felt that Ali was the rightful successor to Muhammad and judged that Sunnis such as Umar (the talented merchant who established the Islamic empire) were more interested in wealth and power than in sincere religious practice. For their part, the Sunnis have regarded Shiites as religious extremists devoid of practical sense.

On the coast I wanted to meet Alawites (also called Nusayris). Alawite belief is based in the teachings of Muhammad ibn Nusayr

130

an-Namiri who lived circa 850 in Basra on the Persian Gulf. One distinctive element of his thought was the deification of Ali. Nusayr's teaching was organized and spread in the tenth century, and during this time Alawites were prominent in Syria's north. When the Shiite Hamdanid dynasty of northern Syria and Iraq fell from power, however, the Alawite sect was without protection and suffered at the hands of the Abbasid caliphs in Baghdad as well as Crusaders, Mamluks, and later the Ottomans. For their own protection, Alawites fled to the coastal mountains (today called Jebel Nusayri, Mountain of the Nusayris) where they joined native Christians who also were seeking shelter from persecution.

In more recent times, and especially since the French occupation following World War I, the Alawites populated the coastal city of Latakia, Syria's main port. The French cultivated a special relationship with the Alawites as a way of exerting control over the country as a whole. As a favor to the Alawites, the French built the first roads and schools in many rural districts. The Alawites were poor rural folk who often hired out to service. Hasan the architect grew up in Syria's northern city of Aleppo and although his family, which survived on his father's school teacher's salary, was not wealthy, they were able to afford an Alawite girl as a live-in maid. Alawites also were attracted to the military as one of the few means of advancement open to them during the 1930s and 1940s when the Sunni urban elite was busy doing business deals and managing lands. After independence, ironically, it was the military—not urban Sunni merchants and landowners—who were in a position to exert power. And the once scorned Alawites found themselves ruling over a proud, sophisticated class of urban Sunnis who had been Syria's power brokers going back hundreds of years.

As I neared the castle, a young Alawite man joined me. Jabir had a large, gentle face, wide-spaced, friendly eyes, light brown skin, and a faint mustache. He was nineteen years old and had been to Homs, but never as far as Damascus—two or three hours away by bus. Still, he had met people from all over Europe who had come to see Crak des Chevaliers.

When I met Jabir I had no idea that

A stone staircase in Crak des Chevaliers.

131

an hour later we would be running from the secret police. Neither did I guess that he lusted after my body. The most significant surprise, however, would be his family. Alawites could not bear to talk about their religion. This was *taqia*, a habit of secrecy that authorized them to deny their faith to avoid harm and had equipped them to endure centuries of persecution. Yet they were otherwise free and open and were especially friendly toward Christians. Alawite women did not conceal themselves, but joked and laughed with a visitor as easily as they did with brothers. Later that evening in a stone house on the steep mountainside,

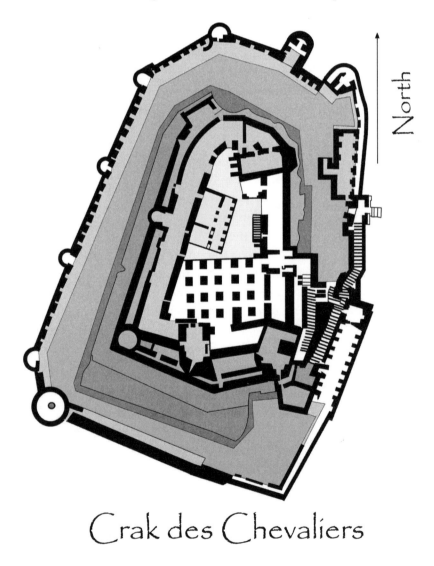

North

Crak des Chevaliers

speaking and eating with members of this strangely secretive Shiite heresy, I would find myself entirely at home. Jabir and his sisters and brothers, unlike the stern monks of Marjurjos, were my kind of people.

I had arrived late, the castle was closed, so Jabir and I walked to the base of the fortress, then circled. Soon we were joined by Ahmed, a twelve-year-old Alawite boy of unusual sprightliness who enlisted in our expedition as though it were an adventure into the unknown. I plodded along behind and climbed goat paths to inspect the lowest blocks of the castle, which were fitted into bedrock. Thousands of limestone blocks were piled on top, joined without mortar. High on the walls I saw slits that had enabled archers to shoot at attackers without exposing themselves, and ceilings with holes for boiling oil.

A stone arch at the "hall of the knights," Crak des Chevaliers.

Jabir and I continued to walk, and soon we had come full circle. It was getting late, and I still had no place to spend the night. I looked out: low sun streamed through the clouds and streaked the valley with light. Then, on the switchback below, I saw the nose of a gray Mercedes coming toward us. The twelve-year-old ducked behind Jabir, who turned to me in explanation.

"*Eshabi,*" he said with a look of contempt, My best friends.

The car pulled back out of sight, then came forward again. The driver was a man of fifty, sinister-looking with dark hair and a narrow face. As we approached, he pulled a cigarette from his lips and let the smoke drift from his mouth and nostrils. He leaned out the window and cursed Jabir in a low voice. I now could see two other men in the back who had weapons, AK-47s.

Suddenly, like a grouse flushed by hunters, young Ahmed ran from behind Jabir and passed the car. The driver shouted and snatched at the air with his free hand but did not get out, and the boy made it to the stone stairs of the footpath and disappeared over the edge into a maze of stone houses cut into the steep slope. By now Jabir had passed the open window and the driver spoke again but Jabir did not respond.

I was careful, as I passed, to say nothing. Jabir was clear of the car now. When I caught up, he jerked his hands in front of his stomach.

"Mukhabarat," he said.

We walked quickly down the steep, stone stairs, then a woman screamed at us from an upstairs window—she had seen the police car and was warning us: the men with machine guns had gotten out and were coming after us. We moved more quickly, turned a corner to throw our pursuers off the track, then another corner, then doubled back, entered a courtyard and an old stone house. Jabir warned his brother, an emaciated man of twenty, but where could he go? His brother flattened himself against a wall.

We sat in silence for a few minutes until the woman who had given warning appeared and turned on Jabir, raging at him in Arabic and slicing the air with her hands. Jabir stepped back against the onslaught. Then another woman appeared and screamed more accusations. Jabir was silent but held his ground. When the two women had run out of steam, he gave them a sentence or two, calming them, reassuring them. Suddenly, conversation ceased.

During the controversy I had huddled against the back wall. We appeared to have escaped the police, who apparently had hesitated at the top of the stone stairs, then returned to their car. Would they come back this evening?

While the brother and the two women sat and sulked, Jabir explained. "The women fear the police," he said. "In Syria every man must serve in the army for three years, but not the fathers. My brother is now a father—but not in the eyes of the police." Jabir's brother had chosen to evade the draft by bringing an orphan—the same Ahmed I had met at the castle—into the house with him and his wife. Ahmed had been orphaned when his mother married an American and moved to Detroit.

Technically, Jabir's brother qualified for a draft deduction, but the police didn't see it that way. For one thing, he had married a woman who was Ahmed's older sister and who, before marriage, had cared for him and lived with him in their family house. Ahmed had not moved into Jabir's brother's house. Actually, it was the other way around. So even though Ahmed had been formally adopted, he lived in the same house as before and his older sister—who was now his adoptive mother—cared for him as before. The only thing that had changed was that Jabir's brother had gotten a draft deduction out of the deal. Was the marriage a matter of romance or simply a way to dodge the draft?

The police ordered Jabir's brother to report, whereupon he dropped out of sight. So the secret police passed the word that they intended to catch him, take him to Homs, and torture him before turning him over to the army. Jabir's brother was upset because our run-in at the castle showed that the *mukhabarat* were hot on his trail.

At the castle, Jabir continued, I had witnessed an attempted kidnapping. Word was out that the secret police had decided to grab Ahmed and put him in an institution in Homs—if he is an orphan, they reasoned, why not give him a home? When they had removed Ahmed, that would leave Jabir's brother without a dependent of any sort and in clear violation of the law. Then they would hunt him house to house.

Jabir's brother walked out, and the tension in the room eased. I entertained Jabir and the women with my small collection of Arabic words, then they went down to the kitchen, on the floor below—beside the room where their cows slept. Jabir and I watched television until the two women returned with food. The draft evader returned, and Jabir's younger brother joined us. The main dish was string beans with small chunks of lamb. Side dishes were rice and yogurt. We sat and ate. By now everyone seemed to think that the police had called it a day. For the time being, we were safe.

A little later Jabir, his younger brother, and I retired to the other room. The boy sat in a sofa and read a school book until Ahmed the orphan came in and challenged him to a wrestling match. While they struggled on the sofa, the two women—Jabir's sister and his sister-in-law—entered and sat cross-legged on each side of a ghetto blaster. This impressive example of Korean electronics was a guilt payment from Ahmed's mother in America. The women played a tape of Arab music, and asked me to perform. I raised my arms in the air, in my best imitation of the belly dancers I had seen at the Cham Palace, and shook my booty. The two women screamed into their hands. I pulled the boys into the dance. Jabir's sister dropped in a tape of disco, and I pulled Jabir in so that the four of us were discoing until Ahmed, in an exaggerated dance motion, slugged me in the stomach. I held my hands in the air as if returning to belly dance and gave the lad a hip. "Bump dance," I explained. Ahmed got off the floor and perpetrated the bump dance upon Jabir's younger brother. Jabir smiled. Jabir's little brother rolled on the floor and laughed and held his stomach. Ahmed pounced on him like a wrestler and then fell back giggling. Jabir's sister-in-law laughed. His sister laughed and wiped tears from her eyes. It was dark out now. The room was small, the walls were solid, and we were safe in our house on the mountainside.

Later I took a trip to the outhouse, and when I returned Jabir's younger brother was asleep under his comforter. I lay down on a sleeping pad and pulled a comforter over me. Jabir turned out the lights and lay down next to me.

It was quiet now, and Jabir talked about his plans for the future. Perhaps he would go to Homs for more schooling, perhaps not. He told me about his past, the people from other countries he had guided. He kept a diary. Ten French, five Dutch, three Italian, three Spanish, four Swedes, two Greeks. All were young people, most were men. Many Japanese had come to the castle, but Jabir hadn't guided any as yet. He had been earning money as a guide since he was twelve years old. And many of his clients asked for something other than information about the Crusaders and their limestone castle. In the dark vaulted recesses of Crak des Chevaliers, they asked for sex. "I earn much more money this way," Jabir explained.

Since leaving Marjurjos that afternoon, I had seen farm workers, school children, secret police, and a fugitive. Now I was preparing to sleep three inches from a man who wanted sex from me and who outweighed me by fifty pounds. This morning on the bus I had thought to take shelter in the monastery. I reasoned that the priests would protect me from the people of this district, but it worked out differently: I had escaped the priests and taken sanctuary among the people. And now, despite the delicacy of my situation, I felt safe. I trusted the native goodness of this man and his people.

Jabir was still on the subject of sex. What did I think of such sex, Jabir wanted to know, "*shebab-shebab*," boys to boys. I gave him my views. Jabir seemed disappointed. Under the circumstances his question was a request, and my reply could only be interpreted as negative. But his disappointment seemed to be more than that of a frustrated seducer. I was spoiling his dream. As an American, I had standards to uphold. He tried to explain.

"America leads the people of the world," Jabir said. "In America the people are free, they do anything they want. In America the women are thin and beautiful and the men have large shoulders and always suntans. America is famous for sex."

6 — Another Patriarch of Antioch

SAFITA. SUNDAY, OCTOBER 25.

In the morning Jabir fried eggs in olive oil for breakfast and then took me on a quick tour of the castle in the morning sun. I saw high crenellated stone walls, slits for the archers, an inner and outer wall, soaring arches supporting tons of earth and stone. In 1910, after graduating from Oxford, T. E. Lawrence (later known as Lawrence of Arabia) had come to the Holy Lands to sketch and study Crusader castles, primarily *this* Crusader castle, the most magnificent of all.

I caught a bus down to the valley and other buses that took me into the hills closer to the sea. We traveled through well-watered fields, then began climbing dry hillsides covered with slabs of limestone and little terraces with a few olive trees. At the top of a steep ridge we reached the old Crusader town of Safita where I climbed into the loft of the White Castle, a stone fort with a church below. On a clear day you could see inland to Crak des Chevaliers and the other direction as far as Tartus (the Syrian seaport, not to be confused with the apostle Paul's home town of Tarsus in Asia Minor). But on this day the haze interfered with the view. From this spot the Crusaders had communicated with signal fires, though they also had learned to use carrier pigeons from the Arabs. Safita was a Christian enclave, and its church had been in continuous use since Crusader times.

After the White Castle, I walked the narrow streets of this hillside town, and a Christian woman called down to me. I climbed the stone steps to her balcony above the street and met her family. We sat and looked out toward the Mediterranean and talked as the woman cooked lamb sausage for me on their charcoal grill. "Our faith has broken away from the Orthodox and is in communion with Rome," she explained. "Like the Orthodox, we have our own Patriarch of Antioch, located in the old city in Damascus."

She asked my denomination, but did not seem to care that the details of my worship of God varied from her own. "At Marjurjos," I said, "the priests told me that I was a heretic."

She laughed. "They talk the same way to us," she explained. "But we are different, more tolerant. We are a minority within a minority, Christians in a Muslim land, and Greek Catholics or Melkites in a religion dominated by Orthodox Christians. So we are kind to all." I ate, and repeated the Arabic words she taught me. *"Taibeh,"* I said, Delicious. *"Tammam,"* Perfect.

Since leaving Damascus I had met Christians, both Greek Orthodox and Greek Catholic, and I had stayed with a working-class Alawite family. Now, if possible, I wanted to meet another class of Alawites: educated, professional people. I bid adieu to my gracious Greek Catholic hosts who kissed my cheeks before sending me off. Then I caught a bus to Dreykish, an Alawite resort town on the mountainside above the Mediterranean that was prosperous and sophisticated by rural standards.

7 — Fatima

My bus traveled down the hillside, through a valley of olive trees, and up another mountain ten miles north. On the steep slopes near the crest we entered Dreykish where I chose a hotel with a view of the valley. Tourist season was past, restaurants were closed, so I purchased a soda from the cooler in my hotel lobby and went to bed without eating. That night I rested well.

Dreykish was famous for its pure, sweet water, which was bottled and marketed in competition with Boukein. The following afternoon I walked out to see the springs and had gone about a mile when I saw several teenage boys sitting on a front porch. I was definitely getting the hang of the language, so I greeted them in my best Arabic. *"Marhaba,"* I called. A block later, one of them caught up with me.

"My sister speaks English," Fadi said. I followed him to a downstairs apartment, and he invited me to sit in a living room with a sofa and several chairs.

Fatima was an Alawite woman, about twenty-three years old, dark-haired, fair-skinned, buxom, and dressed in jeans and a man's dress shirt. She was studying for her master's degree in English at the university in Latakia, a city famous for its student politics during the 1940s when young Hafez al-Asad attended secondary school there.

Fatima's mother had died, and now Fatima returned home as her schedule permitted to cook for her father and look after her younger brother and sister. On the wall opposite was a photo of a proud-looking man with a handlebar mustache.

"My grandfather," Fatima explained. "He and his brothers owned many sheep in the old days and grazed them up and down the hills. Sheep were wealth, and we were a family better off than many in this town. But my grandfather grew old and, in 1957, he and his brothers lost their good health so that they had to hire people to follow the sheep. In 1962, they died, and the sheep went to others who did not care for them well. So our family is no longer wealthy. My father has a shop in town. My older brother teaches Arabic literature at the high school. And for me, I have not decided what to do."

We talked a few minutes more, then Fatima stood to welcome a friend of her older brother's, a Christian whom he had met in the army. Jade had dark hair and a carefully trimmed mustache. He wore a white shirt, open at the front to reveal his hairy chest and a heavy gold chain. His monogrammed socks were thin and white. Jade dressed and acted like he was God's gift to women, but once you got past that he was a pretty good guy. He was twenty-six years old, yet had a worldliness and confidence that made him seem older.

Jade came from a small village near Safita where the majority were Greek Orthodox, the next largest group were Protestants, and the minority were Greek Catholics. Jade was a Protestant, a Presbyterian. That meant he was born into a Presbyterian family. "If you want to know," Jade explained later, "I was only two times in a church: once when I was baptized and a second time when my brother was married." If the Orthodox did not like Protestants, perhaps they had cause. "Everyone was once Orthodox," Jade continued. "But the Presbyterians sent missionaries from Beirut, which is how we became

Fadi and Boushra.

Protestants."

Jade was educated in Damascus at a school for diplomats and now worked in a bank in Tartus. He held a responsible position—but later, when I bumped into him on the street in that city, I got the impression that he had a job but very little to do. Jade spoke Arabic, English, and French, and had picked up Hebrew during his stint in the army where he spent his time eavesdropping on the "cousins" to the south. Half of Jade's family had moved to the United States before World War I. They owned a shoe factory in the Midwest, and his cousin was a lawyer in Kansas. Like most ambitious and well-educated Syrian men, Jade thought it only fitting that he have an American wife. It was not a matter of the beauty of American women, but of the advantages an American passport could confer. Jade had tried to visit the United States last year, but the consul refused his visa application. "The consul keeps me out," Jade said later, "because he does not want me to take an American wife. But I have ways. If I ask, my aunt will send a woman to Syria. We will be married. Then the consul will see that he is a foolish man."

Jade and I moved onto the balcony where the view of the valley had been blocked by a newer building a few feet away. We could still see out to the side, however, across the town itself. The balcony was warm from the late sun. Fatima joined us, and a dark-complexioned man, Fatima's older brother Jamal, pulled up another chair and sat down.

"Our schools are no good," said Jade. "We should know our history better, so that we will understand how to act in the future."

"What is your history?" I asked.

"For one," he replied, "the Turks were here for four hundred years, from 1514 until the First World War."

"They made us barbarians," said Fatima. "They cut us off from Europe."

"They stole our culture," said Jade. "They took our industry, our good people."

"Those were black times," said Fatima.

"Many of our problems today come from the Turkish occupation," said Jade. "They put us under the Islamic caliph. After the Turks came the French, but we learned something from the French. They built some schools here in the hills, and we learned some good ideas from the French Revolution, ideas about freedom. On the other hand, we struggled against the French occupation. We were one country, but they and the British split us into Syria, Lebanon, Palestine, Jordan. Still, the French were nothing compared to the Ottomans, you know, the Turks.

"In school I studied Martin Luther, John Calvin, Machiavelli, Bismarck, Cromwell," Jade continued. "Our schools would be better if everyone would study history." He paused to let the fact of his own erudition sink in.

"Are you hungry?" Fatima asked. Since the day before in Safita I had eaten nothing except some apricot jam that I had purchased in Damascus and carried for emergencies. Still, I wanted to be polite. I asked Jade if he was hungry, then passed his *"La"* on to Fatima. But Jade was thirsty. A younger sister came onto the balcony. "I'll make you tea," Boushra said to Jade, "if you give me one lira." He smiled, and she disappeared into the other room.

We talked of more current affairs, including the protest of Iranian pilgrims at Mecca that July which had turned into a riot and left 402 people dead. "The people in Iran," said Jade, "brought guns to Mecca, and they give money for the Hezbollah in Beirut. They are ignorant. They want to export a revolution of Islamic fundamentalism." He paused to look at Fatima. "The Iranians," he continued, "think we are begging for their help." Jade laughed, Fatima's older brother Jamal laughed, and Fatima laughed and wiped tears from her eyes. For several years after the rise of Khomeini, the best minds in the United States had talked soberly about the possibility that the Iranian revolution would catch fire in Lebanon and Syria, a possibility which always had seemed logical to me. They might have been comforted to know that here, in the mountain town of Dreykish, two Alawites and a lapsed Christian found that proposition ridiculous.

Young Boushra returned with hot tea and sugar and small glasses. She poured tea and handed me a glass. I gave her a one-lira coin, and she blushed. Jade accepted his tea and made teasing remarks. Boushra answered back and laughed, and Fatima talked with the two in Arabic, pausing occasionally to enlist her older brother's support for the good-natured insults she offered to Jade and her sister. Jade laughed. "Women," he said. Fatima corrected Jade's English, then he corrected her. Fatima looked at me. "This Jade," she said, "is our *mahabooli*, a beloved funny man." I was more impressed with Fatima. Her features did not have precise symmetry, yet she was animated, alive. She was quick in repartee, a happy woman surrounded by family and friends, a woman of warmth and beauty. I wondered how Jade could resist her. Now that tea was served, Jade returned to politics.

"Iran is big problem for Syria," Jade continued. "We buy oil from Iran, on credit. If they say 'pay up' we are dead. We trade with Yugoslavia and Eastern Europe because they don't ask hard currency for payment. Without these trading partners we would have no place to go. We want to have a good economy. We must become an industrial land, invest in the right way." As Jade spoke, Fatima withdrew to prepare the meal. Jade continued.

"Of course Israel is also a problem for us," he said. "They want to take land to protect themselves, and we don't know where they will stop. Israel takes American money, makes promises, then does whatever it pleases.

"Israel gets weapons from the United States, more than all the Arabs combined. The Americans say, 'OK, but only for defense.' Then the Israelis invade Egypt and Syria and Jordan, and later they invade Lebanon. Is this defense?

"The Americans say, 'OK, but no nukes.' Then Israel steals the nuclear plans from France and builds its own warheads and even sells them to South Africa. And when Vanunu exposes them, they kidnap him in Italy and take him to Jerusalem for torture and prison. He would be executed but someone says, 'Quick, give him the Nobel Peace Prize.' What do the Americans do? Nothing." Jade was preaching to the choir.

"He'd trade these complaints in an instant," I thought later, "for a peace treaty and open borders." A Syria that was part of the modern world would need Jade's skills. He'd be busy, in demand, instead of languishing in a position that gave him little to do.

Fatima and her sister served a meal on the coffee table inside. Afterwards we moved back onto the balcony. The sun was low by now, the air was cool, and we talked of music. Jade favored Paul Anka songs and sang a few lines. (Later I learned that Paul Anka had been born in a village nearby.) Fatima laughed. I liked these gentle, lively people and allowed myself to think that I was one of them. The town was spread out before us, and we were young and facile and trusted that God would grant us American spouses.

We decided to take a walk, and Fatima changed into something less comfortable, a full-length dress, nylons, and makeup. She seemed stiff, not as appealing as before. Was she dressing for the public? Or for me? We left the apartment and walked back toward the commercial district. The last light of the sun was lost. It was our turn for power conservation, so the street lights did not come on. We switchbacked downhill on a sidewalk promenade with concrete benches and looked across the valley at the lights of mountain villages. We talked, and in the darkness Fatima seemed beautiful again. I marveled at her rapport with Jade.

"I had a dream last night," said Jade.

"Tell me the dream, and I will tell you what it means," Fatima replied.

"In my dream I got a letter from a former lover. And with the letter was a golden ring. In the letter she said her new love was a man whose name started with J, but when she inscribed the ring, her gift to him, she had it inscribed with another name entirely, a name beginning in F."

"This means that you will lose someone dear to you," said Fatima. "And you won't know that you love this dear one until she has gone."

"Ahhh," said Jade. "That is right. I am always losing the women I love, and I never really love them until they are gone."

We walked farther down the promenade, and Jade began talking about American literature, stories of Jack London that I did not remember. Fatima brought up John Steinbeck, and Jade countered with Hemingway. We reached the end of the promenade and doubled back, taking care to avoid the concrete benches in the dark. They knew American stories, my stories, but I knew nothing of theirs. When I asked, Fatima mentioned the story of the Sleepers. I encouraged her.

"Long ago in Syria," she said, "there was a king called Dukyanus. This is a Greek name, so he must have been a Byzantine king. And there were four men, Arabs, and they had a small dog named Karn-teere. One day the king put out a call for them, to come to trial and then to execution. So the men fled with their dog, escaping the city in the night and traveling for ten days and ten nights into a ridge of mountains where they found a deep cave and crawled inside. They were exhausted, so they lay down to sleep, and in the darkness of the cave they did not awake the next day or the day after or the day after that. They slept for month after month and their hair grew and their beards grew and their fingernails grew long and curved. When four hundred years had passed, the men and their dog woke and were hungry but still they feared the king. So one of them took their money and walked to the nearest village to get some food.

"In the market the people wondered at the man's old-fashioned clothes and his beard, and, when they saw the old coins he offered them, they knew that he had been gone four hundred years. He asked about the king and, learning that the king was long dead, the man returned to the cave, oblivious to the villagers who followed. In the cave the man explained to his friends that the king was dead, and the four of them came from hiding. When they and their dog emerged into the light, however, they saw the mass of villagers and dropped dead."

We walked for a time in silence. "What does this story mean?" I asked.

"I don't know," said Fatima. "But the men have Arab names, so they must be Arab tribes fleeing from the Byzantines, then sleeping for four hundred years under the Ottomans."

"Yes," said Jade. "And they come from the cave into the modern world. There are no families or tribes anymore but only nations, blood-less things that have no breath, no face. These nations have armies and make wars that destroy the life of the people."

"When the men came to light," said Fatima, "they were independent, they did not have to run or hide any more. Yet they had lost the very things that they had hoped to save. They had lost their tribes, their families, their souls."

By now we had reached my hotel. I said good-bye. "When you return to America," said Jade, "send me back a woman, intelligent and beautiful, a woman with knowledge of the world."

"I couldn't find a better woman for you than we have right here," I said. I thought I saw Fatima smile in the gloom. Did she appreciate my effort to turn Jade from his calculated infatuation with American women? We exchanged farewells. I returned to my hotel and drank an orange soda with the manager before retiring.

Looking back now, this night, as much as any other that I spent in Syria, was a collection of the finest things that this land had to offer. This evening was possible because Syria in 1987 was a place where people held jobs that ended each day and allowed them to come home from work and talk to one another, a quiet place where conversation, wit, and repartee were celebrated, where present company did their best to represent the world instead of referring all questions to specialists, where electronic entertainment— canned music or video—were not allowed to diminish living voices and gestures, where all attention turned to insight, humor, and offhand eloquence.

Later that evening, as I fell asleep, I thought about the story of the Sleepers and about another story I had heard, the story of the Forty Saints.

8 — The Forty Saints

Several days before my evening with Jade and Fatima, in Maalula, I had met a young man named Jacob at the church of Saint Sergius. This ancient church, as I've mentioned, sits atop the ravine where the town is situated. We walked down the narrow passageways cut into the side of the cliff, around houses carved into the limestone and looked across at sheer cliff faces with spindly, homemade ladders leaning against the openings of caves in the vertical face.

"The villagers hid many times in those caves," Jacob said, "to escape the Ottoman armies. One cave is very big. It holds three thousand people."

When we reached the small square in the center of the village, Jacob invited me into his upstairs apartment where I met his father and mother. He told me about his medical studies in Damascus and spoke in Aramaic so that I could hear the sound of this ancient language. Just before my bus arrived, he gave me a story to take home.

"You ask if there are books in Aramaic," he said. "We do not have such books, but at one time there were many—old volumes of wise sayings, Christian works that we guarded carefully. But the Ottoman soldiers sank four hundred books in the river, and so they are no more."

"Nothing survived?"

"Nothing. Still, the old people make some talk. They say that when the Ottomans were marching up the valley, burning the Christian villages, killing the men, abusing the women, that forty religious men of Maalula gathered the most precious of the books and crawled beneath the church—the church you see today at the crossroads where your bus will stop. The rock beneath the church is limestone, and there are caves. So the forty saints climbed down into the earth with the light from candles and torches and placed these books in a chamber with a narrow entrance. Then, from inside, they mortared stone blocks in place. And so the most precious books were saved from the Ottomans."

"Where are the books now," I said. "Are they being used? Can they be seen and read?"

"The books are ours, safe from the Ottomans," Jacob replied, "but we can't read them. We really don't know where they are. No one ever has made an excavation below the church."

"And what of the forty saints?"

"The saints? When they made a safe place for the books, they sealed their own tomb."

~~~~~~

Years later in Seattle I talked to Farouk, a professor of cultural anthropology, a small man with glasses who chain-smoked and muttered, between drags, that smoking was a "terrible habit."

Farouk had lived in Paris for many years and had come under the spell of French philosophers—at least to my ear his philosophic reveries had a French quality to them. At the same time he was analytical, always forcing my observations to some political conclusion. I told him two stories: Fatima's story of the Sleepers and the tale of the Forty Saints.

"The Sleepers," Farouk said, "is a familiar story from the Quran and, I think, the Bible. What is interesting here is the setting, the way it is told. Certainly Jade and Fatima were talking about themselves, young people with dreams and aspirations, who are caught in a police state—they spend their time sleeping, waiting for the political climate to relax and the economy to improve, waiting to begin their lives."

"But Jade and Fatima said nothing about the present," I protested.

"Still, it fits too well to be a coincidence. Whatever the intentions of the people who told the story, it is a tale from the past that interprets the present."

"And what of the other story, the one from Maalula?" I asked.

"I can't say what it means," Farouk replied. "It's not traditional. It's an original, a local tale that has been passed down in one small, isolated village. It does not interpret the present, does not have a point—but for that it is more powerful: a simple story of life and death, of faith and the things that destroy faith."

9 — Mukhabarat

By this point in my travel through Syria's coastal region I was beginning to understand one fact: the secret police within Damascus stayed out of sight, but those in the back country were far less inhibited.

My first encounter with the *mukhabarat* had come a couple of days earlier on the main highway from the interior to the coast. My bus let me and a dozen locals off on the side of the road, so that we could make connections. The bus pulled away with a ragged blast from its engine, and I lifted my expedition pack and swung it on. Then I heard a shout from behind. I turned to find, one foot from my face, an AK-47 held by a swarthy man with two days' growth of beard, sunken eyes, and thin, tight lips. Sweat glistened on his forehead.

My antagonist wore dirty blue jeans and a short-sleeved shirt with circles of sweat under each arm. His rifle had white medical tape wrapped around its clip—tape that was dirty from handling. A spare clip was taped to a bandoleer over his left shoulder. The man was growling at me in Arabic, but he must have been speaking *fusha*, formal Arabic, with the idea that a foreigner would never understand *shami*, the local dialect. Yet I had studied *shami*, so I couldn't understand. Then he tucked the rifle under one arm, turned his left hand palm up, and slapped the side of his right hand against his palm in an angry hacking motion. I assumed that this guillotine effect described the consequences of failing to follow his orders, and I was ready to cooperate, but what did he want me to do? I pulled out my passport. He grabbed it and began to finger it with sweaty hands. I had satisfied his request.

By now my feet had come back to earth and my internal organs had resumed their proper positions. Still, I was worried. Would he search my sack? I did not realize until later that with this sack on my back I was a caricature of an Iraqi bomber with his parcel of explosives. Only a year earlier bombs had gone off on Syrian trains, trucks, and buses in this section of the country. The word on the street was that Iraqi infiltrators had sold picnic baskets in bus yard markets, baskets with false bottoms, timers, and Semtex.

The man with the machine gun eyed my pack. It was a Lowe-pack—blue nylon, black padded shoulder straps—and it was huge. No one in Syria had seen anything like it. While he thought about the mysteries that my pack must contain, I felt as though my body was balanced on the tip of an ice pick. By now, my fear was giving way to anger. Forget the notes I carried, the addresses, the dozen or so people I could send to prison. "This guy has my passport," I thought. "I'm at his mercy, without rights or recourse. And he seems to enjoy it. The monks at Marjurjos were rude, but this is a new low."

By now I was seething. In all my days I had never, even once, kept silence when I felt such anger. I took a deep breath—then smiled and said nothing. I was spending my tourist dollars in his country.

And now, as a thank you, I was shamed, humiliated, degraded. In a few minutes the man with the machine gun returned my passport, and I was free to go.

I followed the other passengers to an intersection. The sun was hot, the sky blue. I was nauseated, shaking. Later I would hear Syrians talk about this peculiar condition, an aftereffect of a visit with the secret police.

An hour later the connecting bus arrived. It was crowded, and I was forced to sit in the aisle amidst slimy gobs of spit and sunflower shells. The assistant bus driver handed me a small stool that kept me off the floor, but put me half a foot lower than other passengers. We had traveled a mile when a tall fleshy man in a perfectly pressed black suit stood up from his seat in front and slowly walked my direction, then put a stool down in the aisle and sat facing me. He had a round head with thinning black hair, a round face with plump sagging cheeks, and small, close-set eyes. Flaky white dandruff covered the shoulders of his jet black suit. On his lapel I saw a gleaming gold pin which made me think that he was a government official, a mountain mayor. He possessed a pompous air, as though he was a diplomat or head of state, and I realized that he was going to conduct a formal interview with me while squatting in the filthy aisle of this decrepit bus.

The mountain mayor settled himself, held out his left hand, palm up, perfectly flat, and made a precise and slightly effete hacking motion with the side of his right hand. The hacking motion! I handed over my passport, and he smiled slightly, pleased that I had responded so quickly to his request. Then he snapped back into character, gave me an offhand scowl, opened my passport, and began to read.

In a few minutes the assistant bus driver or *jabi*, a boy of fourteen, approached and leaned over the shoulder of the older man to assist in the inspection of my documents. A gray-haired old man in a red headdress, a passenger, seemed convinced that the other two would bungle the job. He leaned into the aisle and peered past the official's shoulder, pointing and offering advice in Arabic when he spotted something of importance.

I was indignant, and the man in the black suit knew it and did not hide his pleasure. I guessed that he spent most of his time brown-nosing his superiors. Now he could force me to get my nose dirty. He sighed, looked at the *jabi*, looked at the old Arab, then plucked out my travel permit and examined it. Without my passport I was going nowhere. I smiled. He gave me a serious look and glanced back at my passport. "I might let you off," he seemed to be saying, "but it won't be that easy." I tried to guess what author Syrian bureaucrats and police read in their spare time and settled on the Marquis de Sade. If they were sadists, they also had a sense of their own power. Would he let me go? Or was this the end of the line? I smiled again. At last he handed back my documents.

It was getting to be that kind of day. After two run-ins with the law in two hours' time I realized that I would survive without convulsions, though I still felt a pre-convulsion tightening of the stomach, a nascent dry heave. The guy with the machine gun and the mountain mayor had simply sharpened and focused the twisting apprehension that I had felt every minute since I entered this country—nothing big but a little at a time all the time.

My third encounter with the authorities came a couple days later on the island of Arwad, just off the coast from the Crusader town of Tartus. Arwad had a long history as a Phoenician center and was the last bit of the Holy Lands to be occupied by Crusaders. I caught a boat to the island and wandered narrow passageways separating honeycombed apartments built shore to shore. The place smelled of urine. Women cursed me. Children chased me, splashed water in my face, and laughed. At last I broke out onto the beach which was covered with boulders that were exposed only at low tide.

I was circumnavigating this island, I realized, taking a good look in the direction of Italy, the direction the last Crusaders sailed when they abandoned this island in 1302. When I finally found someone friendly, the son of a fisherman, a secret policeman suddenly appeared and gave the dreaded hacking motion. He was wearing slacks and a tweed blazer—a far different get-up than the sweaty T-shirt of my first policeman or the black suit of the mountain mayor. This fellow was young and polished and his sandy hair was cut and combed over in a Western style. Yet he was more frightening than the other two. His smooth face had no expression, his eyes were flat and gray and looked at me with faint recognition. This man was not angry or quaint, he was efficient, ruthless, and in a hurry. I handed over my passport and other papers. "Did those angry women sic this guy on me," I wondered. "Or is he going to come back and really nail me when they complain."

The policeman fingered my documents, and, as he turned the pages, the corners of his mouth turned down in an expression of disgust. "I'm sorry," I told him in English. "I should have stayed in the tourist area, stayed away from the houses. But I like architecture and I was curious and so I started wandering. I guess when the women shrieked at me I should have turned back immediately. Of course, I'll never do any of this again. I wouldn't even think of it. Nope. And I'll return to the tourist area immediately, post haste, you know, pronto."

Unlike the mountain mayor with gold pin and dandruff, this guy was all business, no ceremony whatsoever, no theatre: a sinister and evil man. My stomach tightened. He took no notice of my blathering, scowled at me again, barked some orders that I did not understand, returned my papers, and walked off as suddenly as he had appeared. My day was ruined. I began to walk the hundred feet or so to the tourist beach but my legs were like jelly and I stumbled on the barnacled rocks. When I reached the beach I sat on the first chair I saw and stayed there for an hour shivering, sweating, and swatting flies—trying to calm myself. I thought about my interaction with this policeman and the others who had confronted me in the previous few days.

In my first encounter, on the highway, I was quiet, tense, and very, very careful. AK-47s will do that to you. In my second encounter with the mountain mayor, I was peeved but forced myself to be polite. And now, with this last plainclothesman on Arwad, I seemed to have crumbled. I had confessed my sins—I had indeed ventured beyond the tourist area beside the harbor—even before he questioned me. But why should I sing? The tourist area, after all, was not rigidly defined, and no signs marked a boundary. No one had told me to stay back. I hadn't broken any laws. Why had I become so quick to admit guilt? Why had I become so compliant?

I realized that a security state would fail without the cooperation of its citizens, and that I was fast becoming a cog in the machine. Collaboration was hard to avoid. You don't start out on an even footing against the police because they surprise you, shock you—thugs with guns can do that. And this shock is the tip of the wedge. Your apprehension is a form of cooperation. You are tainted, ashamed that you allowed yourself to be intimidated. Then the police play on your lack of self-esteem. "Wouldn't it be easiest," they suggest, "to help us a tiny bit more?"

I had been warned about Syria's secret police before coming to this country. "Keep your mouth shut!" was the advice that Rita, my travel agent, had given me.

"You need to be very restrained," said Alex Bertulis. "You need to do exactly what they ask." Rita and Alex were two of my friends from Seattle. They were fairly sure that I would say the wrong thing when confronted by the police and would end up in detention. They worried about me. But neither Rita nor Alex mentioned the one thing that could have saved me: luggage. In Syria, tourists carried suitcases. Only renegade psycho Iraqi mass murderers humped enormous expedition packs with strings and straps all over the back and everything piled on top.

I'd brought the backpack because it was the easiest thing to do. It was the luggage I took everywhere I went. Also, it gave me flexibility. It allowed me to skip taxis and hike about looking for a hotel. Or I could hike from one village to another and carry my things with me. Or, if I had to escape across a border, fleeing men with dogs and AK-47s, I could cut away from the highways and head for the hills, sleeping in caves during the day, traveling at night by the light of the moon—my version of the Walter Mitty "ta-pocketa-pocketa" fantasy, to be sure. But the real reason I brought the backpack and other mountain gear was because mountains were the setting in which I had proven myself as a young man. I hoped, somehow, that my mountain gear would summon forth from my middle-aged soul a solid effort against the rigors and challenges of third-world travel.

As a teenager growing up in a suburb of Seattle I never had competed in football, basketball, or baseball—the sports upon which a boy's social standing hinged. I tried to avoid sports that involved balls—that included tennis, golf, and bowling—and instead turned out for wrestling. I did OK as a wrestler, but my letter came too late and I never wore a letterman's jacket. Instead, I took up mountain climbing. In those days climbing was an unusual sport, and mountains became my badge of distinction. I climbed Mt. Rainier and Mt. Baker, made other small conquests, and learned that I could survive without the acclaim of my peers.

On my tour of Syria I carried the following bits of mountain gear: a Silva compass with a plastic base, a Lowe expedition pack of dirty blue nylon, a small blue nylon day pack with a zippered top, and a Goretex cagoule or hooded windbreaker. I had the feeling that these were my secret weapons—that they might get me out of a tight spot. I still felt that way after my escape from the AK-47-toting policeman on the coastal highway, even though, to this point, the large pack had only brought trouble.

I suppose that I was as odd in my own way as some of the people I had seen in this country. At the festival in the temple of Zeinab the Shiites had worn photos of Khomeini in plastic covers that hung from the buttons of their shirt pockets. At the Saydnaya convent Greek Orthodox pilgrims had knelt and kissed the wooden door that covered the sacred icon. I thought these people to be a little foolish, yet they might have concluded that I carried a few cherished objects of nylon and plastic for equivalent reasons. I hoped, a little foolishly, that these pieces of matter would help me ascend a summit of soul and spirit. The Shiites had amulets, the Greek Orthodox had icons, I had mountain gear.

If the secret police regarded me with suspicion when I carried my big blue backpack, the larger problem was that I was a tourist traveling in the off-season to villages where tourists were a rare sight. The secret police in these back country regions in 1987 were no fun for a person on holiday, and I was beginning to understand that they were equally unpleasant for Syrians. What I hadn't figured, however, was the way that Syrians with a grudge might throw an unsuspecting tourist to the *mukhabarat* for their own amusement.

10 — Qardaha

On a bus heading to Latakia I met a local man named Rasheed who, as it turned out, resented Americans. Rasheed had the window seat and I sat on the aisle. He glanced at my Nike walking boots, looked straight at me, and said nothing.

"Aesho bil Amerika," I explained.

"An American," Rasheed said in measured English. He paused for a moment, then continued. "I am a student in Tartus. I will become engineer. And you?"

"Ana najar beyout," I said. Rasheed jerked his head back, then gave a short, sneering laugh.

"A house carpenter," he said. He shook his head and looked out the window. In Syria house carpentry meant mixing and pouring concrete, heavy work. And such construction workers were positioned in the poorly paid underclass. Here a person with education separated himself from commoners, from people like construction workers. Rasheed seemed to be facing the point that however hard he studied, he would never rise higher than Americans, even unworthy lower class Americans such as myself. We traveled in silence, then Rasheed made an offer.

"Come with me," he said, "to my village. I live near the birthplace of our president. This afternoon I will take you. We will visit Qardaha."

Qardaha. The Christians in Safita had paled when I mentioned this name. In Tartus people had shushed me. Two years before, in Seattle, a visiting Syrian had given me his business card, then, after I mentioned my interest in Qardaha, demanded that I hand it back. "An American in Qardaha," he sighed. "Big troubles, big, big troubles."

Since Crak des Chevaliers, I'd had three run-ins with the secret police. I was gun-shy and was aware that Qardaha may or may not have had more secret police per square foot than any other village in the country. Still, I was curious. And I figured that a side trip to Qardaha would work well in my narrative. Besides, the secret police would not be a problem because Rasheed had offered to guide me. This was the code of the desert—the noble Bedouin code of honor—still alive in the present day: I would be under Rasheed's protection.

Half an hour later we were standing by a country road waiting for a connecting bus to Qardaha. The first bus that came was full, and the next was even more crowded—young men hanging out of windows and doors and clinging to the rear bumper. The sun was hot.

"Show me the money," said Rasheed, with no idea how his line would catch on in the United States a decade later. I hesitated, but how could I refuse? Rasheed was my host. I handed him a dollar bill. Rasheed gripped each end of the bill, stretched it tight, and held it close to his face as though he were looking for the hidden source of its power. I gave him a few seconds, then pulled it out of his hands.

"You will hire a taxi," Rasheed said. "Why should we wait? It will cost five dollars—what is that to you?"

On my budget, five dollars was a lot. In Damascus, living at Saad's farm, I walked three miles to Zeinab to save thirty cents. If I saved thirty taxi fares, I reasoned, I'd be able to afford another night at a hotel in Aleppo or a gift in the covered market. But Rasheed was making me feel cheap. "Yeah," I said. "I'll spring for a taxi." Rasheed smiled.

The next vehicle, however, was a bus with standing room. Rasheed and I climbed aboard and moved halfway down the aisle. The bus pulled out, and I saw land covered with grass and dark rock, basalt that had a sinister look compared to the pink limestone of Dreykish. Rasheed was silent, almost sullen. After a few minutes he walked forward and nudged the *jabi*, or assistant bus driver. The *jabi* glanced my direction, then smiled and said something to the driver who glanced at me in his mirror. Was the joke on me?

Our bus climbed the side of a valley. Pink-yellow limestone replaced the coastal basalt, and I saw patchy grass and olive trees. Rasheed rejoined me, but said nothing and, when our bus came to a halt, walked quickly to the door. I tried to follow but the *jabi* blocked me. "*Rouh*," he shouted, Go. The bus pulled out, and I took a seat by a window. My stomach was in knots, and I felt those familiar dry

Modern Roman	A B G D E F Z H	I K L M N	O P	Q R S T
Early Latin	A B C D E F Z H	Z K L M N	O Γ	Q R S T
Greek ↑	Α Β Γ Δ Ε Ζ Η	Θ Ι Κ Λ Μ Ν	Ο Π	Φ Ρ Σ Τ
Phoenician	(Phoenician glyphs)			
Early Aramaic	(Aramaic glyphs)			
Nabatian	(Nabatian glyphs)			
Arabic	(Arabic glyphs)			

At Ugarit, archaeologists found a rod of clay inscribed with the Phoenician alphabet.

heaves. Rasheed and the others had conspired to set an American loose in Qardaha.

Fifteen minutes later we passed a nine-story concrete building jutting above the olive trees, the local residence of President Asad. Next we passed houses of rough-cut limestone, others of concrete block and stucco, concrete roofs, steel utility poles streaked with rust. At the far end of town our bus circled a large, bronze statue of Hafez al-Asad, then worked its way back to its station on the main street. This was the end of the line, and the *jabi* and driver motioned for me to leave.

On the sidewalk, clutching my expedition pack, I looked back and forth, trying to pick out the plainclothes police. They usually approached from behind, surprised me, then made that awful hacking motion. I forced myself to concentrate. Now that we had arrived in Qardaha, the driver and *jabi* were counting on me to make their scheme a success. I was supposed to exhibit innocent folly, to walk with a smile into the arms of the *mukhabarat*. I looked across the street where a sidewalk shop sold *mushabak*, fried dough, and saw a young man squirting the dough into a vat of boiling grease. Qardaha seemed an ordinary town. Perhaps I had been wrong. On the other hand, maybe I was just one more lump of dough in the grease.

I turned and walked back to the bus, instructed the *jabi* to replace my bag, then climbed aboard and tried to look invisible. The *jabi* was apologetic. "Rasheed a bad man," he said, "not good, not happy." Twenty minutes later, our bus pulled out, and I was safe.

When I reached the coastal highway, I caught a connecting bus north to Latakia, then (since the bus broke down) took a taxi to the resort town of Kassab on the Turkish border. For the next couple of days I ate crisp apples from the local orchards, pulled late grapes from the vines on the terrace of a hotel where I stayed, and relaxed in the autumn sun. Then I hiked down to the Mediterranean through pine woods that reminded me of the Pacific Northwest.

11 — Phoenicians

LATAKIA. SATURDAY, OCTOBER 31.

On my return to Latakia I passed the turn off to Ugarit, the ancient Phoenician commercial settlement located to the north of town. These days Ugarit consisted of five-foot-high stone walls with grass growing all around. This ancient city dated from the eighteenth century BC and featured a royal palace with ninety rooms arranged around eight interior courtyards. Here in 1929 archaeologists unearthed four libraries that included thousands of clay tablets covering a wide range of subjects—religion, scholarship, government administration. Twenty of the tablets contained poetry more ancient than the Iliad and Odyssey. One of the libraries belonged to Rapanou, a diplomat who possessed an inquiring mind. He saved tablets containing correspondence from his work, as well as tablets with lists of animals, records of weights and measures, and a list that compared words from Ugarit, Babylon, Sumeria, and Haran.

The most famous find at Ugarit, however, consisted of a small rod of clay about the size of a pinky finger. This rod was inscribed with cuneiform stylus marks defining a thirty-letter "phonetic" alphabet dating from the fourteenth century BC. Most historians consider this alphabet to be the oldest in the world and the basis for the Greek,

Roman, Hebrew, and Arabic alphabets used today. Cuneiform was derived at least in part from Egyptian hieroglyphics. The difference was that cuneiform built up characters using wedge-shaped stylus marks and used those characters to designate word sounds rather than complete objects or ideas. Hieroglyphics worked well for an elite caste of scribes who devoted their lives to mastering language and who, one would assume, jealously guarded their prerogatives as the keepers of language. The phonetic system was simpler than hieroglyphics and allowed merchants, landowners, and government administrators the benefits of language—the result was a flowering of commerce and culture all along the Fertile Crescent.

After arriving in Latakia, I took a hotel near President Assad's bronze statue in the center of town. I turned off the lights, lay on the bed, and listened to the sound of cars passing on the street below. The air was wet, and my body seemed weightless. I wondered what I was doing in this place, at this time, and then I smelled the sea and imagined Phoenicians from long ago on this coast. In ancient times, 1500 BC, the Phoenicians were thriving. They used written language and kept commercial records. They occupied solid port cities on the Mediterranean coast with docks, shipyards, and warehouses. Their

At Ugarit, a stone pot and my taxi driver.

158

seamen sailed trading vessels across the eastern Mediterranean.

It wasn't Phoenician skill as sailors that ensured their success. More than anything, the Phoenicians were strong because they had mastered the caravan route which brought goods from the East. Ships from Cathay docked in the Persian Gulf. Here, near present day Basra, caravans formed to carry goods overland, following the Fertile Crescent. The Syrian coast was the place where this trading route played out on the shores of the Mediterranean.

Stone fortification at Ugarit.

I imagined caravans unpacking their goods. I saw sailors boarding ships for Palestine, Cyprus, Egypt, and the Aegean Islands. I saw ships with sails moving across sea lanes, feeding and nurturing men, women, and children camped along the shores. Sailors brought common commercial goods to the markets of ordinary people and silk and spice to the palaces of their rulers.

12 — Ismailis

LATAKIA. SUNDAY, NOVEMBER 1.

On my way back to Damascus I would travel the watered plain on the eastern slope of the coastal mountains to see the city of Hama, the Ghab wetlands on the Orontes River, and Apamea, one of Alexander's stone cities. The prime attraction of the eastern slope was Masyaf, the ancient home of one of Islam's most intriguing sects.

In Masyaf and surrounding villages, Ismailis had made a place for themselves by pushing aside the Alawites—two secretive Shiite sects in conflict. Today the Ismailis are known as an especially intellectual faith that is represented by the Aga Khan prize in architecture and the Aga Khan IV himself who was born in Switzerland, attended college at Harvard, lives in Europe, travels in society circles, and continues his grandfather's interest in breeding and racing horses. Far more mysterious and sinister, however, were the origins of this branch of the Ismaili faith.

Many Muslims, especially Shiites, judged that the Sunni Umayyads of Damascus were too secular and concerned with the practical necessities of administering their empire. In 750 the Umayyads were overthrown by the Abbasids and their Shiite followers. As soon as they were in power, however, the Abbasids disavowed the Shiite claim that authority resided among the descendents of Muhammad and affirmed their Sunni faith, the better to control a predominantly Sunni empire. Needless to say, the Abbasid betrayal fueled Shiite resentment.

An important element of Shiite faith was the imamate. Imams, or spiritual successors to the Prophet Muhammad, brought his teaching and spiritual authority down through history. In 765, when the sixth imam Jafar ibn Muhammad died, the main group of Shiites (Twelvers) accepted Jafar's younger son as the seventh imam. A minority, however, accepted Jafar's eldest son Ismail as the seventh imam. This was the origin of the Ismailis.

In the ninth century Ismaili missionaries across the Islamic empire had preached rebellion against the Abbasid caliphate in Baghdad. After failing in several uprisings, the Ismailis organized a secure base in Yemen and then expanded to East Africa.

From East Africa the Ismailis marched north. And in 909 in Tunis they established the Fatimid dynasty (taking their name from the daughter of the Prophet), then proceeded to conquer north Africa and Egypt. In 969 they founded Cairo and made it their capital city. Now they were a power to rival the Abbasid caliph in Baghdad.

As the story goes, the Fatimid Ismailis exercised power over their dominion, but were slowly overcome by the necessities of administration. Realpolitik replaced idealism. And in the judgment of some of their followers, the religious thrust of their movement was lost.

After the death of the Fatimid caliph al-Mustansir in 1094, a disillusioned Ismaili named Hasan ibn al-Sabbah refused to recognize his successor and instead vowed his allegiance to Nizar, the dead caliph's elder brother. Before long Sabbah left Cairo and returned to his native Persia. There he formed his own sect around a delicate and finely wrought spiritual doctrine. In 1090 Sabbah captured the mountain fortress of Alamut in northern Persia and made it the first in what would be a series of strongholds and castles across Persia and Iraq. In the following century the sect spread to Syria where they came into conflict with both the Crusaders and the Islamic armies whom the Crusaders opposed.

Sabbah, the leading thinker of the Nizari Ismailis, wrestled with problems of faith and power. How to protect one's faith in a world devoted to conquering, holding, and administering territory? Sabbah designed an unusual strategy. His followers worked their way into the confidence of distant leaders, and then, sometimes years later, killed on orders. Sabbah used fear to defend his faith and his *fidais* (for followers or faithful ones) claimed two Abbasid caliphs in addition to numerous Abbasid military leaders and court advisers among their victims.

In Syria, Sabbah's followers were known as the Assassins, and their descendents live here, in towns like Masyaf, to the present day.

If the Assassins were stealthy killers, they also had a reputation for the bizarre use of hallucinogens. For that matter, the term "assassin" was an Anglicized version of the Arabic *hashshashin* for "grass eaters," as the Syrian branch of the sect was called. A slightly different form of the word designated

Logo of Aga Khan University.

cannabis sativa, or hash, which was used in the Middle Ages both in Europe and in Muslim lands. Crusader accounts and the stories of Marco Polo (never confirmed from Ismaili sources) depicted the Assassins employing hash and other drugs to induce loyalty in their *fidais,* or trained killers. The term "assassin" has since been loosely applied to the sect as a whole. I wanted to visit the old Assassin headquarters in Masyaf and meet modern day Ismailis who still lived here.

13 — A Stranger in a Strange Land

I woke early to gusting wind and crashing rain, and taxi shouters on the sidewalk below. I felt awful. Three weeks of new people, new language, new culture were enough. Now, what? I felt a long way from home. In Seattle my wife had listened to my babbling for hours on end. Such comfort! In Syria I had no one to listen. I had spent an evening with Fatima and Jade and felt as though I belonged and then, a day later, they were gone, never to be seen again. I did not belong. I went back to sleep, and when I awoke I was still in Syria and still alone.

A little before eleven I walked out front. Rain was warm and heavy and filled the streets with water. I walked half a block to a plaza, modern and bleak, a marble island in the middle of the boulevard that supported an immense bronze statue of Syrian President Hafez al-Asad. I had hoped to meet Fatima at eleven. I hoped that she would introduce me to Latakians who were like her friend Jade, who were articulate and could bring this place alive for me.

At the time appointed for our meeting the plaza was deserted, while sidewalks and shop fronts on either side of the street were crowded with people, even in this torrent.

"Fatima didn't show," I thought.

I passed hundreds of people every day and did not recognize a single face. I was an outsider, a stranger. In this land of families I was unattached. I ate hot hummus with olive oil in a sidewalk shop and, a little past noon, caught a bus heading east.

PART FOUR

الحشّاشين

Assassins
Two Days' Travel to Masyaf

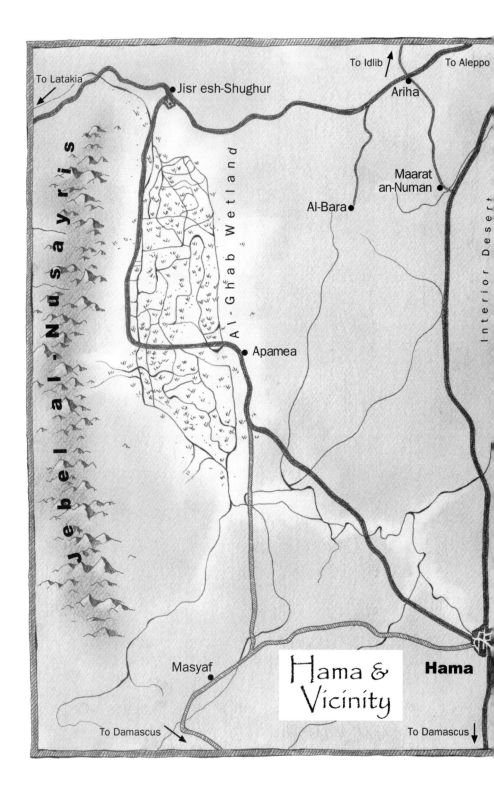

1 — A Long Day's Journey

ON THE ROAD. SUNDAY, NOVEMBER 1.

Our bus was crowded and smelled of wet clothing. I was wearing my precious Goretex cagoule, a necessity in this weather. Cigarettes smoldered on all sides, waiting for me to shift my attention elsewhere so that they could melt holes in the green nylon.

We headed into the mountains, climbing into fog and rain, switch-backing on the hillside, careening around corners. On the shoulder of the mountain the bus stopped at a small village, then pulled out and worked higher and higher on the narrow road until it surmounted the crest and began to descend. The land was severe and beautiful in the gray light, and rain came down like fine needles. Somewhere in the mist we crossed the Orontes on a stone bridge, a *jisr*, which had spanned this river since the time of Alexander and had been rebuilt by Romans and Mamluks, among others. Somewhere on the soggy plain to our south stood Apamea (a-fam-ea), an ancient treasure city and military headquarters where Alexander and his generals kept 30,000 horses and 500 elephants. (The city took its name from the Persian princess who was married to Alexander's general, Seleucus Nicator.) The rain grew stronger as we entered the town named for the ancient bridge: Jisr esh-Shughur, bridge of the border forts. We drove down a narrow street past old store fronts with dirty steel screens.

It would be dark soon, and I had planned to stay the night in this town. I got out of the bus and collected my bag. The other passengers were in a panic, dragging their bags from the underbelly of our vehicle and running down the street to a connecting bus, the last ride out of town on this day, a bus headed—where? I had no idea. A forty-year-old man in a cream-colored turtleneck sweater screamed at me in Arabic, then ran down the street. Something was wrong. I ran after him, and when I caught up made him stop to explain. He demanded that I follow to the hotel where we would share a room. The connecting

Instead of a health warning, cigarettes advertised the 1987 Mediterranean Games.

bus was nearly full by now, the last passengers pushing their way aboard. I had to think fast. Was it possible to stay in the town's only hotel and not find myself in a room with this man? Was he a deviant? A member of the secret police? Or was the hotel simply overpriced?

I abandoned my plans to stay in Jisr and ran for the bus where I was shoved to the rear, crushed against an old man wearing a *kaffiah*. I lost my balance, but we were wedged so tightly that I could not fall. The air was heavy with cigarette smoke and the smell of sweat and wet wool and cotton. We pulled out, and after several stops the crowd thinned so that I had room to crouch beside my bag and look out the window. The land was bare and rocky, and I saw terraces with fruit trees.

"*Wane?*" I asked, Where?

"Idlib," a passenger explained.

I wondered where that was. Then I remembered. It was a town to the north and east famous for apricot, cherry, and olive trees. I had wanted to go south, but the main north-south highway was not far from Idlib. I would spend the night in Idlib, then make sense of things in the morning.

In an hour we arrived in the town of Ariha where I was surprised to learn that I needed to catch a connecting bus to Idlib. It would be three hours before the bus arrived, and darkness would fall in less than an hour. I couldn't find a hotel or waiting room or cafe. I had no place to go, and two dozen school children were crowding around, asking questions, laughing, making it impossible to think. I fended them off the best I could, but soon I was exhausted.

A bus would leave shortly to al-Bara, a village to the southwest which was known for its Greek ruins. But there was no hotel in al-Bara and no connecting bus. I glanced at my map and saw a cutoff going southeast to Maarat an-Numan, an old city that was now on the recently constructed main highway. I remembered that my guidebook had listed a class-A hotel and Roman ruins of exceptional interest.

I decided to go to Maarat an-Numan, but learned that there would not be a bus until midnight. I asked a taxi driver what his charge would be. *"Khamsein,"* he replied in Arabic, Fifty lira. This was a couple of dollars, an unusually low price for the long ride, a very good deal. But I did not understand. I thought he was telling me that the ride would cost five hundred lira, over twenty dollars, an outrage. The reason for my confusion? I had been expecting some-

I survived long bus rides by munching chocolate-covered coconut bars.

thing on the order of three hundred lira, the price I had paid for the taxi that took me from Latakia to Kassab a few days earlier. Also, I was not entirely clear that the Arabic *khamsein* meant fifty whereas *khamsmea* meant five hundred. And one more thing. I did not understand the difference between a shared taxi like this one, which followed a rough schedule and where the fare was split among the riders, and a private taxi like the one in Latakia where the driver charged each passenger the full fare for the trip. The vehicles, after all, were the same yellow color. Also, I hadn't practiced my higher numbers. Food in the market place was ten or thirteen lira. Even roasted chicken or a banana, the most expensive things, were only twenty-five lira. I never dealt with denominations as large as five hundred, except in a bank where the clerks spoke English.

A bus official confirmed that *khamsein* was the standard fare. "I'm doomed," I thought. The spirit of Saleh the Shiite stirred within me. My situation was desperate, yet I could not allow myself to be robbed.

I was stuck in this town, through my own ignorance, and I couldn't think with all these kids jabbering at me. In an effort to shake the school kids, I walked into the bus repair shop. Only two followed me. Inside, a bus employee motioned me over. He was about thirty years old, heavy set, his face pocked with acne. He took off his cheap nylon jacket and ordered me to remove my Goretex cagoule. I couldn't believe it. This fat guy wanted to trade. His jacket had cost about three dollars, my cagoule was worth a hundred and twenty dollars. And how was I to survive the rain without my cagoule?

"La," I said, No. The man held his jacket in the air, explained its virtues, and again ordered me to take my coat off and make the trade. No. By now the other school kids had caught up and were crowding around, not giving me much room. The fat man boasted to

the children that he would convince me to trade. Then he made a grand gesture with his right hand, pulling his red and white headdress off and unfurling it before our eyes. Three dozen school children watched without a sound. Since he was a generous man, he would throw in his headdress. I noticed that its design was printed, not woven, which meant that it was worth five dollars at most. I refused. He offered in addition to take me home, tuck me into bed, kiss me good night, and give me a blow job. He pantomimed his final offer, and the school children laughed. He smiled for a few seconds, but as the laughter continued his look turned sour. He had failed to convince the American and now the rabble of his village were laughing—at him. He lowered his arms, his face flushed with embarrassment. I had an idea that I was in trouble.

I tried to force my way out of the crowd but the children resisted and tugged at me. I glanced back at my antagonist. He stepped toward me, and I pushed again, broke free, and reached the plaza once more. Would the fat guy follow? In a few minutes the school kids caught up and swarmed around me. I had no place to hide, the school kids jammed themselves against me, and now I was worried. By wounding the guy's pride I had broken the cardinal rule of travel in a police state: never make enemies. His uncle was probably a member of the *mukhabarat*. What if he framed me in a drug bust? That was easy to do. And the secret police in this burg, starved for promotion, would be happy to assist. I looked back into the garage, but the bus employee had gone into the next room. Was he using the phone? I clutched at my passport. It was still with me—at least until the police arrived. I stared, across the plaza, at the taxi.

2 — The Blind Poet

The taxi drove south and east for an hour through small, bare hills, red dirt, dark limestone, and occasional bunches of grass. The driver was polite, but silent. I sat in the front, and three other passengers climbed into the back.

I looked forward to exploring Maarat an-Numan and tried to remember what Hasan the architect had told me about the town and about Abu al-Ala al-Maarri, the blind poet who was born here at the turn of the millennium. "When we walk, we must step softly," al-Maarri had written, "for the earth is the body of our ancestors."

The sky was still gray, the rain had stopped, and, by the time we arrived, it was nearly dark. In the town I saw ancient walls and a few new buildings. No one was around. We drove through the commercial district to the freeway where we let out the other passengers. I was glad that I did not have to spend the night waiting for a ride on the side of the road. We drove back into town and stopped to ask directions of a man selling persimmons from a cart.

The vendor told us that there was no hotel in town. My guidebook, I insisted, could not be wrong. I rummaged in my pack. "The Abu al-Ala," I read out loud, "a class-A hotel."

"*Aewa,*" replied the vendor, Yes. He pointed to a building across the street that was vacant and coated with soot, its windows and doors boarded.

"*Leesh?*" I asked.

"Monsieur," the vendor said, then pantomimed a hypodermic injection and placed his hands beside his face in a gesture of sleep. The hotel was gone, the hotel keeper dead. For that matter, the whole town was dead, a cold monument to a blind poet. "Does it matter if one laughs or cries?" al-Maarri had written. "The scream of a woman giving birth is like the sob of a woman mourning her dead."

It was dark and I had nowhere to go. In the time of the poet there had been dozens of stopping places among the villages. But since then technology had improved our lives. The new arterial had brought hundreds of visitors to the convent of Saydnaya and turned the Monastery of Saint George into a backwater. Likewise it had boosted Homs and Hama and turned the commercial district of Maarat an-Numan into a ghost town. We returned to the highway.

The passengers we had let out earlier were gone, they had caught rides. Yet my prospects were not so good for by now it was completely dark, and I doubted that a bus would see me, much less stop. I got my pack out of the trunk, then handed the driver a five hundred lira bill. He complained. I did not like the idea that the fare had gone up since our earlier negotiation, so I argued a little, then held out my wallet, placing myself utterly at his mercy. He replaced the five hundred lira bill and took in its place a fifty lira note. Thank God for an honest man. So that is how I learned the difference between *khamsein* and *khamsmea*, fifty and five hundred.

The taxi driver spoke to a soldier who was standing by the side of the road and told him to look after me. Then he left, and the soldier and I were alone in the night. He was trying to get to Damascus, and I was heading south to Hama, a city not far from Masyaf and the Assassin's castle.

In fifteen minutes an enormous Mitsubishi truck pulled over, and the driver got out to wash his headlights. The soldier inquired, but the driver was going only as far as Hama. In that case, the soldier asked, could he give me a lift? The driver accepted, and, shoving my sack before me, I climbed into the cab. The driver was about thirty years old, muscular, with sandy hair and a red and white *kaffiah* around his shoulders. In a few minutes we pulled out.

If the town was dead, the highway was surging and throbbing with life. Heavy trucks jammed our lane and on a curve I could see that they extended in a line a mile long. Buses passed us going the other way, and passenger cars, and more trucks. The principal commerce of Syria, and also commerce between Europe and Africa, flowed along this highway. These two lanes were the scene of Syria's participation in the world economy.

My driver was in a hurry. We pulled out to pass one truck, then another. As we hurtled down the road, he reached out the window with his left arm to slosh water on the windshield from a green plastic bottle. Traffic safety? We passed on a curve even though we could not see what was coming, then we passed on a hill, and later we passed on a curve on a hill. I clutched the seat. There was no seat belt.

My driver sloshed more water on the windshield and switched on the wipers again. We were jammed behind three trucks that were going up a slight grade. We pulled out to pass and a Mercedes taxi followed us into the wrong lane. My view was no longer blocked by the trucks in front, and at the top of the rise I could see lights coming the other direction, a car I thought, heading straight for us. I wanted my driver to pull back in line, but he was abreast of the middle truck now, and the front truck speeded up with the downhill grade. My driver saw what was coming toward us and blinked his lights. Now we were closer, and the oncoming traffic was driving down a slight hill. I could see three distinct sets of lights: three vehicles, two of them big. They were bearing down on us. The trucks to our right were keeping pace, and the front truck had pulled ahead so that a small hole had opened behind, but it was too far in front of us and too small. I looked to the shoulder on the left and there was the Mercedes taxi. Yikes! It was passing us on the shoulder while we were passing the trucks. My driver saw it and shouted an insult and waved his fist and gave it more gas, and at the same time the Mercedes accelerated and pulled a little in front, and still my driver coaxed some more out of his rig. The oncoming traffic was a few seconds away now, and the Mercedes surged and swerved across our lane into the hole between the middle truck and the one in front—but for us it was too late: the Mercedes blocked our only possible escape, there were three vehicles on our right, and the three oncoming vehicles were upon us now, just a few seconds out, but my driver seemed calm. I thought of President Sadat of Egypt, standing tall, reviewing his troops, when members of the Muslim Brotherhood who were part of his army lifted their weapons. He refused to take cover, refused to duck, but opened his arms to death.

3 — Assassins

In three flashes a car and truck and bus were past us, and we were still alive and still in the wrong lane. The Mercedes taxi pulled out again and was pushing to get past the last truck and into the clear, and I could see more lights in the distance, coming toward us. How had we escaped? The shoulder—the oncoming traffic had swerved onto the shoulder.

Later that evening my driver and I reached Hama, a town famous for its Roman water wheels. The bathtub in my hotel room was covered with crud, some of which may have constituted living organisms, but the water was hot so I showered, at least until the shower head broke off in my hand and the hot water ran out.

The next morning I rose early, traveled in a taxi past buildings scarred by artillery shells—Hama's old town had been destroyed by federal troops in the fracas with the Muslim Brotherhood in 1982—and caught a bus to Masyaf and the castle of the Assassins. The highway passed empty fields where wheat had been cut and ragged stubs jutted out of the ground. This was the Ghab, fertile land at the headwaters of the Orontes reclaimed from marsh by the Baath regime. Before long we climbed to a town on the dry, eastern flank of the coastal mountains, and I saw a castle on a limestone cliff overlooking the valley. The sun was out, and cold wind blew through the streets of the village. From the bus stop I climbed a cobbled path to a great, heavy wooden door at the castle entrance. The door was locked, so I walked slowly along the castle wall while I waited for the gatekeeper to arrive.

The Crusaders told a story about this fortress. In 1198, Count Henry of Champagne was returning from Armenia when he stopped in Masyaf, climbed the stairs of the castle, and was given a tour of the battlements by an Assassin leader who was called Sheik al-Jebel, the Old Man of the Mountain. As the story goes, Count Henry and the Sheik began to talk shop. "You've wondered at our success in battle," Count Henry said. "I'll tell you. The secret is the obedience of our knights."

At this point the Sheik caught the attention of two of his *fidais* who were making repairs high on the castle wall. "Jump," the Sheik shouted. As the men plunged to their deaths, the Assassin turned to the Count. "I agree with you," he said. "Obedience is very important."

According to Marco Polo, such obedience was carefully cultivated by the Assassins over many years' time. Polo traveled through northern Persia on his return journey from Mongolia in 1273 and reported on Alamut, the headquarters of the sect established by Hasan ibn al-Sabbah. The leaders of Alamut conscripted naïve peasant youths whom they tutored in languages, arts, and sciences, Polo reported. Then they drugged the youths and carried them into the inner sanctum of the hideaway, a beautiful garden. Here the young men awoke, surrounded by beautiful women, and were offered every conceivable pleasure. Then they were drugged again, taken from the garden, and upon awakening told that they had experienced heaven and would only return upon death. If they died on carrying out the orders of their leader, they were told, they would reach paradise that much sooner.

One modern scholar calls these tales improbable, yet they circulated in medieval Europe and earned the Assassins a reputation for loyalty that was only later surpassed by their reputation for cunning.

I took shelter from the wind on the south side of the castle. The sun was warm here, and I saw a snug cave, the front built up with mortared stone. An old man walked out wearing black Turkish pants with an extra fold of cloth that drooped down between his legs. No one knows the origin of this style—the extra cloth between the legs has no practical purpose—and scholars have speculated that it prepared for the reappearance of the Islamic al-Mahdi who was supposed to be born from a man. In a few minutes the old man's wife came out of the cave as well. She left the wooden door open but closed an improvised storm door of plastic sheeting tacked to a wooden frame that allowed the sun to enter. "Their stone nest will be warm this evening," I thought.

I saw a local teenager wearing an army jacket and sandals who used a slingshot to chunk rocks at small birds. He grew bored with his sport and began to climb the castle wall, winding to the right. It was never good to disobey the rules in a police state, but by now I was tired of waiting for the gatekeeper and followed the teenager's lead—except that I chose a more direct line, a small buttress at the base of the smooth, south face of the castle. At the top of the buttress I worked my way out onto the face. It was steep, and the holds were rounded and covered with dust. Some of the blocks lifted out when I tested them, others were held in place by moss and grass. From below, this route had not looked so exposed. At the top of the wall I reached a chest-high ledge, sloping and covered with dust. A mantel move (a pull-up followed by a push-up) was required. Still, I hesitated. Mantling requires a fine sense of balance, and I was out of practice—a slip and I would land at the entrance to the cave below. I thought how embarrassed I would be, but then realized that, falling from this height, I could count on death to save me from shame. How different the vanities of the Assassins had been. The *fidais* had jumped from these walls and landed with honor intact. I supposed that being an Assassin was not easy, but at this moment it seemed more difficult to be a recycled rock climber on holiday. I took a breath, made the mantel,

Castle of the Assassins, south tower.

and, as I explored the castle, wondered how I would reverse the move.

The castle was built of stone vaults—unbelievably strong—supporting tons of earth covered with grass. Stone ridges and walls protruded here and there. I looked out at the valley as the wind drove clouds across the sun. In medieval times, great powers commanded vast armies. What could a small sect do to protect its religious life?

Sabbah positioned the leadership of his sect in remote mountain fortresses and kept the caliph and his generals at bay with slender, pointed blades of gold. Sabbah's followers worked their way into the confidence of great men over many years' time. Then, on orders, they murdered their victims in their courts and bed chambers, baths and mosques. The defenders of Muslim orthodoxy regarded the followers of Sabbah as bloody terrorists, yet the sect nevertheless had scruples. They did not use poisoned daggers, presumably because they wanted to give their victims a fighting chance. And it was a point of honor that the *fidais* die along with their victims.

The Assassins were expert at disguise and had an uncanny ability to lull victims and their bodyguards—even when they were on alert. In 1113, for example, Mawdud, the Turkish emir of Mosul, came to Damascus with a small army under the pretext of helping the locals defend against the Crusaders. The Damascenes didn't need this kind of help, but Mawdud had a knife at their throats, so they gave him a courteous reception. Was it possible, however, that they also whispered to the Assassins out the back door? In any case, a few days later Mawdud walked into the Umayyad Mosque. He knew that everyone loved him—that's why he had a gang of men with swords and daggers that surrounded him wherever he went. These bodyguards were poised, their blades drawn, but as they walked through the mosque a humble, pliant-looking man shuffled out from the crowd and cowered a little, as though he were a beggar who wanted the great man to bless him. When Mawdud got close, however, the beggar grabbed Mawdud's belt, pulled him forward, and stabbed him twice in the stomach.

The Assassins were just as happy to intimidate enemy leaders as to actually kill them. After the *fidais* came close to taking his life, for example, the Islamic general Saladin began to sleep in a wooden tower which his aides carted around from battle to battle. Later Saladin concluded that the Assassins were more trouble than they were worth. He called a truce, postponing indefinitely his plans to eradicate them.

Over a century and a half the Ismaili band at Sabbah's Persian headquarters had turned aside all forces sent to conquer them. At last they learned of the approaching Mongol armies and appealed to the Kings of Europe to make common cause. Saint Louis is said to have replied, "Let the dogs eat dogs."

The techniques devised by Hasan ibn al-Sabbah had made the leaders of his sect players in the world game of power. They defined a strategy for those who are small in number yet strong in belief. But no one is saying whether Sabbah succeeded in his larger goal. Had he made the world safe for ordinary Ismailis? Or had the power of the caliphate corrupted Sabbah and his followers as certainly as it had the caliphs themselves? By 1273, the Assassins were history. Yet in villages below the fortresses, ordinary Ismaili men and women lived on.

To descend the castle, I followed the lead of the teenager, an intricate but comparatively easy route that did not force me to reverse the dusty mantel move I had made on the ascent. From the base of the castle I walked into the center of Masyaf and stopped at a butcher shop where half a sheep hung in the window and liver kebabs cooked on the grill outside. I ordered five lamb kebabs and one onion kebab for twenty-three lira, less than a dollar. Soon my meal was cooking on the charcoal grill, a trough about four feet long that had been welded from sheetmetal and old auto parts and stood waist-high on the

Castle of the Assassins, front gate.

narrow sidewalk. While the assistant butcher watched my kebabs, I gazed at his boss who was making sausage, feeding lamb into a grinder along with tomatoes and spices. Light rain splashed against the windows, driven by blustery wind. When my meal was ready I sat inside at a small table across from an elderly gentleman wearing a full length shift and a red and white checked *kaffiah*. He seemed to be enjoying his lamb kebab. The assistant butcher placed a large circle of flatbread on the table in front of me, then lay the spits with their sizzling kebabs on top of the bread, folded the bread over, and extracted the steel spits. I opened the bread and began eating the meat and onions. The lamb was sweet, but the onion was scarcely cooked and crunched between my teeth.

The elderly man finished his meal, removed his teeth, cleaned them against his shift, and then reinserted them. Nothing left to do, he watched with disapproval as I munched on meat and onion, using the bread only as a utensil. "You must roll the bread around the meat and onions," he explained, slowly, with gestures, in Arabic. "You eat together, a sandwich."

"Are you trying to make me fat?" I replied. He laughed. The bread was heavy with flour and would have filled me two times over.

"Look at me," he said. "I am seventy-three years old and still thin."

As we talked, I watched two young boys, one blond, the other with dark hair, school children with gray cases strapped to their backs who stood outside, downwind from the charcoal grill. They warmed their hands in the heat until the butcher, who apparently was their father, motioned them inside, gave them a couple of large bills, and sent them off to the bank to get change.

4 — The Wisest Man in Masyaf

After eating, I walked the village for forty-five minutes and thought of reasons to catch an early bus back to Damascus. I had come to the ancient Ismaili stronghold, climbed the castle, eaten in the butcher shop. "I have done Ismailis," I thought. "That makes Christians, Alawites, Ismailis. Mission accomplished."

I knew that my effort toward Ismailis had been half-hearted. This was one of the most sophisticated and interesting of Syria's religious minorities, but I was tired, I'd been on the road for days, and I just needed to get back. So it was decided, I'd head home early. By now I had learned that the best way to catch a bus was to find the bus depot (which Syrians referred to as the "garage"). That way you could ask questions of men in authority who knew the answers, then ask again of women standing in line. You could get the right bus and could climb aboard and wait in comfort until the bus pulled out—far better than waiting on a street corner for a bus that might be the wrong one or might never come.

I asked a man on the corner for the "garage," but he insisted that there was no garage and that I could only get to Damascus by riding with him in his taxi. I finally shook this guy, kept walking, and eventually found two garages, the old one, no longer used, and the new one, with concrete roof and arches still under construction. It was raining heavily by now, and I was standing at the edge of a shop for shelter when a tall, thin young man of perhaps twenty-four began talking to me in English.

Aref was a local who rode the bus to Homs every day where he studied English literature at the university. I asked him about Ismaili religion, and—as though he did not hear me—he responded with ideas about Christianity and Islam. Very strange behavior. "Wait," I thought. "Alawites did the same thing."

Below the Crak des Chevaliers, Jabir the Alawite had ignored my questions about his faith. For that matter, Fatima in Dreykish had pretended not to hear. So had an Alawite youth I met in Kassab. At the end of my travel I would find the same to be true of Druze families I visited in the Haran area south of Damascus. I was witnessing the doctrine of *taqiya*, or secrecy. Finally it struck me.

"This modern caution," I thought, "has been passed down from earlier centuries. The caliph from Baghdad and the sultan from Istanbul used to be pretty rough on Alawites, Ismailis, and Druze." What continued to puzzle me were the Christians. The sultan had persecuted Christians, but modern Christians did not shrink from speaking about their faith. For that matter, the priests at Marjurjos said a little too much. I guessed that Christians wanted to bear witness to their faith. They had a tradition that honored martyrdom. Also, Christians were not an Islamic minority. Perhaps the caliph and sultan and been far more severe in their persecution of Alawites, Ismailis, and Druze.

Aref seemed pleased to have discovered an American in his hometown. "Come have tea at my aunt's," he said. His aunt lived directly across the street and we had time before the bus, so I walked across with him, he banged on the door, and a steel screen opened above. A woman leaned out, and Aref talked back and forth for a few moments. "A problem," he said. By now I was walking back to the garage. The Damascus bus would pull out before long, and the next bus wouldn't leave until four thirty. "We could have tea at my friend's," Aref said.

"*Yala*," I replied, gotta go. The Damascus bus was revved up. I climbed aboard and walked past empty seats to take a place in the back. The bus doors closed and the bus pulled forward. "We're on our way," I thought.

Then the bus stopped for some reason, and the driver cut off the engines. We did not have a full complement of passengers and were not on our way but I was in travel mode now and felt as though I was miles from this place. Already I was filled with regret. I had traveled quickly since leaving Dreykish five days earlier. I had seen things but hadn't talked at any length to the people I met. "I am skating across the surface of this country," I thought, "I'll never get inside." I glanced through the window. Aref was nowhere to be seen. I could hardly search the village for him. And besides, it was too late. In a second or two we'd pull out and I'd leave this town forever.

I was very discouraged now, mourning the loss of experience. "Eventually I'll get back to America," I thought, "and my life will go on. But I'll never hear the words that this student might have spoken. I'll never see the faces of the people to whom he would have introduced me."

A moment later someone in the aisle nudged me and I looked up to see Aref. "Come have tea with my friend Muhammad," he said. "It is OK."

Aref's friend Muhammad had graduated from Aleppo University but could find no work and for two years had helped his family operate a small grocery on the north side of Masyaf. He rattled off a Masyaf variation on a speech I'd heard from educated Christians in Tartus and would later come to regard as the Educated Young Syrian Unemployment Speech.

"In this country a man can't afford to get married. He can't get a house, even rent one room. If he can pay for a house, a room, he can't pay for a family, for food. I work in this grocery in the morning and in a falafel sandwich shop in the afternoon. Not much, but at least I'm working. In the last fifteen years, the poor get poorer and the rich get richer. They earn plenty of money and put it in Swiss banks. If they have a problem, they go abroad. At two o'clock every afternoon I listen to the BBC in Arabic. I hear that in Denmark they are throwing meat and butter into the sea—here we have no meat, no butter. In Brazil they throw coffee into the sea—here we have no coffee. Thank God that at least I'm working. I have a son, a daughter, and my mother lives with me."

When Muhammad's spiel wore down, Aref told me about the rigors of his English course at Homs. He was preparing to take an oral exam and to defend his Master's thesis. One of his teachers was an American woman who had lived and taught in Homs for six years. When Aref paused, I explained how helpful the Shia had been in expounding their faith.

"At Sayida Zeinab," I said, "the young believers found important sheiks for me who sat patiently and explained their faith. But here, I can find no one to tell me about Ismaili religion." After I spoke, Aref muttered to Muhammad in Arabic. The Shia comparison had turned the trick. No Ismaili really wanted to talk about his faith. On the other hand, no Ismaili wanted to leave an American thinking that the Shiites had a superior religious doctrine.

"There are many Ismailis in Masyaf," Aref said, avoiding the question of his personal faith. "I know one man especially who could speak to you. Abu Taleb, a very wise man." We left Muhammad and walked into the center of town. Some streets had been cobbled by the French during their occupation. Others were covered with asphalt.

Aref and I approached a windowless, one-story concrete building where a Mercedes flatbed truck was parked. Workmen were loading sacks of flour onto the truck and beside them was an old man wearing an insulated Army jacket. Abu Taleb had horn-rimmed glasses, a day's growth of white whiskers, and, when he spoke, I could see that his teeth were mostly gone. He spent his days here, in the single room that doubled as his warehouse, serving as manager of a wholesale flour company. After work, however, he became a man of letters. He read books, wrote treatises, and engaged in rarefied dialogues with other neighborhood philosophers. According to Aref, Abu Taleb was a learned man indeed: he had read more than four thousand books and had memorized the Bible and the Quran verbatim.

"The American," Aref said, nodding in my direction. "He has come to us to know the secrets of Ismaili religion." Abu Taleb smiled, and I could tell that he was a kind man, not a wealthy guru with expensive gowns and wreathes of flowers around his neck, but more of a working-class guru—a wise man who nevertheless stood in the cold all day to earn a living. He paused for a moment, which gave me an opening.

"What is the reason that some men are willing to sacrifice themselves in order to kill others?" I asked. "Do they see God more clearly? Or are they only seeing themselves, their own minds, their own egos? And what of the leaders who order such killing?"

"This is big," said Abu Taleb. "This may take two hours, two days, two years to say. And now I must work. I have no time." As he spoke, Abu Taleb edged out into the cobbled street to get away from the noise of the workmen. He gestured to the truck and to the sacks of flour stacked in the room behind.

"The Christians say they need bread only for one day," said Abu Taleb. "That's their daily bread. But we need a truckload." He smiled at his joke. Now that we had reached the other side of the narrow street, he stood still. Two teenage boys walking past saw him and came close to listen.

"Are you from here?" I asked. "And when were you born?"

"I was born in 1926," Abu Taleb replied. "And I am from here all of my life. I have traveled. In 1942 I went to Palestine and Egypt."

"Why did you leave home?"

"I was hungry," Abu Taleb replied. "All of us in Syria were hungry in those years. I joined the British army, fought Rommel, marched to Libya, then fought in Sicily and Normandy, and joined Montgomery for the march to Berlin."

"And what about your faith?"

"The Ismailis," Abu Taleb said. "Socrates was an Ismaili, and Hypocrites, Democritus, Plato. Ismaili religion includes all science, all chemistry, mathematics, engineering, astronomy, physics. All knowledge is Ismaili religion." He kept speaking in English, helped out by one or two words from Aref. By now several young men had joined our circle. They were quiet, yet their respect was apparent. I wondered if there was a town in the United States where teenagers greeted the words of an old man with wonder, respect, reverence.

"What about Muslim fundamentalism, Shiites like Khomeini?"

"The Shiites have too much feeling," he said. "We believe in knowing God, in understanding God with our minds. The mind leads us to God, the body follows." While I pondered this one, he continued.

"We believe that God can be expressed in numbers."

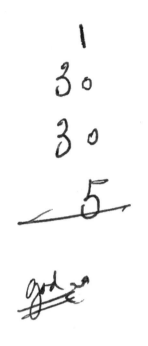

Abu Taleb wrote the numbers— I added the English explanation.

In high school I had read about the Neoplatonists, men who believed that numbers contained mystical knowledge. But it never occurred to me that people who lived near the ancient Greek centers of learning in Alexandria and Antioch might still be working on such theories, long since discarded by mainstream Western thinkers. I handed Abu Taleb one of the pink 3 x 5 cards which I carried for making notes. He wrote in a column the numbers 1, 30, 30, and 5, then drew a line and added them up: 66.

"The total," he said, "is God."

Abu Taleb was impressive, but I had the feeling that I was missing something. Was his math trick a joke for a gullible tourist? He seemed utterly serious. But what could these numbers mean? I would need more time, but now I had a bus to catch. As I turned to leave, the wise man offered to talk again. At the bus garage, Aref agreed to make the arrangements.

~~~~~~~~

"Abu Taleb's notation is clear," said Carool Kersten, a Dutch Arabist, scholar, and man of the world who emailed me years later from Thailand. "You need to consider the Islamic science of number symbolism—the rough equivalent of the Jewish Cabbala. Take a look at the monumental work on Sufism by Annemarie Schimmel, *Mystical Dimensions of Islam.* Individual alphabetic characters had number equivalents. Aside from their religious use, these numerical values had a very plain and practical application. Prior to using what we call "Arabic numerals," the Arabs used their alphabet letters for counting just like the Romans did with their alphabet (i, v, x, l, d, m). What we call Arabic numerals are in fact Indian symbols adopted by the Arabs once they realized how much easier mathematics become through application of the decimal system.

"Abu Taleb was explaining the numeric value of the letters that make up the word 'Allah'—and he was using the same values that Schimmel records in her book.

"In Arabic we do not write short vowels (in this case the second "a"), so the word 'Allah' has four letters: alif, lam, lam, and ha. The numerical value of alif is one, of lam is 30, and of ha is five. The total, indeed, is sixty-six."

5 – The Second Wisest Man in Masyaf

MASYAF. FRIDAY, NOVEMBER 6.

It was pitch dark and raining on the night I arrived for my second meeting with Abu Taleb. Aref did not meet me at the bus—and local teenage boys whom I asked said that Aref had left early to return to the university at Homs. The boys guided me to the house of Abu Taleb, but his housekeeper explained that he had gone to Tartus to attend a concert. I was hungry, and this town had no restaurant, so the boys took me to a grocery where I sat on a box in a corner and ate a canned meat sandwich which had been cooked by being mashed in what looked like a waffle iron—the closest thing to hot food in this place. I was discouraged, and the teenage boys who had been guiding me felt that they had let me down. Then one of them got an idea. I followed into the gloom and rain and a few minutes later was sitting on tubular chrome furniture in the brightly lit living room of Mustafa, the second wisest man in Masyaf.

Mustafa was light-complexioned, perhaps thirty-three, and dressed in a white shirt and slacks. If Abu Taleb had been traditional, Mustafa was avant-garde. He offered me matte, a drink from Brazil, a dish of green sugar to sweeten my drink, and a metal straw. The drink had a heavy taste, and after a quick sip I learned that the metal straw was too hot to touch with my lips. Mustafa had studied English at the university in Aleppo. I told him that I had missed Abu Taleb.

"A scholar and a very wise man," Mustafa said. "He is old now, but he stops always to talk with the people. The young people, the temporal life is heavy on them. They ask Abu Taleb for a way to go, for answers to their problems."

"What problems?" I asked.

"The problem of being," Mustafa said. "They want to know what is this being. Do you think on this subject?"

"In college we used to say 'being is becoming.'"

"Yes. In this life man can try for absolute goals, but can never reach them because he does not have absolute powers. Still, he needs to try for absolute goals or he will accomplish nothing."

Apparently Ismaili children were philosophers from birth. "If their only problem is the problem of being," I thought, "they aren't doing too bad."

"What are you looking for?" Mustafa asked. "Why have you come

Sheep graze on the plains where Alexander, centuries before, kept his horses. Behind are the stone columns of Apamea.

here?" By now my straw had cooled. I sucked my drink and thought about the trained killers who had made their headquarters in this village centuries before. Had they sought the answer to the problem of being? Or were they merely sucked up by cruelty and killing?

"I am making a tour of Syria," I said, "talking to people, taking notes."

Mustafa listened carefully. "What you must do is to write a book," he said. "But not just any book. It must be a book of ideas, a philosophy that is detailed and above what we see and do every day. Such a book of ideas will lift the people out of their misery."

As Mustafa spoke, I stirred the residue of green sugar into the last of my drink, and my mind drifted. Had the *fidais* been weak, the dupes of their leaders? Or had they been men of conviction who died to protect innocent people from the powers that be? I looked at Mustafa.

"Tell me something more," I said.

"The enemy is never outside," Mustafa said. "No matter how big the enemy, how powerful, how violent or wicked. See it this way: if you are strong inside, what is outside will be weak."

The next morning I left my heavy pack in the hotel in Masyaf and took an early bus to Apamea, the abandoned Greek city where Alexander kept his horses. Then I rode back to Masyaf so that I could retrieve my gear and continue my travel.

6 — The Man with Ten Wives

ON THE ROAD TO MASYAF. SATURDAY, NOVEMBER 7.
"You are a beautiful man," the woman said. "Too many beautiful."

She was young, perhaps twenty-two, dark-haired with fair skin and perfect features. She was an Ismaili and sat a few feet from me on a rickety bus to Masyaf.

The other passengers suddenly became quiet, and I felt as though I had been pushed onto a stage. I blushed, and then the passengers began to sigh, cluck, and whisper, not all at once, but one row at a time as the translation of her remark worked its way back. I looked at the dark-haired woman and her equally attractive companion—her sister, I guessed. I stammered a reply but before I could capture the initiative she continued. "In America how many wives do you have?"

I confessed that I had only one wife, and she seemed disappointed. "In Syria," she continued, "a beautiful man like you has more wives. You must have more wives."

"That is how you have a large family, many children," her sister added. I heard the other passengers murmuring and, when I glanced in their direction, caught some sly smiles among the old men.

"One wife is plenty for me," I replied. "At least it has always seemed like enough. Is there really an advantage in having two wives?"

"No, no. Many more, five, six. A beautiful man like you should have ten wives, maybe more." She turned to the other passengers. "For this too beautiful man, how many wives?" She spoke to them in Arabic, translating for my benefit. "Ten wives?" she asked, as she surveyed the crowd.

"*Aewa, aewa,*" the other passengers replied. Her poll complete, the young woman turned to me.

"Ten wives," she concluded.

I tried to protest. Sometimes I secretly thought of myself as an admirable person, yet it had been decades since anyone besides my mother had come to that conclusion. Even so, ten wives seemed excessive. Five or six would be plenty.

I mumbled a few phrases but my Arabic was garbled, and she cut in. "You need nine more wives, only you do not know our ways, so how can you?" She turned and translated to the other passengers who seemed to follow her logic.

"My sister and I, we will assist you." By now the other passengers were on the edges of their seats. "You will come with us to our house this night. You will sleep in our house. We will make you very happy."

I sensed that we were play-acting, but otherwise had no idea what was going on. Village society in Syria was conservative—actual seduction was out of the question, and all of us knew it. I glanced at the other passengers. They had a glazed, soap opera look. In their fantasies I was being seduced—not by one woman but by two. And the seduction was entirely pure and wholesome and breath-taking because, they understood, it would never take place.

What, if anything, did these sisters want? I guessed that they wanted to bring a foreign visitor home to meet the family—that's the way it had been in Dreykish with the Alawites. So be it. They were inviting me to dinner, an invitation that I would have to decline because I was in a big hurry. And after my evening in Dreykish I already had a dinner scene for my book. "On the other hand," I found myself thinking, "sometimes the cause of international understanding requires a person to make sacrifices."

"*Aewa,*" I replied in Arabic, Yes. "So long as your mother approves." As I spoke, a rush of whispers filled the bus. I glanced to the rear and saw an old guy roll his eyes and sink in his seat. A woman to the side suppressed a grin and stared out the window, refusing to meet my gaze, then glanced quickly my direction as I turned my head away. I realized later that my affirmative reply in Arabic had been understood by all. My conditions, however, had been in English and never quite got through.

Before long our bus climbed a grade, entered the narrow streets of Masyaf, and came to a stop in the market. I stood to let the sisters pass, and, by the time I had stepped onto the cobbled street, they had linked arms. The sisters set off at a brisk pace, giggling, made a quick turn, then dodged in unison around the carts of sidewalk vendors. I stumbled at the corner and was not so quick to work my way past the women with bundles and the gray-haired men who stood beside the produce. Now the sisters increased their speed. I called, but they did not look back. In a few minutes they had turned another corner and left me, alone, in the street. The old men were staring at me.

~~~~~~

"You have captured something here," said Farouk.

It was night, and we were outside on the deck of my house in Seattle. Farouk talked precisely, eloquently, sounding more like Sartre than Arafat. He was a surprise, a cultural anthropologist who made sense, and I listened carefully as he critiqued the manuscript recounting my Syrian travel.

Farouk finished one cigarette and began another, trying to overcome a deficit that had built up during the long meal. "All over the Arab world it is this way," he said. He was talking about my manuscript, referring specifically to the Ismaili women. "About sex I mean, very different from America. The Arab world is very, very traditional. You have heard of young women who have premarital sex and then are killed, for honor, by their brothers? 'Honor killing' it is called. It happens. We are very conservative. Yet women are allowed to play with sexual allusions—you say 'flirt'—and their flirting is far more intense than it would be in America because of the conservative situation. The flirting, since it is language, is OK. It is a way to desanctify what is sacred or forbidden. This seems illogical to you as an American, yet Arab men find this normal. But don't dare touch."

PART FIVE

فاصل

Interlude
Three Days in Damascus

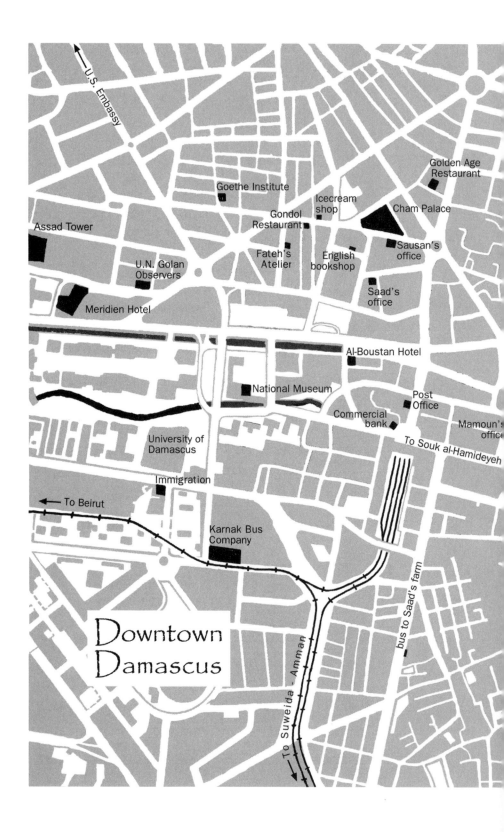

U.S. Embassy

Golden Age
Restaurant

Goethe Institute

Icecream
shop

Cham Palace

Gondol
Restaurant

Assad Tower

Fateh's
Atelier

English
bookshop

Sausan's
office

U.N. Golan
Observers

Saad's
office

Meridien Hotel

Al-Boustan Hotel

National Museum

Post
Office

Commercial
bank

Mamoun's
office

University of
Damascus

To Souk al-Hamideyeh

Immigration

To Beirut

Karnak Bus
Company

bus to Saad's farm

Downtown
Damascus

To Suweida – Amman

1 — City of Fear

DAMASCUS. TUESDAY, NOVEMBER 3.

Between meetings in Masyaf I returned to base camp in Damascus. By now I could distinguish the different sections of this city, the most important being the district surrounding the Cham Palace and Saad's office where I had discovered the Gondol cafe. This establishment was clean, reasonably priced, and served a variety of European foods, some with sauce or gravy. After days in the outback, I was tired of chopped up sheep and roasted chicken. On the other hand, I had to concede that the spare diet had taken the curve out of my midsection. Across the street from the Gondol was the finest treasure of Syria, a gourmet ice cream shop. *Azeem*, Fantastic. The stuff was good. The shop offered a dozen flavors, but I chose chocolate each time. That's the secret to survival in a police state: chocolate ice cream.

Three days earlier I had stood in the rain in Latakia and watched the people crowding into sidewalk shops, ducking beneath the awnings to protect themselves from the deluge. I felt disconnected. Years before, I had adopted the dictum of Descartes, "I think, therefore I am." And I had added a few sayings from the Bible as well. On this day, for example, I had read from Paul in *I Corinthians*, "In Christ shall all be made alive." Both statements were noble and powerful. Yet in the gushing rain in Latakia I realized that they were untrue. Or at least they were not the only truth. There was something else, and it was made of clay. I realized that I was not nearly so self-sufficient as I thought. I needed other people. Despite my intellectuality and my religious beliefs, for the most part I lived from day to day—not by thinking, not by Christ—but as a member of a clan.

Now, in Damascus, I felt better. On this day I would see Saad in his office, then pick up a *Herald Tribune* (minus the portions razor-bladed by censors) at the English bookshop nearby. I would stop by

The takia. *Saad Shalabi's father and his dervishes danced in the courtyard behind this stone wall and lived in the apartments above.*

the Golden Age restaurant to schmooze with the entertaining ex-tank commander who ran the place, and maybe make another try for the Patriarch. This evening I would see the Eritreans at Saad's farm. I was still homesick, yet an ad hoc family was coalescing, and my heart was repairing itself.

I wondered now how I could ever have feared Saad Shalabi. He was my first real Arab, and I had worried that he would hate me. Yet, as it turned out, he was courteous, a compulsive host, and his generosity was making things possible.

If Damascus had been a city of fear during my first days here, it now seemed neutral, a place like other places that gave shelter to men and women of widely varying habits and opinions. As I ran errands, I explored blocks adjoining my bus stops, the bank, the post office, the stationery store. I was expanding my repertoire. One thing made me feel more at home: I kept seeing vintage American cars. This was the place where 47 Fords, 57 Chevys, and 53 DeSotos had come to die. Syrians added a third seat to the DeSotos, installed diesel engines,

194

and used them as service taxis. American cars with their muscle were especially favored for the run over the pass to Beirut.

One of my more interesting excursions took me close to the old city. My companion was Sausan (in English "Susan;" pronounced in Arabic Sows-ann), a friend of Saad's who was about thirty-five and worked in a small, modern storefront near Saad's office. Sausan's name, in Arabic and Hebrew, signified a kind of flower.

I met Sausan at her office and we walked down the hill past the al-Boustan Hotel where I had stayed my first night in town. In a few minutes we had reached a district with narrow streets, buildings six or seven stories high, crowded storefront shops at street level, sidewalks jammed with cars. We opened a battered wooden door to a musty, poorly lit building, hiked up six flights of stairs, opened another door, and found ourselves— shazzam—in an ultramodern office fitted with Danish furniture and Japanese electronics: a bright cubicle with no windows. Our host was Mamoun, a young man of twenty-two who had just taken over a manufacturing plant from his father. "Sausan," Mamoun exclaimed. "It's been too long." He gave her a hug, she flushed, then she cut to the

Outside the al-Boustan Hotel, a man sold small boxes of matches.

chase, quizzing him in Arabic about the French sweaters he had promised to find for her at cost. As she spoke she fingered a garish white designer telephone with large, square buttons. Occasionally she looked down at the phone with disgust.

Mamoun was a new industrialist, part of an experiment by the regime to allow just a little non-government commerce, and he was taking advantage of the opportunity by working fourteen-hour days. He manufactured sweaters on machines governed by American Macintosh computers with German software that wove Spanish yarn according to French patterns. The sweaters were then exported to France where Parisian labels were sewn on—and the sweaters were sold to American tourists.

Other Syrians Mamoun's age were enjoying life, attending college, meeting women. On the other hand, when they graduated they had little to do—I had seen MDs in Tartus hanging out on street corners, and then there was Aref's friend Muhammad in Masyaf who worked at the family grocery. "For me," Mamoun said, "I'm glad to have a job."

By now I thought of Damascus as a city where old and new mixed freely. Saad Shalabi's business was slow, so he attended international conferences to rescue prestige from a career that could never yield much income. Neither Saad nor the other Damascenes I had met were flaming zealots. They were Muslims, yet approached their lives with a mix of reason and emotion that could be found among ordinary Americans.

After an hour Sausan and I marched down the stairs. It was cold now, almost winter in the desert, and Saad's farm had no heat. Sausan took me to a shop where I bought a blanket—my sleeping bag was no longer warm enough. Then I said good night and caught a bus to the farm. The next time I saw Sausan we rode in the back seat of a friend's car to Zebdani, the smuggler's town on the Lebanese border. Sausan was in a meditative state of mind. As we rode, she talked.

2— Sausan

"I hate the police," said Sausan. "The intimidation, the attitude that they are better than you because they have guns. I shiver every day when I see these men. I get sick. Once I went to Malta. Wonderful, very nice. There were no policemen, no weapons, no boxes of bullets, no threat of killing and death. In Malta a person can have some self-respect."

Sausan rolled a Turkish cigarette from ingredients in her purse, lit up, took a drag, and shook her head and shoulders a little. Then she continued.

"You have heard about our families," she said, "our famous families. It is true. Our families are large and widely known. And certain families have lived in certain neighborhoods for hundreds, even thousands of years. Damascus is a safe place for children, because our families protect their young from the temptations that destroy children in New York and London. We don't have crime on our streets because families do not allow it. Damascus is a place where everyone has a home because everyone has a family. If a man has a brother who is unable to work, the man will support him or be disgraced."

Sausan was reciting the virtues of this city, yet she seemed cynical. She crushed out her cigarette in the ashtray in the car door.

"You have heard about our families, but there is another side, believe me. You can get married, for example, but where can you live? Since families own all the houses, and there are no apartments for rent, you live with your mother or his mother. And if the mothers do not approve, you do not marry.

"You have noticed that here in Damascus we have more freedom than in Saudi Arabia. In certain sections of town a woman can drink beer in a restaurant, no problem. But we have no money, so what can we do with our freedom? You can go out with a man, but all you can do is walk in the park. You don't have a house, he doesn't have a house. How do you entertain?

"Sometimes I wish I could get away from my family, have my own place, play music. Once I ran away and came to Zebdani where we are going now, lived in my brother's weekend apartment which I'll show you, and took a cab to work each day. But it cost me two hundred lira each way in the taxi. Too expensive.

"You have experienced our split work day, everyone leaves at noon or one o'clock to be home at two for the midday meal. Then, at four o'clock, shops and offices open up again, private ones, and government offices simply stay closed. You think we prefer this system because we are lazy or because of the heat. But no. The younger people would prefer to work straight through.

"We tried it for a while—an unbroken work day. It was very fine, very efficient. But the families eventually killed it. If there is no midday break, you see, people can live a distance from their work, they can have houses of their own away from town where land is cheap. Then they do not depend on their families, they can lead their own lives."

"You seem to resent your family," I said.

"Not really," said Sausan, "though I complain sometimes."

"You talk of marriage. But you are not married yourself."

"I was married," she said. "It ended in divorce and now, a year ago, my husband is dead."

"Do you miss him?"

"No."

"Why not?"

"He was a little older than me. He was a sheik from the Gulf. For me it was an unhappy marriage."

"Why were you unhappy?"

"To be truthful he was many years older. He was rich, my family was poor. I was forced. My family arranged the marriage when I was twelve years old."

3— Do You Know Saad Shalabi?

The night that Sausan and I met Mamoun I saved a dollar by riding home to the farm on a bus instead of taking a taxi—a big mistake, as it turned out.

Half an hour after leaving Damascus I was walking the last mile from the bus stop to Saad's farm. It was dark by now, and I was carrying my day pack at my side to be a little less obvious. A jeep drove past, then stopped, and a man in uniform motioned me over and offered in Arabic to give me a ride. Wonderful. I loved to ride at night with the *mukhabarat*. So I climbed in, and we started moving.

"*Aina Tathhab?*" he asked, Where are you going? He waved his hand at the surrounding gloom—it was only seven o'clock, but it was dark. He was speaking *fusha*, the formal language, so I did not understand. Still, his meaning was clear: You are a tourist, you should be back in town.

"*Ana sadeik* Eritreans," I said, I am friends with the Eritreans.

"*Sadeik al-Eritreen, ayeh.*" Yeah.

Of course I wasn't here because of the Eritreans, not exactly. I was stretching the truth—anything to keep from breaking my vow not to mention Saad's name. When we got to Saad's farm, my driver kept going and then pulled off at a place with no lights. I got out and saw another jeep and four men with AK-47s. I wondered if they had death squads here like in El Salvador. When my driver gave the hacking motion, I handed over my passport.

"*Amerikee,*" my driver said as he fingered my papers. Then he muttered to one of the other men. Why would an American be walking along the road at night, twenty miles from Damascus? Had he come to see the Eritreans? Later, I learned that I had managed to say exactly the wrong thing. They knew Saad and his association with the United States. If I was his guest from America, no problem. My explanation, however, was something dangerous: two kinds of foreigners, meeting secretly far from town.

My driver was fingering my passport. "*Ma ismuka,*" he barked, What is your name. He pointed at my chest. "*Esmi* Scott Davis," I replied. He paused for a moment, trying to match the words I pronounced to the strange characters on my passport. Suddenly he looked up, as though he had caught me in a lie. "*Bi Arabi,*" he demanded, "*bi Arabi.*" The man wanted to know my name in Arabic, but—what could I say?—a name is a name in any language.

I shrugged and muttered, "*Ma fehmet,*" I do not understand. My interrogator seemed pleased. He had suspected that I was skirting the truth when giving my name and now he knew for certain. To his mind, I was refusing to answer, playing dumb, intentionally thwarting the security forces of a sovereign state. I sensed that things were becoming more serious now and hoped that something would happen to lighten the mood.

While my driver talked, another man took my day pack, emptied it onto the hood of their jeep, and pawed through my stuff. "A bad sign," I thought. "On the coast, the police respected my privacy. None of them searched my bags, not even close." He held up my tourist map and unfolded it for all to see.

"*Shouf, shouf,*" he said, Look. Only a spy would have such a document. All of the men were looking at me now, ready to gauge my response.

"*Min Wazir al-Siyaha bil Sham,*" I said, From the Minister of Tourism in Damascus.

The men talked more rapidly and I kept hearing an accusation: "*Arabi, Arabi.*" My Arabic had meant nothing to my original interrogator but for the others my few poor words set the hook. Everyone in Syria knew that Americans were disdainful and ignorant, they seemed to be saying. So how was it that this American could speak the language?

My captors were second-string secret police, a little slow, and added AK-47s and official sanction to the tendency of many Syrians to accept bizarre plots and conspiracy theories as plain fact. It suddenly struck me—could this be?—that to my captors the map was proof that I worked for the CIA. My meager facility with the language only made the evidence more damning. But it was worse than that. According to common knowledge in the coffeehouses of Damascus, CIA agents were a dime a dozen in Syria and were considered clumsy and dense by the government. Only a CIA agent, for example, would have been stupid enough to be caught with a map on the outskirts of Damascus after dark not far from the hilltop missile batteries that protected Damascus from Israeli bombers.

My captors did not seem unduly upset with the idea that I, like most American "tourists," was CIA. Their real suspicions seemed to lie deeper. Iraq deployed spies and saboteurs as did Israel's Mossad. Iraq was a grudge match. Embittered Baath party cadres had fled Damascus for Baghdad and then, from exile, sent agents to hurl grenades at the Syrian president and to explode bombs on buses.

Israel was worse. Israel was officially at war, and Mossad agents were anathema—put to death instantly once caught, hung in the public square. My captors looked at me in the darkness and seemed to consider who, besides CIA, I really was. After a few minutes I sensed that they were coming to a verdict. Iraqis were good, but not *that* good. Only a Mossad agent would have been clever enough to pose as a clumsy CIA man posing as a tourist.

By now another policeman had returned from the farm with one of the Eritreans, Askia's friend Umar, who translated the headman's questions into English. He wanted to know about my movements in this country. I replied in Arabic.

"*Metajit Souriye?*" When did you come to Syria?

"*Min Shahreen.*" Two months ago.

"*Wane kunt fi Souriye?*" Where have you gone in Syria?

"*Ana rouht ila Saydnaya, Marjurjos, Tartus, Latakia, Masyaf. Ana shouf Qalaat Hosn.*" I have gone to these places, seen Crak des Chevaliers.

Then he asked if I knew Saad. I paused and looked at Umar. What should I say? He gave me no clue, not even a raised eyebrow. My captors were watching him to detect signs of collusion. "*Aewa,*" I said.

"*Trucko rouh,*" the policeman replied, Let him go.

In a moment's time my status changed from public enemy to honored guest. My captors offered fresh tomatoes along with their apologies. On the way back to the farm I was nauseated and shaking a little.

Umar was OK and, as we entered the farm compound, he consoled me. "Your Arabic very good," he said, "very perfect." I had learned some things in traveling on the coast but not nearly enough. To mention or not to mention the name of Saad Shalabi—I was still too green to judge. I had thought I was ready to launch forth to Aleppo and the Roman Bridge. Now I wondered. "What will I do when this scene replays itself," I thought, "when I am hundreds of miles from here, near the Roman Bridge, when I do not have Umar to intercede for me?"

The following day I felt weak and spent most of my time in bed. I was devastated, totally in pieces, and could not understand why, amidst the carnage, I felt a warm glow of accomplishment. "I remembered my Arabic," I thought.

I saw Umar again at dinner. "I went back and talked to the police this afternoon," he said. "They asked, 'How is the American after last night.' They were worried that they frightened you too badly.

"'He sleeps all day,' I told them, 'sleeps in the bed.'

"'Yes, yes,' they said."

The next day I saw Saad Shalabi in his office. "The police apologized," he said. "That's their way of saying that they will not report the incident to higher authority. I asked you not to use my name, but these police know me. In this case it was OK."

From Saad's office I left Damascus heading north.

PART SIX

حلب

A Caravan City
Three Weeks in Aleppo

Mediterranean Sea

Turkish Border

Alexandretta

Kafrjanneh

Azaz

Afrin

Ceded to Turkey in 1939

Qalaat
Samaan

Daret Aziz

Antioch

Bab
al-Hawa

Aleppo

Caravan route to

Idlib

To Latakia

Aleppo &
Vicinity

To Beirut

To Damascus

1 — On the Run

I traveled in darkness. We were moving north on the highway, heading toward Aleppo. This Fiat bus was large and dirty, filled with cigarette smoke, crowded with passengers—a few women in scarves, a few men in Western dress, but for the most part working-class men, "Arabs" wearing *galabeas* and *kaffiahs*. I sat halfway back and watched the city lights move past and then darkness and highway lights in the distance when the road curved out ahead of us. I remembered my ride in the truck coming the other direction on this highway a week earlier. Would we meet an equally stubborn truck driver tonight? Now the highway ran straight so that I could not see to the front or gauge the traffic, could not calculate or worry. My bus driver, an expressionless, pale-skinned man, seemed predictable, a creature of schedules who was in no particular hurry. I trusted him. Our bus moved through the gloom, and I rested my mind.

I thought back. Saad's farm had been my base camp, a place where I felt safe. The compound was surrounded by thick adobe walls with barbed wire on top, a steel gate with a stout lock, and a vicious dog who lived on chicken bones and would tear a leg off anyone who came within range. And then, two days earlier, the police had unnerved me, taken away my only sanctuary in this country. That night I had been surrounded by men who were stupid and dangerous, and their leader had walked to Saad's compound, breached the steel door, skirted the circle of death defined by the dog's chain, and fetched the Eritreans from their caretaker's quarters. After that night I knew that at any moment the police could knock on my door. I had long worried that police would stop me on the road and discover the note pads in my sack—one reason I had carried just two pads with me on the coast and left the others at Saad's farm. Now I feared that police would invade my base camp, uncover the stash I had hidden behind dusty ledgers in Saad's living room cupboard, and find damning evidence in the dozen note pads, the broken miniature tape recorder, the camera.

I had planned to leave Damascus, to travel to Aleppo and then to the Roman Bridge. I wanted to meet people, to conquer my summit. Now I *had* to leave. My only chance to become invisible to the police, I reasoned, was to hit the road, to run and keep running.

I looked out the window at vague, dark countryside while the other passengers stared into the shadowy interior of our bus. Were these men alive, I wondered, or had their lives been suspended for this passage? Our engine sang a steady song of heat and rage and constant purpose that cradled me, rocked me. My life was put on hold, my mind at peace. The bus moved on into the night, carrying me forward, and I felt that nothing could stop us, nothing could slow us down or shake us from our course. I felt secure once again. Then, for no reason, we slowed and braked and came to a halt, our engine idling. We were nowhere: no lights, no refueling station, no resting place for weary travelers. Our driver and his *jabi* got out, closed the door behind them, and we lay helpless like a long animal missing its brain. Something was wrong.

I heard noises, looked out, and saw men in uniform—this was a police roadblock. The luggage compartment below my window was thrown open, and now I saw men with machine guns flashing sharp, narrow lights at our underside. They were checking our baggage, looking for contraband—no, explosives. I wondered how long it would take them to find my bulky sack. Would the *jabi* remember that it was mine? I scrunched down a little in my seat. Here, inside this bus, I was safe. If they pulled me out I would have explaining to do. What, for example, were these notes that I had jotted down? By now I had two hundred pages or more, and though I had taken the opportunity to hide my earliest notebooks in Saad's farm, though I had sent carbons and even some originals home in the mail as a hedge against confiscation, the full notebook and the six blank ones that I carried would betray me. I was not, simply, a tourist. And if I was a spy, what did that make the Syrians whose names and addresses I carried?

208

Our driver came aboard but the luggage compartment was still open, and then someone slammed shut the luggage door. The *jabi* came aboard and I felt better: we had passed the inspection. I waited for the door of our bus to close, but there was something more—and then I saw a man in dark clothing waiting in the doorway. He stepped up, turned, and stood in the aisle facing us, his head in shadow. I could not place this man, yet I sensed his arrogance. Had he found something below?

The man in dark clothes turned, spoke a few words to our driver, then stepped down. The door closed, the engine revved, and we pulled back onto the highway.

We traveled on, the same bus, the same passengers, but I was not the same. My peace of mind had been shattered. Now I knew that I could neither hide nor run: nothing could make me safe in this country.

2— Hot Water

I arrived in Aleppo at nine o'clock that evening and took a room in the Hotel Baron, an elegant, aging structure. The young T. E. Lawrence

The Baron Hotel in 1911. A third floor was added later.

had made the Baron his base in 1910. A year later he returned to the Baron on a graduate fellowship to assist an archaeological excavation down the Euphrates. After World War I he stopped here a third time. By then he was a different person, no longer an innocent child of the British Empire but a legend with a man inside. Agatha Christie was a frequent visitor to the Baron when her husband, the archaeologist Max Mallowan, was in Syria sniffing out antiquities. She wrote *Murder on the Orient Express* in several of these rooms. During World War I, the Turkish leader Jamal Pasha made the Baron his headquarters, and, when the British pushed north, Allenby stayed here as well.

Baron Hotel, "Blanket of the Knight."

The ceilings of the Baron were high, the walls had not been painted for thirty years, and the roof leaked. High ceilings are nice, but you pay for them every time you climb the stairs. Six long flights led to the third floor where I had taken a corner room. Under construction from 1907 to 1911, the Baron had a Victorian flavor. The blankets on the beds were wool, made in Dewsbury, England, and bore an embroidered label. "Blanket of the Knight," the label announced in red Arabic script. Above this brand name was an Arab warrior astride a rearing white stallion. His free right arm held a rifle in the air.

The outstanding feature of the Baron was its plentiful supply of hot water. My first deliberate act in this hotel, undertaken only minutes after my arrival, was to draw a bath. The bathroom was located across the hall from my room, but I didn't mind. The tub was deep, and few other patrons occupied third-floor rooms, so I could count on an hour's uninterrupted soak. Hot water was something I had not experienced since the Cassion Hotel in Damascus fifteen days earlier—and there I had been allotted only a shower, no tub, and the shower stall featured a bare electric bulb with exposed wires which made for short, nervous showers. The Baron was different, however.

The old city of Aleppo surrounded the citadel.

Here I could relax and meditate.

Thus far in my expedition I had survived scowling men with machine guns, buses with spit and sunflower shells on the seats, and moldy hotels with WCs that featured smooth rocks instead of toilet paper. Still, sitting in this bath, the grievances of my recent past seemed not so bad. I found something comical in my earlier assumption that the inconveniences of third world travel (my version of Thoreau's busk) would benefit me. Exactly what had I figured to learn from dirt, grime, and cold water showers?

I reached for the faucet with my toes and let more hot water into the tub. The first 29 days of my journey had changed me. Bereft of the people and places that steadied me, I turned instead to the people I met, the places I visited, the sounds and smells of this land. Of necessity, I made them mine. After requesting admission to the lives of Syrians, after asking them to talk with me, to remember me, to care about me, would it ever be possible for me to dismiss them or to dismiss people from other distant lands as "foreign?" Didn't we all belong to an emerging world culture? By now I thought of myself as Syrian even though I knew I was also American.

One more thing: my assumption that Syrians would be original, unsullied, and clear-minded because of the comparative simplicity of their lives needed revision. Life in a third-world police state is simple? How could I have been so naïve? As far as I could tell, Syrians of every class were preoccupied with complexities that did not exist in the United States. Syrians had to show their identity cards when they rode the bus or walked the streets, to submit to questions and searches at every checkpoint, to weigh their actions, guard their words. How many Syrians had washing machines? Clothes dryers? Syrian lives

Boustan Kul-Aab means "flower orchard," and it lived up to its name 75 years ago. Now it is an auto parts district.

were governed by bus schedules and shortages. In order to purchase sugar, a Syrian might have to spend eight hours running all over town—that's what I'd done one day in Damascus.

What surprised me about Syrians was their resilience. On the coast I had talked in private homes with people so frightened that they only would whisper when it came to the name of president Assad's home village. I met young men, highly trained, who had little or no work. I met older men with years of experience who had work for only a day or two each week. Against these conditions, I would have expected Syrians to be close-mouthed and dour. And they were—when it came to politics and jobs. On other subjects, however, Syrians were whimsical, irreverent, raffish. How could this be?

3 — Desert Traders

Aleppo was old, steeped in history, and owed its character to the surrounding landscape. In early years before all-weather highways and automobiles, when vagabonds and thieves roamed at will, there was a sharp difference between the desert and a settlement in the desert. Caravans spent weeks crossing arid lands. Full sun beat down during the day and, at night, camels huddled beside their loads, drivers slept in tents or under the stars, and lookouts kept watch against marauding tribes. Journey's end was a city such as Aleppo or Basra: men and animals passed through a gate in a thick stone wall to find a well, a cistern, buildings with foundations. A walled city took meaning from the surrounding waste. The desert was an undivided emptiness that threw civilization into relief.

As early as the fourteenth century Aleppo welcomed traders from Genoa and Venice. A century later the French were established in this city, and in 1543 they received commercial concessions from the sultan. In 1580 the English received similar concessions and a year later established their Levant Company here. In time fifty merchants operated from the British "factory," and riders traveled back and forth to the Gulf carrying the Indian mail. The Cape of Good Hope had been opened by the Portuguese in 1479, and nineteen years later Vasco da Gama sailed from Lisbon to India and returned with a cargo of spices. The Cape gained popularity as a trade route in succeeding centuries, yet Aleppo prospered. The overland route to Basra was more expensive, but it was faster and more convenient.

Under the Ottomans, Damascus became a holy city, the staging point for the *hadj*, and a place that was hostile to foreign merchants. Aleppo, on the other hand, emerged as an international trading center and the primary commercial city of the Levant. It had a port on the Mediterranean at Alexandretta, great *khans*—hotels where traders could rest in upper rooms and shelter their animals in enclosed yards below—a vast covered market where goods could be sorted and sold or repackaged for transshipment. Aleppo was the terminus of great caravans which ran back and forth to the Gulf and commonly included three thousand camels. Each season caravans arrived from Basra laden with silk from Cathay and spices from the Indies. In Aleppo camels and drivers were assembled and goods of Europe packed and loaded. Aleppo was the gateway to China, the link to India.

Medina Qadeeme, the old city.

I wanted to spend a couple of weeks in and around Aleppo before following ancient trade routes from Aleppo to the Roman Bridge. In this town I wanted to meet Armenians, urban working folk, peasants in their traditional villages, and I wanted to explore the Aleppo souk. Most of all I wanted to experience urban intellectual life. Hasan the architect had told me that Syria's finest artists and writers—and those most politically independent—were to be found in Aleppo.

213

4 — The "Singing" Boy

The artists and writers I met in Aleppo looked and sounded similar to those I knew in the United States. Like Americans they lived in apartments, worked day jobs in offices, and did their creative work at night. The difference was that in Aleppo people still knew medieval village life, an existence keyed to the seasons and to the survival of the community. The artists and writers of Aleppo were less personally ambitious than Americans I knew. They felt that they painted, sculpted, wrote, or spoke on behalf of ancient classes of people: peasants, craftsmen, urban poor—earnest, simple, ordinary folk. In Aleppo I met some of these "ordinary" people, most notably the singing boy.

A few days after registering at the Baron Hotel, I came to the Umayyad Mosque, a worthy monument. I removed my shoes, then walked into a large courtyard enclosed on all sides. The place was clean except for a single scrap of persimmon peel. As I watched, an old Bedouin stooped to pick it up.

The place was quiet, nearly empty. I walked across the courtyard and passed a small domed shelter with faucets. This was a *mawda*, or place of ablutions. Several men sat here, their trousers and shirt sleeves pulled up, washing feet, hands, and faces. At the edge of the courtyard, women in long dresses and black gauze veils sat in silence. When I reached the other end, I sat on stairs in the sun. It was too hot, so I moved into the shade and made another run at memorizing the Arabic alphabet, which I had copied onto blue note cards. There were twenty-eight letters, three of them vowels. Eighteen letters had distinct shapes, the ten others were distinguished by dots.

Before long, a boy of about twelve walked to my end of the courtyard. He was wearing an old dress coat, brown slacks, and an over-large pair of sunglasses. I turned back to my cards and a few minutes later heard a voice of great purity "singing" (Muslims would say "reciting") lines from the Quran. It was the boy, sitting cross-legged near the place of ablutions. His voice echoed and reverberated, filling the courtyard, touching us all. Then it rose above the rooftops, carrying me with it, and soared higher and higher until I imagined that the boy was sitting at the most slender point of the minaret. And what did he see? Laid out below were the intricacies of human life, tiny dwellings, narrow passageways, and the pettiness in those enclosures—the tangled reasoning, the folly, the deceit. The singing boy seemed to rest atop the minaret and still his voice soared, lifting itself to heaven, and then it curved and came down on the city like a ray of light in a dark and troubled land.

When the boy had finished, two men wearing long, white tunics approached and began to chat with him. A Bedouin gave him money, which the boy folded and put into his coat pocket. Then he stood and smiled and poked the ground with a skinny bamboo cane, a toy cane like that of Charlie Chaplin. He was a showman jesting with his friends. He laughed and walked to the fountain to splash water on hands and face.

By now I was feeling less harried. This place was restful, contemporary, alive. It was unlike the other monuments—or perhaps the change was in me, perhaps I was seeing differently. The Bedouin who had spotted the persimmon peel passed me and stooped to pick up a peanut shell. I was cold in the shade, so I moved back into the light.

The youth was sitting once more, reciting lines that ended with the name of the Prophet. "Muhammad," he sang—sonorous, emphatic. He began a free-floating melody, his voice

Aleppo rooftops.

supple and clear, rising and falling in eastern modulations. Then he was joined by the older men sitting at the sides of the courtyard who had low, droning voices and provided a rough, steady chorus to the brilliance and clarity of the young voice.

This boy was a *moukrey*, practicing his art. These days he performed for pocket change for the few souls who took refuge in the mosque on an afternoon. In later years, when his name became known, he would recite his lines at weddings and funerals, lending solemnity to formal occasions. He would bring a gift to those affairs, not an object of gold or silver, and something more than his pure tone and perfect technique. The worried, the self-important, the mournful—men and women caught in the grim particulars of life: he lifted their heads, opened their eyes.

It was time to leave. I returned my note cards to their envelope and walked in stocking feet to the doorway. I heard something, then turned and saw the singing boy. He was standing now, still wearing his sunglasses, and was walking toward me with his cane. I realized, suddenly, that he was blind.

5 — Hasan the Architect

ALEPPO. TUESDAY, NOVEMBER 10.

My friend Hasan the architect, in Seattle, had given me the name and phone number of his colleagues and old school friends in Aleppo. The first one I contacted was an urban planner named Faisal, a wiry, gray-haired man who drove a white pickup with a green government insignia crudely spray painted on the door. "I work for the government now," he said. "That's where the jobs are. I just got back from Australia. I was there for eight months, looking for work. But I found nothing. Why? I'm not sure. Probably because my English is not so smooth."

Faisal spoke quickly in a thickly accented English. "In America," I thought, "foreign languages are optional. In a country such as Syria, a foreign language can be a survival skill. I'm glad that my job does not depend upon my ability to speak Arabic."

Upon hearing of my interest in intellectuals, Faisal insisted on throwing a party. "I will invite all of Hasan's friends," he said, "the whole *shellah*, as you say, the whole gang. Three of them met here in Aleppo, went to school here together, very close in the university. Plus one other who they met in Damascus after graduation, a close friend and an honorary member of the *shellah*."

"Who's included?" I asked.

"Zouhair Dabbagh the sculptor," Faisal replied. "Then I'd invite

Umar the architect but he just moved to Los Angeles. And I'd invite Youssef Abdelke the painter (whom Hasan and Zouhair met in Damascus), but he lives in Paris. Hasan of course is in Seattle. Really the only member of the *shellah* who's still here is Zouhair."

"Oh," I said.

"So I'll invite Walid Ikhlassy the writer, a little older than Hasan and his college mates, but he will talk enough for everyone who is absent."

The first thing that I learned about Syrian artists and intellectuals was that most of them no longer lived in Syria. Another thing I learned: they were close-knit. Intellectuals in Syria were a small group that gossiped and bickered but also welcomed and nurtured. They gave each other a stage. They were collegial and reminded me of jazz musicians in the United States who welcomed new members because of their concern to perpetuate the art form. They reminded me also of American expats in Paris during the 1920s, Hemingway, Dos Passos, Gertrude Stein—a small group creating very fine work.

Later Hasan the architect explained that my observations failed to mention the most important point. He and his college friends were collaborators who had been battling to create a specific kind of art. And they met overwhelming opposition—not from Westerners, but from their Arab overseers. "In college," Hasan explained, "Zouhair, Umar, and I were inseparable. Later, in Damascus, Zouhair and Youssef were very close and I saw them whenever I could. We wanted something more than to make the same business that our parents had made. My father was a teacher, yet I wanted to create great designs, to build classic buildings. Zouhair's father was a leather worker, yet he longed to create great sculpture. We could not bear business-as-usual. We could not bear the strictness and conformity of the *ulama*, those who organized religious worship."

"It was the 1960s," I said. "You guys were in revolt. Not rioting in the streets. More like the 1950s rebels, like James Dean. You guys had no T-shirts, no cigarettes, no sneers. You were pretty well-scrubbed. Still you had anger and anxiety."

"As you say," Hasan replied. "But really that is wrong. James Dean? Who is this? We were thinking of the Arab past."

"I get it," I said. "You were the first generation of Arab youth born and raised in independence. You felt shame because your people had

Hasan's artist friend Youssef Abdelke reflected on Syrian life from exile in Paris.

been dominated for centuries by the Turks and French."

"That's closer," said Hasan. "And also Israel. The Israelis won the battles in 1967 and that left us angry. 'The world,' we thought, 'does not understand us. We need to explain.'"

"What's to explain?" I said.

"We believed in the greatness of the medieval Islamic empire, the architecture, the mosaics, the calligraphy, the science, the math. We wanted to make that greatness live again in the present."

"So you were taking on the ignorance of the West," I said.

"Of course," said Hasan. "But really you do not understand. Our battle was to make a place in world art, literature, and scholarship for a distinctive Arab and Islamic style. But that was a distant battle. The immediate struggle in those years was against the local authorities. In Aleppo it was OK to worship the past, intact. But it was not allowed to do modern work inspired by the past. Completely forbidden."

"I don't understand."

"The *ulama*, or men of learning, were in charge in Aleppo, a very conservative community that had choked Syria for centuries under the Ottomans," said Hasan. "They exalted the past yet blocked any effort to create variations on the past. And it was worse in the university where we studied Western texts, debated Western ideas. Some of our teachers were French, and most were Arabs who had studied in France or at the American University in Beirut. We were dominated by Western texts, thinkers, ideas."

"But Western learning and art for a long time was the ally of Arab culture," I said.

"What do you mean?" said Hasan.

"Remember that the Ottoman Turks were trying to maintain power while expending as little effort as possible. Scholars have praised the Ottomans for their tolerance and their ability to adapt their administration to the needs of each local culture. Their flexible and unstandardized approach may be far better at integrating diverse societies than the national model we are using today. Still, for the Ottomans it was a matter of incentives. The Ottomans wanted peace and quiet and wanted to collect their tax money. They had no reason to keep Arab culture and literature alive and to encourage people to read and think and debate the issues of the day in Arabic. The Ottomans may or may not have suppressed Arabic or discouraged the development of Arabic. Scholars will argue the fine points. But they really had no reason to encourage the modernization of Arabic language or to push the development of modern Arabic literature.

"In those years you had the Classical Arabic of the medieval poets and the Quran which was used in religious study. And you had spoken dialects in different regions. What about modernizing and standardizing the Arabic language into a common tool for the exchange of ideas? That was for Syrian poets and thinkers to do, using the opportunity that Europeans provided in Egypt and Lebanon.

"You could say the Arabic revival got going when, in 1798, Napoleon invaded Ottoman Egypt and brought in his wake European scholar-ship, libraries, civil administration. Subsequent regimes like that of Muhammad Ali were more open and more linked to the West than others in the Ottoman Empire—a point which attracted writers and thinkers from the Levant who in the mid-1800s began a revival of Arabic literature. They were looking both at classical Arabic literature and at contemporary European literary forms like the novel.

"During the same years the French who were Catholics and the Americans who were Protestants were gaining influence in Lebanon. They had a motive to revive and modernize Arabic: they wanted to convert people, to get them thinking and talking and writing about new religious ideas, to wean them away from the influence of the Ottomans. These missionaries brought modern printing presses to Beirut and before long French and American missionary schools in Beirut were teaching Arabic, translating the Bible into Arabic, creating new Arabic typefaces, and printing the Bible and other religious books in Arabic. They called it *nahda*, renaissance, and scholars often associate it with the teacher and writer Butrus al-Bustani. Between 1863 and 1883, Bustani created an Arabic dictionary, completed eleven volumes of an Arabic encyclopedia, and founded several journals. The American University played a big role. And Arabs were going off on their own, organizing, printing secular journals and books. By 1900 Beirut was the center of Arab journalism and a seedbed in which Arab nationalism could take root."

"OK," said Hasan, "but that was way in the past. I'm sure the French gave us many good things as well as many bad things. And of course for a time we thought that Western learning was the key to expressing our past. For one thing, the idea of personal artistic expression—painting, sculpture, figure studies—is a Western concept. In our tradition we did not hang art on walls, instead we made the walls themselves works of art with tile and calligraphy and massed sculptural form. We did not create an art work and then sign it, instead the artist was an artisan who devoted himself to a project but did not claim personal credit.

"By the time we got to the university, we knew that we lived in an emerging world culture with formats adopted from the West. What we wanted was to express Arabic culture within the new format."

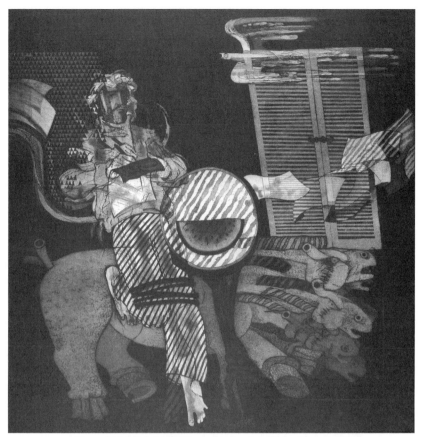

Youssef Abdelke's bound figures depicted the Palestinian cause.
"The Israelis won the battles in 1967 and that left us angry," said Hasan.

"So what was the problem?" I said.

"In the university, pretty quickly we found that 'glass ceiling,' as you say. We were completely free to study Western masters, but no one would let us apply their insights to traditional Arab or Islamic themes."

"What do you mean?"

"In architecture, for example, I was free to study Le Corbusier but I could not do a project with Arab content to apply the inspiration I had gained from the French master. It was OK to imitate the ideas and projects of the great man, to repeat his work, to plagiarize his work. It was forbidden to go out on my own. To put it bluntly, my senior project was blocked by the faculty."

"Your project?"

"Yes. I wanted to design a new neighborhood that adopted traditional Arab urban design: curving, narrow passageways, honeycombed dwellings built one upon another, no public space but instead interior courtyards. The faculty said it was OK to do 'Arab' houses, but I had to put them on individual lots on a street grid—kind of like a 1950s suburb in the United States. Of course, that destroys the whole thing. The point of traditional Arab dwellings is their interdependence, their connectedness, the way they preserve privacy and yet pull the community together. The Western concept is very different; it creates public space and pushes dwellings back from the street so that they can be observed from a public position. The public face of a building is very important in the West, but in Arab design it is the interior space that is important."

"Why this opposition from the faculty?"

"Their expertise was in Western texts, Western architects. They had studied in Paris. They could teach us what the French, Germans, and Americans were designing and saying about design. They had no idea how to make Arab architecture that was great in its own right. If we had started a trend, they might have lost their jobs. The professors were hostile to the ancient architecture of our city."

"How so?"

"I remember a class project in my fourth year. The professors asked us to plan a demolition of the Aleppo *souk,* the ancient covered market. It was here in the time of Marco Polo. It's unique, part of our priceless architectural heritage, but we were to tear it down and build something new and modern in its place. And I've told you about the official city plan at that time."

The city government in Aleppo had maintained town plans since the 1930s that expressed the same sentiment: get rid of the old stuff. Broad new streets were to cut through the old city—just like the designs Le Corbusier was turning out during those years. The current Aleppo town plan, devised by a French architect in 1955 and not overturned until the 1980s, wanted to use the citadel as the hub for highways that would gouge big slots through the traditional stone-walled alleys and houses. The many-layered, many-textured old city, built up since Roman times, would be cut into sections like pieces of pie, exposed to view instead of integrated—an Arab

Disneyland on the desert.

The destruction of the old city never happened, partly through the efforts of a friend of Hasan's, an architect who was a little older, a son of the old landowning class who lived both in Aleppo and in Seattle. In the 1970s, architectural activists in Seattle were fighting to prevent demolition of Pioneer Square and the Pike Place Market. Hasan's friend launched a parallel fight to preserve the ancient Aleppo *souk*.

Hasan's complaints about his college professors made me wonder how such men had been selected. "Politics," said Hasan. "This has happened all over Syria under the current regime. People make political connections, and soon they are running things. So they have a life, a career, but what of the job that needs to be done?

"The school of architecture held classes and gave diplomas," Hasan continued, "but it was always two steps behind the Europeans and Americans. In the end I had to come to Seattle to study Islamic architecture."

Given Hasan's experience with the school of architecture in Aleppo and the sagging Syrian economy, no one was surprised when he chose to stay in the United States after getting his Masters degree. Hasan savored American life and his daughters grew into American teenagers who played in their own rock 'n' roll band, but that did not make Seattle his home. On the other side of the world was a bare stretch of arid, flat ground, a town of bleak, stone buildings, and a people whom he knew as his own.

~~~~~~

"You are holding back here," said Farouk. "You come to the edge of a very brilliant and profound conclusion—then you hesitate, you back away, and the point is lost." Farouk, as you may recall, was an Arab intellectual from North Africa who had spent many years in Paris. I was talking to him at my house in Seattle, seven years after my journey through Syria.

"State it plainly: Arabs such as Hasan are traitors to their people. If they wanted to advance the culture, they would return to their countries and speak their minds."

"How does a Hasan in jail benefit anyone?" I said.

"He suffers, he bleeds, he clogs up the prison system—but the regime cannot ignore him, the regime must take him into account. Every single Arab regime is a dictatorship. Why is this? It is because the people who know better, people like Hasan, are cowards. They leave for Paris, London, and Moscow. Even in exile Hasan is very careful. He can go home to visit, to work, because he has done nothing to anger the regime. His friend Youssef, in Paris, is the opposite. He is not careful. He says what he thinks. And as a consequence, he can not go home again."

"What about you?" I said. "You are here in the United States, working for an American university."

"No, no," he said. "I am going back home. Always I do this."

"Why?"

"My contract ran out, of course. And I am trying to set something up at another university, but they are so slow to decide. I will go home until I hear from them."

6 — Socks

FAISAL'S APARTMENT, ALEPPO. TUESDAY, NOVEMBER 10.

Faisal and his family lived in the modern west end of Aleppo in a walk-up apartment. On the night of their party, he and his wife set out delicacies on their coffee table while Zouhair the sculptor, Walid the writer, and I sat in stuffed chairs and made small talk. Walid regaled us with stories from his recent lecture tour at American universities. "Think of it," he said. "In America you can say anything you want. Absolutely anything. The government doesn't care. It's no problem."

Soon conversation turned to the members of this circle who were not present. Umar the architect first had moved to the Gulf to get a job, then to Los Angeles where he had no work but was free to say whatever he pleased. Youssef the graphic designer and printmaker had moved to Paris where he found a job and sent back to the government five thousand dollars in cash rather than serve in the Syrian army. As thanks, the Syrians had yanked his passport—so now he couldn't travel out of France. Hasan the architect had served in the army, then, as

I have mentioned, moved to Seattle for an advanced degree. Now he had a family and ran his own business.

I began talking to Zouhair the sculptor who explained that he and Hasan had been roommates at the university in Aleppo. Zouhair was thirty-five years old, just under six feet tall, and had a smooth, round face that seemed open and innocent. Our host handed Zouhair a portfolio of Hasan's work, and the sculptor paged through. I recognized early sketches of desert nomads and horses galloping through the sand. Hasan had started out as a visual artist, but switched to applied art when he realized that very few people ever would see a painting displayed on a wall in a museum or private home. He enjoyed architecture and loved graphic design, especially designs that involved Arabic lettering.

Whereas early Christians had decorated their churches with icons depicting Bible figures, Muslims were ever mindful of idolatry and for the most part avoided graven images. Instead Muslims decorated with geometric designs, floral patterns known as arabesque, and Arabic script. Hasan was particularly interested in a style of script developed in the Iraqi city of Kufa in the eighth century. Kufic had a clean, angular look that lent itself to architectural decoration.

The Bismallah in Kufic style lettering. Ever mindful of idolatry, Muslims traditionally decorated with Arabic script rather than human forms.

As Zouhair paged through Hasan's portfolio, I told him what I knew about Hasan's recent work in Seattle. Later he gave me the inside story on Hasan during university days.

"In the winter it was very cold in our dormitory," said Zouhair, "so Hasan did something strange, something secret, and I think he left for America because here in Aleppo the secret leaked out."

"Tell me," I said. "I will never let Americans know the truth."

"In the evenings," Zouhair continued, "Hasan put on his pajamas and thick socks. Then he tucked his pajamas into his socks."

"I'm shocked," I said.

"Truly he did this," said Zouhair. "He looked like a man who was not intelligent."

"And now he is rich and famous in America," I said, "but for you he still has his pants stuffed into his socks."

"As you say," replied Zouhair.

7 – Zouhair, the Sculptor

ZOUHAIR'S APARTMENT, ALEPPO. WEDNESDAY, NOVEMBER 11.
In Aleppo's intellectual circles one good party deserves another. We broke up at midnight and, the following evening, met at the walk-up apartment of Zouhair the sculptor where we sat on stuffed chairs and ate delicacies prepared by Zouhair and his wife. This time the sculptor and I paged through his portfolio while Faisal and Walid the writer argued about freedom of speech, the first item on the wish list of every Syrian intellectual should the regime decide to liberalize. Faisal and Walid were tired and left early, and Zouhair's wife and children turned in. I sat alone with Zouhair and talked into the night.

Zouhair had begun sculpting at age thirteen. In those days he studied photos of sculpture by Michelangelo and Rodin. Later he experimented with the cubist ideas of Pablo Picasso—who was, after all, an Andalusian—only to return to a more realistic rendering of human form. "I like to have good anatomy," said Zouhair. "Good anatomy and good plastic form." He showed me photos of clay models he had made for larger works that he would create in bronze. "Bronze is a very good material," he said. "Bronze and marble. But bronze is better, though it is hard to do in Syria because the manufacturers do not know sculpture."

Zouhair had a family, a car, and an apartment. His wife ran a small retail shop downtown, while Zouhair designed tiles for a construction company—a job which had kept him a little too busy for the past several years. On Friday, the day of prayer, Zouhair forsook the mosque for his studio.

"This keeps my fingers limber," said Zouhair, "but is too little time to make good art." Before long he planned to quit his job, work with his wife in their shop, and devote himself to a series of new sculptures.

Zouhair was ambitious in his own way. He already had a large body of work to his credit, and had been honored by the national museum which acquired several of his sculptures. Zouhair joked about his success. "It is true that my sculptures are at the national museum," he said. "But they gather dust in a storage room in the sub-basement." Zouhair was a peaceful man who had a sense of his calling as a craftsman.

"I know artists and architects," Zouhair said, "who want to do good work and get much money and become famous. For me, I only want to do good work." I asked about his father. "My father and grandfather worked leather for a living—that's what *dabbagh* means, 'one who dyes leather.' They worked hard and were happy, for they were simple men. Do you know this word *simple?* I too am a simple man."

I asked Zouhair if he would follow Hasan and his other friends into exile. "You have seen my sculpture," he answered. Some of Zouhair's most moving pieces, like one of a wild horse whose legs had been bound, referred to Palestinians who had been moved from ancestral lands when Israel was established in 1948. "My work is here. My heart is here. How can I leave?"

Zouhair had relatives in Toronto who begged him to emigrate. He would visit them soon, but saw no chance that he would move away from Aleppo. A better idea, he thought, would be for his college friends—the whole *shellah*—to return home. This would be an especially good idea for Hasan.

Zouhair Dabbagh still lived in Aleppo. *"My work is here," he said.*

"In Aleppo we must have a coalition of artists," said Zouhair. "We must join our thoughts so that our work will blossom for the world. There is one man to lead this coalition, one very good man: Mr. Hasan."

Later in Seattle, I conveyed the sculptor's remarks to Hasan. Whereas the sculptor was a large man with broad features, the architect was small and fastidious. Hasan blinked a few times and then sighed.

"To hear these words," he said, "makes my heart almost break."

8 — Civilization, Then & Now

Zouhair the sculptor and his friend Hasan the architect celebrated the art and architecture of the medieval Islamic empire. They studied individual works in depth but did not pay much attention to chronology, the social setting in which those works were created, or the underlying power relationships. Historians, however, place these accomplishments in time, link them to specific regimes, and judge the ebb and flow of creative production against a linear measure. Historians, in other words, tell a story of rise and fall. And they might say that Hasan and his friends, at this moment in history, are trying to get another rise going.

The rise of the Islamic empire began in the Arabian desert, in Mecca and Medina. Muhammad was born in the oasis town of Mecca in 570, began preaching publicly in 616, and died in 632. Three years later, under the leadership of Umar, Muslim horsemen gathered in Medina and rode north. They overcame Damascus, which they made the capital of their empire, and went on to conquer a territory larger than that of Rome—a territory that stretched from the Atlantic in the west to Persia in the east. Umar was a merchant and a brilliant administrator. The empire he established was managed after his death by the Umayyads (a clan of merchants from Mecca), who won acceptance from Christians and Jews for their tolerance. Some Muslims, many of them Shiites, judged the Umayyads to be secular leaders who, in their efforts to govern, lost the spiritual import of the faith. The most powerful of these critics were the Abbasids. They took their name from al-Abbas, Muhammad's uncle and companion, a devout follower who was the first scholar of the Quran. The Abbasids bridled under rule of the Sunni Umayyads. They objected to caliphs such as Walid II, the Umayyad who liked to spend time hunting in the desert, taking baths in tubs of wine, and frolicking with maidens. In 750, Abbasid insurgents overthrew the Umayyads and moved the administration of the empire to Baghdad.

For all their ruthlessness in acquiring and consolidating power, the Abbasids were resourceful and in some ways enlightened. They constructed an ingenious irrigation system that took water from the Euphrates and Tigris and fed it to parched land, causing the desert to bloom. They recruited teams of scholars from Persian towns where Indian and Persian learning already was being exchanged, and brought Greeks, Jews, Christians, Persians, and Indians to translate Greek, Syriac, Pahlavi, and Sanskrit texts and to copy them into books, a modern invention made possible by using paper which had come west along the Silk Road from China. By 800 the library possessed thousands of manuscripts and was probably the largest repository of learning in the world.

Wealthy men of pure Arab lineage, devout Muslims, nevertheless prized Greek philosophy which was taught and passed down, apparently in secular schools which the caliphs protected from the *ulama,* the conservative religious class. At a time when Europeans are commonly thought to have believed the earth to be flat, Arab mathematicians developed algebra and calculated the circumference of the globe, partly basing their calculations on experiments conducted in the Syrian desert near Palmyra. Three styles of counting existed simultaneously in the Muslim capital, including the Indian method which used decimals to express fractions and featured ten characters which could be combined in a place value system to create numbers (the origin of our modern base-ten numbering system). The craftsmen of Damascus forged highly polished blades of tempered steel that they decorated with gold and silver inlay, damascene, that was prized throughout Europe. Intricate damask cloth was produced here and traded across the empire.

The achievements of Islamic civilization, the work of builders, poets, philosophers, and scientists, were made possible by the empire's prosperity. Arab horsemen had preserved the infrastructure of the lands they conquered and spared the people. As I've mentioned, Christians and Jews and others among the conquered population who chose not to convert to Islam nevertheless were treated with tolerance and included in the wider economy, so that the human resources of the region, the skills of farmers, craftsmen, and merchants, were conserved. After the conquest, economic life continued as before with certain advantages. By crushing the Persians and beating back the Byzantines, the caliphs were able to eliminate the warfare that

Zouhair Dabbagh saw the Palestinian dilemma in the figure of a bound horse.

had cut the region in two. In an immense common market, trade flowed freely from Morocco to Afghanistan. Trade routes to India and China once more became secure, and the riches of the Orient and Central Asia flooded the markets of Baghdad, Damascus, and Aleppo. A quickening of trade created the wealth which made all else possible. In the centuries before the turn of the millennium the lands under control of the caliphs were prosperous, advanced, civilized—far outpacing Europe.

By 1100 the Muslim empire had reached its apex and was beginning to decline. For a time the Crusades preoccupied the caliphs, although the real shock came in 1258 when Hulegu, the grandson of Genghis Khan, sacked Baghdad, overturned the Abbasid dynasty, destroyed the irrigation system, and returned fertile farmlands to prairie and desert. Later Tamerlane the Great (also known as Timur the Lame), an invader from the steppe who made war in the Mongol style, wreaked even greater havoc. Hulegu and Tamerlane laid waste, and, in the story that Syrians had been telling me, the Ottomans who followed blocked the rebuilding of devastated Arab and Persian lands.

The Ottomans, in the analysis of traditional historians, were preoccupied with their European ambitions and did not mind leaving the Levant in ruins. They preferred to divert the wealth of Arab lands to their treasury in Istanbul where it could finance the Ottoman presence in the Balkans and fuel their drive for Vienna. In the last decade revisionist historians have begun to tell a more complicated story that emphasizes the beneficial interplay between Ottoman rulers, their Janissary troops, the Anatolian motherland, and Arab subjects. For many years of Ottoman rule, for example, Arab delegates attended the *mabuthan* or parliament in Istanbul—hardly the mark of an empire that was corrupt and despotic. On the other hand, Syrians, whose forbearers hid in caves on the cliffside whenever Ottoman troops pulled a raid, can be forgiven for not accepting this line of argument.

During these same years, much of the Syrian interior turned to desert. The Syrians themselves burned grasslands as a defense against the Mongols and some scholars argue that in an era of lessening rainfall these grasslands lost the ability to recover, lost their topsoil. In earlier years one could walk from Baghdad to Aleppo on the banks of the Euphrates and travel in shade for the entire journey. Now the rainfall was too scarce to support trees on the interior and, on the coastal hills, the forests were cut and the soil eroded to leave bare rocky hills. The population of Syria's great cities declined, and of the three thousand villages in the north at the beginning of the Ottoman reign, only four hundred still existed when the Ottomans withdrew following World War I.

Although Aleppo prospered even in competition with the longer route around the Cape, the profits went primarily to foreigners—Venetian, Genoese, British, French—who sent their earnings abroad. Under the Ottomans, Arab and Persian lands grew poor and learning and technology slipped backwards. Education fell under the control of the *ulama*, who fixed the curriculum and emphasized rote learning over speculative inquiry. The *ulama* had grown strong under the Ottomans and saw no point in giving away their position to an educated class of philosophers, scientists, and technocrats. And so the *ulama* blocked the development of secular learning and technology at every turn.

By the time that Arab people began to emerge in the 1800s, they had missed crucial developments of science, technology, and industrialization. They also had missed the chance to forge a unique political creation: the nation state.

Why was it that Europe, which had been crude and weak during medieval times, surpassed Arab lands? During the centuries in which the Ottomans governed Arab lands, Europeans were moving forward. The sometimes shaky distinction in Christiandom between secular and religious spheres nevertheless was strong enough to allow the development of rudimental science and technology, sometimes even with the assistance of the Church. In the 1400s religious war broke out in Europe between Protestants and Catholics, a slaughter over doctrine the likes of which has never occurred within Islam. Yet this turmoil, two hundred years later, resulted in a limit on Church power and the creation of a secular realm where scholars and scientists were comparatively free to pursue their work.

Thus Europeans found themselves in a position to make better use of Arab learning than could the Arabs themselves. The Umayyad libraries in Toledo and Cordova survived the Christian reconquest, became an important source of Greek and Arab science and math, and helped to fuel the European Renaissance. In Britain and France tribes and feudal allegiance were weakened, and "nations" of language, culture, and military organization began to demand fealty. The genius of the Europeans was displayed in their application of ideas taken from others. Gunpowder, for example, had been invented by the Chinese, but Europeans developed cannons and learned to mount them along the sides of their ships. The Indian base-ten numbering system which the Abbasids had refined and adapted was passed on to Europe (where these characters were called Arabic numerals), along with algebra and the concept of zero. Arab math was instrumental to Europeans as they learned to make machines and engines for com-

Ottoman-era house in Aleppo old city.

merce and for war.

Within the boundaries of emerging European nations, wealth and manufacturing became concentrated and routinized. The notion of progress was afoot, and nation-building became a linear project pursuing ever greater levels of wealth and power with no designated end, no stopping point, no marker that suddenly would turn the nation from aggrandizement to balance, from growth to survival, from the linear to the spatial. The growth of European nations was fueled by exploiting vast, comparatively disorganized territories in Africa, Asia, and South America. By 1800 Britain and France were quintessential nations, highly structured, rapidly industrializing, recently freed from domination by the Church, and learning to use science and technology to exercise power far from their borders. Ninety years later, according to one estimate, four European nations controlled eighty-four percent of the earth's land mass. In the new century, with no more territories to conquer, European nations turned on one another, ushering in World War I.

After World War II, Arab lands achieved independence and could present themselves to the world as nations with fresh, new borders. But it was too late to duplicate the national development of Britain and France. For one thing, there were no more "disorganized" spaces for them to exploit. For another, the gap in science and technology was so great that Arabs were forced to borrow wholesale from the West. And, at least in the short term, imported learning and technology never worked as well as that which a country developed on its own.

At present, after two world wars, even the most ambitious of the large nations see little to gain by provoking a third. Thus national development has been checked by its own success. The linear, aggrandizing thrust of human activity continues, and has even picked up speed, yet to a surprising degree the new linear project is not national but post-national. It is the wildfire of global commerce raging above, below, and through national boundaries, a movement that is shifting power to international business—and to international media such as CNN and Al-Jazeera. Global commerce has elicited global opponents: the environmentalists, labor organizers, social activists, skinheads, survivalists, and anarchists of the West as well as the Islamic and other radicals of the East.

During the rise of high tech and what seemed to be the invincible power and righteousness of global businesses based in the US or Europe, nations began to seem obsolete. Yet things look different after the high-tech bubble of the 1990s burst in 2001 and stock fraud was discovered in Enron, World Com, and other US corporations in 2002. As the US responded to the 9-11 attacks, occupied Afghanistan, and threatened an unprovoked war on Iraq, it became clear that "transnational" global capitalism flourished on a platform established by national power. It now became apparent that, since World War II, the United States has worked intensively behind the scenes to make the former British Empire safe for American business. The US invaded Afghanistan on the pretext of stopping terror. But isn't it true that Afghanistan is the logical route for an oil pipeline that will unlock the treasure of Central Asian oil? The United States has proposed to invade Iraq and depose Saddam Hussein because of his interest in acquiring weapons of mass destruction. On the other hand, can we discount the lure of Iraqi oil in the minds of administration planners?

As the US administration's war on terror progresses, it becomes clear that nations still count, however adept global corporations have become at avoiding national obligations and regulations in the interest of turning a profit.

In this new world of global commerce, girded with national assertions of power, individual Arab entrepreneurs and investors will flourish, and Arab oil promises to be a source of wealth for years to come. Yet most Arab small business owners will face foreign competition and (like their counterparts in Europe and the United States) will do well merely to survive.

In Syria manufacturers and would-be global traders are held back by a restrictive credit and banking system, a stifling bureaucracy, corruption, inadequate Internet access and phone connections, poor conditions for foreign investment, and the state of war with Israel. Although Bashar al-Asad has appointed new ministers trained in the West and begun the legal reforms needed to modernize, the delicate balance which keeps him in power requires concessions to interest groups which will make wholesale reform difficult.

Hasan and the rest of his Aleppo *shellah* are now scattered around the world. Yet they still feel that their ideals are a match for worldly money and power. Today they are consciously attempting to overcome obstacles of historical development to build a new Arab and Islamic civilization, something more profound than a mere rejection of the West. They are working in a space "beyond history," beyond the linear thrust of national development. They are stepping past the "clash of civilizations" and the violence of dominant nation states as well as the terror of Islamist extremists.

Hasan the architect and Walid Ikhlassy, Youssef Abdelke, Zouhair Dabbagh and dozens of other Syrian are working in a realm where survival, balance, and harmony are beginning to replace perpetual growth as goals, and where the world's cultures are beginning to be valued, like rare plant forms in remote jungles, for the practical wisdom and spiritual insight they contain. Amid these signs of an emerging world culture and against the arid wastes of modern life—the worship of a dead past and the lust for consumer goods—Hasan and his colleagues are attempting to create a place with order and purpose, a city with stone walls, a well, and foundations of its own.

At the Baron Hotel, Sarkis, the paunchy, Armenian desk clerk, bristled at the attitude of Americans and Europeans who, he seemed to think, had no conception of how carefully and at what cost a civilization is built.

"An American was here once," Sarkis said one afternoon, "an attaché

Matthew: Armenian Patriarch
1844–1848

with the consulate. He stood with me on the verandah and looked at our city, and I nearly pushed him over the edge. 'Why don't you have high-rise office buildings here,' he said. 'In the United States we have hundreds of high-rises. Look at New York.'

"I wanted to say bad words to him," Sarkis said. "We are not in the same situation as the United States. We are at war with our cousins to the south. We have not accumulated wealth. For two years after independence in 1946 we had peace, then in 1948 the war with the cousins began. Always this war is on our backs. Most of our money goes for the army. In France they have an army of four hundred thousand. We have a larger army than France. Yet France is an old country and has accumulated wealth over centuries.

"We are young. The Mongols burned our cities to the ground, and then we were under foreigners, Turkey and France, for hundreds of years. They took our wealth. We have not had time to save and build up. And always this war."

That evening I stretched out on my bed and thought about wealth and civilization on a different scale. In order to find time for this expedition, I had been forced to let my construction business run down, and it might take a year or two to get things rolling again. Syrians like Sarkis were discouraged about the economic prospects for their country—how could it achieve prosperity like that of the United States? I was even more discouraged, because I knew that in many ways the paradise was a hoax. I could not dream about economic security in America because, in America, I had no work lined up.

My money worries only increased after watching the evening news one night in the Cassion Hotel in Damascus. The anchorman reported on a disaster in my dear, far distant home: Black Monday, the largest US stock market crash since 1929. Would another Great Depression ensue?

I felt as though I had rowed a small boat out from shore, then looked back to see the entire North American continent sink into the sea.

9 – The Armenian Expulsion

If Syria's intellectuals wrestled with the implications of medieval Islamic civilization, this country's Armenians set their compasses by an event which occurred in 1915.

"The Armenians were massacred," said the owner of the Baron Hotel. "I use this term because the word 'killing' implies mercy. And the Turks showed no mercy."

Krekov "Coco" Mazlumian was an elderly Armenian who wore blue blazers, spoke Oxford English, and haunted the hotel's back offices. His father had built the Baron. "But why should I say this?" Coco continued. "You Americans know nothing of Armenians, and you don't really care."

"Not true," I said. "William Saroyan was a famous American writer. And Damon Runyon. The Armenians I know in America are very fine people. And a couple of weeks ago I was at the Hagop Hotel in Kassab. I spent an evening talking to Dickran, an Armenian teenager, a fourteen year old, who lived there with his aunt and uncle. He was a serious and likable young man, intent on emigrating to Ontario or Los Angeles where other family members had gone before. He had mastered Armenian, Arabic, and English, had a striving mentality, and I think he will be a tremendous success wherever he ends up."

"Yes, yes," said Coco. "Since the massacre our history has been one of movement—refugees, émigrés, always living in someone else's homeland."

"Dickran and I talked about his church," I continued. "I learned that Armenians have their own Patriarch of Antioch. Like the other Patriarchs of Antioch (the Greek Orthodox, the Syriac, and the Greek Catholic), the Armenian Patriarch now lives in Damascus." I counted the Patriarchs on my fingers as I spoke.

For centuries Armenians had protected the Christians of the Mediterranean from the Zoroastrian Persians, yet Christendom expressed

A Roman road near Bab al-Hawa.

slight gratitude. In 449 the Persians ruled that all inhabitants of lands under their control should worship Zoroaster. Instead, the Armenians decided to fight the superior Persian armies and were too busy fighting and dying to attend the council of Chalcedon in 451. In absentia they were judged to be heretics. Later, in a fit of remorse, the Byzantines and their Eastern Orthodox Church offered grudging approval of Armenian doctrine if the Armenians would hand over ownership and operation of all their churches and church-owned lands. The Armenians refused this deal, and their church has been independent ever since. In 1453 when the followers of Uthman (named for the third caliph to succeed Muhammad; the source of the name Ottoman) finally pushed the Byzantines out of Constantinople and renamed the city Istanbul, one supposes that few Armenians shed tears. Armenians were tolerated by the Ottomans until the massacres and expulsions began under the sultan Abdulhamid in 1894 and the Young Turks in 1915.

"On the expulsions," I said, "Dickran explained it to me this way: 'In the First World War,' he said, 'the sultan wanted to kill all the Armenians and leave only one and put him in a museum. And then he threw all Armenians out of Turkey. The Army put children in places and put gasoline on them and burned them. They left Armenians in the desert, no food, no water, and many died.'"

"That's right," Coco said. "And the year before, in 1914, the Turkish army had taken over our Baron Hotel for their headquarters. General Liman von Sanders, head of the German mission, stayed here as did Jamal Pasha, the Turkish general fighting on the Suez front.

"I remember one evening, the German general gave a banquet for Jamal Pasha who was visiting from the front. We made all kinds of splendid food and the banquet was a success. The next day Jamal Pasha asked my father to supply an equally grand banquet in honor of the German general and to serve the same food. When my father refused, Jamal Pasha was taken aback. Then my father said, 'I will not dishonor myself by serving the same food twice, but will provide a banquet far better.' Jamal Pasha was pleased with the results.

"Several years later, during the massacres, our entire family was ordered to leave for Mosul, the city in northern Iraq where thousands of Armenians were sent to their deaths. We were worried. But Jamal Pasha, who by now was stationed in Palestine, learned of the order and arranged for us to travel quickly to Jerusalem where he could protect us."

Others were less fortunate. Forced off their land in Turkey, they were herded south on foot down the Euphrates. At Dier ez-Zoir they were driven east, into the desert. As Sarkis, the desk clerk, explained it, "Fierce tribes on horseback killed them by the thousands, killed them with clubs so that they would not waste their bullets."

Another time I asked Coco how some Armenians had escaped the death march. "Some did not go down the Euphrates but turned right to the coast, to places like Kassab and farther down, to Lebanon. Others hid out in villages around Aleppo. One Armenian was a wheelwright, he made wheels for wagons and was rescued by Arab villagers in a town on the Euphrates. They thought the man would be useful to them. Those who did not hide or run were destroyed."

I mentioned to Coco that I was headed for the Roman Bridge. I'd be on the Turkish border and was thinking about making a day trip into Turkey. Was there anything worth seeing?

"Why go to Turkey?" Coco replied. "Three thousand years ago the Armenians were living there, a civilized people, when the Turks were still riding their horses in Central Asia. Then the Turks ran us out, forced us to begin again with nothing. The Turks descended from Tamerlane the Great and Genghis Khan. They plucked a few Slav women here, a few Armenian women there. But mostly they were Central Asians. Scratch, scratch, scratch a Turk and you'll find a bloody savage."

10 — Peasant Women

This was my day to visit Qalaat Samaan, also known as the Basilica of Saint Simon Stylites, one of the most popular tourist destinations in Syria—a magnet that, even in medieval times, had drawn visitors from as far away as England and Russia. Other guests at the Baron had aroused my curiosity about Qalaat Samaan. I had met two French stonemasons and a Vietnamese woman from San Francisco who was their photographer. The masons were union men, documenting early stonework techniques for an encyclopedia of crafts that their union was publishing. For their purposes, Qalaat Samaan was the most important of Syria's monuments. "Here is the first time," said the older mason, "that an arch is built from a scaled drawing."

My bus drove west for an hour across flat, cultivated earth to Bab al-Hawa on the Turkish border. Along the way we passed a stretch of ancient Roman road, still visible. Then we doubled back and took a side road to the town of Daret Aziz, a village surrounded by limestone hills sprinkled with Roman ruins. Hundreds of villages on these highlands had been abandoned during Ottoman times, no one knows exactly why, and now nothing was left but pediments and pillars of cut stone. The bus did not go all the way to Qalaat Samaan, so I hired a taxi for the last three or four miles to the ruins themselves.

The Basilica of Saint Simon (also known as Simeon) was a series of stone structures atop a rocky knoll that looked toward Antioch, the ancient Christian center. (As I've mentioned, the French gave this Syrian city to Turkey in 1939.) Some say that Qalaat Samaan was the largest Christian structure built before the great, European cathedrals of the Middle Ages. Qalaat Samaan was the original from which Citizen Hearst modeled his palace on the California coast.

On this day the sky was clear, the sun hot, and the rock had a pinkish cast and was warm and coarse-grained; "friendly rock" we had called it back in my climbing days. I walked through the ruins and checked out Simon's pillar, which once had been fifty feet tall. Simon spent thirty-six years living atop this pillar—night and day. Here, in full public view, he dictated letters to men of power, performed bodily functions, and bowed hundreds of times a day in prayer. Twice each day he preached to assembled pilgrims. Imitators sprang up in the surrounding hills and in Beirut, Constantinople, and on the far side of the Black Sea. Simon's pillar has steadily grown smaller since his death, as pilgrims have taken chunks home with them, and now it is about the height of a kitchen counter.

I stood atop stone rubble and looked west toward Antioch and north toward Alexandretta where, in 333 BC, Alexander defeated the Persian king, Darius III. After an hour at the monument I walked down to the parking lot, failed to catch a ride with another tourist heading into town, and began to walk across the valley to the nearest bus stop. It was a nice day, but I was getting nervous. If I missed my bus from Daret Aziz I would be stuck without a hotel—easy pickings for the secret police. I had walked about a mile when a tractor pulling a steel cart passed, then slowed and came to a halt. I thought that it was stopping for me, so I ran. As I caught up, however, I saw that the tractor had let off a passenger, but by now I was committed. I climbed atop the tire and swung over the steel wall of the cart as the driver pulled out.

Inside, packed tight, were thirty Bedouin women wearing rumpled clothes and plastic shoes. They cheered and made a small space for me on the steel floor. These were village women coming in from the fields—old women with arms curled around their knees, and young women on the tailgate with their legs dangling. One young woman had a gold tooth. Her hands were smeared with red earth.

We trundled along the highway, then turned up a dirt road toward a village on a hillside amidst Roman ruins, the remnants of a village that had been abandoned centuries ago and only recently resettled

The pillar of Saint Simon Stylites once had been fifty feet high.

241

Qalaat Samaan

by squatters who improvised dwellings that leaned against the ancient structures. "A village of the Druze," said one woman. The dirt road was rutted, the trailer lacked springs, and I put my hands beneath me to cushion the blows. As we drew near, the women started clapping in unison, and one made a trilling cry, a *zaghradah*, the same yell I had heard in the Cham Palace to the music of the *debka*. I clapped along with them, let loose my own trill, and they smiled and laughed (I did not realize that the *zaghradah* was for women, not men) and continued their chant.

We stopped, the passengers got out, and half disappeared into the village while the rest of us stretched for a few minutes before the journey resumed. Several older women offered an immense sandwich of flatbread and yogurt, and three young women offered something else. "Come," they said in Arabic, "stay with us tonight." An older woman was scandalized. "He is sleeping in Aleppo," she said in Arabic, "at the hotel." The young women weren't listening. This was their chance, a free trip to America. They continued to plead until the old woman became disgusted and turned her head. This time I wasn't going to act the fool. I followed the old woman's lead, turned my head, and soon the young women walked off to converse among themselves until the driver called us to climb aboard.

Qalaat Samaan was a beautiful piece of stone work, something that the masons and their Vietnamese photographer could document and preserve. But what of traditional life in an agricultural village?

For years, men and women had been abandoning Syria's villages to move to the city. This was especially true since World War II, when the Syrian nation came into being. This nation was an abstract, political entity that levied taxes, required military service, and defended strange, invisible boundary lines across the desert. The nation curtailed trade, gave jobs to bureaucrats and secret police, and broadcast TV news and entertainment. Of course the regime in power needed to have a constituency to maintain that power. And Hafez al-Assad's regime knew that city dwellers, most of them Sunnis, would never give whole-hearted support to Islamic minorities such as Asad and his fellow Alawites. So they courted rural folk, paved dirt roads, sent buses through the countryside, started schools, and broke up the feudal system that allowed city dwellers to own agricultural villages and their fields. Under the feudal system, you farmed the land as your parents and grandparents had done or you went hungry. When land passed to the people, to farm or not became a choice. Later I talked with a disenfranchised former landowner. "In the old days acres and acres were under cultivation. But now, no one wants to work the land and so the fields lie fallow. People would rather move to the big city and live by spreading a blanket on the sidewalk and selling cigarettes one at a time."

Even villages that had not lost their inhabitants, I supposed, had been changed by radio, television, and walkmans. The old virtues had become obsolete. The authority of the village headman, the authority of the elders, the lore passed down from parent to child—all had been altered or surpassed. Nowadays Syrian children, like their American counterparts, spent hours in front of the television where they learned the lore and language of their culture. Glory and power no longer lay entirely in the esteem of one's village. The man of authority was one who had been anointed by the world shown on television. He was a doctor or a soldier—a man of learning or a man with a gun.

The modern world pulled at the young. The closeness and intimacy of village life, a structure of classic lines and perfect joints, was in danger. Where was the photographer of the heart to document this life? Where were the craftsmen of blood to jot notes for their encyclopedia?

At my hotel I filled the tub, relaxed in the warm water, and allowed

An abandoned village near Qalaat Samaan.

my mind to go blank. I thought of the village women, their camara-
derie, their rummage-sale clothes, skirts and dresses worn over pants,
bits of straw sticking in sweaters and scarves. I wondered what would
become of them and their village. I thought of the three young women
who had been eager to meet a foreign man. Would they be willing to
spend the rest of their lives with red clay on their hands?

Years later, in Seattle, I asked Hasan the architect to tell me what
I'd seen.

"The women you met near Qalaat Samaan were *fellahin* or peasants,
very different from women in the cities."

"Traditionally, women in the cities did not work outside the home.
They were cloistered, protected from public view. When they traveled
in the city they wore scarves or veils. In old times it was different for
peasant women because they worked in the fields all day. So they
had far more freedom and were less restrained in public. Traditional
city women never would have flirted with you as the young peasant
women did. The *fellahin* women you met were among other women,
and were open and spontaneous.

"Of course, if their husbands and fathers had been there, the
situation would have been entirely different, very restrained and
subdued, and your contact would have been more formal—for certain the young women would not have invited you to stay the night,
even as teasing."

11 — Walid, the Writer

"Our villages are the treasure of Syria," said the writer. "We have cities, very modern, and people come from the villages to the cities because they want this modern life. Here it is dirty, noisy, overcrowded. What they get is not a good life. And so our national treasure is lost. And for what?"

Walid Ikhlassy was fifty-three years old and one of the finest novelists of the Arab world. He had also written short stories, plays, and essays. A large man for an Arab, Walid was clean-shaven, had a slight paunch, and was dressed neatly in a gray flannel suit. He was married with children, and he also had a job of some importance as an agricultural engineer—yet he was innocent and eager in conversation. I was honored that he had agreed to meet. Certainly no writer of comparable stature in my country would have done the same. But I was a friend of Hasan the architect, and in Aleppo writers and artists were close.

As Walid and I took our table in the cafe of the Siyahi Hotel, a radio gave a news report. "Something important," said Walid. "Iran says it will launch the great war soon."

"What do they call the war they have now?" I asked.

"This is simply a practice war. Iran is always preparing for the Great War."

"What do you think about Islamic fundamentalism?" I asked. "In the United States we think Muslims want a *jihad*, to sacrifice themselves to God and kill us in the process."

"When religion guides the state," said the writer, "it makes a problem. I think we should be free to believe as we wish, not to hurt anyone."

We were sitting near the large windows that enclosed the hotel's ground floor. Each slab of glass had its own poster of the Syrian president, the largest had two posters. There were not enough posters on our window, however, to keep the sun from streaming in and falling across Walid's shoulder. He rose and closed the curtain behind him,

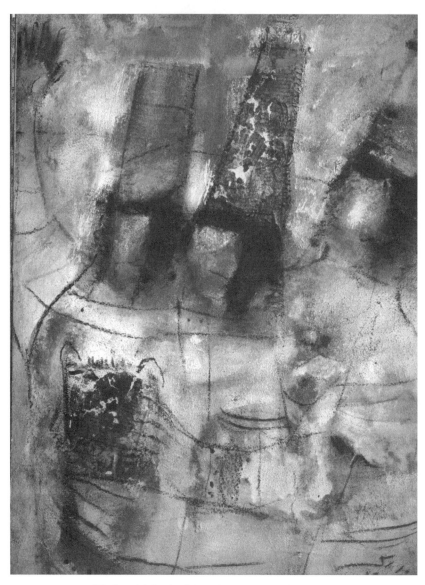

The Dervish by Fateh Moudarres. (Original in color.)

then we ordered espresso from the waiter. When it was served, we
sweetened it with cube sugar.

"What is the source of your work?" I asked.

"Always you need location. But notice that, within one place, you
are writing about the whole world. Also, I depend on my dreams.
Ideas come during dreams. I have no plan, no agenda for writing. I
start with a dream. I write, and the characters come smoothly, otherwise I cannot continue. My own mind is very little organized. But

during writing surely I am another man." Walid paused, and looked down at his small cup. Then he lifted it to his lips and emptied it in two long sips.

"Do you begin with an Arab or an Islamic consciousness?"

"In my normal life I am grounded in the Quran and the great Islamic tradition. As a writer, however, I am a different man. Always, there is a ready-made culture that we are supposed to accept as it is. But I'm for something new, something positive. God is inventing the future, not just the past."

"What does that mean?" I asked. "'Inventing the future not just the past.' You mean that worshipping the past is not the only thing to do? That God can create something equally good in the future? That the Islamic tradition that was great in the past can be great in the future as well?"

"Right," said Walid. "If everything were perfect, there would be no need for art. But the world is not perfect. Art is our effort to make a change in history. I have admired Arabic writers and philosophers from Egypt who shared in the modern Arabic renaissance during the 1930s and 1940s. They confronted the idiot thinking of the past.

"We need brave, intellectual people. Many in Islamic countries are afraid, so they only repeat the past. Those who are courageous and try new ways give us the power to think."

Our table was small and the feet were improperly adjusted so that, as I scribbled notes on pink cards, the table rocked back and forth. By now Walid had gotten tired of talking about himself.

"What is your object in coming to Syria?" he asked.

"I want to collect the thoughts of people from this culture," I said, "and put them into a book of ideas. I want to write about Syria as a way of writing about the world. In Tartus I met a teacher. 'Syria,' he said, 'is the entire world in a single, small place.'"

"Yes," said Walid. "In Syria and especially here in Aleppo we have many cultures—the Kurdish tribesmen, the Bedouins, the Syriac Christians, the Armenians, the Turks."

"And in Masyaf I met a young man who they say is the second wisest person in that town. He suggested that I write a philosophy from my trip, something like Heidegger. The Ismailis love philosophy, but it's too bloodless for me, so I am thinking more of a travel book like *Gulliver's Travels* or *The Canterbury Tales*, except that in my version I am trying to reach the Roman Bridge."

"These are good models," said Walid, "but you need a plan, a design, and a way to execute the design."

"If you take a map of Syria," I said, "and draw a line on it that represents my route, the map becomes a chart—not simply of a place, but of a consciousness."

"And what of the villages and towns and monuments that you visit?" said the writer.

"Each of them becomes an idea in the larger mind. So that the map of my travel is a way of structuring and linking ideas, of putting them in relation to one another. And when it's done you have a totality, a whole. That would be a lot more fun than keeping track of Heidegger's theorems."

"This is an ambitious project," said Walid. "If you are ever to succeed, you must meet more people, not simply village philosophers, but the finest artists of our culture. Painters, for example. We have excellent painters here in Aleppo. Fateh Moudarres is from here and now lives in Damascus. He has studied in France, exhibited all over the world, won many awards. He is regarded as one of the foremost painters in the Arab world. Many red and brown colors go through his work, for this is the soul of our people, the red earth of the villages, the soil from which we spring. Fateh Moudarres himself came from the village of Afrin, north of Aleppo. You should see the work of Fateh Moudarres, and go to the villages and see the red soil that gives him inspiration."

When our conversation eventually wound down, I thanked Walid and returned to the Baron. That evening I met Zouhair the sculptor at his favorite restaurant. I asked about the artist Fateh Moudarres, and it turned out that he and Zouhair were old friends. "A great man," said Zouhair. "He spent hours talking with me when I was in college, guiding me, nurturing me as an artist. An inspiration."

Zouhair was the one Syrian who was utterly sincere when he complimented Fateh Moudarres. The painter's widely acknowledged success had spawned a distinct strain of humor. Among Syria's intelligentsia, a favorite thing to do was to poke fun at this man. They loved him and also kidded him without mercy—a favor which the painter was quick to return. "Fateh is a dreamer and visionary," Hasan the architect told me later. "Still, he does not always separate fiction from fact. And his studio is filled to the ceiling with junk, especially the piano."

"On Monday," Zouhair said, "I'll be in Damascus on business. Why not come down? I'll introduce you to Fateh Moudarres."

Did it bother me that Moudarres was in Damascus? You bet. The trip south would make spaghetti of my route to the Roman Bridge and would ruin the symmetry of the book I was trying to write. Still, I had to meet Fateh Moudarres. He was the next bread crumb on the path I was following, the path which seemed to be leading me deeper and deeper into the psyche of the Syrian people and propelling me steadily toward the Roman Bridge.

On the Sunday afternoon before my meeting with Fateh Moudarres I caught a bus to Damascus and took a taxi to Saad's farm. When I arrived, it was cold and dark and there was no food at the farmhouse. For dinner I nibbled a coconut bar which I had saved. At ten o'clock I walked across the compound to see the Eritrean caretakers. Their single room was warm, but thick with smoke. I crouched to get under the haze and located an empty olive oil bucket where they were burning sticks for warmth. At this lower elevation there was air to breathe, warmth from the fire, and even a TV set. Askia sat on the floor, and his friend was tucked into bed. We watched Arabic dancers, then an old Australian cowboy movie. For some reason, I felt that I had come home.

12 — Fateh, the Painter

DAMASCUS. MONDAY, NOVEMBER 16.

Fateh Moudarres was a slight man who stumbled in the darkness and clutter of his low-ceilinged *atelier,* located in the embassy district. Fateh's digs consisted of several basement rooms filled with knick-knacks and featured an upright piano festooned with photos, coffee mugs, and ashtrays. He was preparing for an exhibition to be held December 25 in Aleppo, a one-man show. He needed to create thirty paintings, which calculated out to five per week or about one per day if you allowed time for drying and crating before the show. When I looked into his paint room, however, I saw only one finished canvas, and it was done in tones of green rather than red as the writer had promised. Zouhair the sculptor had told me that Fateh Moudarres always painted three canvases at once. Standing beside the green painting were two blank canvases, covered with white primer, ready for the master's brush.

Fateh Moudarres, however, seemed more interested in entertaining visitors.

"I hope we are not interrupting," I said as Zouhair introduced us.

Sartre and Moudarres.

"No my dear," replied Fateh Moudarres. "I must make you some coffee, and then you can tell me about your tour of Syria." As Fateh searched the debris for cups, coffee, and sugar, Zouhair excused himself. Already Fateh Moudarres was babbling as though he had known me for years. "You must see Syria slowly," he said. "If you go quickly you will see nothing. But if you go slowly you will see it all."

I told him of my desire to reach the Roman Bridge at the far tip of Syria. "al-Jazira," said Fateh. "We call this *jazira* or island because it is an island of desert and steppe surrounded on one side by the Euphrates, on the other by the Tigris. This land still is ancient—the people are very poor and live the way all of us in the villages lived centuries ago. Jazira is an old place and also bizarre, filled with Kurdish tribes and strange Christian people, the last surviving clans of ancient heretics. Not many Westerners travel this way. Something keeps them out, I think. They get the headache, the stomachache, and they always go another way, to Aleppo or Palmyra. Probably you will not go to Jazira, but if you do the place will put a mark on your soul like a mark of birth that will last until you die."

I mentioned Walid Ikhlassy, the writer from Aleppo.

"Ah," said Fateh. "This Walid speaks much. Sometimes he says things that are worth hearing."

Fateh Moudarres mixed coffee and told the story of how he had met Jean-Paul Sartre one night in Rome. Fateh had been a young man on scholarship and in the late hours rescued a drunk whom he found staggering in the street, took him back to his *atelier*, and made him spaghetti. Jean Paul Sartre returned every day during his two-week visit, ate more spaghetti, met the painter's friends, and came to admire his painting and also his poetry, some of which Sartre translated into French. Fateh Moudarres and his friends told Sartre about the Palestinians. The philosopher later saw similar abuses in Algeria and wrote an article critical of the French government's dealings with that country. "Come to Paris," Sartre told Fateh Moudarres. "I will make you famous."

"But I never came to Paris," said Fateh, "not for nine more years until I went to get my doctorate. By then Sartre had adopted a Jewish girl and thought of Arabs as the enemy. So it was not the same, and he did not make me famous. Years later, when I was in Paris again, I saw Sartre at a magazine stand buying tobacco. He was old, almost blind, and I felt sorry for him. Sartre was a good man, a funny man."

Fateh's wife came in and introduced herself and made a place to sit while her husband rustled around in search of coffee. I asked about her husband's other successes. She told me how he had won a grand prize for a painting in an exhibition in Florida. "We were very proud," she said, "until the painting returned and we unpacked it and found that it had been hung upside down." By now Fateh had resumed his seat as his wife's coffee warmed.

"Walid the writer says that the red earth and village life are in your painting," I said.

"This is true," said Fateh Moudarres, "but also my mother. I wrote a poem about my mother." He found a photo of the two of them. She was in black, small and wrinkled. They were sitting on a stone bench, his arm around her. "Sometimes I say of her, my sister or my daughter," said Fateh. "I say this because I love her."

"That is the sadness of his life," Fateh's wife said, "that he was kept from his mother those many years, never knew her until later. She was a young woman, a Kurd—and you know we Arabs have

Fateh's mother

always thought of Kurds as thieves and beggars. His father was an aristocrat of an old and wealthy Arab family with houses in Aleppo and villages to the north, villages with peasants and many lands. After Fateh was born his father died, from an accident they say. This was in the late 1920s. The father was progressive and gave money to the politics of change. He gave family money and others in his family were jealous. The French authorities did not want his money going to the independence movement. Politics, I think, was behind his accident. Also, of course, his brother."

"How old was Fateh when his father was killed?" I asked.

"He was two and a half years old," his wife replied. "And then he was taken from his mother for many years until he cried so much that they gave him back to her when he was ten years old. But no money. Fateh lived again with his mother, but they were very poor."

"What kind of accident killed Fateh's father?" I asked. "A car accident?"

"No, an accident with a gun."

"What do you mean?"

"His brother shot him in the head."

13 — The Poetry of Fateh Moudarres

On Wednesday morning I met Saad Shalabi at his office, and we checked next door for the Christian lawyer. He was not in, so that meant that my effort to locate the Patriarch of Antioch was still on hold. Which was too bad but, at the moment, I was curious about something else. The painter Fateh Moudarres had given me a copy of the poem that he had written about his mother. At the top was a photo of a fierce-looking old woman wearing a scarf. I asked Saad to translate from the Arabic.

"My Sick Mother," Saad read. "Now I see the light smile on your face from the ID picture / As for the eyes, there is a wall of glass between them and me. / Your hair is not completely white, and your chin is a piece of gold. / I wish I held it in my hand to touch my heart . . ." Saad stopped reading and puckered his lips as if he had been sucking a lemon.

"This is terrible," he said, "too sentimental. I can read no farther."

Now that he had dispensed with the painter-poet, Saad tackled my current travel problem: my travel permit would expire in a few days, and I didn't want to go for another interview with the immigration police. What if he kicked me out of the country? "An idea," said Saad. "Take a bus over the border into Jordan for the day. When you return the border police will stamp your passport again. You will get another fifteen days on your permit."

I took Saad's advice and returned in time to meet Fateh Moudarres.

14 — Green Canvas

DAMASCUS. THURSDAY, NOVEMBER 19.

When I reached Fateh's *atelier*, no one answered my knock, but the door was open, so I walked in. In the paint room the green canvas was still drying, the two blank canvases were still a pristine white. I found Fateh in the next room, on the phone. He motioned me to sit, but every possible sitting place was stacked with books and ashtrays. I cleared a space on the sofa.

When Fateh finished his phone call I offered him gifts of sugar and instant coffee.

"No, no, my dear," said Fateh Moudarres. "You must save your money, otherwise you will have none, and I will have to help you."

I asked Fateh what advice he had for the painters of America.

"There must be a bridge from the person within to the beauty of humanity," Fateh replied, "—not the ugliness, but the beauty of soul, the face, life, women, poetry, science. We call it beaux-arts. Real

American art should not be an imitation of Cézanne. One must paint from one's own influence—not that of the art schools—so that we can enrich the art of the world."

"In Seattle," I said, "the big corporations have high rise office buildings with immense lobbies. They use art to cover up blank walls. It's merely decoration, so what's the point?"

"Art," Fateh replied, "gives humanity a sense of honor."

As a leading Syrian artist, Fateh Moudarres sometimes did favors for the government. On the following Monday, for example, Fateh had agreed to visit a small town just north of Aleppo to judge the artistic merit of a statue of President Asad. He invited me to join him, and we made plans to meet. In the meantime I wanted to know more about Fateh Moudarres, so I decided to visit the countryside near Aleppo where Fateh had grown up. That afternoon I caught a ride back to Aleppo and the Baron Hotel.

15 — People of the Red Earth

ALEPPO. SUNDAY, NOVEMBER 22.

After breakfast I caught a bus to Afrin, one of many outlying villages owned by Fateh Moudarres's family until the Baath party came to power and land reform set in. This excursion wasn't my idea, really, but the writer Walid had convinced me. I was going to Afrin to better understand Fateh Moudarres. I wanted, as Walid had put it, to "find the soul of the Syrian people" in the red earth of Fateh Moudarres's village—an embarrassing, romantic notion, I admit, but I was comforted by the thought that no one else need ever know.

Afrin was situated on the side of a gentle ridge overlooking a small, cultivated valley with sharp knobby hills protruding here and there. According to my tourist map, one of these hills supported a Byzantine castle, but today I just wanted a view of the land itself. My bus arrived in the town square at one o'clock in the afternoon. Walking up the main street, I passed small shops and looked through open doorways to see men weaving flat rugs on ancient looms made from poles and twisted rope.

At the crest of the ridge I sat and rested and looked out at the valley. The earth in the valley bottom was black and rich but here, on the hillside, it was a pale red color. The scenery was nice but the people of this town, who were Kurds, turned away when I greeted them. Later I learned why.

I walked back toward the town square. When I passed a tiny candy store, the proprietor, a big beefy guy of about thirty, blocked my path and made a violent hacking motion. "Police," he said. "I am police." My stomach got tight, yet I was not entirely convinced. "I am police, I can throw you in the prison and slap you around, and you be crying for mercy," he said, half in English, half pantomime. I handed him my passport, whereupon he motioned me into his store and blocked my exit. I was his prisoner. He gave me a small hard candy in cellophane wrapper. That was the formula: terrify the tourists, then display your generosity. He read my passport carefully, though I noticed that he was holding it upside down. When he had finished, he closed it in his big, meaty hand and began to interrogate me. "Who do you come to see?" he said. "Names! Names! How long since you come from Israel? Carpets! Why do you wish to buy our carpets? Only to smuggle them from the country!"

Since the secret police in Syria did not wear uniforms, how could I know for certain who the guy was? After a while it occurred to me that the *mukhabarat*, if nothing else, had a sense of their own dignity. A member of the *mukhabarat* never would go undercover as a mere candy store operator. I grabbed my documents, wormed my way past my captor, and bid him adieu. Just then a swarthy looking man on a motorcycle pulled up.

"Police," he said. "I am the police." He looked a lot more official than half the people who had stopped me thus far on my trip. He did not have a weapon, but neither had the black-suited mountain mayor with dandruff on the bus to Safita or that man in the sports coat on the island of Arwad.

"You can't be police," I said and pointed at the big guy from the store. "He's the police." I looked over at the kids and at an old woman who had come to buy something. "Are all of you police?"

The guy insisted, however, so I handed over my passport. At least he read it right side up. "Washington," he said as he handed it back. Then he spoke to the candy man in Arabic, to the effect that perhaps they should arrest me. I was getting tired of this and the children crowding around were curious, not terrified, so I knew that these guys were impostors. I snatched my passport and began to leave. Then the man on the motorcycle ordered me to get on the back of his motorbike so that he could be a good host and give me a tour. Intimidation and generosity, the tactic of people who enjoyed the exercise of power. "These guys are the detritus at the bottom of a police state," I thought. "When do they get to exercise power? Only when a hapless tourist stumbles along."

I declined the tour and walked away. As I turned the corner to the main street which led to the bus stop I picked up the pace. I wanted to run, but that would have attracted too much attention. I needed to get on the bus to Aleppo before any other guardians of public order decided to detain me. I was in sight of the bus stop now, a block away, then half a block away.

"*Qiff! Qiff!*" I heard. Stop! Stop!

"Someone's shouting," I thought. "I wonder what that's about?" I resisted the tendency to turn and check out the commotion, just in case I was the object. "I might still slip through," I thought. I was just a few feet from the bus now. Something startled me, and I looked up: two men with AK-47s blocked my path. One was tall and angry-looking and seemed to be in charge. He made the hacking motion. I handed over my passport and prepared to wait while he examined it. But he slipped my passport into his pocket. "*Mukhabarat* in a hurry," I thought, "an ominous development."

"*Idkhil al-sayyarah,*" my captor ordered, Get in the truck. His companion motioned with his machine gun toward their rusty Toyota pickup. I was pretty sure that these guys did not run a candy store. I squeezed into the front, the lieutenant rode in the back. We drove a few blocks to an unmarked concrete building, crude and dark, concrete walls, unlit cells with brown stains on the walls and floors. Bloodstains? Then my captors, the tall one in front, the lieutenant behind, led me up two flights of stairs until we reached an office with a window that admitted shady light. My escorts stood to each side in a quick, formal movement, military precision, parade ground showmanship. They were reporting. They were presenting their captive, a dangerous spy from America. My captors looked straight ahead and said nothing.

I faced the window and, before it, a gray steel desk. Behind the desk, outlined against the window, fierce and strong, was a man with a shaved head, a man whose face was in shadow.

I had thoughts about the way that this man was dressed. In this country where children wore identical smocks from the earliest grades, uniforms were scorned as the mark of the ordinary. The higher the rank of an individual, the more casual the dress. My captors had been dressed informally in blue jeans and army jackets, which was a bad sign. My stomach had been jumping around a bit and it only got worse when I saw that the man who sat before the window was dressed very casually indeed. He wore a bright blue jogging suit with white trim.

One of my captors handed over my passport, and their chief examined it slowly. His face was large and fleshy, his eyes small, darting. At last he sighed and looked at me. "How long since you came from Israel?" he asked in English.

"I, well, I've never been to Israel," I mumbled.

"How many friends you have in Afrin? Names! Please, it will be easier if you give me the names." This was a great chance to repay the candy store owner for his hospitality, but I did not have his name.

"Sorry," I said, shaking my head. "I don't know anyone here."

"Carpets! You have come to Afrin to buy carpets! Women! You want our women! Tell us, why are you here in Afrin?"

"I came to look at the scenery," I said. This sounded lame. My captor, the tall one who still carried his AK-47, puckered his lips at my lack of creativity. Couldn't the American invent a lie that was a little more plausible? The headman looked at me with a blank expression, as though waiting for me to say more. My captor glanced at me and offered a single sound, a sucking sound between his tongue and the roof of his mouth. *"Tch!"* he said. Then he looked at the floor. I was his catch, he had paraded me with pride, and now I was turning out to be not much of a prize. I felt that I had let him down.

The *mukhabarat,* like other government officials, were recruited from Syria's traditional underclass. Now they had power but little respect. So their dealings with an American became a way of asserting status. I needed to show them that I took them seriously. I needed to feed them a flagrant or ingenious lie. My statement was pedestrian, an insult to their *rujoolah,* their manhood, but I could think of nothing better. And still, it was a vast improvement on the truth.

The headman sighed once more. He had given me the chance to upgrade my story and regretted that I was making such a poor showing, but he could wait no longer. He jotted down my response on a piece of white paper, clipped it to my passport, and placed my passport in an envelope which he licked, sealed, and placed on the table. And now for more serious business. The headman's face became rigid. He stood quickly and spoke rapid, clipped lines to my captors who stiffened at their posts. "It's happening," I thought. He strode across the room, closed the door behind him: I was alone with two silent men and their automatic rifles.

I heard a noise at the door, scratching and bumping. "It's the headman," I thought, "returning with some kind of paraphernalia." I decided to run. I wanted to be outside where there were witnesses, but my captors grimaced and fingered their weapons, and it struck me that they were waiting for an excuse, that they wanted me to make a move. Then the door swung open, and it was the headman, his face angry and red and dripping sweat, and I tensed and started to move, but those weapons! I slumped back in my chair, looked at the floor, then I heard a clattering noise and looked up. The headman carried in his hands—what was this?—a tray with four small teacups and a steaming samovar. He set the tray on his desk and, now that he was no longer in danger of spilling, his face regained its normal color, the lines of strain relaxed, and he looked at me with a slight smile. *"Chai?"* he asked.

After our tea party the headman explained that my offense was serious, and I would have to be interrogated at police headquarters downtown. I still didn't know what my offense was, but decided to go along with the program. He handed the envelope with my passport to another man who motioned me to follow. Driving to town in a new Suzuki, we listened to a station that broadcast Western music. A few miles down the road I was surprised to hear the strains of "Yankee Doodle Dandy." "This," said the radio announcer, "is the Voice of America."

At the immense, concrete headquarters in Aleppo I was tortured by guards who forced me to sit alone in a windowless cell and watch Lassie reruns on TV. My suffering only increased when I considered that the guards thought that they were being hospitable. At last, just as Lassie was swimming to retrieve the canoe paddle before her master was swept over a waterfall, the chief inquisitor called. I went into another room, sat in a straight-backed chair and then, as the questioning was to begin, the inquisitor realized that his subordinate had gone to dinner—and taken my passport with him. What prestige to carry an American passport! After the subordinate was located and chastised, the inquisitor had nothing but charm left for me. "Ah, you are from Washington," he said. "My brother is in Washington. Two months ago he got his green card. Here in Aleppo we have a big party to celebrate, the whole family." Still, he was curious about one thing. "Why didn't your wife come with you?" he asked.

"I didn't think she'd like the way you treat tourists," I said. The guy winced and tears came to his eyes. He turned away from me and began dabbing with a handkerchief. Great. So now I felt guilty for having hurt the feelings of the secret police. You never could win. "I'll bring her next time," I said. "She's never seen anything like this country. The hospitality of Syrians has been quite unusual."

With these words my inquisitor recovered his composure enough to jot down my answers to a dozen questions. I waited an hour for forms to be drawn up, then signed my confession in triplicate. Yet something still blocked my release: I would have to pass a more rigorous exam before the director. An hour later a short, fierce-looking man in a blue suit arrived, examined the documents, and explained that in a situation this serious justice could not be obtained through normal procedures.

"You see this coin," he said as he held a half-lira piece for me to inspect. One side had an eagle, the other side the number 50. "I will flip, you call." The coin came up eagle for me, three out of five, and I was free to go.

16 — The Bust

ALEPPO. MONDAY, NOVEMBER 23.
Two days later I met Fateh Moudarres in Aleppo at the Brazil Cafe. Fateh had a rasping cough.

"These cigarettes," said Fateh. "I must stop with these cigarettes."

Fateh had brought a friend, a government minister with bushy hair and a mouth with more gaps than teeth. The minister was a tough guy.

"Last week," he said, "Fateh and I visited three villages whose mayors wanted to build statues. We cut them off here." The minister motioned across his neck. That was his way of saying that the proposals had been killed. As the minister continued to speak I realized that the statue we would judge today in the village of Azaz had not yet been built. The mayor of Azaz could proceed only if Fateh Moudarres and the culture minister certified that it possessed artistic merit.

We left the Brazil Cafe and found a shared taxi (called a service taxi) that ran back and forth to Azaz—just a few miles from Afrin, the town of red earth where the secret police had detained me two days earlier. Our taxi was a '53 De Soto with two back seats, a diesel engine, and a Plymouth hood ornament. Twenty minutes out of town Fateh stopped the taxi so that I could see the monument where, in 1918, the last battle of World War I had been fought between Allenby's British troops from Egypt and the Ottoman Turks.

The flat land was punctuated with small hills that seemed to be aligned. "The Romans built hills," said Fateh, "and put signal fires on top."

I was more curious about modern history, especially the habit, peculiar to this country, of erecting statues of Hafez al-Asad.

"What are you looking for in good public sculpture?" I asked.

"Form is most important," said Fateh Moudarres. "The anatomy must be correct, the proportions. A good public sculpture must have the common sense of the people.

"It is hard," he continued. "You have a standing figure, you put the arms this way, that way. There is not much you can do, and these things are terribly expensive, though smaller pieces, like busts of President Asad, are far more reasonable. Yet none of the mayors wants a bust. They all want full statues. You tell me why. And the government money that is wasted, well, couldn't that be better used to sponsor art exhibitions in Damascus or Aleppo?"

Fateh worked a string of green prayer beads in his right hand. The minister of culture had white prayer beads in his left hand. Even some Christians—for example Jade whom I had met in

Dreykish—carried these beads (as a Christian, Jade called them worry beads). They had become a national habit.

Aside from public sculpture, what about Fateh Moudarres? "How did you become a painter?" I asked.

"At eleven or twelve I started painting," said Fateh. "I didn't know how to mix the paints. I used kerosene—the wrong kind of oils. Reds turned brown, whites gray, yellows green. I asked a local painter how to mix paints but he refused to talk. 'This is my secret,' he said. Then a Syrian painter who had studied in Rome came to Aleppo and taught us."

We passed fields with women planting. I had yet to see a man working in the fields, though men did drive tractors. "An experiment with winter wheat," said Fateh.

"Your family did not approve of your father's marriage," I said.

"No. He was an aristocrat. His family had many lands. Our village near Afrin had a thousand hectares, another near the Kileh river was smaller. She was a commoner, a Kurdish tribeswoman. They met when she moved from Turkey—the Kurds are always moving about—into an area where my father was working."

"Did it ever occur to you that you had this burst of creativity—your first painting—when you were reunited with your mother?"

"It's true. I was living in Aleppo but I insisted on being with my mother, and, finally, they brought her from Turkey. My father's mother came to live with us, too—she was saddened by the death of her son. We had no place to live so we rented a small house. I painted by candlelight to save money on kerosene. The family took everything. The family was living high, and we were poor."

"So your father's brother shot your father?" I asked.

"No, his father shot him," Fateh said. "My grandfather hired bandits to shoot him, like out West in your country."

We arrived in Azaz, and Fateh and the minister went into conference with the mayor and his aides while a member of the local secret police gave me a tour of the town on his motorcycle. Today I was on the side of the law. Three hours later the mayor emerged, looking pale. The minister of culture had a wicked smile on his face, and I guessed that it had not gone well for the locals. We piled into a Land Rover and drove to Kafrjanneh, a village which featured cafes and restaurants on the highway to Afrin. We pulled in at a roadhouse where we were the only guests. Our meal of many courses lasted until dark.

The food was good, but I nibbled with caution at two delicacies: river eel and sheep's brain with split tongue. Near the end of the meal Fateh picked up an eel, nothing left but the head, spine, and tail. The eel's chin jutted forward, and its top lip lifted up like a trash can lid.

"You've got it upside down," I said.

"No," said Fateh. "It's not a shark. I used to catch these from the river when I was a child."

"Which river was that?" I asked.

"The Qweg River. It's in one of my stories, the one about a Kurdish girl. I'll have to give you a copy. Many of my stories happened in this area. They all are tales I heard when I was growing up. Each year in the spring and summer I came from Aleppo to the village near the Qweq River to live. The goat's milk and especially the sheep's milk in the spring were very sweet and good for children. I knew the girl—she actually spoke the words that she says in my story. For example she passes the tomb of a Kurdish saint near the river and there is a tree beside the tomb. So she says to the saint, 'Oh you holy man who is dead, why are there no fruits on your tree?' And in another place she says to the little frog in the river, 'I love you. Is there a lot to eat in there, little frog?' These are her words.

"We were the same age, and many afternoons we went to the river together. I was in the area when the sad ending of the story took place."

We were cleaning up the meal. I was happy to act the part of a dignitary, feasted at government expense in a restaurant with salmon-colored table cloths and matching cloth napkins. I had a hard time believing that, two days earlier, I had been detained by the police in a town only ten minutes down the road.

By now the culture minister, who had been drinking an especially potent, clear beverage called Arak, was nearly under the table. Fateh told how a Chinese diplomat visiting Damascus had mistaken the culture minister for a fellow countryman, and the minister had played along. The minister gave us a few lines in a pidgin Chinese of his own creation, a dialect that had mystified the diplomat. Fateh and I laughed, the mayor and his entourage smiled. Things were degenerating. Fateh Moudarres stood and emptied a tray of pistachio nuts into his coat pocket.

We moved to a second table for oranges and apples. During the meal, conversation had been personal, convivial, no business. Now, the laughing stopped and no one spoke. Something

Women washing clothes.

serious was at stake, the prestige of the mayor and his men, stuck in an ordinary town with little hope of advancement. I had missed the negotiations from earlier in the day, but I got the gist of it from Fateh's remarks on the drive from the town hall to this restaurant. The mayor and his guys wanted a bronze statue and bigger was better. I realized now that Fateh and his "Chinese" friend had not intended to judge the artistic merit of the design, not really. They had been dispatched by the regime to put the kibosh on the statue, to satisfy the locals but to spend as little as possible in the process. President Asad had better things to spend money on than a statue in some decrepit border town.

I sat next to Fateh Moudarres. The mayor took a chair across from us, positioning himself for a final plea but saying nothing. Fateh waited a few minutes, then drew the figure of the president on a paper placemat. The mayor looked at the drawing and then at me. He seemed confident now but kept his silence. Fateh Moudarres put down his pen, slowly peeled his orange, and then put one section at a time into his mouth. When he had finished, the mayor was still looking at him. Fateh lifted his pen and made a swift, cutting stroke, drawing a line through the statue at the chest. The mayor winced, as though his own body had been cut in two.

"You should think about a bust," said Fateh Moudarres in languid, lucid Arabic. "A bust we might approve."

17— Circassians

I wanted to read the story that Fateh had written. He had given me a copy, in French, and Sarkis the desk clerk at the Baron had offered to translate. One morning at breakfast Sarkis gave me his report.

"This is the story of a little Kurdish girl named Alo. She lived in the north near the Turkish border, in a village on the Qweq River which the Turks, in defiance of international conventions, have since cut off and used for irrigation. The father has previously fallen into the river and drowned, although they never recovered the body. The girl's mother is sick, and appeals to their landlord for the medicine she needs to be well. He is a wealthy Arab who doesn't think much of Kurds, so he refuses. Then the mother asks the daughter to pick some mint to make tea for her to drink to recover her health.

"Alo walks across the countryside until she comes to the river and finds a place where the current is strong and the growth is rich. She sees a mint growing at the edge of the water, reaches for it, and falls in."

"That's the end of the story?" I asked.

"That's the end."

"What's the point of it?"

"The injustice of the landlord, the misery of the family, the description of the countryside—very local."

"That's nice," I said. "So simple, mythic, profound."

"I wouldn't say so," said Sarkis. "It's not very convincing that such a small girl would know the words put into her mouth. They seem simple in translation, but the French words are obscure." Sarkis picked up the xeroxed text, then began to narrate the story and to quote the dialogue.

"The girl Alo gets close to the river and sees women on the riverbank who are finishing their laundry.

"'Hey, little one,' a woman says, 'are there any men on the bank of the river?'

"Another woman calls. 'Alo, you should go back to your mother, little albino.' In Arabic the word 'albino' is a derogatory term, as the author tells us, which was used in medieval times to refer to lepers.

"Another woman says, 'What are you coming here for, little devil? Don't you know that the water is deep? Do you want to follow your father?'

"Another woman screams at her, 'Hello, little one, what are you looking for? You'll die if you stay like that in this harsh sun.'

"Alo replies to the women, 'I want a stem of mint for my mother who is sick.' But by now the women have left and the girl is alone. Alo sees some mint at the edge of the river. 'There are some big fish here behind the mint,' she says. Then she sees some frogs in the water who croak, 'Come on. Come on.' She talks to the frogs, then jumps into the water, even though she cannot swim. As she is carried away she screams 'Mama!' Her mother is not present and her father is dead. But they nevertheless reply to her.

"'Take my hand, Alo, sweetheart,' her mother says.

"'Grab some plants to hang onto, Alo, my little one,' her father shouts.

"Very sentimental," Sarkis concluded. "If you ask me, it's not a good story at all."

Sarkis the desk clerk had no use for Fateh Moudarres and his artistic pretensions, and he hoped that I would leave the painter out of my book. Sarkis assumed that I was writing a book, because all the English and Americans who stayed at the Baron Hotel were writing books—you could see them at breakfast jotting notes, then throwing napkins over their note pads when they thought that they were in danger of being spotted. Sarkis hoped that I would include the part about the Armenian massacres, of course, but there was one other subject which he required as well.

"The Cherkas," he said. "You must see the Cherkas, a magnificent people intertwined with the history of this region. You call them Circassians. They are from the Caucasus Mountains, now in the Soviet Union, where they once had their own republic. They say that Cherkas are born on the back of a horse—such horsemen and bravery and skill in fighting the world has never seen."

"They sound like Genghis Khan," I said.

"No," Sarkis replied. "The Khans were Mongols, bloody savages from the high deserts to the east. The Cherkas were warriors, only more civilized and with brilliant costumes. For four hundred years, whenever things got bad in their mountains, whenever the Tsars closed the fist too tight, the Cherkas came south, whole families and tribes.

"They have very fair skin and look like Europeans, yet they converted to Islam and settled here on the desert. Forty years ago you still could see them in Aleppo, walking the streets in their native

The Aleppo citadel had been built by the son of Saladin in 1290.

costume. Even before that, of course, the cream of the Cherkas warriors had come south to work as mercenaries or as slave warriors to the great kings of Egypt. The palace guard of King Hussein of Jordan is Cherkas to this day.

"When the Communist Revolution came, the Cherkas declared independence and were happy to be free of the Tsars, but then the Red Army invaded and brought the area back into the empire. In World War II when the Nazis invaded, the Cherkas convinced them that, as Muslims, Cherkas were not Communists. So the Nazis liked them. But when the Communists regained control the Cherkas paid the price—and more moved south. Unlike Armenians, they are becoming assimilated very quickly now, their language dying out. You must meet some Cherkas."

Saad Shalabi had told me a story of the Cherkas, perhaps the only small victory in the military embarrassment of 1967. "In the midst of battle," Saad explained, "we needed to communicate over the radio, but how could we? The Israelis were listening in and had broken our very most secret codes—nothing was too tough for them. What to do? Each of our units had a Cherkas in uniform, and one of them spoke up. The two men simply talked in their native tongue, and the Israeli code-breakers were utterly bamboozled."

I remembered stories by the young Tolstoy about the dashing horsemen of the Caucasus, a people the more mysterious for being buried in an immense continent far from Western eyes. An Armenian would know the true story, I reasoned, for the Armenians had shared the highlands with the Cherkas. The two civilizations must have come in contact slowly, over centuries. The Armenians fought the Cherkas, or perhaps they had made common cause against the Persians or Tsars or Turks. "How do you know so much about these people?" I asked.

"I read *National Geographic*," Sarkis said.

18 — The Carpet Seller

During my days in Aleppo I avoided many of the travel problems that had beset me on the coast. On the other hand, the ancient Aleppo market presented a mercantile challenge greater than any I had faced thus far in Syria. How do you tour the souk without being played for a sucker? Faisal the architect had warned me to stay away from the labyrinth of covered souks surrounding the Umayyad Mosque in the heart of the old city. I did not believe that I would face ruffians in the market because it was a commercial setting, and I figured that the merchants would keep the place safe for tourists. The real threat, I judged, would be the merchants themselves. Unlike my mother-in-law, who had lived through the Depression, I had low sales resistance. Fortunately, I had a plan: carry only a small amount of cash.

One morning I toured the magnificent citadel with its towers, glacis or apron, moat and heavy front gate. Across the street was an opening to the market. The place was eight hundred years old, the most terrific living archaeology in Syria. It was dark inside, crowded with people, cluttered with trade goods. *"Ma leesh,"* I thought, Why not?

I walked into the souk and at once was overcome by sensory overload. Dozens of shops no more than ten feet wide stood side by side along narrow alleys sheltered by domes of stone. I saw heaps of raisins, barrels of olives, and stacks of laurel-scented soap. I stopped and bought a pancake from a Druze, distinguished by his white lace skullcap. I came to shops filled with textiles and discovered the singer with the smiling mustache, the leader of the musicians who had performed at the Cham Palace. He ran a shop that sold *kaffiahs*. I splurged and bought three in red and white for six dollars each—gifts for friends.

Built for access by donkeys and people, the market was an urban designer's paradise: no cars, no parking, everything close and open where you could see and touch and smell. The market was impressive and the people were friendly, too. A smiling college student named Ahmed appeared in my path, introduced himself, and offered to give me a tour. "I'm not buying," I said.

He lead me down a narrow side street and, to make a long story short, two hours later I owned three dirty carpets. It turned out that my desire to save money was not nearly as important as my friendship with Ahmed and his need to sell me some carpets. (Ahmed sold carpets when he was not attending class.) I was happy, if a bit dazed. And my lack of money was no problem. Ahmed would go with me to my hotel to pick up my traveler's checks and then accompany me to the bank so that I could change money. An assistant showed me how to clean the carpets. He took a sip of water in his mouth and sprayed it over a carpet, then scrubbed it with a stiff brush. "Snow is all over America," Ahmed said. "Best is to put it in snow, then brush."

Now that we had finished our business, Ahmed took me on a tour. From the narrow, covered alleys we saw small entrances to little mosques where shopkeepers could perform their prayers. In the textile district we saw rooms filled with machines making cotton into thread, wool into yarn, hemp into rope. The crafts were grouped into individual souks in the larger labyrinth. We passed shops selling hardware, dates, sheepskin capes, candles, and more laurel-scented soap—an Aleppo specialty. Eventually we reached the jewelry shops where Ahmed recognized a friend, a sixty-year-old Armenian jeweler with gray hair who had family in Los Angeles. As Ahmed and I exchanged pleasantries, the jeweler began pulling out silver necklaces, bracelets, brooches.

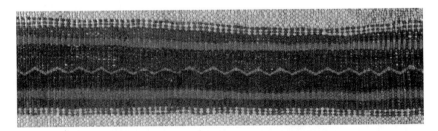

One of the carpets I bought may have come from Baluchistan.

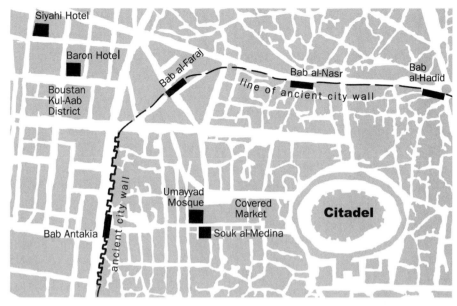

Medina Qadeeme, the old city, was near the Baron Hotel where I was staying.

"I'm not buying," I explained.

The jeweler paid me no heed. Wasn't this great stuff? I pointed at one necklace that was not as bad as the rest. "I'll come back some time," I said and stood to leave.

By now Ahmed was challenging the guy on price, bringing him down, then further down. The old man resisted, he was being bled. The entire exercise lacked only one thing: a buyer. By now Ahmed and the old guy were eyeball to eyeball. I stood again to leave but Ahmed was in my way. "Just give him a price," said Ahmed. The Armenian had written down 950 on a slip of paper for one turquoise necklace. It didn't look that bad, and my wife liked this sort of thing.

"Pick another one," the Armenian said. I chose a jade necklace. "Where did this stuff come from?" I asked.

"Bedouin women sell their silver, buy gold now," the jeweler said. I had heard about this: Bedouin women swapping ancient silver jewelry and silver-embroidered dresses for new stuff, gold and synthetics.

"My wife would love one of these necklaces," I thought. "And my mother would go for one too. But I'm still not ready to spend the money." The Armenian wrote down 1,850 lira, or about 60 dollars, for both necklaces, and I stood once again to leave. "Just give him a price," said Ahmed. I thought 1,500 lira would be a good price, but since I wasn't buying I didn't expect him to come down that low.

"Let's go," I said. Ahmed wrote down 1,500 and the jeweler wrote down 1,750.

"Let's go," I repeated.

"Just a minute," said Ahmed. "I'm trying to do something good for you."

The Armenian wouldn't agree to the low figure, but Ahmed pointed at it. "There it is, let's shake." He got the guy to shake and the deal was done. The Armenian was pretty sour and wouldn't shake my hand, but I insisted. I didn't have any money but that was no problem. Ahmed knew where there was a bank.

Two days later I registered the stuff at the museum so that I could send it home. I learned that I had paid too much for the carpets, which were Kurdish, except the small one, which may have come from Baluchistan. The jewelry was not ancient stuff from Bedouin women. On the contrary, the chain was recently manufactured and only the coin pendants were a hundred years old. The value of the chains was in their design, not in an ancient provenance. The turquoise in one necklace was actually a turquoise substitute, manufactured in Taiwan. The other necklace had jade, which turned out to be blood-stone—a cheap substitute, not jade at all. The man at the museum said he would have paid 1,000 lira for both chains, so I was 500 lira or 20 dollars off the pace.

I returned to the souk, found Ahmed, and took him to see the jeweler. "You told me it was jade," I said to the jeweler.

"Why put jade in a necklace?" he replied. "Jade is expensive."

Ahmed and I were still friends, of course, and Ahmed had promised me a more thorough tour. The Aleppo covered market was composed of more than forty individual souks, each one devoted to a trade or product. The largest was Souk al-Medina which featured vegetables and other food. After the souks Ahmed showed me the *khans* where traders had stayed in hotel rooms above the stables for their camels and the store rooms for their trade goods. We saw the consulates where European agents had worked. Coming out of the Khan of the Ministers, built in 1682, Ahmed asked me about America.

"Is it true that American girls wear no clothes?" he asked.

"Of course," I said.

"All the time? In all the places?"

"Not during winter," I said. "And not all women. Usually when a woman gets married, then she starts wearing clothes."

Ahmed was silent as we walked. I had paid too much for the carpets and the necklace, but now I was getting my money's worth. I would set him straight later on. We visited a factory where machines make cotton cloth for T-shirts. I asked if he had taken a commission on the necklace sale. "No," he said. But as we walked through shops I realized that he must have. He could only sell a tourist so many carpets. He spoke good English, got the tourist in a buying mood, showed him the market, then dropped in on his friend.

The jeweler's shop was a counter with a bench on each side. Ahmed had invited me to slide into the bench first, which seemed courteous but meant that he blocked my exit. Three times I stood to leave, but couldn't get out. The jeweler kept showing stuff, as had Ahmed when he was selling me the carpets. Ultimately I had to buy something in order to escape. There was a distinct choreography to their sales. I remembered that, in the carpet

These shopkeepers in the Aleppo market are displaying their merchandise: kaffiahs.

shop, Ahmed had invited me to sit deep in the space so that I would have to trample the merchandise to leave. I had been trapped and couldn't escape until I acceded to their charm and purchased some goods.

I had been hustled a little, even mildly bilked. But that was the price of wisdom. Ahmed continued his tour of the souk until we grew tired and needed a place to sit and rest. Fortunately his uncle's fabric shop was nearby. We took seats. In a few minutes the uncle came in, congenial and full of compliments. "I love Americans," he confided. "Here, take this seat over here." The seat he indicated was farther into his shop. If I moved and the uncle laid out his goods, Ahmed would be blocking my exit.

"No. I'm comfortable right here," I said. The uncle raised his eyebrows.

"He's not buying," Ahmed explained.

Salesmanship and deal making of the sort that Ahmed displayed were the grease that kept Syria's economy from binding, and had been for centuries. Syria had flourished as a trading nation—a crossroads of many cultures. And commerce had a personal point of contact. Today borders were closed and, for the most part, the trade of nations no longer flowed through Syrian trading houses. Still, Ahmed reminded me that civilization was more than a sculpture gathering dust in the sub-basement of the national museum. Civilization consisted of things of immediate importance to ordinary people, things like laurel soap and woven scarves. Civilization required commerce.

19 — Leaving Aleppo

ALEPPO. WEDNESDAY, NOVEMBER 25.

Ready or not, it was time for me to launch forth to the Roman Bridge. This effort would be a test of my travel skills, yet I also had some pieces of the Syrian puzzle that I hoped to fit together. Specifically, I wanted to meet Bedouins and Kurds.

To reach the Roman Bridge I needed to cross a stretch of territory which would grow progressively more primitive and difficult. I was following the Fertile Crescent and, in Aleppo, that arc had flattened and curved east and south. First I would descend the Euphrates valley to the river town of Dier ez-Zoir (literally "home of hardship"). Here I would turn from the Fertile Crescent and travel northeast up the Khabur River, a tributary of the Euphrates, to the town of al-Qamishly on the Turkish border, just a few miles from the Roman Bridge. The leg of my journey which followed the Khabur River would take me across al-Jazira, which, as I've mentioned, designated the "island" between the Euphrates and Tigris rivers—a wedge-shaped body of land just a few miles wide at Baghdad that expanded to a width of more than three hundred miles at the Turkish border. Al-Jazira was a forlorn place of desert and steppe, the territory that Fateh Moudarres had told me would leave a mark upon my soul.

My tourist map showed small Kurdish villages, large police out-posts, and an international border which I assumed to be defended with mines, barbed wire, and machine guns positioned with intersecting fields of fire. The map gave raw information, and, as a mountain climber, I understood what the information meant. This was the summit pyramid, the final challenge of my expedition.

My journey from Aleppo to the Roman Bridge would have to be comparatively quick and careful, for the territory that separated me from my goal was crawling with secret police, especially the far eastern lands which were heavily populated by Kurds. One American who had visited this district a year earlier had been interrogated by the police, then thrown into jail. He was an archaeologist, but no one would listen. The police thought that he was—what?—a Kurdish sympathizer? A weapons dealer? Eventually his university noticed that he was missing, made inquiries, wired his credentials, and arranged for his release. He survived the ordeal, but I expected that things would be worse for me. I had no credentials, no institution, no back-up.

Still, I had some ideas about how to outfox the secret police. And why worry about it now? It would be a few days before I reached Dier ez-Zoir and crossed into al-Jazira. That's when I would be vulnerable to the *mukhabarat*.

I rose early, packed my bag, and checked out of the Baron Hotel. Before leaving I found Sarkis the desk clerk in the study where he nibbled a roll with cream cheese and sipped tea. I said good-bye, then mentioned an incident I had heard about a few years before. Armenian terrorists had blown up the Turkish Ambassador in his car.

"Was this OK?" I asked.

Sarkis reddened, swallowed, and put down his roll. "These are young hotheads," he said, "and I do not personally think this is good. But you must believe: it is the Turks that have killed the Armenians. The Armenians have done nothing." He paused for a minute and looked at me. After all he had told me, he seemed to be thinking, I still did not understand. "Sometimes it is better," he said, "not to speak of these things." He turned away and picked up his roll. I walked to the door. Then he turned toward me again.

"I myself had seventy-two members of my family," he said. "Only three survived."

PART SEVEN

Al-Jazira
Two Weeks on the Steppe

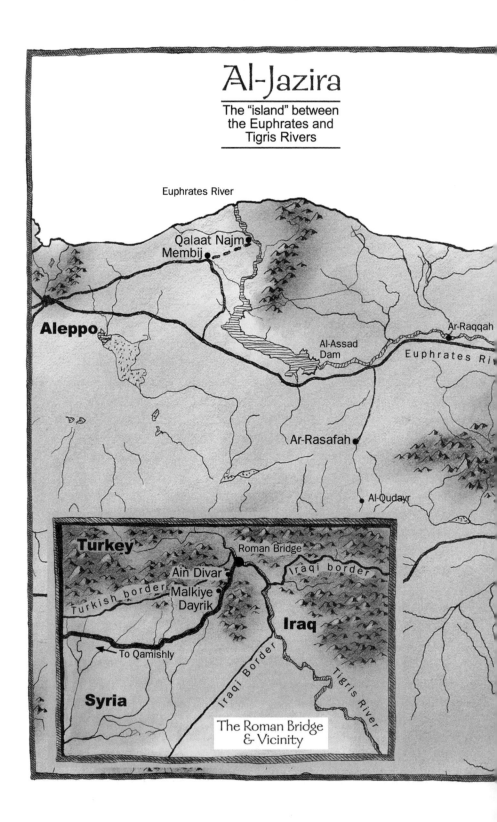

Al-Jazira

The "island" between
the Euphrates and
Tigris Rivers

Euphrates River

Qalaat Najm
Membij

Aleppo

Al-Assad
Dam

Ar-Raqqah

Euphrates River

Ar-Rasafah

Al-Qudayr

Turkey

Roman Bridge

Ain Divar

Iraqi border

Malkiye
Dayrik

Turkish border

Iraq

To Qamishly

Iraqi Border

Tigris River

Syria

The Roman Bridge
& Vicinity

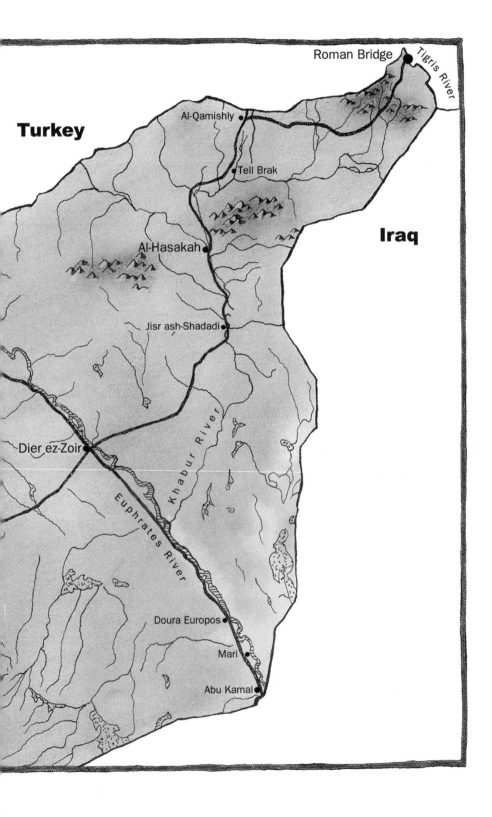

1 — Brothers

On the road from Aleppo. Thursday, November 25.
My bus left Aleppo at 11:00 AM and traveled through cultivated land, sweeping furrows without a village in sight. This was farming on an industrial scale, the ground tilled with immense John Deere tractors and harvesters and sown with hybrid seed purchased from America. At noon we arrived at Membij, a dusty town in the plain.

"Taxi?" A Kurdish youth who spoke a little English offered to help me find a taxi and show me around. Haidar had black hair, brown eyes, and a smooth, expressive face covered with wisps of beard. He was open, trusting, and utterly relaxed.

"American?" Haidar asked. "Never here, an American." I was a surprise, and Haidar seemed to think that surprises were always good.

"*Bidi rouh la Qalaat Najm,*" I said, I'd like to go to the Najm Castle.

"Oui, Monsieur," replied my driver.

Haidar and I wedged ourselves into the Suzuki—a three-wheeler, a typical underpowered conveyance—and our driver carried us four or five miles to Qalaat Najm, a stone fortification high atop a cliff overlooking the Euphrates. I stood on stone arches and looked down, down, down. At this point the river was wide and shallow. It had served as a ford since Roman times. On the far bank I saw willows, forty feet tall, planted in rows (a wood crop) and beyond, flat, furrowed fields. The air was cool, still, buoyant. The sun was warm.

Haidar took delight in every small discovery. He scrambled among

Haidar snapped a photo of the driver and me.

Haidar at Qalaat Najm.

the ruins, pointing at arches and secret chambers, urging me to follow. Afterwards, on the plain beside the castle, we explored a village of old-style mud houses, carefully plastered with fine-grained finishing clay. On the leeward side of these dwellings I saw flecks of straw glistening in the light. The houses were soft, smooth, and beautiful against the turned earth of the fields and the packed earth of the village square. The houses were scrupulously maintained, and I did not see a scrap of paper or a single tin can cluttering the landscape. Women inside the largest house displayed their loom and a Kurdish-style carpet twenty-five feet long.

Our return to Membij brought us from medieval times to the present, for Membij had grit and dirt and was bulky with crude concrete apartment buildings. The builders might return one day to add another story, one never knew, so they followed the Syrian custom of leaving the tops of supporting columns uncapped, reinforcing bar jutting into the sky. When I saw the rebar in silhouette, I thought of the fingers of suppliant women. Red stains, rust from the rebar, bled down the sides of the columns.

The air was fresh, neither warm nor cold, the autumn air of arid highlands, and the light was low and golden. Haidar walked me through his town. We knocked at the door of Haidar's friend, a Cherkas or Circassian with blond hair and blue eyes, but no one was home so we kept walking. School let out, and children shouted and laughed and ran back and forth. Haidar skipped along with them for a block. He was loose-jointed and casual, dressed in baggy, ordinary clothes: ill-cut slacks, a sweat shirt, tennis shoes. He smiled and jabbered at me and pointed out every feature of his town. Here was the hotel. Here, the pastry shop of his friend. Here the Roman columns unearthed in the latest effort to install utilities. Membij had been a resort and bath

In a village of old-style mud houses wool was washed and dried before use in carpet-making.

during Roman times, and now the most minor excavation turned up capitals and columns of limestone and marble. What would have been prizes in museums in my country were scattered about the streets—in this town they were nothing more than nuisances that made construction difficult and expensive. "Digging," Haidar explained. "All the time digging."

Later, at Haidar's house, the power was off for conservation. We were eating stewed vegetables by the light of a candle when Haidar's brother walked in. Bakeer was twenty but seemed much older. His hair was short and black and carefully combed, his sideburns cut at a rakish angle with sharp, precise razor strokes. His shirt was carefully buttoned, his jeans tight and cut to resemble Levi 501s, his shoes carefully polished. Bakeer had strong shoulders, a thick muscled neck, and a sharp brow. His eyes were hardened, focused, and always looked down. His face was blank. Bakeer moved slowly into the room. He was powerful and intent and did not smile or speak words of greeting. To me he seemed weary. He was a man of the world, a man preoccupied with . . . I could not say what was on his mind.

Bakeer sat and ate. The sun was going down by now, it was getting cold, and, after the meal, Bakeer put a sheepskin on the floor, then sat on it and pulled over his shoulders a heavy cape covered with black cloth and lined with sheepskin. He lit a cigarette and held it between his first two fingers with his palm up, cupping the cigarette, then turning his hand when he brought the cigarette to his lips—a strange, almost feminine affectation. He smoked slowly, kept his silence, and I guessed that he was angry.

Suddenly Bakeer turned to his younger brother and let loose a stream of Arabic. Every so often he looked at me, and I realized that he was quizzing Haidar about the guest that he had brought home. Was I unwelcome? I should go, but where? I had seen the hotel: it was a million years old and looked as though it had not been painted since Genghis Khan's grandson had spent the night. Then the brothers came to an agreement, I could stay. The hotel would not be needed and I relaxed a little. There was no heat, so I pulled on my blue nylon pile mountaineering vest against the cold. By now Bakeer knew that I was an American. "The commandos won the Marines," he said in English, "in Beirut."

"Ma jayid," I said, Not good.

Bakeer looked at me for a moment, then turned away. He was referring to the 241 Americans killed early one Sunday morning—October 23, 1983. The man who killed the Marines drove a Mercedes truck and smiled as he turned his rig down the driveway, wheeled past the guard post, and pulled below the concrete building where our men slept. He was an Arab, a fundamentalist associated with the Hezbollah, and he died for his faith—or so the world would assume. Bakeer, on the other hand, was a Kurd, a very different brand of Muslim. Kurds were not known for sympathy toward any cause other than Kurdish independence. So far as political ideology, Kurds liked Communism—not Muslim fundamentalism. Bakeer's words were boastful, and, for a few seconds, I thought that he was proud of the suicide bomber. But that was not it because his expression did not fit. He looked distracted or, more exactly, as though he were trying to distract himself. What was on his mind?

Bakeer said something to his younger brother, and, as they spoke, the fluorescent tube on the wall above the table flickered to life. Haidar rose, blew out the oil lamp, and put a tape in the player. The music was by Selah Rasool, a Kurdish musician from Qamishly who played strange, violent strings. Bakeer closed his eyes to listen and let his cigarette burn down. His face was smooth-shaven, light brown in color, well-proportioned. And now, once again, it was unreadable.

As the music continued I looked at Bakeer, and for a moment I thought I knew what was going through his mind: Beirut, the smiling suicide bomber, the sound and smoke of the explosion—American soldiers his age who had died serving someone else's cause.

At a pause in the music, Bakeer got out a plastic chess set. He invited me to play, but I deferred to his younger brother. By now Selah Rasool had moved into another song which consisted of frenzied plucking. Bakeer's initial moves brought him control of the board, but then, when checkmate was nearly within his grasp, he seemed to lose concentration, and his brother pulled even, then closed. The chess game was over. The tape ran out. Bakeer finished a third cigarette and walked out of the room.

I spoke to young Haidar in Arabic, and he answered in English.

"*Bakeer ma said,*" I said, Your brother is sad.

"Not sad," said Haidar, "only he worries. He worries if someone will shoot him."

"*Ma fehmet,*" I don't understand.

"Maybe tomorrow a man will shoot him."

"*Leesh?*"

"My brother is in the army, the Syrian army. Tomorrow he goes to his group, to Beirut. You know Beirut?"

"*Aewa.*"

"In Beirut, the Syrian army guards the streets. The Arabs—the Hezbollah—shoot them from the buildings."

2 — Two Mercedes

A CROSSROADS IN THE DESERT. THURSDAY, NOVEMBER 26.
I waited for a bus to Rasafa, a shining ancient city with walls built of gypsum stone which sparkled in the sun. Nearby, a Mercedes truck was pulled over, an old one, 1967. Its driver was a Bedouin in a white

headdress and a long gown who poked under the hood. The truck had stake sides extended with steel pipe and was packed fifteen feet high with mattresses, bundles of clothing, saplings cut into poles, and sawhorses. I guessed that the truck was coming from the city with loot purchased for almost nothing at the Syrian equivalent of yard sales. Now it was headed into the desert, probably toward the home village. Nothing seemed sinister and, although I had questions about the reliability of their vehicle, at least it was here. My bus was nowhere to be seen. I stared at the truck.

"You want to ride?" A man who stood beside me waiting for the bus had no interest in riding on the Mercedes. But he was willing to help me get a lift.

"*Aewa,*" I replied. He approached the driver, and I could hear them negotiating in Arabic.

"OK," he said.

I climbed up the side of the load, lugging my expedition pack. On top I found a red, stringy-haired sheep, two chickens, a dozen empty olive oil cans, and—hidden from view among the mattresses and comforters—two young women. One had long, dark hair, tattoo marks on her chin, and wore a silky red dress. Her skin was smooth, her eyebrows dark and perfectly arched. She invited me to sit beside her in the one spot not cluttered with sharp-edged objects. I was happy.

By now the Bedouin had gotten the engine running. The truck lurched onto the highway and slowly accelerated, the clutch grinding as the driver searched for higher gears. The land was flat and dead and covered with rock and dry dirt and clumps of dead grass. The sun was bright yet the air was cool, and we pulled the bedding around us against the breeze. The women were winsome and attractive. They seemed innocent, along for the ride, and I was alone with them except for an old man who sat on a bundle with the two chickens and, also, two boyfriends who had climbed aboard at the last minute.

The young men did not like the idea of sharing their women with an American. They glared at me, then threw sunflower seeds into their mouths. To my amazement—without aid of the human hand—they turned the seeds in their mouths, crushed them, and spat out the hulls. Their front teeth were worn away in half circles, a

Smugglers?

testament to years of shell-shucking. After firing a few warning shots over my bow, the older of the two, the one who claimed the woman in red, offered me a handful of seeds. This guy had a fierce look as if he were proposing a duel for the hand of the woman. We would turn the seeds in our mouths, snap off the shells, and spit them out. May the best man win.

I hesitated. My opponent was a sunflower acrobat, world-class, and I didn't stand a chance. I refused the seeds, taking away his opportunity to humiliate an American, and that made him even more angry. He shoveled another handful of seeds into his mouth, like coal into a steam engine. Soon his pressure was up, and he was spitting great globs of saliva and sunflower hulls into the wind while the women applauded. I could not help but be impressed. The old man sitting in the rear wiped the slobber from his face and said nothing. The young women still seemed innocent and uncalculating, although I sensed that the one sitting next to me was taking pleasure at her boyfriend's furious display of manhood—all inspired by her invitation to me to sit beside her in the place, I now understood, that he had occupied before my arrival.

Half an hour later we reached a police checkpoint where a man in khaki motioned us from the highway to the backyard of a station house. While he was interrogating our driver, another man waved at me with his AK-47. I climbed down. "Smugglers," he said, "not good

In the center of Rasafa lay the ruins of an ancient church.

people. Very bad." This road was an entry point to Syria's interior desert—an unpatrolled route to Jordan and Iraq. Perhaps, beneath the junk, were objects of value. By now the young men had climbed down and were shouting at the police while a soldier probed the load with a long, pointed steel rod. On top, the woman in red stood and shrieked and cursed. She was making life difficult for these men of order and rules.

The woman in red had seemed pliant and attractive when meeting an American, but now I could see the steel in her character. Were they smugglers? Did she have a stake in the enterprise? Or were they simply yard sale scroungers taking their sorry merchandise to sell to their neighbors? One policeman escorted me to the roadside where he suggested that I hitch a ride. From my vantage point the Mercedes truck was obscured by the police house. I could not see or hear what was going on, and I was surprised when, ten minutes later, the truck pulled out and continued down the road. Had the smugglers been cleared? Or had money changed hands? (Several times in the eastern lands of Syria I saw police take bribes.) I wondered: were these real smugglers, as the policeman had insisted, or was that simply an excuse to get an American out of the way? How could their truck, which broke down on the highway, survive a rigorous off-road excursion to Iraq? It seemed more likely that the woman in red and her entourage were simply small-time merchants who dodged as much as they could on taxes but never managed to smuggle anything of significance.

I spent an hour at Rasafa where the walls did not shine in the sun because the sun had disappeared behind a layer of cloud. The walls enclosed a field of dirt, pockmarked from the digging of local entrepreneurs. In the center were stone arches, the remains of an ancient church, and immense, polished granite pillars lying in the dirt. I wondered how these columns had been shaped, transported, and lifted into place. Near the north wall I saw an ancient well, seventy feet deep (according to my guidebook), and only two or three feet across. How had it been dug in the days before power augers?

When I returned to the roadside there was no traffic, and I was wondering how many hours I would have to wait for a bus when I spotted a car parked among the ruins. I put on my blue blazer, tidied my hair, and stood in front of my expedition pack to make it look smaller. In a few minutes a glossy, white Mercedes sedan pulled over. This was my second Mercedes on this day, but the ride and my companions could not have been more different. Inside the sedan were two men neatly dressed in slacks and sport shirts—Damascenes, as it turned out, who spoke perfect English.

"Antiquities," said the driver. "We've seen Palmyra and Mari and now Rasafa."

"In your Bible," his friend added, "they called the place Rezeph. It's where Sergius was beheaded by the Romans, back in 305. He became a martyr, very famous, nearly as famous as Saint George."

"You're kidding," I said.

"Really," said the driver. "Also, the water system is very famous. The town was dry, so the Romans constructed stone basins to collect rain water and stone trenches to bring the water to town."

"Like an aqueduct?" I asked.

"Yes, only on the ground," said his friend. "And the cisterns are still there. They held enough water for the ancient town for two years."

As they spoke, my companions passed me a plastic bag with carrots that had been carefully peeled and sliced. My seat was deep and cushioned, and we accelerated with scarcely a sound from the engine. They drove me to the main highway, where I caught buses down the river to Dier ez-Zoir, a city so dull that no one would protest if it dropped off the earth tomorrow. Largely built in this century, Dier ez-Zoir is the one city in the world to utterly escape urban design, Eastern or Western. This place, not Aleppo, cried for Le Corbusier's bulldozers.

I took a room at the Ragdan Hotel, an establishment that gave new meaning to the word dingy. Even so, it was the best in town. The following evening, I got into an argument with the manager over traveler's checks. He said that he couldn't accept them. He could only take cash dollars or other hard currency like German marks or British pounds. I had a little cash, but none to spare—I was saving it for the more remote hotels to come. A geologist happened in, took up my case, and, when the controversy died down, invited me to dinner at the Cairo restaurant.

3 — The Geologist

"I think human beings start from water," the geologist said in lightly accented English. "Water is the beginning, protozoa at first and in the end multi-celled beings."

I had just finished a meal of chicken barbecued over a charcoal fire. *Taibeh*, Delicious. The restaurant was crowded with locals, including three old men in gray suits who sat at the next table, bickering with one another while they ate. My dinner partner was a short, chunky man with a heavy mustache and glasses, a Syrian who worked for an oil company.

Mahmoud was that rarest of educated people, a man whose curiosity and love of knowledge had not been killed in the process of acquiring his PhD. He spoke forcefully about the origins of life, leaning forward and jabbing his forefinger into the table. His face was heavy, masked by his glasses, and it made me think of a powerful truck with a divided windshield. Still, after making his point, Mahmoud straightened up in his chair and smiled sheepishly. "Perhaps we should order a kebab," he said. "We could divide it between us." We ordered a skewer of lamb and another of onions and tomatoes and then our conversation shifted from food to less important subjects.

"The whole universe is like the atom," Mahmoud said, "the same rules, principles, components. If we can understand the atom, we can understand the universe."

As Mahmoud filled me in on the nature of the universe, I remembered the long bus ride down the Euphrates that had brought me to this city. I had traveled past fields white with salt, and I had seen white sheep with brown heads, women watching the sheep, and lambs walking behind their mothers—fields ripe with cotton, women plucking the cotton, and donkeys loaded with sticks, immense bundles with only a nose and four legs sticking out. After the river, the city was a disappointment, large and dirty and nothing to see.

The waiter came with our kebabs, and Mahmoud and I divided them between us. I told Mahmoud about Abu Taleb, the Ismaili holy man I had met in Masyaf. "He said that God could be expressed in numbers," I explained, "and he wrote down several numbers on one of my note cards. 'These are God,' he told me."

"God as numbers?" Mahmoud twisted his face into a knot. The semi-truck had broken down on the quirky formulations of an old man whose forebears had killed with golden daggers. "I believe that God is in the laws of the universe, the physical and thermodynamic laws—and those laws can be quantified." Mahmoud had gotten his truck back on the road. "So I suppose that is a way of saying God can be known through numbers." While he spoke I noticed that the old men in gray suits were smiling as they argued with one another. To them, bickering was a form of entertainment.

"But Abu Taleb is kind of a Greek thinker," I said, "like the Neoplatonists who felt that numbers were connected to reality and that by understanding numbers we could open the universe." The Neoplatonists had reached their zenith eight hundred years before the Ismailis. Still, the Ismailis and the descendents of the Neoplatonists had lived in the same coastal towns. Had they traded philosophical insights when they bumped into one another at the local sheep markets?

"Neoplatonism is farfetched," said Mahmoud. "God says, 'Use your mind to understand the universe, and in the end you will understand me, because I embody the universe.'"

The old men in gray suits had finished eating and now were ready to contest their bill. As they argued with their waiter, Mahmoud paid for our meal, and we walked down the street to a sweetshop. Standing on the sidewalk outside, we ate pastries with syrup. "America," I said, "is at a low ebb for ideas."

"I disagree," said Mahmoud. "The United States has more ideas, more publications, more expression and free thought than any other society."

"But history is here," I replied. "Here the great civilizations are physically within reach. All these societies have left traces, castles, people, customs that come down to the present."

"This is true," he said, "but—"

"A person who grows up here, who is educated and thinks, has a breadth that people in America normally lack."

"Good," he said. "But don't forget that our past—the Arab past—has been written in America and Europe. The data we use to understand our past has been provided by Western researchers."

"I find many Arab scholars, from every Arab country."

"Today you are right. But fifty years ago, a hundred years ago? It was Westerners building the foundation while most Arabs were held down by the Ottomans and French."

By now we had finished our pastries. Mahmoud did not let a single sliced almond escape. The syrup was too sweet for me, so I ate as much as I could, then jettisoned the remains when Mahmoud was not looking. We began to walk toward my hotel.

"In the United States you can publish anything you want about the Middle East," Mahmoud said, "about our history, about anything. You have give and take. You can try out ideas. We have good minds, but we don't have good voices."

"It's not so simple," I said. "The test for a society comes when it is poor. What will happen in America if the pie starts shrinking? At the moment we are rich. We spent the last two hundred years turning trees and rivers and topsoil into stocks and bonds. We haven't had time to squander our inheritance. Or to be invaded. Didn't the Mongols destroy the wealth of Syria?"

"Sure," Mahmoud replied. "The Mongols were killers, but they did not stay too long in any one place. The Ottomans were far worse. They lasted for centuries."

Mahmoud and I walked and talked until we had no more to say. It was dark, the air was cool, and the excitement of the evening had passed. I felt empty, and something vague and sinister lurked at the edges of my thought. We passed a charcoal grill on the sidewalk where I had eaten liver kebabs the day before. The proprietor stood behind his grill and turned the skewers to the rhythms of popular Arabic music from a small plastic radio placed on the sidewalk. We crossed the street to a fruit stand so I could buy oranges, then walked past the Damascus Hotel and the tearoom on the corner where a dozen old men in *kaffiahs* drank sweet tea and played backgammon. I thanked Mahmoud and said goodnight.

4 — Pity and Terror

My room at the Ragdan Hotel smelled of mold. I sat on the bed and peeled oranges and thought. This journey had changed me. My incipient pot belly was a thing of the past, a victim of missed meals and my habit of walking to save taxi fares. I suppose that I should have felt young and fit. Instead I felt old and decrepit. I was tired, worn down, exhausted. I felt worse when I thought about my plans for the following day.

I had come to a spot on the Euphrates near its confluence with the al-Khabur river. This was the end of my travel along the Fertile Crescent. Now I would cut across desert to the al-Khabur, then follow it upstream, traveling north and east into al-Jazira, the most isolated part of Syria. This final leg of my journey to the Roman Bridge would be difficult, demanding—a real pain—and the chances of being apprehended by the police were great. Was this last portion of my trip really necessary?

I ate one orange after another and slipped deeper and deeper into my orange peels. I did not look forward to another ride on a country bus. If something went wrong, I did not want to spend a week or a month in a dirty, provincial jail. I had seen the high points, the most famous ruins, the ancient cities. No one would object if I bypassed the old, obscure, and difficult territory between two rivers. Most Syrians—Hasan the architect, for example—had never come east themselves. I had intended to travel from border to border, from west to east. I had intended to see the whole country, all the way to the Roman Bridge, not just tourist spots. But now I wondered what difference it would make. I missed the ice cream shop in Damascus and the Gondol cafe with its greasy Western food. I missed Saad Shalabi, the urbane engineer, and the Eritreans in their caretaker's hut. I had seen a lot of this country. I wanted to return home—and when I thought of home it was images of the capital city that came to mind. So that was that. In the morning I would take a bus heading west to Damascus.

I was nauseated at one o'clock when I went to bed. Three hours later, I woke and stumbled across the hall to the toilet where I fell onto my knees, grasped the rim with both hands, and retched into the bowl. I rinsed my mouth with water from the tap, but did not want to swallow tap water and therefore could not remove the acidic slime that burned my throat. I returned to my room and sat on the side of the bed. The dinner was lost, the high-minded conversation gone. I was sweaty, my head ached, my stomach was in revolt. I was sick—not from the food, but from the accumulated weight of my own failures. I considered my journey and my life.

My journey was going OK, but I was tired of grimy buses, dilapidated hotels, and rude men waving AK-47s. Most of all, I was tired of being afraid.

The secret police had made me tense, weary, and nauseated from my first hour in Syria. Also the dirt, garbage, and bombed-out ambiance of these third-world cities had seemed to be part of the adventure until now. When I was twenty-two, I had thought that hitchhiking around and sleeping on floors was fun—no schedules, no itinerary, very spontaneous, just bivouac wherever I happened to be when it got dark. I had traveled this way in college, and I still thought of myself as vigorous and capable of living a life on the edge. Yet now I was nearly forty, and after seven weeks on the road I had to confess that I missed small comforts. I had come to Syria for elevated reasons, and in there somewhere was the hope that travel in Syria would prove to me that I was still young. Only now I was forced to accept the opposite conclusion. I was no longer young. I was not immortal.

I had to laugh at myself. The young Islamic fundamentalists in red headbands who had dominated American news coverage of the Middle East for the previous few years also had tried to prove their immortality. But their approach was different. I sought to extend my length of years on this planet, they sought to cut theirs short. I had mocked these martyrs since my first day in Syria, and Syrians had been quick to join me. But now I wondered if they didn't have one thing right. A life dedicated to its own perpetuation—did it have meaning? Hasan the architect, the most reasonable of men, was no martyr. Yet I had no doubt that he would sacrifice—perhaps even sacrifice his life—for his vision of Islamic culture. What did I have that meant more to me than life itself?

I had exchanged my ambitious, linear workaday life for the uncertainties of travel in a foreign land. I had forsaken lulling domestic comforts, left a woman on uneasy terms—a woman who had loved me for years. And now I was sitting in a room in a hotel on the bank of the Euphrates River. The river stank, the hotel sagged with age, my room was scarcely wider than the bed. Here I sat, a lone sentinel in a sleeping land, washed in weak, blue light from a single bulb mounted on the wall. In this place, at this moment, I concluded that I had traded my youth for a workaholic's routine which was useful in earning money but otherwise of slight value. And then I had made things worse. By coming to Syria I had impaired what little I had attained, put in shambles the order, the symmetry, the surface perfection of my life.

I loved Christianity, a religion of ideals, fine thoughts that contradicted the weakness and decay of the flesh. These thoughts had helped me, made me happy. But now I was alone, swimming in gloom, stealing quick, shallow breaths of stale air, and my ideals had lost their buoyancy.

I ran for the toilet again, but the spasms were too quick so I grabbed the sink in my room, bent over, and croaked out my guts. When the heaving ceased, I rinsed my mouth, made an attempt to clean the sink, and returned to my seat on the edge of the bed.

My life seemed less satisfactory than my journey. I had come to this country with faith in ordinary people. I had expected Syrians to lift my spirits and to show me that there was more to life than money and success. Some Syrians had done just that. But at this moment I could think only of the casual encounters, the stares, the words of envy. As a tourist I attracted those who were convinced that they lacked the things which made life worth living—who lusted after America and the pleasures and possessions that they felt it could provide. I would have to go a lot farther than Syria to escape the corrosive effect of Western culture.

"Instead of improving myself by meeting Syrians," I thought, "I've taken on their materialism."

At first I was able to fend off curious Syrians with their rude questions. As the days passed, however, the despair of these Syrians and others who were not rude, just unemployed, added up in my mind. I carried their worries with me for week after week until now I caught myself thinking their thoughts. I, too, lusted after unattainable riches which the heavens had reserved for those blessed people, the Americans.

I ran for the toilet, and once again came up short. After one heave into the sink, my stomach was empty, but my body kept retching. My face was hot with sweat yet my back was cold. At last the spasms stopped. I rinsed my mouth, then tried to clean the sink but the drain was clogged. I lay down on the bed and closed my eyes. As I drifted into sleep I thought about al-Jazira, the island, a place of mystery and ancient practice—one of the lures that had drawn me to Syria. I did not want to cross the desert. I did not want to be locked up.

I listened for a few moments.

"Now that I am sick," I thought, "the matter is settled for good. I'll return to Damascus."

The next morning I felt wasted, yet managed to accompany the hotel manager to the bank where a short, balding man in a three-piece suit explained that policies in this jurisdiction were different than those in Aleppo, Damascus, or Tartus. In this town I was required to pay my hotel bill in US dollars—traveler's checks would not do. (Why have an efficient economy when senseless bureaucratic regulations were so much more fun?) Saleh the Shiite would have given a stiff protest, but I was only half alive and had no spirit. The hotel manager agreed to a compromise: he would hold my traveler's check until I returned with cash. Now that the traveler's check problem was out of the way, I collected my bag, took a taxi to the place of buses, and boarded the first bus going—not to Damascus—but east to al-Jazira.

"Readers will not understand this passage," said Farouk. "They will not see the threads that you are weaving so subtly, so delicately."

"Oh," I said.

"When you talk of this illness, you are alluding to the earliest work of literature. You are giving a soliloquy, a religious meditation on life and death—Christians, Muslims, and Jews share a distinctive spiritual view of life, so deep in us that we can't challenge it. So you have this spiritual meditation in al-Jazira, on the banks of the Euphrates, the exact land, the exact river where an ancient writer created *Gilgamesh*, the very first meditation on immortality, thousands of years old."

"Hmm," I said.

"And you need to tell more about this sickness," Farouk continued. "You ate good food, yet you were sick. Why was this?"

"Well—"

"It was not your body but your mind. It was fear of emptiness, fear of the desert. You did not want to cross the desert. All your life, the life of all Americans, is an effort to avoid emptiness. In your country people work a lot, keep themselves busy, divorce a lot—all to avoid the fear, to forget that we're born to be alone, that we travel alone, that we die alone. The desert is severe, extreme, ultimate. In the desert we can not keep from seeing who we are. The desert brings us to our deep selfness."

5 — Maasalama

On the road to al-Hasakah. Saturday, November 28.
Because of my bulky sack I sat behind the driver in a sideways seat over the wheel, and found myself looking straight at the other passengers including a Bedouin woman who might have been twenty years old. She was accompanied by an older man, fifty or more, and at first I thought that she was his daughter. His hands were lined

and cracked, and he wore a gold wedding band. A little later, I saw her raise a hand that was still smooth and soft to show an identical band of gold. She was his wife.

The young woman had followed her husband aboard. She had walked behind him, very deferential, an example of traditional Arab womanhood. He had waited for her to sit on a seat and slide toward the window. There had been no discussion. She did what he indicated that she should do, mirrored his every movement.

Our bus pulled out and headed along the river, passing quickly through flat land lush with cottonwoods and growing vegetables. Farther from town the land was dry, and short green stalks of winter wheat grew in plowed fields. I saw two Bedouin girls riding a donkey to fetch water. Yesterday had been the day of rest, and now our bus was crowded with Bedouins returning from their families in Dier ez-Zoir and nearby villages to work at an oil installation a couple hours' ride across the desert. Many of the passengers were women traveling with their husbands, women with facial tattoos, front teeth of gold or silver, and long gowns of blue or red or purple.

The young woman across from me had brown eyes and strong, black eyebrows. She was covered up, but in a way that distinguished her from religious women. She wore a dark green gown and had a black scarf pulled around her chin—garments that identified her as a traditional Bedouin. She was wearing a *thoub* like I had seen in the airport on the nursing Bedouin woman—not the black gauze veil and black *abiah* of Shiite women at the temple of Zeinab. Her *thoub* had color and weight and a different purpose than the *abiah*. Saad Shalabi had explained to me that Bedouins did not conceal themselves out of religious zeal as some Shiite women did, but simply for privacy in a world where men felt free to stare at women in public. This was Bedouin custom and may well have predated Islam.

Our bus was up to speed by now, and the land was passing by, cultivated land covered with salt. I saw cotton and women with hand scythes cutting cotton stalks for firewood. I looked back. The Bedouin woman's husband wore a white headdress and black cape. His head was turned, but she looked in my direction. Her eyes danced.

I turned away. Out my window I saw sand and rock. We were entering serious desert where nothing grew and the only creatures were inanimate: great steel towers carrying high tension wires.

I looked back at the Bedouin woman. It was warmer now, and she had loosened her scarf so that I could see the smooth line of her neck. Did she have designs on me? She ran her finger along the end of her scarf in a motion that was slow and methodical. Our eyes met, straight on, and I felt as though I had been thrown through a plate glass window. I blinked a few times and tried to break away, but she held my eyes. I resisted, but her eyes drew me in. They were deep and expressive.

At last I managed to break away. The Bedouin woman was attractive but my throat was dry, and I was still queasy from the night before. I was not in any condition to appreciate her good looks or to fathom the intricacies of her relationship with her husband. I wanted her to go away.

I watched the land moving past. Nearly seventy years earlier, tribesmen had crushed the skulls of thousands of Armenians on this land. I expected to see broken bones in the sand, but there was nothing. I glanced back. The Bedouin woman's husband was looking out the opposite window. He had not turned his head in my direction, had not warned me off, yet when his wife looked at me it was across his line of sight. He must have known. I wondered what the punishment was in this country for looking at another man's wife.

After an hour we emerged from desert into steppe and reached a village with mud houses. I saw small trees at the edge of a river, children running in the grass, and women herding sheep. This, I thought, is Central Asia. Twenty minutes later we reached another village. While a dozen of our passengers disembarked, I moved to a seat which was more comfortable and had the added advantage of facing forward, thereby keeping my eyes out of contact with those of the Bedouin woman and adding a few years to my life expectancy. Now that I could not see her, she filled my thoughts. I wondered if it was possible to deduce her life.

Why had the Bedouin woman married this older man? In this part of Syria, I realized, jobs were especially scarce. Young men with initiative moved to the Gulf to find work. They were not around to marry. And those who stayed home were unemployed and in no position to support a wife. I guessed that her husband, like most of the others crowding this bus, had a good job at the oil installation. And I supposed that he had a family home in Dier ez-Zoir. A young man her

Mamoun Sakkal

age would not have a place of his own. Her marriage, I guessed, had been arranged. It was not romance. It was logic and tradition.

We reached a village where sand had drifted against stone fences. I was feeling a little better, hanging in there at any rate, trying to survive until the first city, the first hotel. When we pulled onto the highway once again, I looked at the ground racing past and found myself thinking back to my first few days in this country, to the Shiite festival at the temple of Zeinab. My friends Jamal and Muhammad occasionally had recognized young women in scarves and smocks and made small talk for a few minutes. These were city dwellers and Lebanese, yet they were religious and their relations with women friends, I guessed, were formal—no dating, no going steady, definitely no premarital sex. When these conversations came to an end, the women took leave in a way that acknowledged their affection and yet was chaste and quaint. They placed their hands over their hearts, bowed slightly, smiled, and spoke words of farewell. "You are close to my heart," their gesture said.

An hour later, we arrived at the village of Shadadi where the oil installation was located, the one modern place in a land that seemed very old. Most of the passengers stood, crowded into the aisle, and filed out carrying babies and bundles tied with cord. The husband walked past me toward the door, then something hit me hard on the head, and I looked up. The Bedouin woman was standing beside me, her eyes waiting for my glance, her left hand closed—she had rapped me on the head with her knuckles. She put her right hand over her heart. *"Maasalama,"* she said, Good-bye.

6 — Bedouins

If Syria's agricultural villages have gradually lost their inhabitants to the cities since World War II, Syria's Bedouins have been even more deeply affected by the loss of their nomadic existence. By the 1950s the income to be gained from guiding and protecting desert caravans was long gone, and the income to be gained from breeding and trading camels was largely gone as well. Some Bedouins continued to wander, following sheep rather than camels. They began trading—some would say smuggling—across international borders. Others settled in villages along the Euphrates, hastening a trend that was centuries old. During and after the construction of the Asad Dam on the Euphrates in the 1960s, the movement to villages increased. Work on the dam pulled Bedouins from the desert, introduced them to a cash economy. Most found it hard to return to a nomadic life.

European travelers from the 1700s who accompanied the great caravans from Aleppo to Basra commented on the movement of Bedouins from the desert to villages located along the Euphrates. They noted a decline in the Bedouin code of honor among tribes that had moved to the river valley.

Pure Bedouins were warlike tribes, yet their fierce habits were strictly governed by rules of honor. Their desert code bound them to care for lost travelers. Bedouins would defend to the death those whom they had accepted as guests and placed under their protection. Although a caravan could be regarded as a legitimate military target, subject to straightforward attack, a pure Bedouin would never use the safe passage agreements of his sheik as a cover for petty theft or murder by stealth.

Caravans that chose a route crossing the deep desert and negotiated safe passage with tribes that controlled this territory normally were safe from attack. Those which traveled close to the river were also unlikely to be attacked—riverine tribes had lost their warrior mentality and the authority of their sheiks had waned—but such caravans were often robbed in the night. Of course the Ottoman sultan had something to do with this change in behavior. Bedouins who lived in the desert were out of reach of the sultan and could live according to their own rules. But clans that had settled in villages were punished, often severely, for breaking the sultan's laws. In the villages, an independent spirit could express itself only in small nocturnal acts of sabotage and lawlessness.

During my travel in Syria, in passages of desert, I saw rough wool tents with old Mercedes trucks rather than camels parked beside them. For all the lure of modernity, at least a few of Syria's Bedouins still preferred the open sky, the tent with a carpet beneath, the fire pit, the pot of hot, sweet tea.

7— Crossing the Steppe

The land was arid and severe, a high plain swelling and dropping away as our small bus crossed on a ribbon of asphalt. We traveled in full sun but the light was colorless. There was nothing to give it color, nothing but flat, muted tones of earth and stone. The air was cold, and wind came upon the land in fitful breaths, the first bleak winds of winter, wind from the heart of Asia.

I looked out the window of my bus and thought of the lords of the steppe: Genghis Khan, his grandson Hulegu, and, the most feared of all, Timur the Lame, or Tamerlane the Great. For twenty-four years after the death of Genghis Khan, the Mongols consolidated their empire, improved their administration, built roads, enjoyed their wealth. Then Genghis Khan's older grandson Mangu came to power, took away gold and jewels from noble families to finance vast armies, put home territories on soldier's rations, and drew up plans to carry the Standard of Genghis Khan to the corners of the earth. From his felt-covered throne in Karakorum, Mangu sent armies—or the golden horde, as they were called—on the attack to the east, south, and west. The strongest army Mangu gave to younger brother Hulegu who headed toward Baghdad and Cairo—the centers of Islamic power—in a bid to bring the land from the Caucasus to North Africa under Mongol control. Hulegu left Karakorum, the desolate, eastern center of Mongolia, in 1253 and moved slowly westward with a force that included geographers, Chinese engineers, and technicians who had mastered the art of hurling naphtha fire bombs from wooden siege machines.

Hulegu had sacked Baghdad and Aleppo, occupied Damascus, and was poised to attack Cairo when he received word that his brother Mangu had died. Tradition required Hulegu to travel home to Karakorum to choose a successor. But his favorite wife Dokuz and his favorite general, Kit Boga, begged him first to take Jerusalem and give it to the Crusaders as a way of enlisting their help in the siege of Cairo. This approach seemed logical to them, in part because Dokuz and Kit Boga were Christians and also because a few weeks earlier the knights of Antioch had joined them in the siege of Damascus. Over the preceding 600 years, the Nestorian Christian faith of Dokuz and Kit Boga had won converts among many of the Tartar tribes and had penetrated as far east as Lake Baikal. If the advice of Dokuz and Kit Boga had prevailed, then Christians very likely would have taken control of Persia, the Levant, and North Africa.

Mamoun Sakkal

Hulegu hesitated, then chose clan loyalty over religious opportunity. He departed, taking Dokuz and her prayer wagon with its clapping iron bells and flapping wooden plaques. He left behind Kit Boga with twenty-five thousand men.

In the meantime, in Cairo, the ruling Mamluks were bent on defeating the Mongols. The Mamluks were warrior slaves who had overthrown their masters to take power years before. The Mamluks idolized the Mongols and wore their hair long in the Mongol style. As the Mongols entered Persia and the Levant, slowly working their way toward Cairo, the Mamluks confiscated the gold of Cairo's merchants and princes and scoured the deserts to raise an army. After Hulegu turned back toward Karakorum, the Mamluks approached Kit Boga with a force of a hundred thousand—mostly rabble, peasants who had fled to Cairo in the face of the Mongol advance plus a few fleet Bedouins.

Mamoun Sakkal

The Mamluks used their light cavalry to lure the Mongols into an attack, drew them away from their Armenian foot soldiers and then, when the Mongols were committed and were tiring in the heat, the small, elite band of Mamluk cavalry attacked their rear. They split the Mongols, chased them as far as the Tigris River. And Kit

The victories of Hulegu and Tamerlane depended upon their extraordinary horses.

Boga? The Mongol general refused to flee. The Mamluks killed him and played an exultant round of polo with his severed head. The leader of the Mamluks was Baybars, the one-eyed slave king, who, as I have mentioned, later wrested Crak des Chevaliers from the Crusaders.

A century and a half passed, and the Levant had still not recovered from Hulegu when it suffered another great invasion of mounted warriors from the steppe. This wave was led by Tamerlane who rode forth in the name of the Mongols and installed as his puppets men who were the descendents of Genghis Khan. Yet Tamerlane bore no relation to the great leader—for that matter, he was of Turkish, not Mongol, descent. Tamerlane was the most brilliant tactician of cavalry that the world has known. He began by pursuing the remnants of the Mongol armies across the Hunger Steppe. When he had destroyed them, he turned south.

In 1400 Tamerlane came upon Damascus with vengeance as a Shiite seeking retribution for centuries of scorn from the capital of urbane, reasoned, Sunni faith. When their city walls failed, the people of Damascus fled into the Umayyad Mosque and bolted the doors. Tamerlane set fires against the doors and, the next day, stacked the heads of his thirty thousand victims in three great piles. Tamerlane wrecked the mosque and took the fabled craftsmen of Damascus—the weavers of silk scarves, the forgers of damascene blades—and those of Aleppo, Baghdad, Teheran, and returned with them to Samarkand where he was building a city of symmetry and grace on the steppe.

Later Tamerlane marched south into India, introducing Shiite Islam into the lands which today are known as Pakistan, India, and Bangladesh, and doing his best to exterminate the Nestorian Christianity of his Mongol predecessors. Always the warrior returned to Samarkand, to the market with its spectacular fountains, and to the immense Bibi Khanum mosque which he had constructed—the largest structure ever built of unfired, unreinforced mud brick.

The lords of the steppe came and went. Hulegu died in 1265 as he was returning to Karakorum—poisoned by his enemies, and his wife Dokuz died shortly thereafter from the same cause. Tamerlane died on the march to China in 1405. To Syrians like the geologist I met in Dier ez-Zoir, their quick, brutal conquests now seem benign beside the plodding, stifling, centuries-long repression of the Ottomans who achieved control by corrupting and diminishing their subjects. Hulegu and Tamerlane called their opponents out, asked them to fight in alliance or fight in opposition, to fight or die. Hulegu and Tamerlane and the extraordinary horses they rode to victory have long passed from the scene. From one angle they defined barbarism. From another, however, their daring captures the imagination.

At last our bus emerged from open steppe into the outskirts of al-Hasakah, a plain and primitive town. I saw a hill capped by an ancient ruined fortress, and I closed my eyes and saw rough long-haired men with lances and swords and others, on horseback, with quivers and bows—riding slowly, deliberately, and behind were crude wagons and captives in rags and, farther behind, the fortress in flame, gates smashed, blood covering the stone pavement. I heard the sobs of women, the low groan of dying animals, and I smelled smoke. I saw the captives up close: they were boys, lost sons cut from their families, boys with wounded hearts walking south across the plain to the next river ford, the next city of walls, the next battle. I saw these things, and I was there. I was with the horsemen, proud and cruel, the plodding men on foot, the awkward wagons. I was a child, walking in silence, eyes down, a child who dreamed of tender life.

I opened my eyes and looked again. Below the castle was a stream and beyond the stream were buildings and streets, gray and crumbling. Shops were small and dirty and had little to sell. Streets were quiet and nearly vacant.

8 — Theodora's Double-Cross

"Welcome," said the hotel keeper, a large, Turkic man with a heavy, black mustache. "Not so many Americans in our place." In fact there were no Americans. The Nadizerai Restaurant & Hotel was located a block from the original Ottoman police outpost on the banks of the Khabur River and two blocks from the old souk. It was on the second floor of a stucco building and featured a fleshy, blonde nude—a German pinup—on the wall beside the counter. My room was clean and filled with sunlight. Three dozen flies circled. The manager gave me a plastic swatter which I broke in my enthusiasm. I bathed in steaming hot water and at three-thirty in the afternoon fell asleep on the bed and didn't wake until six-thirty the next morning.

On this new day I felt a little better. I rose, entered the restaurant, and ate a breakfast of rolls and tea while chatting with the hotel manager. As he explained, the hotel and restaurant were owned by Souriyani (Syriac) Christians who had fled the barbarous Turks on the other side of the border. "Turks killed the Armenians," the manager said. "True, true. But what no one knows is this: the Turks killed the Souriyani Christians."

After breakfast, I went to the bank to cash a traveler's check. Nothing doing. Mr. Daod (David), the bank manager, was a slight, dapper man with gray hair. "My family," he said in careful English, "are also Souriyani Christians. We came from Mardin, in Turkey. The soldiers pushed the Souriyani Christians south in 1916, and many died. So we live here, on the farm, making the tomatoes and the squash, and after thirty years we move into Hasakah to make business. And now, Sweden. Many of us move to Sweden. A church is there. And here in Hasakah we have two churches, old and new.

"You call this area Kurdistan, but you are wrong. Kurdistan is to the east. Really there never were any Kurds here, just Bedouins and then Syriac Christians. The Kurds came only in the last years as we moved to Europe. But the Kurds have big families, so now Kurds are everywhere."

"I'd like to see your church," I said.

"You must not," he said. "The police, always the police. It will be very bad."

Scholars identify Souriyani (Syriac) Church as the West Syriac, Syrian Orthodox, or Jacobite Church, a remnant of early Christian worship that has remained largely unchanged over the last 1700 years, uninfluenced by the Renaissance, the Scientific Revolution, or the Protestant Reformation—uninfluenced by the pipe organ, among other developments. These were the folks I had heard about in Damascus who currently were negotiating a merger with the Greek Orthodox or Eastern Orthodox, the Church of the Byzantines. Apparently attitudes had softened since ancient times. If the fathers of the ancient church had had their way, the Souriyani faith would have died an early death.

In the sixth century Byzantine emperors sent armed men to break down Syriac churches and jail their clergy. One of the worst culprits was Justinian I (the most famous Byzantine leader and the founder of the Saydnaya convent near Damascus) who "decapitated" the Syriac Church. He threw its leaders into prison and its followers fell into disarray. The church surely would have perished but for Justinian's wife and a man named Jacob Baradeus. Jacob was a Syrian who in 528—before the worst of Justinian's persecution—had traveled to Constantinople. There he met in secret with Justinian's wife, the empress Theodora, and convinced her of the truth of his teaching. She kept him safe in a monastery in Constantinople, and then, fifteen years later, when all seemed to be lost, she sent him forth disguised as a beggar to recreate the church that her husband had destroyed.

Adobe dwelling on the road to al-Hasakah.

Jacob traveled from village to village, criss-crossing northern Syria. He told of a Jesus who had divinity inside and used it to raise himself

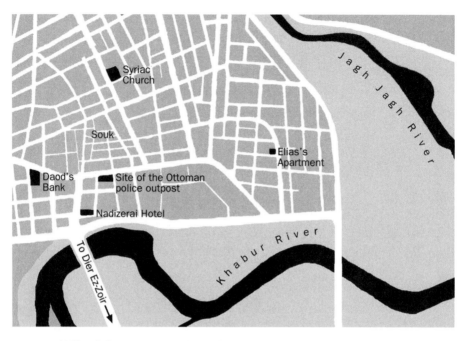

Al-Hasakah was situated at the confluence of the Khabur and Jagh Jagh Rivers.

from the darkness and sin of this world. Most of Jacob's listeners, one supposes, had previously received Christian teaching but had fallen from the faith when the Syriac Church was destroyed or had come under the sway of the more rigid and hierarchical Greek Orthodox Church. Jacob's listeners took away the idea that they too might have light inside themselves, something spiritual that could redeem them and lead them to God—otherwise (as Jacob might have characterized the Orthodox view) they were simply sinners who slithered along the ground, sinners whose fate depended upon favors that originated in faraway Constantinople.

The glory of Byzantine culture and the Greek Orthodox Church was expressed in the gold leaf and soaring arches of the Hagia Sofia cathedral which Justinian I built in 537 in Constantinople. Today the cathedral still stands with its central dome spanning 107 feet. It is praised by historians as the finest late example of Roman building skill, and is a magnet for tourists. In contrast, what monuments express the earnestness of the ancient Syriac Church? Historians and tourists display only slight interest in the town of al-Hasakah. Yet its worn buildings and drab, sooty streets aptly express the humble faith of Jacob Baradeus.

When I arrived at the old church, a man in a gray suit ushered me into a single, large room, plain and old, with immense arched ceilings, stove pipes rising crookedly from potbellied stoves, and, on walls far above, inscriptions in Syriac script. In front I saw a wooden pedestal holding four enormous books and three men and two boys who were chanting and singing the mass along with the priest. The men took the chorus, and their singing was a bass line, steady, cadenced. The priest and then the boys took the solo, bright and melodic. They sang in Syriac without accompaniment, and their singing was casual and beautiful and very sad.

On the walls above I saw a painting of the Last Supper and other icons: Saint George slaying the dragon, John the Baptist being beheaded, Elijah beholding his chariot of fire.

Almost the entire congregation were men, small by American standards and conservatively dressed in dark slacks and coats. They were craftsmen like Elias, the usher—an ironworker who took me home for tea after the mass, or petty bureaucrats like Mr. Daod, the banker, or proprietors of small shops. They were cautious: none of them seemed to possess the fire of Jacob Baradeus. They were men who husbanded their resources. Only by saving pennies could they finance a new church at the edge of town or a new life in a foreign land. They had little sympathy for Bedouins, especially the more flamboyant among them who still traveled from place to place and seemed extravagant in the mismanagement of their lives. That morning I had come to the church to find out the time of the mass. I had seen a Bedouin woman at the door.

Elias the usher had invited me to step inside and see the icons. When he opened the door for me to leave, a Bedouin woman approached and spoke to him in Arabic. She had four gold teeth, a gold pendant hanging from her right nostril, and wore a red gown trimmed with gold and covered by a blue cape. I had never seen such fine garments on a Bedouin. Still, I sensed that she was poor. "I am hungry," she said, "and my children are hungry. Could you give us bread?"

9 — The Archbishop

Historians bypass al-Hasakah because they are interested in old places and this town, like al-Qamishly to the north, is comparatively new. When Tamerlane swept through in 1401, he destroyed the cities of al-Jazira including nearby Tell Tuneinir. This city above the Khabur River had a population of 15,000 that included a thriving Christian community with its own monastery. The Syriac and Assyrian (or Nestorian) Christians who escaped did so by fleeing north to the Turkish mountains.

During the Ottoman reign that followed the towns of al-Jazira were not rebuilt and the primary inhabitants of the region were Bedouins who traveled from place to place tending their herds on the rich but arid land. The Ottomans established a police outpost not far from the site of Tell Tuneinir at the confluence of the Khabur and Jagh Jagh rivers. The local Bedouins referred to the Ottomans as *barghrela,* people who ride mules. And the settlement was called al-Hasakah, from the Syriac word meaning the place filled with trees.

Syriac Christians, many of them from the city of Mardin in Turkey, moved south and repopulated al-Jazira beginning in the first years after the turn of the century and gathering momentum during the persecutions of 1916. Those who reached al-Hasakah established trading posts near the police station where they would be protected from marauding tribes. Here they exchanged sugar, tea, and coffee for the wool, fat, and other products that the Bedouins could provide. In 1920 the Syriac school was established to tutor the children of these merchant families. At this time there were about fifty Syriac families here, and the church had not yet been built.

Al-Hasakah was isolated. It was a long way from Aleppo and the Mediterranean. The old caravan route to the Gulf via Dier ez-Zoir and the Euphrates had not yet been upgraded with modern roads or railways, and the roads leading to nearby Mosul and the Tigris route to the Gulf were controlled by independent tribes.

The story of al-Hasakah and al-Jazira was in large measure the story of Syriac Christians. Yet there is a richer and more complex way of telling this story, as I learned on my return to this town in 2001. I visited the old church again and this time I met Archbishop Matta Roham. The Archbishop is a tall man with a thick black beard who wore a flowing black gown, a broad red waistband, and a tight black hat. Around his neck hung a heavy gold cross. The Archbishop spoke fluent English, thanks to his years studying in New York, and was eager to explain the history of this region and its Christians.

"Ten or fifteen years after the Syriac Christians moved down from Mardin," he said, "the Iraqis in power at the time provoked a confrontation with the last surviving Assyrian (or Nestorian) Christians—the descendents of the few whom Tamerlane had missed, who lived in villages in northern Iraq. In 1933 the Iraqis sent soldiers and ended up killing 200 or 300 Assyrian villagers. Others fled across the border to Syria which then was under French control. Many of the refugees came to Hasakah. So today we have thirty-six Assyrian villages in this area.

The old Syriac church had stovepipes that rose crookedly in front of the windows.

"You can say 'Syriac Christians'," he explained. "But in so doing you miss the unity and breadth of our people. We usually say 'Aramaic' people. In this way we do not have to distinguish between Syriac Christians and the Assyrian Christians or the Chaldeans (who are Assyrians who converted to Catholicism beginning in 1550 or so). These are all the same people, only with differences of religious belief. Also, by using the term 'Aramaic,' you provide a link to ancient times which makes clear the brotherhood of most of the people in the Levant—Christians, Muslims, and Jews."

"How's that?" I said.

"We are all Semitic people. Our languages are sister languages. Somewhere deep in the southern deserts was an original Semitic mother tongue from which our languages derived.

Archbishop Matta Roham.

"And so today when I talk with my Muslim friends I remind them that their history as Arabs is not just 1,000 years old. I explain that the Muslim invasions of the seventh century AD were simply the most recent wave of Semitic people who came north, that many other waves had come before, and that one of the earliest waves brought Aramaic-speaking people who populated the north of Syria. We, of course, are the descendents of these Aramaic people. And our liturgy is still in Syriac (a written version of Aramaic) today."

"Where did Aramaic come from?" I asked.

"Aramaic was written in a script that evolved from the Phoenician alphabet and it came on the scene in the eleventh century BC. Three hundred years later it was the predominant language of the Levant, and by the sixth century BC Aramaic had replaced Hebrew as the spoken language of the Jews.

"The books Daniel and Ezra in the Old Testament were written in Aramaic. And there were Aramaic translations of the Old Testament by the time of Jesus."

"What about Alexander? Didn't he spread Greek far and wide?"

"Alexander's Greek was adopted for government administration. It was a written language for educated people, but it did nothing to dislodge Aramaic. Neither did the Latin of the Romans who followed. And to skip forward in history, neither did the language of the Ottoman Turks who ruled here for so many years. Aramaic was the language of the land until the Muslim invasions in 650 AD, when Arabic took over."

"Why did Arabic supplant Aramaic?" I asked.

"Just because a society is predominantly Muslim does not mean that it speaks Arabic," said the Archbishop. "You have Muslims in Indonesia, Pakistan, Iran, Turkey—none of them use Arabic as their daily language."

"OK," I said.

"In the Levant Aramaic had resisted Greek and Latin but was quickly transformed into Arabic. That's because both Aramaic and Arabic were Semitic languages. They sounded alike. And Arabic speakers kept the Aramaic place-names because they sounded familiar. For example, outside of Aleppo is the old bath which the Greeks and Romans called Hieropolis. Does this sound Semitic? No. We call it today Membij. And take the city of Dier ez-Zoir. The Arabs will translate this as the 'home of hardship' because it sounds like Arabic. Actually it is derived from the Aramaic. 'Der' means 'monastery.' And 'Zuor' means 'small.' So Dier ez-Zoir is the small monastery."

"This is all interesting," I said, "But what is your point?"

"In the Levant," the Archbishop continued, "with the Turks on the north, the Persians on the east, and the Greeks on the west, we had a large body of people who spoke Aramaic. These were Semitic people. So when the Muslims rode north and took control of government administration and Arabic replaced Greek as the language of government, well, Aramaic transformed itself into Arabic. And the Aramaic peoples became Arabs. The whole process happened quickly, over a century or two.

"When you look at our history in this way, you see that Syriac Christians and Assyrian Christians and Chaldeans are not simply leftovers from a Christian past. Aramaic people are an early wave, you could say an original wave, of people from the southern deserts. Modern day Arabs are not simply derived from Bedouin tribes (who have been speaking Arabic since ancient times). Modern day Arabs are composed of many strains of Semitic peoples and one of the earliest and largest is ours."

10 — Minority Report

"I don't trust in God or in any religion," said Youssef Abdelke. "I grew up in al-Jazira in the town of Qamishly, an hour north of Hasakah. I went to the Syriac school, then I quit and went to Protestant school. I refused to learn the Syriac language. For me, Arabic only. And now, of course, French."

I associated Youssef Abdelke with his friends Hasan the architect and Zouhair the sculptor. On the other hand, I knew that Youssef was only an honorary member of that Aleppo artist's mafia, that *shellah*. Hasan and Zouhair were Muslims from Aleppo. Youssef, on the other hand, was a Christian from al-Jazira.

Strange to say, Youssef had a lot in common with the Archbishop Matta Roham—a fellow Christian from al-Jazira. The two men were about the same age. Each had exceptional talent. Yet the paths they chose in life and their memories of this land could not have been more different.

Matta Roham loved the faith, excelled in religious school as a youth, won every award, and made the church his career. He seemed content to serve in a district that most Syrians thought of as a backwater. For Matta Roham, al-Jazira was a hallowed enclave of Aramaic Christians determined to make something of themselves, to scratch out a new life in the shadow of ruined monasteries, and to win recognition for Aramaic culture and language in the history of the region.

Youssef Abdelke, like other Christian artists in Syria, chaffed against what he saw as the petty thinking and restrictive practices of the church. In 1966 at the age of sixteen, Youssef fled to Damascus, and a couple years after graduation he moved on to Paris. In this world capital of art, Youssef's talent expanded. He was invigorated by the level of competition in Paris, his art stimulated by the interplay of cultures. Yet many of the images on his canvases recall the tortured relationships of the nation where he came of age. And the deep unsettled textured gray backgrounds on which his images rest reach even farther back to the primitive, brutal, endearing landscape of his youth.

Years later when I finally caught up with Youssef in Paris, he remembered al-Jazira as a land rich, unspoiled, and peopled by a rough-and-ready collection of sheiks, insurgents, border rats, and smugglers.

Mamoun Sakkal

"A beautiful life," said Youssef. "I lived a beautiful life in al-Qamishly. I am thinking in particular of the years from 1960 until I left in 1966. Many kinds of people lived here: Turks, Bedouins, Kurds, Armenians, Syriac Christians, farmers, soldiers, merchants, herdsmen. Qamishly was an agricultural center, a station on the railroad.

"My grandfather Hanna Abdelke was under a Turkish death sentence from 1910 until 1915—which is why our family came south into Syria. In the 1920s he worked with the French on the first land use plan for al-Qamishly. This was when Syria was part of the French Mandate. For years my grandfather held the position of town planner for the nearby settlement of Hamouda. In the 1930s he wrote a book that criticized the Syriac Christian Patriarch. The church and the Patriarch wielded political power. Who would risk offending them? No one dared to publish my grandfathers' book. So he sent money to Buenos Aires, had the books printed, then smuggled them into Syria.

"My father Abdel Ahad Abdelke was a Communist leader who was imprisoned twelve times for his political views. I grew up listening to political talk. For me, religion did not exist, the church did not exist. Between 1947 and 1958 my father was in and out of jail, usually for periods of two to four months. The longest stint was nine months. His crime? My father was organizing the Kurds. He went to Kurdish villages to make politics—but never to Syriac or, as they say today, Aramaic villages."

"Fateh Moudarres's father was killed for organizing the Kurds near Aleppo," I said. "It must have been a hot topic at the time."

"Yes," said Youssef. "I knew Fateh when he taught in Damascus. The Syrians and the Syriac church did not want to acknowledge the Kurds or to give them rights."

"What did my father do for a living? What did he *not* do? He worked as a grocer, a photographer, a woodworker, a journalist. For a time he was the administrator of wheat distribution and traded wheat on his own accounts. Another time he had a shop on main street that sold TVs and radios and another shop that sold carpets. One other shop he opened was for justice. People came in who were having trouble with the local bureaucrats. He did what he could to help.

"As a child I never knew what the year had in store. One month we were living comfortably in our own home, the next month we had nothing to eat and had to go and live with my grandmother.

"Nature was generous. There were lakes and water everywhere. One area near the village of Amunda was called Ras al-Aain (*al-aain* means the spring). There were dozens of small lakes here, fifty of them fed by springs, clear mineral water. When our family went on picnic, we never took vegetables or salad. We found a place near the water and then picked cucumbers and tomatoes and greens from nearby fields and washed them in the cold water and ate them fresh.

"Every building in Qamishly was made from mud bricks, except for the school and a few stone buildings on main street. The roads were dust in the summer and mud in the winter. There was a market where the farmers and herders came to sell produce and meat. And the market was full of colorful people, the smugglers whom we called *katchaque*, a Turkish word. They would run tobacco, clothes—anything of value—across the borders to Turkey, Iraq, Iran. The borders were new, governments were distant, the taxing authority was nebulous, whereas the caravan tradition was very very old.

"We were also sports-crazy in those days. In Qamishly we had an Armenian soccer team that was very good and competed against the local Syrian team and against the Armenian teams from Hasakah, as well as other teams from Dier ez-Zoir and Aleppo. There is a lot more I can say about Qamishly. What do you want to hear?"

"Give me a story," I said, "a story of murder or love."

"This is not a story, but a fragment of a story, a scene," said Youssef. "I'll remember it forever. It happened on the main street of Hasakah in 1962. It was bizarre, magical, and could have come from a novel by Gabriel Garcia Marquez. This scene marked the coming of age of our community.

"In Qamishly in the 1920s there was a woman of extreme beauty named Goulezar. Men saw her and wanted her and became jealous and fought and killed each other because they simply had to have her. None of them succeeded for long, however, because Goulezar was not interested in joining the entourage of any one man. Still, she liked men. She knew how to entice them, to tantalize them, to seduce them. More than anything, however, she knew how to mask her intentions from them until she could win them over with her charm. Goulezar was more than a simple seductress. She was an ambitious woman.

"Sometime around 1930 Goulezar started a *bait sharaneet*, a house of prostitution, in a villa on the northwest side of town near the Turk-

ish border. Her villa consisted of several
flat-roofed mud brick buildings and a
garden without walls. Goulezar kept
ten or fifteen women in her bordello,
women from Turkey or Aleppo. Custom-
ers came from Qamishly and Hasakah
and from all over al-Jazira. Prostitution
was legal at this time by civil law, but
the church did not approve and worked
to keep the whole thing concealed. The
church never was able to close down
Goulezar's bordello, but there was an
unspoken agreement. She kept her
business at the edge of town. When her

Youssef Abdelke.

women were not working, they tended
the garden and did not come into town, did not flaunt."

"On the face of it," I said, "You were an upright community of
Christians and Muslims. Behind the scenes, however, the men were
out at Goulezar's."

"Yes," said Youssef. "Years passed. The world suffered a great
depression, then Hitler, then a world war. After the war we finally
pried Syria loose from the fingers of the French and became free,
except that our governments were not democratic. On the other hand,
none of them lasted for long. Every few months a new government
was formed. And all this time Goulezar steadily grew in power and
stature.

"The priests and bishops and archbishops could marry a man, and
if they wanted they could grant a divorce. They could baptize your
child, and they decided if you would go to heaven, or not. But Goulezar wielded another kind of power. She was the one who determined
which of her women a man could see. Now men fought one another,
killed one another—not for her love but for her permission to see the
most tender, endearing, and appealing of her women.

"When I was young, my friends and I tiptoed past her villa. We
were curious and afraid. Every man in Qamishly tried to do favors for
Goulezar, tried to be her friend. In her last years Goulezar was living
with the wealthiest man in town. He owned property and businesses
including the coffee shop in the center of the city. The church still did

not acknowledge Goulezar, yet by now she had risen in the esteem of the local citizens. The men admired her and sought her favor for the reasons that I have mentioned, and the women saw that her bordello kept families intact. You seldom heard of a man leaving his wife for another woman, thanks to Goulezar. You did not have the young girls of the town getting pregnant. Why? Because the fathers took their sons to Goulezar. The women of Qamishly saw Goulezar as an ally, a force for social stability, not a competitor or home-wrecker."

"Something else," I said. "Don't you think that Goulezar expressed the aspirations of the women of Qamishly? Women wanted to be taken seriously, they wanted to wield power in public ways. She showed them that it was possible."

"As you say," replied Youssef. "All this brings us to the scene I mentioned. In 1962 Goulezar died. I was twelve years old. The priests would not allow her to have a funeral in the church. So, instead, she had a public funeral—almost like a state funeral—on main street where everyone could see, in the very center of town where all the streets were blocked off, the traffic stopped, the shops closed. The setting was formal and carefully staged. In front of the big stone buildings, main street was arranged like a single large room. The casket was in front on a stand, then a dais for the speakers, then seats for the musicians—saxophone, trumpet, drums—a brass band. Then seating for the audience. And the most remarkable thing: on each side of the audience was an honor guard formed by the women who worked at Goulezar's bordello. They were spaced a few paces apart going down the two sides of the street, and they faced into the audience so that each of these women looked across the audience to her opposite on the other side of the street. The women were young and beautiful and stood silent and motionless. They were draped in an exceptional fine cloth and looked like marble statues in a grand concert hall or museum.

"Everything was solemn. The music played. The most important men in town made speeches. The rest of us watched. And the strangest thing in this town, dominated by a strict and unyielding church: the women from the bordello, the honor guard, the cloth in which they were draped was sheer, and if you looked you could see every naked bit of them underneath. Still, no one objected, no one said a thing."

"What is the meaning?" I asked.

"I don't explain my visual art," said Youssef. "I am not sure that this scene *has* a meaning. I only know that I remember it like yesterday. Besides, you're the writer. You tell me."

"Goulezar's funeral was a local event," I replied. "OK. On the national stage, these were heady days of democracy, because now Syria had Nazem al-Qudsi, an elected civilian president. Newspapers were printing all kinds of things, anything they wanted. Syrians were free as a nation, and, in Qamishly with the funeral of Goulezar, a community of people came to some conclusions in their wrestling match with the church. They stopped the deception. They dropped the hypocrisy. They gave public recognition to a woman who was important to the functioning of the community."

"Is this you speaking, or me?" asked Youssef.

"Mainly you," I said. "*My* philosophy tells me that we should aspire to satisfied lives without physical desire. So Goulezar is not a hero in my view, but a temporary concession, a way to meet the human need while people prepare themselves for something higher. And there is always the question of whether a concession such as this holds people back and stunts their growth or takes the pressure off, removes the element of will, self-righteousness, hypocrisy, and promotes their growth. In any case, I like this scene as a piece of literature, and I approve of the honesty that the community displayed in recognizing Goulezar. To me this scene is, at best, practical humanity and a social turning point—not a philosophical statement."

"But you would go farther. You would say that this scene was the moment that the people of Qamishly admitted that, however spiritual their souls, their minds and bodies still are here in the world and require care and comfort. In that moment Qamishly grasped knowledge and became mature and for the first time allowed the women of dream and desire, the working women of the bordello, a physical presence in the finest part of town."

"Pretty words," replied Youssef. "But you are avoiding the question. What, exactly did this scene mean to me, to my life?"

"You felt as though the new Qamishly was an established fact," I said. "You were young and did not understand that all things in this world change. Even solid civic accomplishments dissolve in rain and dust and sun. A few months after Goulezar's triumph, the Baath Party took control of Syria by force. Syria's new rulers were military men who wanted to run things their way. They declared a state of emergency. They shut down newspapers, outlawed political parties, threw their political opponents into jail. (The democratically elected President Nazem al-Qudsi, for example, went into the Mezze prison.) Elections were no longer free."

"Things did change," said Youssef. "Change came as well to the beautiful land around my home town. The water was pumped for agriculture until the streams and lakes and springs went dry."

"Yes," I said, "I can see it. And even in the rainy season the streams that formed were like trickles, the lakes like puddles, and the water was no longer clear and cold but silted, murky, and thick with chemicals. Who planted vegetables any more? It was wheat, wheat, wheat. Wheat grown from American hybrid seed. Wheat that required heavy fertilizers. Wheat grown for export."

"You writers," replied Youssef.

"For a moment in 1962 Qamishly was the kind of town—and Syria was the kind of country—that could keep you. And then the moment was lost and you were lost. It's been thirty-six years since you left Qamishly, twenty-four years since you left Syria. You have never returned."

11 — Outsmarting the Mukhabarat

Now that I was in the heart of al-Jazira, I was on the alert, as were the people of this town. Police were everywhere. They had chosen to stay in the shadows, yet I knew that they were watching me. I tried to calm myself with the notion that I had a plan. My strategy turned on two insights that had become clear to me in Aleppo.

First, castles. The game that I was playing with the secret police allowed me to wander the countryside, but required that I have a castle or other tourist landmark as my destination. In Afrin, instead of heading uphill through the residential district, I should have walked along the valley bottom in the direction of the Byzantine castle. Tourists walked toward castles, subversives walked in other directions.

Second, hotels. Several days after the Afrin episode I was talking to Sarkis at the desk of the Baron Hotel when a man in a dark blue suit walked in. I recognized the chief of the immigration police—the man who had flipped me three out of five for my freedom. Without saying a word, Sarkis handed over the hotel register and the passports of all the guests. Later it struck me that the primary way that the police kept track of foreigners was through the hotels—you surrendered your passport when you registered. Sure, the cops picked up foreigners during the day, people who didn't have enough sense to be heading toward a castle. But otherwise, examination took place at the registration desk of the hotel. The whole process was discreet, invisible: no hacking motion, no AK-47s. The foreigner was seldom even aware that his passport had been fingered.

My strategy for the Roman Bridge called into play both lessons. The Roman Bridge was a tourist destination like a castle—at least that's what I would claim when I was stopped by the police. I also would take precautions. I would keep to main bus lines and turn down invitations that took me off the beaten track. No more Qardahas. And I had learned from the incident in Afrin. I would avoid villages, especially those of the Kurds.

That left the problem of hotels. Normally a traveler to the Roman Bridge would stay in Qamishly, an outpost on the Turkish border— heavily populated by Kurds. Qamishly was reputed to be the town where Kurdish rebels came for R&R before returning to the battle in southern Turkey. This was a tough town infested with secret police. One American woman I had talked to warned me that the police in Qamishly were very thorough in their ID checks. She had passed through unscathed, she explained, because the *mukhabarat* did not respect women enough to suspect them. A male colleague of hers who stayed in Qamishly, however, had had his passport inspected while he slept and, at first light, was awakened by a knock on his hotel room door. An unusual incident? She had asked around and learned of similar stories from other men traveling alone through this district. "It's no accident," she told me. "Police in and around Qamishly have a policy of detaining and interrogating every male foreigner, traveling alone, who comes through town."

My idea was to avoid the hotels in Qamishly by using Hasakah as my bivouac. In Hasakah the police had a lot less to do, since the town was only at the edge of the heaviest Kurdish settlement and was fifty miles from the border. I expected the police in this town to be omnipresent, but not to be on a hair-trigger. From Hasakah I would dash for the Roman Bridge, then return to Qamishly for my night's stay. I would likely have official visitors the next morning, but by then victory would be mine.

I returned to my hotel at five thirty, sat in the cramped reception room, and watched the end of an old Charles Bronson movie dubbed into Turkish. Charles shot three hoodlums in New York while the hotel manager totaled restaurant receipts. I went to my room and my private bath but this evening the water was only lukewarm. "Tomorrow is my big day," I thought. I bathed in the tepid water, shut out the lights at eight o'clock, and fell into an uneasy sleep.

12 — Nuri

HASAKAH. MONDAY, NOVEMBER 30.

I rose early, butterflies in my stomach. Today I would take on the *mukhabarat*. After weeks of self-deprivation, I felt good, felt strong. I would take on the police *mano a mano*—hand-to-hand—in the crudest, dirtiest, most forlorn corner of this nation. As you can imagine, however, by day's end my bravado, my *mano a mano*, had collapsed, and I was muddling through, as the British say, surviving by any possible means.

I paid my hotel in dollars (traveler's checks were not accepted in this outpost) and caught a shared or service taxi to Qamishly. Things were going well when I noticed, on my map, some Roman ruins along the way. The taxi let me off, and I saw women working in the fields and a half dozen men with motorcycles parked at the intersection, in case some paying customer needed a ride. I hired a motorcycle, then spent an hour exploring Tell Brak. As near as I could see, the entire hill, a quarter mile around, was composed of pottery fragments and tufts of grass. I rode back to the highway, paid my driver, and waited half an hour before catching the next bus. When we reached the outskirts of Qamishly it was past noon.

I was trying to visit Jisr Roman without getting thrown in jail and, as our bus drove through town, I shared my plans with a Kurdish youth of seventeen. Nuri had blue eyes, sandy hair, and sharp features that belied a mild frame of mind. At the bus yard Nuri inquired and learned that the last bus to the Roman Bridge had left an hour earlier. The route to the bridge, it turned out, was not highly traveled, and buses were few.

Why had I detoured to Tell Brak? Now my strategy had come unraveled. Staying at a hotel in Qamishly would be like sleeping in the police station. "Come with me," Nuri said. "Stay the night with me, in my house, in my village."

A Kurdish village! Just what I needed. The last time I had visited a Kurdish village I had spent six hours in detention. According to all my theories, a Kurdish village would mean a quick trip to jail for this American, or worse. And could I trust this young man? What about that other student who had invited me home with him, Rasheed, that guy on the coast who it turned out hated Americans, the one who tricked me into entering Qardaha alone. Not a good idea at all.

"Ma leesh," I said, Why not?

We caught a bus that took us to a small Kurdish settlement surrounded by rich, grassy farmland. Nuri's house was a picturesque adobe with one modern improvement: a poured concrete slab for a roof, far less leaking and less dust than traditional clay roofs. Individual mud bricks were exposed where the surface plastering of mud and straw had weathered away. Maya, his brother's wife, was tall and slender, with long dark hair and small crosses tattooed below her eyebrows. When we arrived, she was crouched on the floor, cooking over a propane burner in a corner by the door.

What unfolded in the afternoon and evening that I spent with Nuri was pure farce. Nuri and his family were the rightful inhabitants of this house. Yet they tolerated the intrusions of two neighbors, both of them boors, who came and went as they pleased, never thinking to knock. While these two were circling, like confused scavenger birds, I was waiting for the knock on the door, the men with AK-47s, and all the while I kept being offered bits of advice on the grim fate that awaited me at the Roman Bridge.

Nuri and family.

Nuri and I sat on a cushion in the living room and talked. In a few minutes the first boor, a schoolteacher, a slender man of thirty-five, walked in and strutted about as though he were lord of the manor, then asked me dozens of questions about America.

Maya brought in a platter with cut tomatoes, an omelet, yogurt, and parsley. The schoolteacher excused himself, displaying discretion that I had not expected from him. I was hungry. We used flatbread for silverware and plates and did not speak as we ate.

Halfway through our meal, the schoolteacher returned and sat on the couch, staring down at us. He was rude, a complete slob, no doubt about it. Nuri poured tea which was sweet and hot, but there were not enough glasses now that the teacher had joined us. Nuri passed his glass to the teacher. When we finished eating, the teacher announced the purpose of his visit.

"I must have your name and address," he said to me in English. "I must have this for my visa to the United States."

"Mumkin," I replied, It is possible. "But later." Since I was accepting Nuri's hospitality, I couldn't really refuse the request of a man who appeared to be Nuri's friend. Besides, it seemed unlikely that the teacher would ever reach America, not to mention my home town.

"Life in Syria is difficult," the teacher said. "The food is expensive, and people have no work. I must go to America." The teacher left, and Nuri and I relaxed for an hour and then, about four o'clock, decided to take a walk. Before we reached the door, however, the schoolteacher returned. "You should know," he said, "that I write in English." He scrawled five words on a scrap of paper, smiled at this tour de force, and handed the paper to me. I examined it for a few moments.

"Azeem," I said, Fantastic. "What does it say?" The schoolteacher made explanations, and I voiced my praise. Nuri told him that I was traveling to the Roman Bridge. "No," the teacher said. "Dangerous, very dangerous. You must turn back."

"Leesh?" I asked. "The Syrian police? You are afraid that they will

jail me like that other American?"

"Not the Syrians," said the teacher. "The Turks. The Turks shoot you and kill you. They all the time do this. It is too unfriendly of them. One man killed just a little time ago. Please, turn and go south."

I didn't know what to think. Several years later I came across a book that cautioned visitors that this "sensitive border area" was "heavily watched by Turkish soldiers." The book stipulated that a police escort was required, and strongly advised against venturing from the high bluff down to the bridge itself. The teacher was an edgy and unpleasant man, a classic pest, yet he was no fool. I accepted his warning. On the other hand, I wasn't about to turn around.

Nuri and I walked out, and the schoolteacher followed, then turned away at the corner. Although the teacher was worried about the Turks, I was still more concerned about the Syrian *mukhabarat*. I expected at any moment to see grim men in blue jeans and khaki jackets.

Nuri and I walked the streets as the sun set over low mud houses with walled courtyards and weathered wooden gates—no concrete apartment buildings, no rebar jutting into the sky. Everything was old and traditional. At the edge of this village we came to a small store in a concrete building, an island of modernity in this ancient land. I purchased a tape of Selah Rasool, the Kurdish musician whose music I had heard in Membij. The man in the store knocked off the tape on a high speed Sony duplicating machine while I wondered about copyright. He informed me that "Selah Rasool" meant "prayer for Muhammad" in Kurdish.

"Is Selah Rasool at home now, in Qamishly?" I asked.

"No," replied the proprietor. "Selah Rasool is gone. Maybe to the war in Turkey, to fight for the Kurds. Who can know?"

Nuri and I walked to a fruit stand on the highway. I was worried about the Roman Bridge.

"No problem," said the proprietor in English. "You are safe at Jisr Roman."

"But the Turks with their guns," I said. "Won't they shoot at me?"

"The Turks," he frowned. "Yes, the Turks kill people there, but only fools and imbeciles. You will be OK."

"*Ma fehmet,*" I don't understand.

"The Turks have put an iron gate across the bridge at the border but their guns are pointed twenty-five meters on our side. The only ones who get shot are those who look at the old stones and go too close. Then the Turk guards jump from behind a rock and shoot quick. Ah! The tourists make big trouble for the Syrians who must find a bag or a box and send the body to France or Germany or wherever."

13 — Lenin on the Steppe

"Lenin," said Nuri, "I love him very much."

Nuri and I were sitting on his living room floor when the second boor, a serious-looking young man, walked in. Hamza's face was hard and old beyond his nineteen years, with strong lines across the brow that gave him an expression that was both pugnacious and smug.

"Lenin," Nuri continued, "his ideas are very good for the life, for the poor people. I study the October battle in Russia in 1917." Nuri had purchased books of Lenin's in Aleppo and smuggled them home. If he had taken such books to school, he would have been arrested—which seems a little strange since, officially at least, at this time the Soviet Union was Syria's patron.

Nuri's friend Hamza had not spoken since he entered the room. As Nuri talked with me, Hamza walked to a chest in the corner and pulled out two large posters drawn on matboard, flow charts featuring boxes, diamonds, and circles filled with handwritten text in very small Arabic characters. One poster represented the life and deeds of Lenin, the other his philosophy.

"Have you ever heard of Thomas Jefferson?" I asked. Nuri had not heard. "Jefferson had ideas of freedom that you should know. He was important to my country, just as Lenin was to the Soviet Union."

I didn't like the franchise system in my country that made every commercial district look alike. I didn't like the intensity of the advertising, the use of sex as a tool to manipulate consumers, the tone of Hollywood movies. I didn't like the way the tax system was rigged so that wealth was concentrated at the top. But to me these were surface imperfections, serious but fixable. My country was based on an ideal that elevated individual men and women and tried to organize life around individual rights. The world had never seen anything like it.

Certainly Marx and Lenin, for all their insight into the excesses of capitalism, had nothing to compare to the plain, primitive truth of one person, one vote. In my country, there is a certain amount of freedom, both political and economic. In the United States, if you have an idea, you can go for it, make it happen, change the world.

Nuri seemed puzzled but his friend Hamza had an answer for every question. "America is good for nobody," Hamza said. "Why did America kill Grenada? America is good only for killing people." I didn't have a quick answer. To me Grenada seemed like a trumped-up military exercise, a pretext for joint military maneuvers, a phony war if there ever was one. Still, I did not like being put on the defensive by a high school student, so I changed the subject.

"Why don't you think critically?" I said—this was a line that my college professors had used to antagonize us when we complained about the military death machine that was killing people in Vietnam. Now I was so old and slow-witted that I had no choice but to toss this old smoke bomb. "Lenin was a critical thinker. He looked at the past. He knew how to pick and choose. Why don't you follow the example of Lenin instead of parroting the words of Lenin?" It took half an hour of searching to find Arabic words for these ideas, but eventually I made my point.

Nuri seemed excited by the notion of intellectual improvising. Hamza, however, felt that he had been bested in an argument with an imperialist and choked on his resentment. Hamza did not need critical thinking for he was past the point of philosophy. I concluded that soon he would have a rifle in his hands. He stood, turned, and left without speaking.

A few minutes later the schoolteacher returned. Hoping to get rid of him quick, I wrote out my address. "Thank you," he said. "Now I will get my visa. I will see you in Seattle in two weeks. I will live at your house, work in your business. This will be my new life in America, very beautiful."

I suggested that he try Australia, and his eyes filled with tears. "I must come to America," he said. "I *will* come to America. America is good."

"Really," I said. "You should talk to the guy who just left."

14 — The Roman Bridge

After enormous effort I got the schoolteacher to leave, then he returned for one more question. At last he was gone for good. "Finally!" I thought. But then he returned to invite me for coffee. I got him to leave a third time and collapsed on the mattress that Nuri had pulled out for me. It was past midnight, and I lay down to sleep beside Nuri, his sister-in-law, and her baby. The baby cried, Nuri pulled the blankets over his head, Maya, exhausted after a week with a cranky child, could not be roused. I stood in my underwear—who's looking?—and rocked the child through the night.

The next morning I rose early and flagged down a service taxi. I was going for the Roman Bridge. The car was a De Soto, this time a '54, with a diesel engine, three seats, and a carrying capacity of nine. The land passed by, and I saw signal hills built by the Romans and oil wells with big cams pumping methodically. The sky was pale and clear and the new sun rose above the eastern hills, painting the valley with light. I was awake, on the lookout for police, and at this moment too worried to feel tired.

Malkiye Dayrik is the most dramatically situated town in Syria, a cluster of low adobes on the edge of a volcanic plain with snow-covered mountains jutting into the sky on three sides. I saw plowed earth, flat and dark, and grass, faded and silver gray. I was in a hurry to get moving before the police descended, so I hired the first car I saw, a Toyota Land Cruiser painted metallic blue. My driver took me down a long hill toward the river and came into Ain Divar, a small village of ancient, weathered adobes at the edge of the plateau. A little farther along we reached a police station on the bluff with a spectacular view down to the Tigris and across to the Tarus Mountains in Turkey. I had been waiting to get busted ever since Hasakah, and my stomach was in knots. I pulled out my passport and waited for an official to give the hacking motion. My driver stopped, a policeman came out, glanced at my passport, smiled, and waved us on. As my driver pulled away I gasped and twisted in my seat: a friendly cop.

We drove to a tourist lookout, then cut over the edge following two tire tracks, which soon became little stream beds lined with softball-sized rocks. Before long I was standing atop the ancient, arched bridge. I looked across gravel beds at the main flow of the Tigris which had shifted to the east so that now only a small current flowed beneath the stone arch of Jisr Roman. The structure had been built by Romans in the second century near the spot where Alexander had forded the Tigris on September 20, 331 BC, and marched to a final, decisive battle against Darius III and the massed

Roman Bridge, detail.

Persian army just a few miles farther east. In the eleventh and twelfth centuries Turks and Arabs had repaired and restored the bridge, adding inset stone panels with Arabic inscriptions that depicted the signs of the zodiac. I looked back toward the Syrian shore. Somewhere in the brush and weeds was the site of an ancient Roman camp called Bezabda.

The sun was warm, the air fresh. This was an idyllic spot, a beautiful no-man's land at the intersection of three countries, a setting of peace poised amidst strife, war, and revolution. I had succeeded in reaching the Roman Bridge. I had taken the road from Damascus, met people I could never have seen at home. I would carry the image of these men, women, and children—and their goats, dogs, cats, and mud houses for a very long time.

How was it that I had reached my goal? Was it because I had carefully honed my skills as a traveler? Since Hasakah I had committed errors which, according to my theories, should have spelled disaster at the hands of the *mukhabarat*. Yet nothing had happened. Perhaps the secret police, with their fine sense of irony, were toying with me. Maybe they were being inconsistent on purpose, to keep me guessing, or, on this day, simply did not care. Were my errors outweighed by the one thing I had done right? I had been heading toward a tourist destination. Still, what seemed most unfair: after days of fear, a smiling policeman.

I took a Landrover down to the Tigris River and the Roman Bridge.

Whether my success was skill or luck there remained a deeper question: what did it mean? "The value of any summit," I found myself thinking, "is in the quality of insight it brings forth."

Saleh the Shiite had been right. I had come to this country for a reason. I was searching for a specific truth. Yet as I sat atop the Roman Bridge, I struggled to pull the object of my search into the light.

I thought of great journeys in literature, and Herman Melville's *Moby Dick* came to mind. The demented Captain Ahab launched forth on his sea journey, months on board ship, sailing the heaving seas, cold storm and hot calm, sea birds and sharks, smells of tar and brine. Ahab searched for the white whale and found it and fought it. The whale smashed a hole in the side of his whaling ship. As the ship sank, it created a vortex that pulled everything under, the whale boats, the men. Ahab died and his men died, except for one. Ishmael, a seaman who sailed before the mast under Captain Ahab's command, lived to tell the tale. As he recited his story, Ishmael sifted his experience, using the flow of his narrative to elicit order, purpose, meaning. Ishmael reflected upon the driving action of the plot. He refracted it, provided conscience, judgment, a larger human perspective. Against linear action that spiraled to destruction, Ishmael provided spatial, circular continuity. Against death, Ishmael affirmed life.

Ishmael gave perspective to Ahab's search for the white whale. He probed particular events to reveal a larger meaning. On my Syrian journey, who was the talkative man, the equivalent to Ishmael? "Saleh's the one," I thought.

Saleh the Shiite placed American life, specifically *my* American life, in a larger context. "Look at the world," he seemed to be saying, "look at the people in the world." I had to admit that Americans could be crazy about their careers, hard-charging to the end, pursuing linear projects of career advancement—a little like Ahab chasing his whale. I had to admit that, in my construction business, I had known a few willful, Ahabian impulses. Yet I had put them behind me, I had escaped America and come to this land. And Saleh was right. This trip was no accident. It was my chance to experience the broader universe in which my particular life in Seattle was set. This was my opportunity to find continuity, balance, perspective.

"So the joke is on me," I thought. In this land my linear, ambitious impulses had quickly reasserted themselves. Now that I was on vacation, I had invented an entirely different career, that of adventure-travel writer, and pursued my literary project with the focus of an Ahab, pushing toward what I thought of as literary success much as I had pushed my carpentry jobs back in Seattle. But Saleh urged me in another direction, and so did every particle of this country.

Would I colonize Syria, divide it, organize it, conquer it for my writing? Or would this land dis-organize me, pull me apart, remake me as a new person, a type of Syrian, a man with new ideas? The contest went back and forth. And then, out of nowhere, my night of agony on the Euphrates. I felt as though I had spiraled into the murk of the Euphrates as certainly as Ahab had been sucked into the clear depths of the Pacific.

The problem, I now could see, was that I was trying to turn this place into my idea of a book, a page-turner, a book with a plot. This was a linear effort if there ever was one, and Syria resisted because it had better things to do. That night on the Euphrates forced me to get rid of my pretensions. Now I was a mere traveler shorn of will. I reached the

Two boys offered to cart my blue sack to the bus stop.

Roman Bridge as an exhausted man without design.

I was still taking notes, and I supposed that I was still writing a book, but the project had utterly changed. I was no longer seeking to entertain Americans with exotic tales from the orient. I was exhausted, and this land had turned me and was using me for its own purposes. It was molding me into a vehicle for carrying a message back to America, the message that Saleh had urged me to acquire.

I casually turned the other direction from my spot at the top of this arched span so that I looked into Turkey. I saw river water, swiftly flowing, like the Snoqualmie River back home. I thought about trout, then explored a little more with my eyes. I saw gravel heaped at the far bank, brush at the water's edge, a small road winding along the river. I saw no Turkish soldiers, no trucks, no cars. Above the road I saw a plain covered with dry grass, then steep, tawny hillsides, covered with grass and rock, with sculpted, folded cones of smoothly covered earth and rock rising up and up—and beyond, in the distance, I could see high blue-gray mountains with snow.

"Insight? Message?" I thought. "I've no idea." It was time to go back to Damascus. I turned toward the Syrian shore. My driver was sitting at the side of the old river bed, throwing small stones into a pool of dead water, in no hurry whatsoever. I pulled a map from my backpack. Here was Hasakah, Qamishly, Malkiye Dayrik, Ain Divar. Here was the Roman Bridge. And just across the line into Turkey and a bit downstream on the Tigris was Cukurça, a tiny village, and above it on the heights was Hakkari. I had picked up bits of news at the Baron Hotel in Aleppo. I knew that in the past few weeks this district had been raided by Kurdish revolutionaries operating from bases in Iraq. Many of the Kurds, I knew, had come over the border from Syria. Villagers had been killed, Turkish troops had counterattacked, and then, in response, Iraqi soldiers had come up to their side of the border. The place was tense, not at all safe.

I had come to Syria for Syria. I had avoided the lure of Istanbul, Jerusalem, Cairo. I was exploring this country, writing about this country. On the other hand, my travel permit was running out, and I needed to duck into Turkey for a day in any case. Hakkari and Cukurça sounded like interesting towns. What would be the view of Syria from the other side of the Tigris? Then it occurred to me: for all my mountain climbing metaphors, the Roman Bridge was not a summit but a bridge. It was a means of reaching the other side. It connected two lands, two cultures, two peoples. I had come to Syria intending to bag a peak, like a good mountaineer, but Syria had changed me and changed my project. I now knew that I was here—not to conquer a summit but to cross a bridge.

The Roman Bridge was a letter drop, in cold war parlance, where the secret agent picked up a message sending him to his true goal. I had something—not an epiphany, not a message for America, but simply an instruction: cross over the bridge, insight to follow in due course. I needed to reach Hakkari.

15 — The Kommando

HAKKARI, TURKEY. WEDNESDAY, DECEMBER 2.

I walked the narrow streets in late afternoon, and the sun on this high, Asian terrace was low, slanted, and filtered. It shifted the colors of my surroundings, desaturating them. We were high, and the air was cool and carried intimations of the bitter-cold winter to come.

I saw pushcarts, stone buildings, and mud houses. Mount Subul, 10,500 feet and covered with snow, rose above the town on one side, and small farms sat in high valleys on the other. The climate was dry, and I saw small streams and irrigated fields that grew vegetables, a little wheat, and also slender trees with fine yellow branches. As I looked from town the trees gave the scene an old and gentle quality.

The growing season at this altitude was short, agriculture was poor, and the town survived as a market for cattle which grazed in the surrounding hills. Hakkari had been part of the Ottoman empire from the early 1500s but it had been governed by local Kurdish emirs who lived in the stone fortress which still stood on the hill above the town.

In the evening I sat in a kebab salon in the market with two locals, Ayoub and Uthman. We ate roasted lamb, salad, and afterward drank sweet tea. Ayoub was tanned from his work as a mountain guide.

"Every year for eight years I have seen young Iranian men on their way to Ankara or Istanbul," he said. "They are escaping the army. This year more than before."

Sitting beside the mountain guide was Uthman, a young man with a crew cut who was a "Kommando" (an elite Turkish troop) stationed nearby at Çukurça (chew-kur-cha), a Kurdish village on the Iraq border. Uthman showed me snapshots from boot camp which he carried in his wallet. Here was Uthman with his army buddies in combat gear, looking like red-faced fraternity boys at a party. Another picture showed him alone with an enormous machine gun and its ammunition belt. In the photo he smiled.

We were speaking casually, piecing together the world, yet at the same time I saw figures in a dream: a Kurd and a Turk. Half a millennium earlier, in the valley of the Tigris, Kurdish brigands on horseback attacked merchant caravans, the calculated investments of Arab traders or French or British or Genoese, and made off with trade goods or extracted a heavy toll for safe passage. And, on the heights above the valley, Turkish horsemen hacked and scattered the last Byzantine troops, the last soldiers of the last outpost of the Roman Empire. In 1453 the city of spires and crosses, the city of golden chalices, the city of Constantine fell to swift, rude cavalry and ponderous, stone-slinging siege machines. More than four hundred years later, the Victorian British would deride the Ottomans as corrupt despots with harems and eunuchs. The British would scorn the Ottoman empire as a decaying, tottering relic propped up by more vigorous powers—Russia, France—kept alive as a place holder, a buffer, a filler of vacuum, kept alive by the British themselves as a calculated move in their Great Game.

Today the Ottomans are stoutly defended by scholars who compare the human face of Ottoman rule to the chilling machine-like inhumanity that characterized the imperialism of nations such as Britain, France, Russia, Germany. As the twentieth century began the world gasped and shuddered at its own modernity. Bands played, soldiers paraded, and civilized peoples were sucked into the stinking pit of war: the first war, the last war, the Great War, a war where men huddled, cowered, died, and machines were king, machines of steel that eviscerated, dismembered, crushed.

The Ottomans were blundering potentates, utterly out-of-date. They were an empire, not a nation. Yet the critics of the Ottomans seem to forget that the early members of the dynasty overran the Byzantines because they were stronger, more persistent, more vital.

Mount Subul loomed above Hakkari. The sign across the street announced to this predominantly Kurdish town, "How happy is the one who says, 'I am a Turk.'"

They forget that the Ottomans began as lean nomads on the steppe, *ghazis,* vigorous, religious warriors. In 1300 the Ottomans began their ride to power on the same living force that had propelled the Mongols: the lightly armed fighting man, a master of warfare by maneuver, a man on the back of a horse.

I asked Uthman how many years the war with the Kurds had been going on. The mountain guide translated. "Fighting for four or five years," he said. "This year the most. Bombs from the air."

A few days earlier in Syria, Nuri had told me the reason for the war. "The Kurds fight," he said, "because the Turks take their land."

Ayoub, the mountain guide, did not agree. "I am a Kurd," he said. "I grew up in a village near here. There is no difficulty between the Kurds and the Turks, here or anywhere in Turkey."

"But the fighting," I said.

"No," said Ayoub. "They are just terrorists with Soviet weapons. They are a cheap way for Iraq to fight Turkey. In October, an Iraqi helicopter dropped a bomb on a Kurdish village near here."

"That was Çukurça, where I am," said Uthman. "It came at night. I was outside. I shot at it with my machine gun but it escaped."

"Was anyone hurt?" I asked.

Uthman took out his wallet and extracted two pieces of crumpled metal, each smaller than a gumdrop. "These came from the bomb," he said. Then he rolled up his right sleeve and showed a small scar on his forearm. "These came also from my arm. Another soldier was hurt bad, and twelve were killed—not soldiers but Kurdish people in their houses, women, children, old men."

Uthman put the metal fragments back in his wallet and the three of us returned to the hotel where Uthman and I were sharing a room. He slept soundly while I tossed. Cukurça was on my mind.

In the morning I rose early to catch my bus back to Damascus. As I dressed, I watched my sleeping roommate. Uthman was strong and fit, undoubtedly a fine soldier, yet he looked a little like his mother's boy. On the way out I paid our hotel bill.

The bus pulled away. We descended down, down, down into a canyon and turned onto the road beside the river that flowed away from Hakkari. Our bus traveled along the river, then crossed a bridge and began to climb.

16 – Hotel Baron

A day later at the Baron Hotel in Aleppo I told Sarkis the desk clerk the details of the bombing in Cukurça. He listened, then thought for a moment. "The helicopter that dropped the bomb could not have been from Iraq," he said. "Iraq is in big trouble now with Iran. Iraq is preparing to meet the winter offensive of the Iranians. The last thing they ask is trouble with Turkey. Many of Iraq's supplies come in trucks on the highway from Turkey."

"Who then?"

"This was a trick to make Turkey fight Iraq and cut off Iraq's supplies. Only one country could benefit."

"Who?"

"The helicopter must have been from Iran."

Unlike the hotels in Dier ez-Zoir and Hasakah, the Baron accepted payment in traveler's checks—the reason for my detour to this city. Sarkis the desk clerk allowed me to pay for my ten dollar room with two traveler's checks: a ten and a twenty. I took change in dollars, slept for two hours, and caught the night train down the Euphrates

Bedouin women and their cow.

toward Dier ez-Zoir. As the train left Aleppo and moved past the last scattered lights, I thought about the bomb and the Kurdish village.

Whether the helicopter belonged to Iran or Iraq, it was a cinch that it had been made by an arms manufacturer in the United States or the former Soviet Union. Arms exports were important to the national economy, officials in Washington and Moscow explained. They were necessary for "balance of payments." On the ground, first-world technology gave a lethal edge to third-world animosities.

What I saw in Cukurça was a snapshot of the future: a nation defending its existence against a clan, a race, a village—against Kurds who valued Sony tape duplicators and loved their large families and close villages but had little use for national governments based in Baghdad, Teheran, or Ankara.

Cukurça was in Turkey, not Syria, yet events in this village posed the question of Syria's national survival. What will happen when the Syrian security state loosens its grip and allows Kurds, Aramaic Christians, Ismailis, Druze, Armenians, and other minorities to express themselves?

Bedouin girl and her pet sheep.

Bedouin elder.

Survival, more immediately, is an individual matter. How do Syrians keep their minds and hearts together? In 1987 the economy was poor and the security of the regime was strict. Nevertheless, Syrians seemed happy. How could this be? In Aleppo I had visited artists and writers and thought that they did something to soften the blows. Yet later, riding country buses, I realized that their importance was national and international. They were testing and probing and creating a path for humankind to follow through Islamic extremism and Western imperialism to a vibrant world culture, governed by law, where idea and difference fueled the engines of intellectual, spiritual, and economic growth.

Still, within Syria, the identifiable influence of artists and writers was narrow, for the most part restricted to an urban elite, and percolated only very slowly, if at all, into the lives of working folk. After traveling to the Roman Bridge and beyond I sensed that I knew the answer. But words failed me. Syrians, against all odds, were happy. That was enough.

I also wondered about the Roman Bridge—what was it? The Roman Bridge enabled me to see Syria, my adopted country, through the eyes of Turks and Kurds. When I returned to Syria I was changed in a subtle yet lasting way: I had acquired the unconscious habit of looking back, of viewing events from two perspectives at the same time. Now I saw the Syrian government straight on and also from the other side of the bridge that separated it from its people and the people of other lands. The same was true when I returned to the United States. Fourteen years later, following the September 11th attacks, I found myself angry and grieving as an American. Yet my impulses for unthinking wide-scale revenge were blocked. For I also saw these events as did silent, innocent men and women from all over the world who waited, in fear, for the American response.

The Dutch Arabist Carool Kersten put his own spin on my visit to the Roman Bridge.

"You had a mystical experience," he said. "You realized that the Roman Bridge was not a summit but a bridge, a way to cross over to the other side and to view the world through the eyes of the Other."

By now my train was lost in desert. It was dark, no lights, and we moved almost silently but for the clack-clack of our wheels passing over the rails. It was a restful sound, the lights in our car were dim, and I tried to sleep.

Images of Cukurça came to mind yet the scene included faces from a different place, faces I knew. I saw young blond-haired Nuri and Maya, his sister-in-law, and her baby. It was evening, the light was soft, and I also saw old men in black sheepskin capes standing beside the highway, small houses of mud and concrete, alleys choked with dust. I was almost asleep now, and the lives of quiet people came to me full and wordless, like a sound or color, and then passed on. My mind was clear and still and empty.

PART EIGHT

Return
A Week in Damascus

Aleppo

Al-Assad
Dam

Ar-Raqqah

Euphrates River

Sabkhat
al-Jabbul

Khanaser

Wadi al-Gharrah

Esriye

Jebel al-Bishri

Dier ez-Z

Jebel al-Bilaas

Hama

Homs

Wadi al-Hajl

Abu Rahba
Hammam

Palmyra

Qasr al-Hir
al-Gharbi

Wadi al-Miyah

Syria's
Interior
Desert

Sabkl
Al-R

Khan Abu Shamat

Damascus

Jebel al-Druze

Khirbat
an-Nbash

Suweida

Key
hammam, bath
jebel, mountain
khan, inn
khirbat, ruin
qasr, palace
sabkhat, dry lak
wadi, stream

Lebanese border

1— Coming Home to Damascus

I woke to gray and sunless dawn. Beyond my window, the land was unpeopled: bleak, dry, covered with salt. At this moment I felt like a returning explorer. I was stumbling down the rough slopes, a weary man, dehydrated, blinded by sun and wind, weak from days of thin air and meager provisions. I closed my eyes and opened them again. The landscape held still as we moved past. We moved without labor, easing our way, our wheels gliding along the track. I could not hear our engine, and we seemed to coast the last miles to Dier ez-Zoir.

I adjusted my seat into a sitting position. By this time I was fully awake, and complications of the coming day's itinerary began to weigh on my mind. I was discouraged. I may have found something at the Roman Bridge, but I was returning with nothing objective or articulate: no trophy, no ringing phrases. Suddenly, an idea. "Articulate wisdom is the domain of patriarchs," I thought. I had to get back to Damascus and find the Patriarch of Antioch.

When we reached Dier ez-Zoir, I paid my outstanding hotel bill in cash dollars and retrieved my traveler's check, then explored downstream on the Euphrates for a day. I saw ditches that revealed the mud walls of the ancient city of Mari, 2700 BC. I also saw the scattered stone of Doura Europos, fourth century BC—Alexander's outpost against the Persians. On the Iraq border, I found a desert town named Abu Kamal that was filled with Bedouins, and in the dusty market I saw chickens scratching in small cages made of lashed sticks.

At ten PM I caught a bus heading west across the desert. At two AM I arrived at the ancient Roman oasis of Palmyra and knocked on the door of the Zenobia Hotel. I couldn't raise anyone, however, so I stopped at a less distinguished place down the road where the tired manager stumbled to the door to check me in.

In the second century AD, Petra (the stone city located in what is now Jordan) and its Nabatean inhabitants fell into decline and gave way to Palmyra, the jewel of the Syrian desert, a stone metropolis in the sands. Palmyra became a way-station in trade between East and West. In the third century, Palmyra was the scene of rebellion and murder—the place where beautiful queen Zenobia challenged Rome.

Zenobia's husband was a loyalist who had battled the Persians on Aurelian's behalf but was murdered (historians have deduced) on Zenobia's orders. She quickly took control, built up her army, then sent troops south to Egypt and north to Antioch. In 272 Aurelian counterattacked, and Zenobia fled. Aurelian's men caught her on the banks of the Euphrates, shackled her in golden chains, and transported her to Rome. Here, as the story goes, she was pardoned, became the wife of a wealthy noble, and lived quietly in his villa until her death.

For the modern visitor, Palmyra is a magnificent jumble of cut stone. On the day of my visit the wind was cold, tourists few. I toured the ruins, inspected Roman water lines made of tile and lead, and caught a bus to Damascus.

The highway was asphalt, and the land was covered by gritty soil without grass. Wind lifted sand and blew it in drifts against the rocks. There was only gray sand and rock and nothing growing until, suddenly, green palms rose against the landscape: an oasis.

I saw black wool tents, Bedouin tents with a single white stripe, and I glanced at my travel map in the soft light and saw in the interior dozens of small *wadis, khirbats, qasrs, hammams, sabkhats,* and *jebels*—streams, ruins, castles, baths, lakes, and mountains. This "empty" space had long been inhabited, I realized, and still was home to a Bedouin remnant.

But that was another question, a project for another year. I was tired now, my bus traveled on, light slipped away, and there were no more palms or tents. All I could see was rock and dirt and sand. Ours was a good bus, a Karnak bus with high-backed seats and an attendant who offered lemon drops and drinks of water. There were no chickens in these aisles, no sunflower shells on the floor, no sheep stowed in the baggage compartments. The engine was steady, the light was low, and I was no longer hungry, just numb and tired.

We reached Homs, stopped to reload, then pulled out and turned onto the freeway to Damascus. It was night by now, and we cruised the highway, moving south, driving in darkness under a black sky. Our bus carried us into desert mountains and then down and down into a valley of lights, a flat, desert valley where the lights were small. We moved on, turned from the highway, and I could see the familiar debris of urban living. The light was gray, did not seem to have a source, and there was no color, only tones of gray. A little farther along I saw dark, plain-faced buildings jammed together at the edge of the street, cars parked on the sidewalks, and everything coated with muddy light from a distant street lamp. The scene moved past slowly on the other side of my window, and I closed my eyes again to rest. Eight weeks earlier I had gotten off my airplane and ridden a night bus into this city. In that hour it had seemed a strange city, a capital of barbarism.

Days and nights had passed since then, and the city had changed very slowly. At first I learned to ride the buses back and forth to Zeinab, met Saad Shalabi, danced at the Cham Palace. And then I ventured into the countryside where it was rough and rude, the police were paranoid, and you carried your throbbing heart in your hands. Each time that I returned to Damascus on some brief errand I could see that the place had grown more hospitable in my absence. And now, after days of fear and sleeplessness on the frontier, Damascus had become an island of order and civilization, a safe harbor, a quiet moorage. I was glad to be home.

My bus came to a halt. Outside it was very cold, and the wind gusted. I pulled on more clothes and walked from the bus yard past the university and toward the embassy district. I wore a turtleneck, a dress shirt, a sports coat, a blue pile vest, a green cagoule, and my nylon expedition pack and was heading for the Meridien Hotel where the brass door handles were perfectly polished, the hotel staff turned out in crisp uniforms, and the hotel guests were expensively dressed. It would be warm inside, and I would walk across the polished marble floors in my cagoule, carrying my bulky blue backpack which was bad enough. But then I would be too hot and would have to unzip my cagoule which meant that everyone could see my layers—my blue pile vest, my sports coat, my button down shirt—and I would be revealed as the king of mismatch, utterly out of place. I would be like an old city with a trench through its gut, no more secrets, but I did not care.

For three weeks the bureaucrats of back-country banks had made life difficult for me, and now the act of cashing a traveler's check seemed a daring statement of principle.

I completed my banking at the Meridien and walked past the office of the UN Golan peace-keeping force, then through the embassy district to the Gondola Restaurant where I ate steak and chips and drank a cola. Then I went across the street and bought chocolate ice cream in a small plastic dish. In Dier ez-Zoir, as uncivilized a city as I can imagine, they had a single ice cream machine but turned it off at summer's end. I walked a few blocks as I ate my ice cream, then caught a cab for Saad's farm.

The moon had risen and shone full and strong upon the valley, giving it whiteness and strength. My taxi driver normally did not travel so far out at night. He was doing me a favor. When I arrived at Saad's farm, the gate around the compound was locked. I climbed the adobe wall, still wearing my sports coat and expedition pack, reached my legs over the barbed wire, then jumped into the darkness on the other side. The dog went crazy, but I was too far for his chain to reach. I left my bag in the house and walked across the compound, stepping on patches of moonlight beneath the cedar trees.

In their single room, the Eritreans sat around a small TV placed on the floor. An old movie was on. The room was warm and the air clear thanks to Saad who, to replace the olive oil bucket where the Eritreans had burned sticks, had installed an oil-burning heater with a stove pipe going up and through the wall. I thought about the immense pile of branches that Askia had dragged into the compound over the previous summer. Now this tangled mass was no longer needed as firewood and would have to be dragged out again. I watched television for an hour, then returned in moonlight to my quarters, empty, silent, and bitter with cold. It was winter on the desert now, and the heat of the previous October was but a memory. I lay down in my sleeping bag wearing all my clothes on a mattress on the tiled floor and shivered through the hours.

The next morning I awoke with the call to prayer. The voice, which came from a loudspeaker in the village, rose and fell and rose again. *"Allaaaaahu akbar!"* God is great! The voice penetrated the stone walls of the farmhouse and filled the room where I lay. It was mournful, resonant. In my first days, this voice had captured my pain, and now it gave dark comfort. The sound carried me, made me dream. I thought back to travelers in history who had come through Syria. I thought of Alexander. He had ventured east, marching through Syria and crossing the Tigris into Persia, defeating the Persians, then moving south into India. He fought every battle, overcame every enemy, then turned back. It was 323 BC and he was in Babylon, near current-day Baghdad. He was still a young man at thirty-three. He was building a fleet and planning to explore the water route from Persia to Egypt. But the story of his last months that's most often repeated depicts a saddened Alexander returned from the wars, a man uninspired by the demands of administration, despondent—no more worlds to conquer—a man who took fever and lay speechless while each member of his beloved army passed silently before him to bid adieu to their friend, their champion.

I was not Alexander and I was not about to die. Still, I had worked for sixty days to reach the Roman Bridge. I had used this goal to give meaning and order to my life, and now I had many things to do but not one thing of pressing importance. I felt empty, depleted.

It was dank and chilly in this room, I was alone, and my life was suspended. When sun came through my window, I rose and climbed to the roof. The air was cold, the sun was bright, the sky was rich, full, saturated—it was steeped in blue. I saw snow on the mountains above the valley.

2 — Tell the Truth

Askia had left to visit his parents in Eritrea and his friend Umar was now in charge of the farm and its small, black-and-white TV. I spent the day relaxing in the sun. That evening when I crossed the compound to visit, Umar was the one who spun the TV dial looking for films of famous directors. If his friend Askia favored Francis Ford Coppola, Umar favored Truffaut and Fellini. I asked Umar his opinion of American movies.

"Not so good for the third world," Umar said, "especially for the young people."

"Why not?" I asked.

"The young people are peaceful and happy," he said, "but the American movies teach fighting and killing."

Umar had a way of delivering a biting critique with simplicity and innocence. If Americans suffered from his chiding, Syrians fared no better.

"The Syrians do not understand East Africa," Umar continued. "One Syrian student asked me, 'Do you have buildings? Do you have cars?' The Syrians are rich, and they are ignorant, you see. They think we are like bushmen. So I had some fun with him. 'No,' I said, 'we live under trees. We have only one building in our land, and that is for the Syrian Ambassador. In my whole country there is only one car, and that is for the Syrian Ambassador. If the president of our country wants to go somewhere, he comes to the Syrian Ambassador and asks to borrow his car.'"

Umar had lived in Damascus since high school and made it clear that I should consider him a Syrian, a member of this country's large expatriate community. Like most Syrians, Umar was quick to offer literary advice. "You must write down the story of your visit," he said, "so the people of America will know who we are. If you write about us, it will not be funny. It will make them cry. You should have information about what it is like, what you have seen. Take us for who we are and what our stage of development is. But if you see mistakes, tell the mistakes along with the good things."

"This is all fine," I said, "but I need to find the Patriarch of Antioch in order to have a successful story. The Patriarch can give my journey a benediction, which would make a formal conclusion. See what I mean? A story needs to have a proper ending. No one wants to read a book that breaks the rules of literature."

"What are the rules of literature?" asked Umar. "Have respect to other people to tell the truth, just the truth—because you are a human being."

~~~~~~~

"The traveler goes far away from his native land," Farouk said. "He travels to a culture which is very strange, very different, and he makes observations, makes notes, makes theories. He is absorbed in this foreign culture and is thinking only of it and has forgotten the land of his birth. This is you in Syria, and since then, writing about Syria."

"OK," I said.

I thought that literary kibitzing would stop when I left Syria, but not so. At home in Seattle, whenever an Arab expatriate heard of my travel, I would likely receive a few more tips. One example was Farouk, the anthropologist.

"But the traveler doesn't know something, he can't sense it, he is looking one direction with such attention that he does not feel himself being gently pulled. And then someone from his home country reads what he has written and understands, it is obvious, everyone can see. Everyone, that is, except the traveler himself."

"What do they see?" I said.

"The traveler's deepest thoughts and feelings, so deep that they are intangible to the traveler himself. It's a signature of thought, impossible to erase, a vocabulary of soul that develops as one's character develops, that grows but never is lost or replaced with another, a style that stays with a person for life."

"Yeah?"

"The traveler, you see, has been writing about his own country from the moment he put pen to note pad. The more diligently he concentrated on a foreign culture, the more certainly and truly and intuitively he was drawn to the deepest troubles, the most central dynamics of his own. He has gone a very long distance to come home."

3 — Searching for the Patriarch of Antioch

The next day I woke suddenly. "I've forgotten something of pressing importance," I thought. By now I was starting to sound to myself like Saleh the Shiite. What was it? Had I forgotten to argue my hotel bill, my restaurant bill, the cost of my bus ticket? Then I remembered: I was searching for something. I needed to find the Patriarch. And besides, I still needed a benediction for my book. One more world to conquer.

I jumped out of bed, splashed water on my face, and set off for Damascus where I found Saad Shalabi in his office. We knocked on the lawyer's door, but no one answered, and Saad suggested that I try later, after the midday meal. In the meantime, what about Fateh Moudarres, the painter? I found Fateh in his basement *atelier* and noticed that he had finished only four canvases. Nevertheless, with eleven days left before the show, Fateh had time to visit. He talked, as eloquent as ever, and I got an idea. Since the Patriarch of Antioch was playing so hard to get, why not use Fateh as a substitute?

The following evening I met Fateh Moudarres again and walked with him to two openings: a photography show, and an exhibit of prints by Turki Mahmoud Bey put on by the Goethe Institute. In the midst of casual conversation Fateh mentioned that he wanted to do a show in the United States, say, in Seattle. "I'll give the gallery a good discount," he said. "I have the customs all worked out." I was willing, of course, to make the deal possible. At the same time, I was crushed. A day earlier I had put this dear man on a pedestal, right next to the Patriarch of Antioch, and now he was jumping back down and acting like an artist concerned about his career. The artists and writers I had met in Aleppo seemed less personally ambitious than Americans,

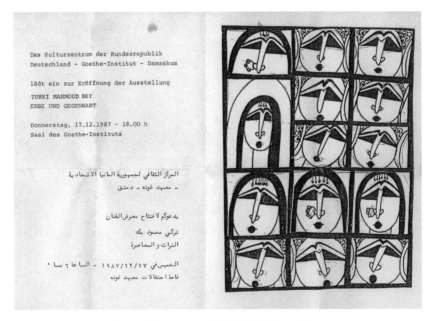

I attended an opening by Turki Mahmoud Bey.

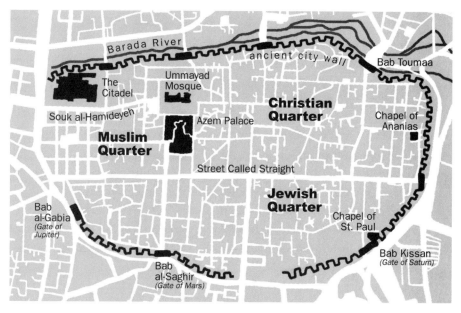

The old city of Damascus.

not so for Fateh and the others I was meeting in Damascus. Fateh Moudarres was both comic and profound, a quotable man, yet he had mentioned the one subject that I assumed the Patriarch never touched: marketing. Try as I could, I was unable to push him back onto his pedestal. He was one of a kind, but not a proper substitute for the Patriarch. Like the rest of us, Fateh Moudarres was a mortal with flashes of something better.

The next day I visited Saad who tried his lawyer friend again, with negative results. It struck me that the lawyer had been stringing me along for nearly three months, that he never intended to put me in touch with the Patriarch. I felt betrayed, although I suppose that the life of a lawyer in a police state was difficult enough without tourists throwing their two cents in. Time was running out.

I said good-bye to Saad and headed for the old city to find the Patriarch on my own. The darkness of this quarter parted before me as I entered, and I had difficulty recapturing the logic of my old fears. Over the next few days, I visited the ancient Damascus citadel (built in 1078 and used as a defense against the Crusaders) and Saladin's tomb which stood nearby. I also saw the Azem palace, built in the mid-1700s, an exquisite dwelling of Azem Pasha who was a governor

Azem Palace. A star-shaped window looking from the second floor into the courtyard.

of Damascus under the Ottomans. I took a steam bath in a domed bathhouse a few blocks away that was three or four hundred years old, and explored the Souk al-Hamideyeh with its high iron roof, built in 1863 and named for the Ottoman Sultan Abdul-Hamid.

I passed through the ancient Jewish quarter but did not stop to talk because I didn't want to get anyone in trouble and because few people were on the street. I visited the house which has been designated as that of Judas on the Street Called Straight where Saint Paul took refuge when he first came to the city. I also visited the house of Ananias, the Christian who restored Paul's sight. Day after day I searched for Der Mar Boulas, the monastery or chapel of Saint Paul, where at least one of the Patriarchs was supposed to be staying. (Later I learned that it was near Bab Kissan, marking the point on the ancient wall where Paul was supposed to have escaped.) The old city of Damascus had been built in Roman times and some of the stones that I was seeing were very old indeed. The stone and mud buildings, the stone curbs, the cobbled streets—everything was Ottoman or earlier, even the woodwork. I saw intricate wooden doors with heavy steel knockers and wooden bay windows cantilevered over the passageways.

I was looking for something in the present, however, and didn't really care. At last I gave up hope of meeting the Patriarch and wandered the narrow streets at random. One evening just before my plane was to leave, I was walking through the Jewish Quarter where I met a nun who was standing in a courtyard. Sister Mary had an Irish accent and ran an orphanage. She could not direct me to the monastery of Saint Paul but invited me for tea, then told stories from her twenty years' work as a teacher in India.

As I was leaving, I asked if there was a mass that I could attend in order to catch a glimpse of the Patriarch from afar. The Patriarch? Why hadn't I asked? He lived next door. Five minutes later I was standing in front of the man himself. My Big Moment had arrived.

The Patriarch of Antioch, Greek Melkite Catholic, had a frizzy, square-cut beard and wore a red robe. Around his neck was a gold chain and a pendant with a porcelain of Virgin and Child. His beard was white—he was an old man—but his eyes moved quickly, analytically, and I had the feeling that they missed nothing.

"From America," the Patriarch said. "And what church?" I told him that I was a Christian Scientist, then waited for the ax to fall, but my affiliation did not bother him in the least. "Ah yes, *The Christian Science Monitor*. I read it all the time, a good newspaper. Really the only newspaper from your country that is fair to Arabs."

The head priest at the Monastery of Saint George had raged at me when he learned my faith. This Patriarch, however, was a kind man. He put me at ease and found a way to compliment me by praising the newspaper put out by my church. He was building me up—which should have pleased me but instead made me a little suspicious. I did not want to be built up. I had high-minded reasons for wanting to meet the Patriarch. But now that my wish to see the man had come true, I could think only of a more more frivolous objective.

I wanted my benediction—something sonorous and dramatic. Was the Patriarch going to play ball?

The Patriarch bantered a bit more, pleasantries, then unfolded a map of North America with half a dozen cities circled in black. He scanned the map, more serious now, as though he were looking at an exotic and scarcely settled territory at the far edge of the universe.

"We have churches all over the world," he said, "especially in more central lands, the Mediterranean and Europe. Out in your country, however, we have but a few." I was not used to thinking of the United States as a minor and very recent addition to a far-

Azem Palace.

351

flung, ancient empire with headquarters in Damascus. The Patriarch shrugged. "In time these churches will grow."

The Patriarch's assistant, a young man wearing a three piece suit, served coffee in small cups, and the Patriarch seemed to relax. "This is Arab coffee," the Patriarch said, "the best, much better than Turkish coffee. If I gave you three cups, you would pass out on the floor."

What? These were the Patriarch's exact words. From his seat in ancient Damascus, the holy man with the square-cut beard had adopted the tone of an American tough guy, a Gary Cooper. He was teasing me, and now I knew that my plans were going awry. The Patriarch was more subtle than I had imagined.

Ottoman-era doorway.

I asked the Patriarch about his relations with the followers of Muhammad. "Muslims are a good people, faithful. Not terrorists as described in your country. We have good times with the Muslims."

"What do you think of the Arabs, apart from their religion," I asked.

"Arabs. Why do you ask me? I am an Arab, my native tongue is Arabic. You must remember that there are many Christian Arabs.

"The stony problems started in 1948," he continued. "Israel took the lands of the Arabs, and the United States helped Israel. Not a good policy at all.

"Yesterday your president signed a treaty with the Soviets. This is good, broadening. But an injustice is made to the Arabs. Recently a Palestinian measure came up in the UN and the only two votes against were the United States and Israel. Always it is the United States and Israel. Israel doesn't want to give justice to the Palestinians. And they don't have to since the United States protects them."

"I have heard all this," I said, "but what is the answer? What about Islamic suicide attacks? How about the hostages in Beirut? What about bombs dropped at night on villages of Kurds? What does it mean?"

"This is a big subject," he said. "You must read *The Christian Science Monitor* and learn more." The Patriarch smiled, gave me a small pamphlet, and showed me the door.

At last I met H. B. Maximos V Hakim, Patriarch of Antioch and all the East, of Alexandria, and of Jerusalem.

I walked through the narrow alleyways of the old city, not knowing what to think. I had expected the Patriarch to act as though he were the pinnacle of a magnificent institution. I wanted him to be pompous and quotable—very good for a formal close to my journey, good theatre, good literature. I gave him the opportunity to step onto his soap box, but the Patriarch had other ideas. He seemed to regard the role of Oriental wise man as wooden and false. Instead he had adopted the persona of a Gary Cooper for a few moments, and had given me plenty of wit and grit.

"Unfair," I thought.

4 — Jet Planes

At the airport, I sat in the same place where Saleh, the Shiite from London, had waited for his plane nearly three months before. He asked me to keep an open mind as I toured the country, and I tried to follow his advice. I was not ready to become a Muslim, but I had to concede his point: the people I had seen were poor yet friendly, extremely hospitable, and for the most part easy to love.

353

On the airplane I found my seat, stowed my carry-on bag, and fastened my seat belt. Before long the stewardess began her safety instructions and, suddenly, I was struck with a strange, visceral sensation: my body, my mind. I tried to figure out what was wrong and, after a few moments, realized that it was something simple: my nausea was gone, my stomach was not cramped. I was no longer afraid, and this was a strange feeling. For nearly three months I had been crawling around with my nose about an inch from the ground for fear of the police. Now I was at peace.

Our engines came to life. We taxied, then rushed down the runway and lifted into the air, climbing at a steep angle. Soon we had lost Damascus, and I could see desert and volcanic cinder cones below.

What about the Patriarch?

"Maybe the Patriarch was driving at something," I thought. I had completed an arduous journey, and when I found the Patriarch I was in an impatient frame of mind. I wanted a quick answer. I wanted flashy words that would finish this project and allow me to go on with my life.

"Not so fast," the Patriarch was saying. "You have no idea what you have just experienced in Syria. You have completed the physical journey, but you have barely started the intellectual and spiritual journey."

During my travel in Syria I had taken the road from Damascus. My performance on that road was fixed, it was in the past. Or was it? I had notes, photos, maps. Perhaps I needed to travel that road again, far more slowly this time—to ponder the words, hands, faces, eyes of the people I had met. And so it was decided. I would resume my life in Seattle, yet in heart and mind I would still be in Syria until this second journey, the mental journey, was completed.

Our airplane turned to the west and in a few minutes rose over the Mediterranean, hidden by cloud. Above us was the sun.

In Seattle I felt out of place. Culture shock. I could scarcely function. For two months I did not believe my life. I felt that I was a Syrian. My house, my car, my occupation seemed false. I could not understand when friends and family treated me like a person I no longer was. It didn't help that I had no work.

After a year I managed to separate, to distance, to conceive of Syria

American eagle from the cover
of my passport.

Syrian eagle from
a customs form.

apart from my life in Syria. Still, I had not yet come home. I felt that I had left important work undone. So I began to follow what I thought of as the Patriarch's advice, to devote myself to perfecting my performance on the road from Damascus. I found myself taking this journey again, very slowly, sifting through my notes, looking for connections, jotting down the story of my travel. I read every book in English on my subject. I corresponded with Saad Shalabi and hosted him when he visited Seattle. I studied my photographs and transcribed a tape of the concert that Saad and I had attended at the Cham Palace. Hasan the architect and his wife helped me understand the nuances. Also, I met with scholars and tried out my ideas on expatriates from the region who had moved to Seattle to study at the university.

My manuscript began to take shape, and a few of the puzzles from my travel pieced themselves together. For one thing, I figured out why Syrians were happy: even with the poor economy and grim political situation Syrians had family and friends. They had time to keep alive an elaborate and extended social network.

I was close when I had surmised that it was Syrian artists who forged the link of happiness. What I had not understood was that the artists in this case were untrained. They were millions of ordinary people whose creative effort went into developing and maintaining a common work of art that had been passed down for hundreds of years. These men and women devoted their lives to maintaining the social fabric. Their happiness came from curbing their ambition, accepting the restrictions of life among other people, and taking pleasure in the practical affection they received from their families, friends, churches or mosques, neighborhoods, and professional groups.

The Gulf War broke out, and Rita my travel agent started a group to raise money for refugees. Hasan the architect created the logo. I attended meetings, my wife Mary ended up working on the project for months. Hasan and his wife organized events for an Arab cultural group, and my wife and I found that our social life revolved largely around our local Arab friends. My construction company flourished.

On Saturday evenings, exhausted from my week's work, I sometimes played the tape of the concert I attended at the Cham Palace. As the music began, I closed my eyes, let my mind drift, and Syria came back to me—immediate, visceral, beyond words—a strange, bitter drink that made any other seem bland and flavorless by comparison.

By the fall of 2000 I felt that the intellectual and spiritual journey was drawing to a close. I had put a great many thoughts into words. Had I grasped the truth for which I was searching? One day I was sorting the photographs I had taken in Syria and noticed that I was missing a few pics. "I need a better image of Crak des Chevaliers," I thought, "And I could use a photo of an old adobe from al-Jazira." What was going on in Syria?

Since President Hafez al-Asad had died and his son had taken over, it appeared that the Damascene curtain was lifting. Was the first act of the real Syria about to burst forth on the world stage? Freedom forums were sprouting up all over the country. People were speaking out. Independent political parties and contested elections were promised, just a couple of years off. "I really do need those photos," I thought.

In February 2001 I traveled to Syria for three weeks. I moved quickly around the country this time, taking taxis, visiting the same towns as before, renewing old acquaintances. Ultimately, I ended up in the old city of Damascus. "I still need my benediction," I thought. The Patriarch, however, had retired.

I returned to Seattle where I polished my manuscript, pondered, waited. In July I read an obituary for the Patriarch of Antioch—my Patriarch. He had been staying at a hospital in Lebanon during my

February visit. I had missed him, now he was gone, and it was too late. What about my benediction? On September 11th I watched with the nation as the World Trade Center collapsed. I had no idea that a friend of mine, a teacher traveling on a National Geographic outing with a school kid of hers, was on Flight 77 when it crashed into the Pentagon.

"What is the answer to terrorism?" I thought. This, of course, was the same question I had asked the Patriarch fourteen years earlier. Since then I had taken the Patriarch's advice. I had read my newspaper, done my homework. Yet the Patriarch was gone now, and I was left to answer the question for myself.

Or was I?

I remembered the pamphlet that the Patriarch had given me. I had read it in 1987 and found nothing of interest. Yet maybe there was something, even a single word, that would help. I kept the pamphlet in the bottom of a dusty cardboard box in my garage.

The pamphlet contained the text of a speech the Patriarch had given in Italy on the 900th anniversary of the "translation of the relics of Saint Nicholas of Myre"—an obvious excuse for a rockin' party, I suppose, if you were a Patriarch. His text circled round and round on the problem of people of different faiths and races living together.

In one passage the Patriarch explained that some of the big Christian churches of North Africa, "those of Saint Augustine and of Saint Cyprian which played a decisive role in the Christian world of the first centuries," had entirely disappeared. His church, on the other hand, still existed in the Arab world by means of a "continuous succession"—a point which made him realize that his church had been preserved for a reason; namely, to carry out the mission of "cohabitation" with Muslims.

The Patriarch noted that in medieval Europe Muslims and other minorities largely had been removed by the Christian majority, or as we would say, they were "ethnically cleansed." In the Near East, on the other hand, Christians, Muslims, and Jews "lived and worked side-by-side for many centuries."

The Patriarch of Antioch made me wonder. The great churches of the past, the churches of Augustine and Cyprian—why had they been lost? Had their leaders been too pompous, too quotable, too quick to state their case? I remembered my interview with the Patriarch.

Perhaps his hesitance to perform for me *was* the wisdom he wished to impart. Had the Patriarch trained himself to think and act in unobtrusive ways, to make his point without drama, to live his beliefs without offending the belief of others?

In this land of many faiths, it is not the supreme spiritual insight or exalted epiphany that has value, the Patriarch seemed to say. Instead of the bold pronouncement on terrorism that I desired, he had given me joking remarks—"We have good times with the Muslims." According to the Patriarch, it is not grand words that matter, it is not the ability to drive home one's point, to triumph, to slay the dragon, rather it is the ability to get along with other people—Muslims, for example—most of whom also have received messages from God.

The Patriarch felt that we should make allowances for one another, just as we do for our brothers and sisters. Personal insight and mystical vision had to yield to the day-to-day needs of actual people who lived in the world. Realpolitik, colonialism, aggressive global commerce, stealthy terror, raw ambition, linear strategies, the entrepreneur who acted like a gunslinger on the loose, the prima donna, the workaholic—all would wane under the Patriarch's prescription. What would we gain? Happiness perhaps. And the ability to live together in peace.

In Biblical times the Apostle Paul received a striking spiritual vision on the road to Damascus. Yet, according to the Patriarch, it is one's performance on the road *from* Damascus that really matters.

Scott C. Davis

Coda:
Dinner with Saad Shalabi

DAMASCUS. FEBRUARY 2001.

"How have things changed since 1987?" asked Saad Shalabi.

"It's much more relaxed now," I said. "I'm completely unafraid. Before, the secret police were everywhere and they carried weapons. And I was worried that I would do the wrong thing and get in trouble. Now most are unarmed and they are polite. And now I know how to be discreet. I went the same places as before, but this time no one jumped me."

I was talking with an old friend, a man who'd been invaluable fourteen years earlier during my first visit to Syria. We were sitting in the upper floor of an ancient stone building, now a restaurant, near the Umayyad mosque in the old city of Damascus. On the platform behind my host I could see musicians preparing traditional instruments: an oud, a canoon, a tabla. Near the musicians I saw two men in white robes chatting to one another. They were Sufis, whirling dervishes, and would dance for us as the evening wore on.

"You have to realize that in 1987," Saad Shalabi said, "we had hostages in Beirut, we were headed toward another war with Israel— instead, just as you left, the Intifadah broke out. We were worried about Turkey and our Kurds, so the northern border was on alert. And that business in Hama was still fresh, as well as the killings that provoked it."

"Back then no one would talk politics," I continued. "Now, no one will stop talking. It's a lovefest for the new, blue-eyed president. In Hasakah the people told me the most startling truth about this man."

"Oh?"

"'President Bashar,' they said, 'visited Aleppo in his car. He came to a traffic light. The light was red. And the president stopped. He waited for the light!'"

"No," said Saad Shalabi.

"It's true," I said. "In Hasakah it's common for people to drive on the wrong side of the road. You don't get a ticket for this, as long as you blink your lights every so often. Red lights are definitely optional. The idea that the President stops at traffic lights, well, that's big news.

"'And in the market no one recognized Bashar,' the people in Hasakah told me. 'He bought something from a merchant. When the merchant realized who his customer was he insisted that Bashar accept his money back. But the President refused. "This is good merchandise," Bashar said. "It is right that you charge for it."

"'Can you believe that?' they asked me. 'A person in government who refuses a gratuity! And it turns out he is the President. He could have had anything he wanted!'"

"Bashar has the right idea," said Saad Shalabi, "although he is only one person."

"OK," I said. "But the real people are below, outside government, and Bashar encourages them. Like Ali Farzat, the political cartoonist. I have no idea how he's survived all these years, publishing in the regime's own newspapers, but his stuff is great. I met him the other night, in a little office off Pakistan Street. The place was crawling with twenty-year-olds and I could feel that spark, that energy.

"So, thanks to a decree from Bashar, independent papers are now legal, and Ali Farzat's will be the first. *Ad-Domari*, he is calling it, 'the man who lights the street candles.'"

"But that's where Riad Seif comes in," I said. "He is saying things like, 'We need an independent political party, otherwise the Baath will have no competition and the government will never improve.'"

"Seif is a Member of Parliament," said Saad, "and he has immunity and can say things if he wants. But you saw what happened at his house, that night."

"You mean that guy who shouted me down?"

"Right. Run that by me again."

"OK. So I heard about the wild, political free-for-alls that Riad has been holding at his flat since last fall. I called, got directions, took a cab. And we were squished in there, nearly 300 people. We couldn't meet in a bigger place downtown because then we wouldn't be covered by his immunity. Everyone was talking about democracy, civil society, freedom of speech. There was a paper on democracy which a local dentist presented to us.

"Then everyone starts making speeches and completely on impulse I whispered to Riad and asked him if I could speak. Hey, I'm an author with a book coming out. I had this translator with me, no problem.

"I stood up with the translator and started speaking into the mike. Of course I mentioned my book by way of introduction. Then I continued.

"'There are no formulas,' I said. 'You may think of other countries as models, but they are not. You are the experts. You are doing something new and creative.'

"These were audience-pleasing remarks, but I hadn't gotten out two words when some guy starts shouting and calling Riad's motives into question. Just what was my reason for speaking? Had the embassy sent me to subvert the Baath regime? Like I was the perfect thing for this guy, an American, and he wanted to use me to bring Riad down."

"Exactly," said Saad.

"At last he calms down and I continued. 'In America we are fighting a similar battle for civil society,' I said. 'Only not against government, but against global conglomerates, huge corporations that commercialize our life. They do not allow us to vote on their boards of directors.

"'America is a very young country. I have come to Syria to learn from you, to understand your families, to capture your energy for reform.'

"I handed back the mike and everyone was just gasping. Because in Syria everyone expects Americans to be arrogant people who have all the answers and want to bully everyone else into submission. They judge us, in other words, by our foreign policy. As I returned to my seat the audience was clapping and Riad was sweating and smiling. If I had said the wrong thing I could have gotten Riad fried pretty bad. So he escaped, just barely.

"And it turns out that my opponent was Faisal Kalthoun, a highly placed official at the University of Damascus, a political appointee, and near the end he made a ripping speech about how great the Baath party was. Everyone was polite, but after a while they started tapping their watches and he started smiling. I shook hands with him afterward. It was a brawl, the stakes were high, but there was also something quaint and sweet about it.

"And actually, there's nothing wrong with the Baath party—if you read how it was created, what it stands for. It sure beats Leninism all to pieces."

"That's my point," said Saad. "The Baath party members who compose our government care nothing about the ideals of the party. They are people who have grown wealthy thanks to their positions. And they would be happy to escape with their loot. But they are afraid. 'If I relax my grip,' they say to themselves, 'I could end up in prison.'"

"Yeah, right," I said.

"So Bashar encourages change from the top, and from the bottom people like your friends Riad Seif and Ali Farzat are pushing for change. But the bureaucrats in the middle—that's where the struggle comes in. And how much power does Bashar really have? Now the counter-attack is beginning. That's what was happening with Faisal Kalthoun at Riad Seif's when he shouted you down. He was defending the Baath party. And Nabil Suleiman, a novelist in Latakia was holding forums, and last week he was beaten half to death.

"No one knows who did it. Suleiman said that he didn't think it was the regime or the security services—maybe it was local politicians who did not want to be exposed. In any case, his forums have stopped. In the next few weeks you are going to see the Baath party rally. They are going to put Riad Seif back in his box. Just wait."

"Even so," I said, "I think we have *Glasnost* here. I think that the Damascene Curtain is falling and I think that the tough old guy, Hafez al-Asad, started it."

"He was tough," said Saad. "And that toughness enabled him to keep his grip, to tighten his grip. Bashar, on the other hand, is a nice guy. I hope he can last."

"Bashar's already lasted," I said. "OK. He's not throwing the country open in one day to free elections, free press, private ownership, free markets. That happened in Russia and it was a fiasco. There need to be laws and institutions in place to receive the change, to govern banking, business, markets. I mean, we are learning now that the freeing of the Czech Republic, for example, was a license to steal.

"Instead Bashar is taking a step-by-step approach to creating an open society, an intelligent man's revolution. Look at his record. *Glasnost* started last April when Bashar's father froze the state of emergency—no more arbitrary arrests."

"And the father purged some officials in an anti-corruption drive,"

Damascus 2001. Skyline of the old city at Bab Touma.

said Saad. "Of course lots of people in the government are corrupt. The ones that went to prison were those who were corrupt *and* who opposed Hafez al-Assad's successor."

"Look at Bashar's record, is what I'm saying," I replied. "In just a few months he has legalized private banks, released movie theaters from government control, released half the country's political prisoners, legalized private universities, and a dozen other things. He's encouraged Riad Seif, Ali Farzat, and others with his statements on the need for public discussion. This isn't some accident. This is *Glasnost* on the desert. What would that be in Arabic?"

"*Infitah*," said Saad, "opening."

"What we are seeing is *Infitah*," I said. "Definitely."

"Let me repeat my question," said Saad Shalabi. "How have things changed since your last visit?"

By now Saad and I were finishing our meal. The musicians had tuned their instruments and were beginning to play.

"I see billboards now," I said. "They advertise washing machines and kitchen ranges. People have cell phones, BMWs, and email. The rooftops of the cities, even remote towns like al-Qamishly, are covered with satellite dishes."

"Those dishes are still illegal, by the way," said Saad Shalabi.

"And everyone is pulling down *Al-Jazeera*, the Arabic version of CNN, so everyone knows what's happening. No more secrets."

"I watch it," said Saad.

"I looked up a lot of the people I had met before. In Aleppo the novelist Walid Ikhlassy has retired from his job exporting cotton. Now he is a Member of Parliament. 'By accident,' he told me. 'Someone died, they put me in there.'

"And I talked to Zouhair Dabbagh the Aleppo sculptor. He has been

The bureaucrat speaks, while the poor live their lives. By Ali Farzat.

working with his wife in their pharmacy. Now he has a studio outside of town and is devoting his time to his art."

"Who else?" said Saad.

"I asked about that contrary and eloquent Armenian desk clerk at the Baron, Sarkis (they called him Kash Kash). As a writer, in my mind, I argued with him for ten years. Which of his comments was I going to include in my book and where was I going to position them? I found out that he had died shortly after my 1987 visit. So he was speaking in my mind and in my text long after he had passed away.

"Here in Damascus I tracked down Shouckran Imam, the widow of Fateh Moudarres. She is turning his *atelier* into a gallery. And I learned that the Patriarch of Antioch whom I met has retired."

"You saw Sausan again," Saad said. "What's she up to?"

"I took her to lunch in the embassy district. In 1987 she was hurting, feeling constrained by her family. 'How can I have a life?,' she was telling me. Now her father has passed on and her mother is sick. She is still single and spends a lot of time caring for her mother. Also, aerobics, and her big thing is dance. She takes classes several times a week and especially likes the Latin dances. She is busy now, night and day, and doesn't date very much.

"In 1987 Sausan took me to visit her friend Mamoun who had an ultramodern office in an old building downtown. He was working fourteen-hour days running his sweater manufacturing business, and to me he was an example of an up and coming young entrepreneur. Well, Sausan says he got burned out after a few years, started going to the mosque, and now is leading the meditative life. I think he started his entrepreneurial surge ten years too early. The government is giving a lot more support now."

By now the musicians were in full swing. The two dervishes I had noticed earlier flung off their dark capes and walked to the center of the floor, a space cleared of tables. They stood without expression. On cue from the musicians, they began to twirl slowly, then faster and faster. Their white skirts flared, and they slowly moved their arms and hands from one pose to another.

"Those gestures," said Saad. "Each of them means something. One, for example, means submission to God's will. Another means seeking God." We watched until the dance was complete and the dervishes had bowed and retired. The music continued.

"What about that woman on the coast," asked Saad, "the one from Dreykish."

"OK. So I wanted to find Fatima and also Jade, the young banker who she knew through her brother," I said. "I was curious. For one thing she had stood me up in Latakia. And I wanted to know if she had gotten married, or what. And Jade. The guy was totally obsessed with American women. Did he find an American wife?

"So I went to Tartus and took a taxi up into the hills and found Fatima's place. But the neighbors said that the family had moved to Tartus. And they thought that Fatima had gone to Australia. I returned to the city and called them on the phone."

"Did they remember you?" said Saad.

"They remembered but even so Fatima was suspicious and pretended that she was someone named Leila and put me off. That evening I was in grief. I had wanted to find these people again. So the next day I asked Aziz, a young guy at my hotel, to call on my behalf. He urged Fatima-Leila to see me. 'Davis is a true man,' Aziz said.

"Well, Leila-Fatima relented and sent her younger brother and sister, Fadi and Boushra, to collect me. When we got to their apartment I met the rest of the family. Fatima didn't say anything, but I knew it was her. 'Fatima,' I said. She kissed me on the cheek and we talked while I cried for some reason I don't understand. I hadn't realized they meant so much to me.

"Anyway, Fatima had been to Australia for seven years, and now she is engaged to an old friend from college, a lawyer from Latakia.

Both she and Boushra look good and are taking care of themselves. But it's funny because Boushra still has that innocence and openness that I associate with Syrians. Fatima seems a little war-weary, more on guard. Her years in Australia have given her an edge.

"'A brother of mine died,' she told me. 'And I was very sad and then I went to Australia to try something new.'

"Fatima was really kind to me, but I missed that flash, that vivacity I had admired in 1987. The next day Jade came to visit, and they were talking back and forth in Arabic. He was teasing her like before, and she became really animated and spontaneous. So I felt better about Fatima—the delightful young woman still was alive inside the polished adult.

"Jade is still working at the bank in Tartus, and he married a woman from his home village. His American-woman fixation, as it turned out, was just a phase. He lives in his village and commutes to work. Before he was such a shark, a lady's man. Now he is looking very smooth and mature."

Ali Farzat, 2001.

The dervishes had left yet the musicians were still going strong. Would they play all night? Saad and I couldn't stay. Saad pushed his chair back from the table to leave. Then he hesitated.

"You understand individual people," said Saad, "but you miss the large scale changes."

"Like what?" I said.

"Our population is exploding. We are growing faster than any country on earth. And everyone is moving to the cities. What about power? What about water? The Turks have dammed the Euphrates. When you were here in 1987 we negotiated a temporary treaty that guaranteed us a certain amount of water. But this agreement no longer applies now that the dams are finished. With the reduced flow the salt content goes up. We have a lot of salt in our fields now. And by the time the water reaches Iraq its too salty for irrigation.

"Here in Damascus the water table has dropped. I had to shut my farm down, the fruit trees, the olive trees. Everything at my farm is dead. The government cuts water off every day for conservation. But they don't want to announce the shortage."

"Are they afraid of panic?"

"Who knows? The trouble is, if I get a meeting together to address the water problem or the traffic problem or the problem of unplanned and illegal sprawl I will be charged with criminality. How do we solve problems when we cannot meet and discuss?"

Civic freedom—in the ten months following April 2000 Syrians made striking progress. What followed, however, was a counter-offensive. Four days after my visit to Riad Seif's forum, the government closed similar gatherings all over the country, and Baath party officials announced rallies to support the regime. Seif's events continued, thanks to his immunity as a Member of Parliament, but attendance dropped from nearly three hundred to seventy. Six weeks after my visit to Riad's, his forums were shut down as well. "As a Member of Parliament," the government told him, "you have the right to confer with people at your home, but not to give lectures."

Also, Seif announced that the Prosecutor General was bringing a civil suit against him on the charge that his proposal to form a new political party undermined the constitution. By now it was clear that Seif and another independent member of Parliament named Mamoun Homsi were headed for prison. The question was simply when.

Seif and Homsi were businessmen who had made money under the Baath and therefore had been close to the regime and then quarreled. Aref Dalila had been a professor at Damascus University and therefore also had been allied with the regime. Now these men were reformers, although somewhat tainted by their previous associations in the eyes of Syrians. A more profound figure was Riyad al-Turk, the Communist opposition figure, who had gone to prison for his views twice in the 1950s and once, for eighteen years, under the Baath. He was released in 1998 at sixty-eight years of age under the condition that he refrain from politics. He made good on that promise for three years, although he did allow the Lebanese film maker Ali Atassi to create a documentary about his life and his views. "In prison I couldn't think about my family, about the world outside," al-Turk says in this film, "or I would be lost." Instead al-Turk concentrated on removing the thin shells from lentils and arranging them in elaborate geometric patterns on his prison bed. "Riad al-Turk is the beating heart of the

Syrian opposition," said one Lebanese journalist I talked to several years later. "He is a big teddy-bear of a man and is as close as Syria ever will get to Nelson Mandela."

Riyad al-Turk was free and was keeping his silence. Seif was free, but his days of freedom seemed to be numbered. Dalila and Homsi? Who could say how long the regime would let them speak out.

The first two issues of Ali Farzat's newspaper *Ad-Domari* were published in February. All 75,000 copies sold out in three hours. Before the third issue reached the news stands—information is sketchy here—the regime apparently leaned on Farzat, his young volunteers accused him of caving and walked off the job, and his sales dropped by two thirds.

Ten months of change versus thirty-eight years of state control. These years will not be shed overnight. The new story is one of advancement and struggle, hope and disappointment. More chapters will be written before the story is complete.

Timeline

[note: scholars differ on some of these dates]

BC

3000   Aramaic people from the Arabian desert begin migrating to Syria.

2700   The city-state of Mari flourishes on the Euphrates.

2000   Canaanites (Phoenicians) migrate to Syria's shores.

1800   The patriarch Abraham, father of Arabs through his son Ishmael and of Jews through his son Isaac, moves to Palestine.

1200   Phoenicians are using a phonetic alphabet and cuneiform script.

1200   Moses leads the children of Israel from captivity in Egypt.

399   Socrates dies in Athens.

331   Alexander the Great wins the final battle against Darius III.

323   Alexander dies at the age of thirty-two.

AD

0   Nominal date for the birth of Christ.

35   Peter the Apostle becomes the first Bishop of Antioch.

40   Paul starts the first Christian church in Antioch.

303   The Roman soldier Sergius is martyred for believing in Christ.

312   Constantine converts to Christianity.

325   The Nicean counsel—the first Christian ecumenical council——meets to condemn the heresy of Arius of Alexandria.

330   The Roman Empire is split into Eastern and Western realms.

395   Syria becomes a part of the Byzantine (Eastern Roman) Empire.

450   The title "Patriarch" introduced for church leaders formerly known as Bishops of Antioch.

547   Justinian I, the greatest Byzantine emperor, erects a church at Saydnaya near Damascus.

613   The Prophet Muhammad begins to teach publicly.

635   The Umayyads occupy Damascus and in 661 make it the capital of the Islamic empire.

750 The Abbasids defeat the Umayyad armies to gain control of the Islamic empire.

756 Abed ar-Rahman, the sole Umayyad survivor, flees to Andalusia (Cordoba) and begins a rule which will last nearly 800 years.

1095 Pope Urban II launches the First Crusade.

1098 Crusaders in Syria occupy Antioch and Maarat an-Numan.

1099 Crusaders occupy Jerusalem.

1174 Saladin (Salah ad-Din) begins his quest to unite the Muslims of Egypt and the Levant in opposition to the Crusaders.

1256 Alamut, the headquarters of the Assassins in northern Persia, is captured by the Mongols.

1258 Hulegu, the grandson of Genghis Khan, sacks Baghdad and overthrows the Abbasids.

1271 Baybars, the Mamluk leader, captures Crak des Chevaliers.

1271 Marco Polo travels from Acre up the Syrian coast to Alexandretta on his way to China.

1302 The last Crusaders leave Syria.

1401 Tamerlane the Great occupies Aleppo and Damascus.

1453 The Ottomans take Constantinople from the Byzantines.

1488 The Cape of Good Hope route is opened by the Portuguese.

1516 The Ottoman Empire begins a 400-year occupation of Syria.

1581 The English establish the Levant Company in Aleppo.

1798 Napoleon invades Egypt and defeats the Mamluks.

1866 A missionary college is established in Beirut that will become known as the American University.

1908 "Young Turks" establish a constitutional government.

1915 Armenians are massacred by the Young Turk government.

1918 Syria is liberated from Turkish rule by British troops.

1920 The French take control of Syria.

1923 Mustafa Kemal Attaturk founds the Republic of Turkey, officially ending Ottoman rule.

1939 Antioch is incorporated into Turkey.

1946 Syria gains independence from the French.

1948	Fighting between Israeli and Arab forces leaves thousands of Palestinians homeless. The state of Israel is established.
1958	Syria joins with Egypt in the United Arab Republic with Gamal Abdel Nasser as president.
1961	A Syrian army coup establishes Syria's independence from Egypt. National elections are held in Syria and a democratic government is established.
1963	Baath party elements within the army gain power and overthrow Syria's elected government. Col. Salah al-Jadid rules under a state of emergency.
1967	The Six-Day War. Israel attacks Egypt, Jordan, and Syria.
1970	Gen. Hafez al-Asad wrests control from Salah al-Jadid.
1970	Black September: King Hussein of Jordan defeats the PLO and its Syrian allies.
1973	Syria and Egypt attack Israeli forces occupying territory acquired in 1967.
1979	Followers of Ayatollah Khomeini take hostages at the American Embassy in Teheran.
1982	Revolt in Hama is crushed by Syrian troops under the command of Rifaat al-Asad, brother of President Hafez al-Asad.
1982	Israel invades Lebanon, in pursuit of Palestinian guerrillas, and the Hezbollah is created among Lebanese Shiites in response.
1983	Hezbollah suicide bomber kills 241 US Marines in Beirut.
1983	Syrian President Hafez al-Asad is incapacitated by illness.
1984	February. Rifaat al-Asad positions tanks and artillery in Damascus in a challenge to his brother's rule.
1985	Rifaat al-Asad is exiled to Europe.
1985	Syria attacks Jordanian interests in Italy and Greece with the help of the Palestinian gun-for-hire Abu Nidal.
1985	December. Abu Nidal bombs the El Al Counters in the Vienna and Rome airports. Libya and Syria are named as sponsors.
1986	US bombers strike Libya, killing Qaddafi's infant daughter. Sixth Fleet maneuvers, to Syrian observers, signal an imminent air strike against Syria.
1986	November. Syrians leak the US-Iran arms deals (the basis for the Iran-Contra Scandal) to Beirut's *Al-Shira* newspaper.

1990   Syria joins the Gulf War on the side of the United States.

1992   The Syrian government allows Jews to sell their property, which makes it practical for them to move from Syria.

1998   May. Under a general amnesty Riyad al-Turk is released after 18 years in prison.

2000   April. The state of emergency under which Syria has been governed since 1963 is "frozen;" arbitrary arrests cease.

2000   June. Hafez al-Asad dies at age sixty-nine and his son Bashar al-Asad becomes president.

2000   October-December. Violence in Palestine destroys the Middle East peace process.

2000   November. Bashar al-Asad releases political prisoners and legalizes private banks. The Mezze prison will become a hospital.

2001   February. Asad legalizes private schools and universities.

2001   September. The Syrian government denounces Osama bin Laden and the September 11th attacks and cooperates with the CIA in assisting the US war on terrorism.

2001   August, September. The regime arrests Riad Seif, Mamoun Homsi, Aref Dalila, Riyad al-Turk, and other reformers.

2002   January. Asad installs new Western-educated cabinet ministers.

2002   March. Asad purges conservatives in the bureaucracy.

2002   March. The *Los Angeles Times* reveals US contingency plans to drop nuclear bombs on Syria and other enemy countries in a "strike first" policy.

2002   March. Syria backs the Saudi peace plan at the Arab summit in Beirut.

2002   April. Riad Seif is sentenced to five years. Rumor says that he will be pardoned late in the year.

2002   April. In response to Israeli incursions into the West Bank, many Syrians stop attending restaurants, and movie theaters shut down. The nation fears that war with Israel is imminent.

2002   June. The *Washington Post* quotes CIA officials as saying that intelligence provided by Syria has saved American lives and that Syria has eschewed terrorism since 1986.

2002   July. The new Syrian cabinet presents a detailed plan for economic reform and invites public comment.

Acknowledgements

Many Syrians extended courtesies to me during my travels, and many have given patient help as I wrote the manuscript. I would like to thank Youssef Abdelke, Zouhair Dabbagh, Ali Farzat, Walid Ikhlassy, Fateh Moudarres, Archbishop Matta Roham, Riad Seif, Abu Taleb and many others (whom I will leave unnamed to protect their privacy).

I have based my account on notes which I took during my travels. In order to place my observations in context I have relied on the work of the scholars I have credited in my Bibliography.

Especially helpful has been the work of Patrick Seale and the commentary of Sami Moubayed. I have also relied on proofs of Moubayed's forthcoming book: *Steel and Silk: Men and Women Who Shaped Syria 1900-2000*. I have been helped as well by reporting and commentary on current events by arabia.com and stratfor.com. I have found the online version of *The Encyclopaedia Britannica* (britannica.com) to be an effective way to check historical facts and dates.

I also am indebted to many individuals who have helped in the years it has taken to develop this book by sharpening my Arabic, making travel arrangements, and giving critical readings of the manuscript. My apologies to those whose names I've inadvertently omitted.

Thanks go to Brooke Anderson, Raja Atallah, Sean Bentley, Charles Bergstrom, Midge Bowman, Upton Birnie Brady III, Lorna Burden, Ellen Collins, Phil Collins, Bruce Davis, Donald C. Davis, John M. Davis, Lyn Davis, Mary McConnel Davis, Peter Davis, Amelie Mel de Fontenay, John Felstiner, Crista Goddard, Natalie Greenberg, Kris Grevstad, Dr. Marwan Hujeij, Brian Johnson, Rawa Johnson, Carool Kersten, Fawzi Khouri, Anson Laytner, Yoona Lee, Joanne LonayChapa, Joegil Lundquist, Ruth Marsh, Pat Matteson, David Maymudes, Nancy Wood Oyler, Cathryn Pisarski, Mamoun Sakkal, Seta Sakkal, Diane Solvang-Angell, Steven Schlesser, Kristiann Schoening, John Sinno, Eric Soderlund, Holly L. Thomas, Robin Trucksess, Talcott Seelye, Daniel M. Streisguth, Dawn Stuart, Dominique Vallila, Kristine Vallila, Martti Vallila, Gulam Abbas Habib Walji, Dan Watkins, and Rita Zwaideh.

Credits

Youssef Abdelke (artwork) was raised in Aleppo, Syria and is currently based in Paris. Email: youssef@cunepress.com.

Zouhair Dabbagh (artwork) is an artist based in Aleppo. Email: zouhair@cunepress.com.

Ian Miller (maps) is a freelance illustrator based in Kent, Washington. Email: ian@cunepress.com.

Ali Farzat is a caricaturist and newspaper publisher based in Damascus. farzat@cunepress.com.

Mamoun Sakkal (artwork) is a scholar, architect, and graphic artist based in Bothell, Washington, who was raised and educated in Aleppo, Syria. He has designed several widely used Arabic typefaces, and his Arabic calligraphy has won international awards. For more: mamoun@sakkal.com or visit www.sakkal.com.

George Manougian is an Aleppo photographer and can be reached in care of the Baron Hotel, Aleppo, Syria.

Bibliography

Al-Asadi, Mohammad Khayr al-Din. *Comparative Encyclopedia of Aleppo*. Aleppo: University of Aleppo, 1981.

Arpee, Leon. *The Armenian Awakening: A History of the Armenian Church, 1820—1860*. Chicago: The University of Chicago Press, 1909.

Bahnassi, Afif. *Guide to Syria*. Damascus: al-Salhani, printer [Published by Ministry of Tourism?], 1987.

Barkatullah, Qazi Muhammad. *Education During The Middle Ages Under the Muslims*. Los Angeles: Crescent Publications, 1974.

Batatu, Hanna. *Syria's Peasantry, the Descendants of its Lesser Notables, and Their Politics*. Princeton: Princeton University Press, 1999.

Bell, Gertrude. *The Desert and the Sown*. London: Virago Press, 1985.

Bianca, Stefano, et al. *The Conservation of the Old City of Aleppo*. Switzerland: UNESCO, 1980.

Bosworth, C.E., E. Van Donzel, B. Lewis, and C. Pellat, eds. *The Encyclopaedia of Islam*, New Edition. Leiden: E.J. Brill, 1986.

Bosworth, C.E., Charles Issawi, Roger Savory, and A.L. Udovitch, eds. "Ilm," "Madrasa," "Ulama," "Umaiyads," in *The Islamic World: from Classical to Modern Times*. Princeton: Darwin Press, 1989.

Brewster, D.P., trans. *The Just Balance*. Lahore: Sh. Muhammad Ashraf, 1978.

Burns, Ross. *Monuments of Syria: An Historical Guide*. New York: NYU Press, 1992.

Carmichael, Joel. *The Shaping of the Arabs: a Study in Ethnic Identity*. New York: Macmillan, 1976.

Carruthers, Douglas, ed. *The Desert Route to India*. Nendeln, Liechtenstein: Kraus, 1967. [Original edition by the Hakluyt Society, 1928.]

Cleveland, William L. *A History of the Modern Middle East*. Boulder: Westview Press, 2000.

———*Islam Against the West: Shakib Arslan and the Campaign for Islamic Nationalist*. Austin: University of Texas Press, 1985.

———*The Making of an Arab Nationalist: Ottomanism and Arabism in the Life and Thought of Sati' al-Husri*. Princeton: Princeton University Press, 1971.

Cowell, Alan. "Trouble in Damascus." *The New York Times Magazine*. April 1, 1990.

Daftary, Farhad. *Assassin Legends: Myths of the Isma'ilis*. I.B. Tauris, 1994.

———*The Isma'ilis: Their History and Doctrine*. Cambridge University Press, 1990.

———*Mediaeval Isma'ili History and Thought*. Cambridge University Press, 1996.

Deighton, Lee C., ed. "Syria" in *The Encyclopedia of Education*. New York: The Free Press, 1971.

Dodge, Bayard. *Muslim Education in Medieval Times*. Washington: The Middle East Institute, 1962.

Douwes, Dick. *The Ottomans in Syria: a History of Justice and Oppression*. London: New York: I.B. Tauris; New York: Distributed by St. Martin's Press, 2000.

Ebied, R.Y., A. Van Roey, L.R. Wickham, eds. *Peter of Callinicum: Anti-Tritheist Dossier*. Leuven, Belgium: Departement Orientalistiek, 1981.

Eldem, Edhem, Daniel Goffman, Bruce Masters, eds. *The Ottoman City between East and West: Aleppo, Izmir, and Istanbul*. Cambridge: New York: Cambridge University Press, 1999.

Encyclopaedia Britannica, 27th ed., s.v. "Christianity," "Clement of Alexandria," "Didache, The," "Eucharist," "Jacobite Church," "Mohammed," "Montanism," "Nestorius," "Origen," "Spain," "Tertullian," "Timur," and "Turkey." London: William Benton, 1959.

Fawaz, Leila Tarazi. *An Occasion for War: Civil Conflict in Lebanon and Damascus in 1860*. London: Centre for Lebanese Studies ; London ; New York: I.B. Tauris, 1994.

———*Merchants and Migrants in Nineteenth-Century Beirut*. Cambridge: Harvard University Press, 1983.

Fedden, Robin. *The Phoenix Land: the Civilization of Syria and Lebanon*. New York: George Braziller, 1965.

Franzius, Enno. *History of the Order of Assassins*. New York: Funk & Wagnalls, 1969.

Frischauer, Willi. *The Aga Khans*. London: The Bodley Head Ltd., 1970.

Fromkin, David. *A Peace to End All Peace: Creating the Modern Middle East 1914—1922*. New York: Henry Holt and Company, 1989.

Gelvin, James L. *Divided Loyalties: Nationalism and Mass Politics in Syria at the Close of the Empire*. Berkeley: University of California Press, 1998.

Ghulam, Yousif Mahmud. *The Art of Arabic Calligraphy*. Privately printed, 1982.

Gibb, H. A. R., J. H. Kramers, eds. "Ali," "Assassins," "Derwish," "Druzes," "Ismailiya," "Mawlawiya," "Nusairi," "Shia," and "Tasawwuf," in *Shorter Encyclopaedia of Islam*. Ithaca, New York: Cornell University Press, 1953.

Glubb, John Bagot, Sir. *Syria, Lebanon, Jordan*. London: Thames and Hudson, 1967.

Grant, Christina Phelps. *The Syrian Desert: Caravans, Travel and Exploration*. London: A & C Black, 1937.

Hamarneh, Samar. *Fateh Moudarres's Point of View*. Nabil Al-Gasser Publisher, 1999.

Hamilton, F.J., E. W. Brooks, trans. *The Syriac Chronicle Known as that of Zachariah of Mitylene*. London: Methuen, 1899.

Hodgson, Marshall G.S. *The Order of the Assassins*. 'S-Gravenhage: Mouton, 1955.

Hopwood, Derek. *Syria, 1945-1986: Politics and Society*. London: 1988.

Hourani, Albert. *Arabic Thought in the Liberal Age 1798-1939*. London: Cambridge University Press, 1983.

———*The Emergence of the Modern Middle East*. Berkeley: University of California Press, 1981.

Hourani, Albert, Philip S. Khoury, Mary C. Wilson, eds. *The Modern Middle East: A reader*. London: Tauris, 1993.

Hureau, Jean. *Syria Today*. Paris: Editions J. A., 1977.

Hurewitz, J.C. *Middle East Politics: The Military Dimension*. New York: Praeger, 1969.

Khoury, Philip S., Joseph Kostiner, eds. *Tribes and State Formation in the Middle East*. Berkeley: University of California Press, 1990.

Khoury, Philip S. *Syria and the French Mandate: the Politics of Arab Nationalism, 1920-1945*. Princeton: Princeton University Press, 1987.

———*Urban Notables and Arab Nationalism: the Politics of Damascus, 1860-1920*. Cambridge: New York: Cambridge University Press, 1983.

Lamb, Harold. *The March of the Barbarians*. New York: Literary Guild, 1940.

Lane Fox, Robin. *Pagans and Christians*. New York: Alfred A. Knopf, 1987.

Laymon, Charles M., ed. "The First Letter of Paul to the Corinthians," James L. Price in *The Interpreter's One-Volume Commentary on the Bible*. Nashville: Abingdon, 1971.

Lent, Frederick, trans. "The Life of St. Simeon Stylites: A Translation of the Syriac Text in Bedjan's Acta Martyrum et Sanctorum, Vol. IV." *Journal of the American Oriental Society*, vol. 35, no. II (1915).

Lewis, Bernard, ed. and trans. *Islam from the Prophet Muhammad to the Capture of Constantinople*. New York: Walker, 1974.

Lewis, Bernard, et al. *Islam and the Arab World*. New York: Knopf, 1976.

———*The Assassins: A Radical Sect in Islam*. New York: Basic Books, 1968.

———*The Muslim Discovery of Europe*. New York: Norton, 1962.

Lewis, Peter. *Syria: Land of Contrasts*. London: Namara, 1980.

MacArthur, J.S. *Chalcedon*. London: Society for Promoting Christian Knowledge, 1931.

Macoz, Moshe. *Syria and Egypt: From War to Peacemaking*. Oxford: 1995.

Magowan, Robin. *Fabled Cities of Central Asia: Samarkand, Bukhara, Khiva*. New York: Abbeville Press, 1989.

Makdisi, Ussama Samir. *The Culture of Sectarianism: Community, History, and Violence in Nineteenth-century Ottoman Lebanon*. Berkeley: University of California Press, 2000.

Mansfield, Peter. *The Arabs*. New York: Viking Penguin, 1985.

Marcus, Abraham. *The Middle East on the Eve of Modernity: Aleppo in the Eighteenth Century*. New York: Columbia University Press, 1989.

McConnell, Brian. *Assassination*. London: Leslie Frewin, 1969.

McCullough, W. Stewart. *A Short History of Syriac Christianity to the Rise of Islam*. Chico, CA: Scholars Press, 1982.

Meagher, Paul Kevin, Thomas C. O'Brien, Consuelo Maria Aherne, eds. "Jacob Baradai," "Jacobites," "Nestorian Church," "Nestorianism," "Nestorius," "West Syrian Church," and "West Syrian Liturgy," in *Encyclopedic Dictionary of Religion*. Washington: Corpus, 1979.

Moore, A.M.T., G.C. Hillman, A.J. Legge, eds. *Village on the Euphrates: from Foraging to Farming at Abu Hureyra*. London: New York: Oxford University Press, 2000.

Morgan, David. *The Mongols*. Cambridge: Basil Blackwell, 1986.

Moubayed, Sami. *Steel and Silk: Men and Women Who Shaped Syria 1900-2000*. Seattle: Cune, 2003.

———"Ushering in the New." *Al-Ahram Weekly*, December 20-26. 2001 (Cairo).

———"Debate blossoms in the Syrian spring."*The Daily Star*, April 19, 2001 (Beirut).

———"An Appeal from a Syrian to His President." *The Daily Star*, August 15, 2001 (Beirut).

———"Threatened by Its Neighbors, Damascus Clamps Down on 'Opinion of the Other.'" *The Washington Report on Middle East Affairs*. December, 2001.

———"Independent Journalism Slowly Returning to Syria." *The Washington Report on Middle East Affairs*. July, 2001.

———"Syria's New President Bashar Al-Asad: A Modern-Day Attaturk." *The Washington Report on Middle East Affairs*. December, 2001.

———"Syrian Era of Dungeons." *Gulf News*. December 13, 2001 (Dubai).

———"A Transformation in Syria." *Gulf News*. December 6, 2001 (Dubai).

———"Damascus Spring Ends." *Gulf News*. November 22, 2001 (Dubai).

———"Syria's Voice in Washington." *Gulf News*. October 11, 2001 (Dubai).

———"Aftershocks of Assad's Passing Hit Lebanon." *Gulf News*. August 24, 2001 (Dubai).

Nyrop, Richard F., ed. *Syria: A Country Study*. Washington: U.S. Government Printing Office, 1979.

Pollard, Nigel. *Soldiers, Cities, and Civilians in Roman Syria*. Ann Arbor: University of Michigan Press, 2000.

Richards, D.S. *Islamic Civilisation 950—1150*. Oxford: Cassirer, 1973.

Ross, Frank, Jr. *Arabs and the Islamic World*. New York: S.G. Phillips, 1979.

Russell, Alexander. *The Natural History of Aleppo*. London: Robinson, 1794. [Republished, Westmead, England: Gregg Intl. Pub., 1969.]

Said, Edward. *Orientalism*. New York: Vintage Books, 1979, 1978.

Salibi, Kamal S. *Syria Under Islam: Empire on Trial, 634-1097*. Delmar, NY: Caravan Books, 1977.

Salisbury, Edward E., trans. "The Book of Sulaiman's First Ripe Fruit." *Journal of the American Oriental Society*, vol. 8, no. II, (1866).

Saunders, J.J. *The History of the Mongol Conquests*. New York; Barnes & Noble, 1971.

Savory, R.M., ed. *Introduction to Islamic Civilisation*. Cambridge: Cambridge University Press, 1976.

Schimmel, Annemarie. *Mystical Dimensions of Islam*. University of North Carolina Press, 1975.

Seale, Patrick. *Asad of Syria: The Struggle for the Middle East*. Berkeley: University of California Press, 1989.

Spuler, Bertold. *History of the Mongols*. Berkeley: University of California Press, 1972.

Sweet, Louise E. *Tell Toqaan: A Syrian Village*. Ann Arbor: University of Michigan, 1960.

Thomas, Davis, ed. *Syrian Christians Under Islam: The First Thousand Years*. Leiden: Boston: Brill, 2001.

Thubron, Colin. *Mirror to Damascus*. London: Century Publishing, 1986.

Tibawi, A.L. *A Modern History of Syria Including Lebanon and Palestine*. New York: 1969.

Tucker, Judith E. *In the House of the Law: Gender and Islamic Law in Ottoman Syria and Palestine*. Berkeley: University of California Press, 1998.

Viorst, Milton. "The Shadow of Saladin." *The New Yorker*, Jan. 8, 1990.

Wright, William. *An Account of Palmyra and Zenobia with Travels and Adventures in Bashan and the Desert*. New York: Thomas Nelson, 1895.

Zwemer, Samuel M. *Nestorian Missionary Enterprise: The Story of a Church on Fire*. Edinburgh: T. & T. Clark, 1928.

Index

The Road from Damascus
is part of the
Bridge between the Cultures Series.
Other titles include:

Searching Jenin:
Eyewitness Accounts of the
Israeli Invasion 2002
by Ramzy Baroud

A Pen of Damascus Steel:
Political Cartoons
from an Arab Master
by Ali Farzat

Steel & Silk:
Men and Women Who Shaped
Syria 1900-2000
by Sami Moubayed

An Intimate Dinner Party:
Essays by New American Writers
in Arabic and English, Vol. 1
by John Milton Wesley, et al.